Online Resources

With our test prep books, we also provide Online Resources to help you in your test prep journey! With this book, you can access -

Conquer the GRE: Stress Management & a Perfect Study Plan - This stress management e-book is specially designed for test-takers to manage the stress experienced when preparing for the GRE. It includes:

- Stress Management Techniques
- A 6-month Study Plan
- An 8-week Study Plan
- Practical Tips to get a good score on the GRE

To access the e-book, follow the steps below:

1. Go to www.vibrantpublishers.com
2. Click on the 'Online Resources' option on the Home Page
3. Login by entering your account details (or Create an Account if you don't have one)
4. Go to the Test Prep section and click on the 'GRE Quantitative Reasoning Supreme: Study Guide with Practice Questions' link and get your e-book!

Have fun learning!

This page is intentionally left blank

What experts say about this book!

GRE Quantitative Reasoning Supreme is thoughtfully organized and easy to use. All problems have step by step explanations and are very easy to follow. I highly recommend this book for students wanting to be well-prepared for the Quantitative Reasoning portion of the GRE General Test.

– **Laura Mischke, Head of Adult Services**
Bellevue Public Library

The range of difficulty of questions feels comprehensive, and the geometry problems in particular are a real workout! This book would work best for mid to high-performing students who need to identify and fill gaps in their Quant knowledge.

– **Michael J. Hartwell, Test Prep Expert**

The book is really good and in my opinion will be very helpful to the students.

– **Mrs. Amita Menon, Director,**
AM Study Abroad

The book contains a breakdown through easy, medium and hard questions so students can start from the level they are comfortable with. I would HIGHLY recommend this book for additional practice on Quant lessons.

– **Jay Padhya, Independent GRE Educator**

This page is intentionally left blank

TEST PREP SERIES

GRE®
QUANTITATIVE REASONING SUPREME:
STUDY GUIDE WITH PRACTICE QUESTIONS

SECOND EDITION

15 Timed
Practice Tests

520 Solved
Quant Questions

Detailed answer
explanations

GRE® Quantitative Reasoning Supreme:
Study Guide with Practice Questions
Second Edition

© 2024, By Vibrant Publishers, USA. All rights reserved. No part of this publication may be reproduced or distributed in any form or by any means, or stored in a database or retrieval system, without the prior permission of the publisher.

Paperback ISBN-10: 1-63651-208-9
Paperback ISBN-13: 978-1-63651-208-2
Hardback ISBN-10: 1-63651-209-7
Hardback ISBN-13: 978-1-63651-209-9

This publication is designed to provide accurate and authoritative information in regard to the subject matter covered. The Author has made every effort in the preparation of this book to ensure the accuracy of the information. However, information in this book is sold without warranty either expressed or implied. The Author or the Publisher will not be liable for any damages caused or alleged to be caused either directly or indirectly by this book.

Vibrant Publishers books are available at special quantity discount for sales promotions, or for use in corporate training programs. For more information please write to bulkorders@vibrantpublishers.com

Please email feedback / corrections (technical, grammatical or spelling) to spellerrors@vibrantpublishers.com

To access the complete catalogue of Vibrant Publishers, visit www.vibrantpublishers.com

GRE is the registered trademark of the Educational Testing Service (ETS) which neither sponsors nor endorses this product.

Table of Contents

1 Overview of the GRE General Test — 1
- Format of the GRE General Test — 1
- Outline of the GRE General Test — 2
- Registering for the GRE — 5
- How the GRE General Test is Scored — 5
- General Strategies for Taking the GRE — 5
- Preparing for Test Day and Taking the GRE — 6
- Frequently Asked Questions — 7

2 The Quantitative Reasoning Section of the GRE — 13
- Overview — 13
- Question Types — 13

3 Arithmetic Practice Questions — 17
- Level: Easy — 17
- Level: Medium — 24
- Level: Difficult — 36
- Answers and Explanations — 42

4 Algebra Practice Questions — 61
- Level: Easy — 61
- Level: Medium — 70
- Level: Difficult — 85
- Answers and Explanations — 91

5 Geometry Practice Questions — 109
- Level: Easy — 109
- Level: Medium — 120
- Level: Difficult — 135
- Answers and Explanations — 145

6	**Data Analysis Practice Questions**	**169**
	Level: Easy 169	
	Level: Medium 180	
	Level: Difficult 191	
	Answers and Explanations 203	
7	**Exercise #1**	**219**
	Answers and Explanations 225	
8	**Exercise #2**	**229**
	Answers and Explanations 235	
9	**Exercise #3**	**241**
	Answers and Explanations 246	
10	**Exercise #4**	**249**
	Answers and Explanations 256	
11	**Exercise #5**	**259**
	Answers and Explanations 265	
12	**Exercise #6**	**269**
	Answers and Explanations 276	
13	**Exercise #7**	**281**
	Answers and Explanations 287	
14	**Exercise #8**	**291**
	Answers and Explanations 297	
15	**Exercise #9**	**301**
	Answers and Explanations 307	
16	**Exercise #10**	**311**
	Answers and Explanations 318	

17	**Exercise #11**		**321**
	Answers and Explanations	326	
18	**Exercise #12**		**329**
	Answers and Explanations	336	
19	**Exercise #13**		**341**
	Answers and Explanations	346	
20	**Exercise #14**		**349**
	Answers and Explanations	356	
21	**Exercise #15**		**361**
	Answers and Explanations	366	

This page is intentionally left blank

Dear Student,

Thank you for purchasing **GRE Quantitative Reasoning Supreme: Study Guide with Practice Questions.** We are committed to publishing books that are content-rich, concise and approachable enabling more students to read and make the fullest use of them. We hope this book provides the most enriching learning experience as you prepare for your GRE exam.

Should you have any questions or suggestions, feel free to email us at reachus@vibrantpublishers.com

Thanks again for your purchase. Good luck for your GRE!

– Vibrant Publishers Team

GRE Books in Test Prep Series

TITLE	PAPERBACK ISBN
6 Practice Tests for the GRE	978-1-63651-090-3
GRE Analytical Writing Supreme: Solutions to the Real Essay Topics	978-1-63651-190-0
GRE Analytical Writing: Solutions to the Real Essay Topics - Book 1	978-1-63651-200-6
GRE Analytical Writing: Solutions to the Real Essay Topics - Book 2	978-1-63651-198-6
GRE Master Wordlist: 1535 Words for Verbal Mastery	978-1-63651-196-2
GRE Quantitative Reasoning Supreme: Study Guide with Practice Questions	978-1-63651-208-2
GRE Reading Comprehension: Detailed Solutions to 325 Questions	978-1-63651-204-4
GRE Text Completion and Sentence Equivalence Practice Questions	978-1-63651-202-0
GRE Verbal Reasoning Supreme: Study Guide with Practice Questions	978-1-63651-193-1
GRE Words In Context: The Complete List	978-1-63651-206-8

For the most updated list of books visit
www.vibrantpublishers.com

Chapter 1

Overview of the GRE General Test

The Graduate Record Examinations (GRE) General Test, while previously required for admission to most graduate programs, is now part of a larger picture. A strong GRE score can provide evidence of a strong scholarship on an application. This book is designed to prepare students for the GRE General Test. The GRE revised General Test was renamed in 2016 and is now known as the GRE General Test, but the content and scoring of the test remain the same. Note that some graduate programs require applicants to take specialized GRE Subject Tests which will not be covered in this book. Before preparing to take the GRE, please review the admissions criteria for the programs that you are interested in applying to so that you know whether you need to take subject tests in addition to the GRE General Test. To learn more about subject tests, visit the Subject Tests section at ets.org.

The GRE General Test is not designed to measure your knowledge of specific fields. It does not measure your ability to be successful in your career or even in school. It does, however, give a reasonably accurate indication of your capabilities in certain key areas for graduate-level work, such as your ability to understand complex written material, your understanding of basic mathematics, your ability to interpret data, and your capacity for reasoning and critical thinking. By using this book to prepare for the GRE General Test, you will not only improve your chances of scoring well on the test, you will also prepare yourself for graduate-level study.

Format of the GRE General Test

The GRE General Test is offered as a computer-delivered test throughout the year. Post-Covid, ETS provides test-takers with the option to take the test from home.

Whether you are taking the GRE General Test at the testing center or at home, the format of the test will essentially be the same. The test consists of three main components: Analytical Writing, Verbal Reasoning, and Quantitative Reasoning. The total time for the test will be about 1 hour 58 minutes.

The first section of the test is always the Analytical Writing component which comprises a single section, after the changes in the test format announced on May 31, 2023. In the section, you will be asked to write an argumentative essay that takes a position on an issue of general interest.

The remainder of the test will be split between sections devoted to Verbal Reasoning and Quantitative Reasoning. There will be two sections devoted to Verbal Reasoning, and another two devoted to Quantitative Reasoning. You will be given 41 minutes to complete both the sections of Verbal Reasoning and 47 minutes to complete both the sections of Quantitative Reasoning. Section 2 (12 questions, 18 minutes) and Section 4 (15 questions, 23 minutes) will be on Verbal Reasoning, and Section 3 (12 questions, 21 minutes) and Section 5 (15 questions, 26 minutes) will be on Quantitative Reasoning. The unscored section has also been removed for the shorter GRE General Test, along with the 10-minute scheduled break, which was granted to the students after the 2-hour mark of the 3-hour 45-minute test.

Outline of the GRE General Test

The Verbal Reasoning and Quantitative Reasoning sections of the GRE General Test are section-level adaptive. This means that the computer will adapt the test to your performance. Since there are two sections each for Verbal Reasoning and Quantitative Reasoning, the difficulty of the second section will depend on how well you did in the first section. The overall format of the GRE General Test will be as follows:

Component	Number of Questions	Time Allowed
Analytical Writing (1 section)	1 Analyze an Issue	30 minutes
Verbal Reasoning (2 sections)	12 questions (first section) 15 questions (second section)	18 minutes (first section) 23 minutes (second section)
Quantitative Reasoning (2 sections)	12 questions (first section) 15 questions (second section)	21 minutes (first section) 26 minutes (second section)
Unscored Section	None	None
Research Section (TBD)	None	None
		Total Time: 1 hour 58 minutes

Note that the GRE General Test at home follows the same format as the computer-delivered version of the GRE General Test.

While taking the GRE General Test, here are some things to remember:

a) You can review and preview questions within a section, allowing you to budget your time to deal with the questions that you find most difficult.

b) You will be able to mark questions within a section and return to them later. This means that if you find a question especially difficult, you will be able to move on to other questions and return to the one that you had trouble with, provided that you stay within the time limit for the section.

c) You will be able to change or edit your answers within a section. This means that if you realize that you made a mistake, you can go back and correct yourself provided you stay within the time limit for the section.

d) You will have an on-screen calculator during the Quantitative Reasoning portions of the test, allowing you to quickly complete any necessary computations.

The following section will briefly introduce the three main components of the GRE General Test.

Analytical Writing Assessment

The first section of the GRE General Test is the Analytical Writing assessment. This component of the GRE is designed to test your ability to use basic logic and critical reasoning to make and assess arguments. The Analytical Writing assessment comprises of a singular assignment, which must be completed within 30 minutes. In the assignment, you will be asked to develop a position on an issue of general interest. You will be given an issue and a prompt with some specific instructions on how to approach the assigned issue. You will be expected to take a position on the issue and then write a clear, persuasive, and logically sound essay defending your position in correct English. You will be assessed based on your ability to effectively defend your positions with supporting evidence and valid reasoning, your skill in organizing your thoughts, and your command of English.

Task	Time Allowed	Answer Format
Analyze an Issue	30 minutes	Short essay on an issue of general interest that clearly and carefully addresses the prompt

The Analytical Writing assessment tests your ability to:

- ❏ Coherently develop complex ideas
- ❏ Write in a focused, organized manner
- ❏ Identify relevant evidence and use it to support your claims
- ❏ Command the elements of standard written English

Verbal Reasoning

The Verbal Reasoning portion of the GRE assesses your reading comprehension, your ability to draw inferences to fill in missing information, and your vocabulary. You will be given two sections on Verbal Reasoning, consisting of 12 and 15 questions and lasting 18 and 23 minutes respectively. Verbal Reasoning questions on the GRE General Test are mostly multiple-choice and will be drawn from the following three types: Reading Comprehension, Text Completion, and Sentence Equivalence. Reading Comprehension questions will ask you to read a short passage several paragraphs long, and then answer questions about the passage. Text Completion questions will have a short passage with 1-3 blanks which you will need to fill in by choosing the best of several multiple-choice options. The Sentence Equivalence section will ask you to fill in the blank in a passage using the two words that will complete the sentence in such a way that the meaning will be as similar as possible.

Time	Question Type	Answer Format
You will have 41 minutes to complete the entire section, which will include a mixture of different question types	Reading Comprehension	Multiple choice: select one answer choice Multiple choice: select one or more answer choices Highlight a section of text
	Text Completion	Multiple choice: fill in one or more blanks to complete the text
	Sentence Equivalence	Multiple choice: select the two options that produce two sentences with the most similar meanings

The Verbal Reasoning section measures your ability to:

- Comprehend, interpret and analyze complex passages in standard written English
- Apply sophisticated vocabulary in context
- Draw inferences about the meaning and authorial intent based on written material

Quantitative Reasoning

The Quantitative Reasoning section of the GRE evaluates your ability to use basic mathematics, read and interpret graphs and figures and engage in basic reasoning involving math and numbers. You will be given two sections on Quantitative Reasoning with 12 and 15 questions and 21 and 26 minutes of allotted time for them respectively. There are two basic question types, multiple-choice and numerical entry. For multiple-choice questions, you will be asked to choose the best answer or answers from several possibilities; for numerical entry questions, you will be asked to enter a numerical answer from your own calculations. Some questions will be designed to test your knowledge of basic algebra and geometry; others will be designed to test your ability to read and interpret different presentations of data.

Time	Question Type	Answer Format
You will have 47 minutes to complete the entire section, which will include a mixture of different question types	Multiple Choice	Select one answer choice Select one or more answer choices
	Numeric Entry	Solve the problem through calculation and enter a numeric value
	Quantitative Comparison	Evaluate two quantities to decide whether one is greater than the other, whether they are equal, or whether a relationship cannot be determined
	Data Interpretation	Multiple choice: choose the best answer or answers Numeric entry: enter a value

The Quantitative Reasoning section tests your ability to:

- Use mathematical tools such as basic arithmetic, geometry, algebra and statistics
- Understand, interpret and analyze quantitative information
- Apply basic mathematical and data interpretation skills to real-world information and problems

On-screen Calculator

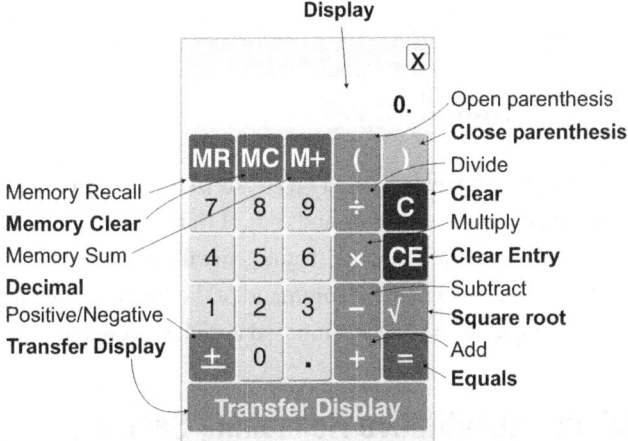

The on-screen calculator in the GRE is a handy tool for you to make computations faster. However, you should only use the calculator for complex equations that will take a longer time to do manually such as square roots, addition, subtraction, and multiplication of numbers with several digits.

Guidelines for using the on-screen calculator

- ❑ The on-screen calculator follows the order of operations (PEMDAS). This means that it computes equations in the following order - parentheses, exponentiation (including square roots), multiplication and division (left to right), addition and subtraction (left to right). So, for an equation like 2 + 3 * 6, the on-screen calculator will give the answer 20 but some calculators will give the answer 30 as they first add 2 and 3 and get 5 which is multiplied by 6 to get the final answer 30.

- ❑ The Transfer Display button will be useful for Numeric Entry questions. The button will transfer the number on your calculator display to the numeric entry answer box. But remember to check the transferred answer as sometimes you may be required to round up your answer; adjust it accordingly.

- ❑ The Memory Recall (MR), Memory Clear (MC), and Memory Sum (M+) buttons work as per normal calculators.

Registering for the GRE

Before you register to take the GRE, be sure to consider your schedule and any special accommodations that you may need. Be aware that the availability of testing dates may vary according to your location. Be sure to give yourself plenty of time to prepare for the GRE and be sure that you know the deadlines for score reporting and application deadlines for all the schools you are applying to. For general information about deadlines and the GRE, visit the GRE section at ets.org. For more information on how to register for the GRE, visit the Registration section at ets.org. For information on special accommodations for disabled students, visit the Disability Accommodations section on ets.org.

If you are taking the GRE General Test at home, there are certain equipment, environment, and testing space requirements that you need to fulfill before you can start the registration process. For more information on these requirements, read the At Home Testing section on ets.org.

How the GRE General Test is Scored

Scoring for the Analytical Writing Section

In the Analytical Writing section, you will be scored on a scale of 0-6 in increments of 0.5. The Analytical Writing measure emphasizes your ability to engage in reasoning and critical thinking over your facility with the finer points of grammar. The highest scores of 5.5-6.0 are given to work that is generally superior in every respect - sustained analysis of complex issues, coherent argumentation, and excellent command of the English language. The lowest scores of 0.0-0.5 are given to work that is completely off-topic or so poorly composed as to be incoherent.

Scoring for the Verbal and Quantitative Reasoning Sections

The Verbal and Quantitative Reasoning sections are now scored on a scale of 130-170 in 1-point increments.

General Strategies for Taking the GRE

There are strategies you can apply that will greatly increase your odds of performing well on the GRE. The following is a list of strategies that will help to improve your chances of performing well on the GRE:

- Review basic concepts in math, logic, and writing.
- Work through the test-taking strategies offered in this book.
- Work through mock GRE tests until you feel thoroughly comfortable with the types of questions you will see.
- As you are studying for the GRE, focus your energy on the types of questions that give you the most difficulty.
- Learn to guess wisely. For many of the questions in the Verbal and Quantitative Reasoning Sections, the correct answer is in front of you - you only need to correctly identify it. Especially for questions that you find difficult, you should hone your ability to dismiss the options that are clearly wrong and make an educated guess about which one is right.
- Answer every question. You won't lose any points for choosing the wrong answer, so even a wild guess that might or might not be right is better than no answer at all.

Preparing for Test Day and Taking the GRE

How you prepare for the test is completely up to you and will depend on your own test-taking preferences and the amount of time you can devote to studying for the test. At the very least, before you take the test, you should know the basics of what is covered on the test along with the general guidelines for taking the GRE. This book is designed to provide you with the basic information you need and give you the opportunity to prepare thoroughly for the GRE General Test.

- ❏ Although there is no set way to prepare for the GRE, as a general rule you will want to:
- ❏ Learn the basics about the test - what is being tested, the format, and how the test is administered.
- ❏ Familiarize yourself with the specific types of questions that you will see on the GRE General Test.
- ❏ Review skills such as basic math, reading comprehension, and writing.
- ❏ Learn about test-taking strategies.
- ❏ Take a mock GRE test to practice applying your test-taking skills to an actual test.

Remember, you don't need to spend an equal amount of time on each of these areas to do well on the GRE - allot your study time to your own needs and preferences. Following are some suggestions to help you make the final preparations for your test, and help you through the test itself.

Preparing for Test Day

- ❏ In the time leading up to your test, practice, then practice some more. Practice until you are confident with the material.
- ❏ Know when your test is, and when you need to be at the testing center or in front of your computer at home.
- ❏ Make a "practice run" to your testing center, so that you can anticipate how much time you will need to allow to get there. For the at home test, make sure to sign in at least 15 minutes before the test.
- ❏ Understand the timing and guidelines for the test and plan accordingly. Remember that you are not allowed to eat or drink while taking the GRE, although you will be allowed to snack or drink during some of the short breaks during testing. Plan accordingly.
- ❏ Know exactly what documentation you will need to bring with you to the testing center. If you are testing at home, you will have to provide a valid government-issued identification document as well.
- ❏ Relax, especially on the day or night before your test. If you have studied and practiced wisely, you will be well prepared for the test. You may want to briefly glance over some test preparation materials but cramming the night before will not be productive.
- ❏ Eat well and get a good night's sleep. You will want to be well-rested for the test.

The Test Day

- ❏ Wake up early to give yourself plenty of time to eat a healthy breakfast, gather the necessary documentation, pack a snack and a water bottle, and make it to the testing center well before your test is scheduled to start.
- ❏ Have confidence; you've prepared well for the test, and there won't be any big surprises. You may not know the answers to some questions, but the format will be exactly like what you've been practicing.
- ❏ While you are taking the test, don't panic. The test is timed, and students often worry that they will run out of time and miss too many questions. The sections of the test are designed so that many students will not finish them, so don't worry if you don't think you can finish a section on time. Just try to answer as many questions as you can, as accurately as possible.

- If there's a question you're not sure of, don't panic—the GRE test allows you to skip and return to questions when you are ready, so take advantage of that. Remember, the value of each easy question is the same as the hard questions!

- Remember the strategies and techniques that you learn from this book and apply them wherever possible.

Frequently Asked Questions

General Questions

What changes have been made to the GRE General Test post Covid-19?

Due to Covid-19 restrictions, test-takers are now able to take the GRE General Test at home. Content and scoring have remained the same. Study materials that reference the GRE General Test are still valid and may be used for test preparation Due to Covid-19 restrictions, test-takers are now able to take the GRE General Test at home. Content and scoring have remained the same. Study materials that reference the GRE General Test are still valid and may be used for test preparation.

What changes have been made to the GRE General Test after the announcement on May 31, 2023?

The main changes to the test are a reduction in the time (from 3 hours 45 minutes to 1 hour 58 minutes), and the removal of the "Analyze an Argument" essay task (which was a part of the Analytical Writing section) and the unscored section. The time has been curtailed by decreasing the number of questions in each section, reducing the total number of questions from 40 to 27. Furthermore, the removal of the "Analyze an Argument" task and the unscored section also aided in shortening the total duration. The official scores will also be delivered more promptly and will now take 8-10 calendar days, facilitating faster applications to their desired institutes by the students. For more information on the changes, visit the GRE section at ets.org.

Can I take the GRE test at home?

Yes. ETS now provides students with the option to take the test from home. If your local test centers are closed or you prefer a familiar testing environment, you can take the GRE from home. You will have to check the equipment, environment, and testing space requirements for the at home test and whether it's an option for you. For detailed information on the requirements for the home test, check the At Home Testing section at ets.org.

Are there any changes in the format and content of the GRE test due to COVID-19?

No. The format and content of the GRE General Test remain the same.

How do I get ready to take the GRE General Test?

To take the GRE General Test, there are several steps you'll need to take:

- Find out what prospective graduate/professional programs require: Does the program you're interested in require additional testing beyond the GRE General Test? What is the deadline for receipt of scores?

- Sign up for a test date. You need to sign up for any GRE testing. Act in a timely manner so that you have plenty of time to prepare and are guaranteed that your scores will be sent and received on time. For the in-center test, testing dates are much more restricted, so if you know that you will need to take the GRE General Test at the center, make arrangements well in advance of the application deadline for your program. There are additional requirements if you're taking the test at home, so make sure to check the requirements well in advance.

❑ Use resources provided by ETS and Vibrant Publishers to familiarize yourself with the format of the GRE and the types of questions you will face. Even if you are confident about taking the test, it is essential to prepare for the test.

Does the GRE General Test measure my proficiency in specific subject areas?

No. The GRE General Test is designed to measure general proficiency in reading, critical reasoning, and working with data, all abilities that are critical to graduate work. However, you won't be tested on your knowledge of any specific field.

Where can I get additional information on the GRE General Test?

Educational Testing Service (ETS), the organization that administers the GRE, has an informative website entirely devoted to information about the test in the GRE section at ets.org. There, you can find links that further explain how to sign up for testing, fees, score reporting, and much more.

Preparing for the Test

How should I start to prepare for the test?

The first thing you should do is thoroughly familiarize yourself with the format of the GRE General Test. Read about each section of the test, how many questions are there per section, and the required format for answers. You can find general information about the structure of the test earlier in this chapter.

How do I prepare for the questions I will be asked on the GRE General Test?

There are plenty of resources by Vibrant Publishers, including this book to help you prepare for the questions you will face on the GRE General Test. A list of books is provided at the beginning of this book. For the most updated list, you may visit the Test Prep Series section on www.vibrantpublishers.com.

How much should I study/practice for the GRE?

Study and practice until you feel comfortable with the test. Practice, practice, and practice some more until you feel confident about test day!

Are there additional materials I can use to get even more practice?

Yes. ETS offers a free full-length practice test that can be downloaded from the GRE section at ets.org. Also, after you have signed up for testing through ETS, you are eligible for some further test preparation materials free of additional charge.

Test Content

How long is the GRE General Test?

The overall testing time is about 1 hour and 58 minutes.

What skills does the GRE test?

In general, the GRE is designed to test your proficiency in certain key skills that you will need for graduate-level study. More specifically:

- ❑ **The Analytical Writing section** tests your ability to write about complex ideas in a coherent, focused fashion as well as your ability to command the conventions of standard written English, provide and evaluate relevant evidence, and critique other points of view.

- ❑ **The Verbal Reasoning section** is an assessment of your ability to understand, interpret and analyze complex passages, use reasoning to draw inferences about written material, and use sophisticated vocabulary in context.

- ❑ **The Quantitative Reasoning section** is an assessment of basic, high school-level mathematical skills and knowledge, as well as your ability to analyze and interpret data.

What level of math is required for the Quantitative Reasoning section?

You will be expected to know high school-level math: arithmetic, and basic concepts in algebra and geometry. You will also be expected to be able to analyze and interpret data presented in tables and graphs.

Scoring and Score Reporting

How are the sections of the GRE General Test scored?

The GRE General Test is scored as follows:

- ❑ **The scores of the Verbal Reasoning section** are done in 1-point increments on a scale of 130-170.

- ❑ **The scores of the Quantitative Reasoning section** are done in 1-point increments on a scale of 130-170.

- ❑ **The scores of the Analytical Writing section** are done in increments of 0.5 on a scale of 0-6.

When will my score be reported?

It depends on when you decide to take the GRE General Test. In general, scores for the test are reported in 8-10 days. You can find your scores in your official ETS account. An email notification from ETS is sent when the test scores are made available. ETS will also send an official Institution Score Report to the institutions you've chosen to send the test scores to.

Check the GRE section at ets.org for updates on score reporting and deadlines.

How long will my scores be valid?

Your score for the GRE General Test will remain valid for five years.

Other Questions

Do business schools accept the GRE instead of the GMAT?

An increasing number of business schools accept the GRE as a substitute for the more standard test for admission to an MBA program, the GMAT. Before you decide to take the GRE instead of the GMAT, make sure that the programs you are interested in applying to will accept the GRE. You can find a list of business schools that currently accept the GRE in the GRE section at ets.org.

How is the GRE administered?

The GRE is administered continuously year-round at designated testing centers, where you can take the test free from distractions in a secure environment that discourages cheating. The GRE Test at home is also available for those who are more comfortable in a familiar environment. For information on testing centers in your area and important dates, visit the GRE section at ets.org.

I have a disability that requires me to ask for special accommodation while taking the test - what sort of accommodation is offered?

ETS does accommodate test-takers with disabilities. For information on procedures, visit the GRE Disability Accomodations section at ets.org.

Will there be breaks during testing?

Yes. You will be given an optional 10-minute break after the third section of the test and multiple one-minute breaks between the remaining sections.

Will I be given scratch paper?

Yes. The test administrator will provide you with scratch paper to use during the test, which has to be returned to the testing center staff without any pages missing.

For the at home test, you cannot use regular notepaper. You may use either of the following materials:

One small desktop whiteboard with an erasable marker.

A sheet of paper placed inside a transparent sheet protector. You can write on this with an erasable marker.

At the end of the test, you will need to show the proctor that all the notes you took during the test have been erased.

Should I bring a calculator to the test?

No. There will be an on-screen calculator for you to use.

This page is intentionally left blank

Chapter 2

The Quantitative Reasoning Section of the GRE

Overview

The Quantitative Reasoning Section of the GRE is designed to measure and test the ability to solve problems that require fundamental skills in arithmetic, algebra, geometry, and data analysis. The section consists of three modules:

- Quantitative Comparison, which involves fewer computations or calculations than the other modules but requires reasoning ability and the skills to describe problems in a logical manner. The module is about 35% of the GRE Quantitative Section.

- Math Problem Solving, which tests basic mathematical skills. Problems in this module are usually multiple-choice questions that can be solved fairly quickly.

- The Numeric Entry module requires entering solutions to math problems into an answer box.

Some of the questions in the quantitative reasoning section are based in real-world settings, while others are placed in formal mathematical contexts. Solving these problems requires basic mathematical skills.

Question Types

There are four types of questions in the Quantitative Reasoning Section. In general, the questions test your ability to:

- Understand and apply basic mathematical skills
- Understand fundamental mathematical concepts
- Use quantitative methods to logically reason and model practical problems

Quantitative Comparison Questions

Quantitative Comparison (QC) Questions are a subset of the Quantitative Reasoning Section.

In Quantitative Comparison questions, you will be provided with information on two quantities, such as Quantity A and Quantity B. From the given information, you should compare Quantity A and Quantity B, and select an answer that is based on these choices:

- Ⓐ   Quantity A is greater.
- Ⓑ   Quantity B is greater.
- Ⓒ   Quantities A and B are equal.
- Ⓓ   The relationship cannot be determined from the information given.

Hints for answering QC questions:

- Carefully examine answers (A) through (C), before selecting choice (D).

- Avoid unnecessary and lengthy computations. Sometimes, you need to simplify the results of the computation in order to find the answer in choices (A) through (C).

- Keep in mind that geometric figures may not be drawn to scale.

- If quantities A and B are mathematical expressions, plug your answer into the expressions in order to validate your choice of answer.

- You may need to simplify the mathematical expressions for quantities in order to use them effectively.

Example:

<u>Quantity A</u>	<u>Quantity B</u>
The number of prime numbers between 1 and 100	The number of odd numbers between 1 and 100

- Ⓐ   Quantity A is greater.
- Ⓑ   Quantity B is greater.
- Ⓒ   The two quantities are equal.
- Ⓓ   The relationship cannot be determined from the information given.

Multiple-Choice Select One Answer Questions

The Multiple-Choice Select One Answer Questions form a subset of the Quantitative Reasoning Section. In the MCSO (Multiple-Choice Select One) section, you will be asked to select only one answer to a question from a list of choices.

The Quantitative Reasoning Section of the GRE

Hints for answering MCSO questions:

- Carefully compute to validate the selected answer.

- Avoid unnecessary and lengthy computations but check your calculations to avoid careless errors.

- Keep in mind that geometric figures may not be drawn to scale.

- If you need to guess the answer, you should perform validation tests (such as plugging the selected answer into the problem).

- The answer is present there; so make use of that fact. Work 'backward' by substituting each option in the problem and see if it fits.

- The answer to some questions is in the question itself. Some direct questions specifically ask for a property that you will be able to answer by looking at the choices and the relationships between them.

- You may need to simplify the mathematical expressions for quantities in order to use them effectively.

Example:

If the average (arithmetic mean) of four distinct positive integers is 11, what is the greatest possible value of any one of the integers?

- (A) 35
- (B) 38
- (C) 40
- (D) 41
- (E) 44

Multiple-Choice-Select Multiple Answers Questions

The Multiple-Choice Select Multiple Answers Section of the GRE is a subset of the Quantitative Reasoning Section. In the MCSM (Multiple-Choice Select Multiple) Section, you will be asked to select one or more answers to a question from a list of choices. Keep in mind that a question may not specify the number of choices that need to be selected.

Hints for answering MCSM questions:

- If the question hasn't specified how many choices need to be selected, you will have to consider each answer carefully and choose all that apply.

- Try to avoid lengthy numerical calculations as far as possible. Look for numerical patterns and make a wise, educated guess.

Example:

Which of the following decimals are greater than 5.04078 and less than 6.1035?

Select *all* that apply.

- [A] 5.1703
- [B] 5.0405
- [C] 5.709
- [D] 5.00231
- [E] 6.123
- [F] 6.046

Numeric Entry Questions

Numeric Entry (NE) questions are one of the four types of questions in the Quantitative Reasoning Section of the GRE. Questions of the NE type require you to answer a question by typing your answer into a box. Your answers may be in the form of integers, decimals, or fractions, and they could be negative quantities.

Because there are no answer choices for an NE question, it is necessary to read the question carefully, and to answer the question in the form that is expected. It is also important to pay attention to units (such as feet, yards, miles/hour, km/hour, and so on), and to give answers that are fractions or percentages, if requested. You may be asked to round up an answer to a certain number of decimal places.

Because NE questions do not allow you to guess at an answer, it is necessary to check your answer carefully after you have expended some time to obtain it.

Example:

What is 21% of 19? Write your answer in the answer box up to two significant digits.

[ ]

Hints for answering NE questions:

- Read the question carefully. Since there are no answer choices to act as a guide, you need to understand what exactly is required.

- Keep aside a larger margin of time for this section, as the computations may take time.

- Make sure that you round up your answer to the exact degree of accuracy specified in the question. If no instructions are given, enter the exact number.

- Your answer should be reasonable in terms of the question and what it is asking.

Chapter 3

Arithmetic Practice Questions

This chapter consists of *80 Arithmetic* practice questions. The questions cover all the question types as explained in Chapter 2 and are segregated into 3 levels of difficulty - Easy, Medium and Difficult. You may choose to start solving the Easy questions first and then move on to higher levels of difficulty or solve the questions in any random order. You will find answers and detailed explanations towards the end of this chapter.

Level: Easy

1. What is 21% of 19? Write your answer in the answer box up to two significant digits.

   [   ]

2. Which of the following decimals are greater than 5.04078 and less than 6.1035?

   Select all that apply.

A	5.1703
B	5.0405
C	5.709
D	5.00231
E	6.123
F	6.046

3. If $(2^{2x+1})(3^{2y-1}) = 2^{3x}3^{3y}$, then $x+y =$

A	−2
B	−1
C	0
D	1
E	2

4.

$$\left\{\frac{m}{n} = \frac{2}{3}; n \neq 3\right\}$$

Quantity A

$$\frac{m+3}{n+3}$$

Quantity B

$$\frac{5}{6}$$

- Ⓐ Quantity A is greater.
- Ⓑ Quantity B is greater.
- Ⓒ The two quantities are equal.
- Ⓓ The relationship cannot be determined from the information given.

5. If the average (arithmetic mean) of four distinct positive integers is 11, what is the greatest possible value of any one of the integers?

- Ⓐ 35
- Ⓑ 38
- Ⓒ 40
- Ⓓ 41
- Ⓔ 44

6. The ratio of the arithmetic mean of two numbers to one of the numbers is 3 : 5. What is the ratio of the smaller number to the larger?

- Ⓐ 1 : 5
- Ⓑ 1 : 4
- Ⓒ 1 : 3
- Ⓓ 1 : 2
- Ⓔ 2 : 3

7. Total income of a family of 5 members is $27,000. The average income of three of them is $4,500. Then what will be average income of remaining 2 persons? Write your answer in the answer box.

$ ☐

Arithmetic Practice Questions

8. The mean value of ten numbers in a list is 7. The mean value of the seven lowest numbers in the list is 5. Determine the mean value of the highest three numbers in the list to 2 decimal place accuracy.

☐

9.

The relationship between the cost and the pounds of laundry washed by two different laundry services is shown below. Compare Quantity A and Quantity B for 30 pounds of laundry.

Laundry A	
Laundry washed (lbs)	Cost ($)
1	16
2	18
3	20
4	22

Laundry B	
Laundry washed (lbs)	Cost ($)
1	6
2	10
3	14
4	18

Quantity A

Laundry A

Quantity B

Laundry B

Ⓐ Quantity A is greater.

Ⓑ Quantity B is greater.

Ⓒ The two quantities are equal.

Ⓓ The relationship cannot be determined from the information given.

10.

Quantity A

The number of prime numbers between 1 and 100

Quantity B

The number of odd numbers between 1 and 100

Ⓐ Quantity A is greater.

Ⓑ Quantity B is greater.

Ⓒ The two quantities are equal.

Ⓓ The relationship cannot be determined from the information given.

11. A pie divided into 3 equal parts. The first part is divided equally between 2 people, the second part is divided equally between 4 people, and the third part is divided equally between 5 people. What percentage is the ratio between the smallest serving of the pie, to the largest serving of the pie (to the nearest integer)?

    [   ] %

12. A cricket player played 3 matches against team A with an average of 42 runs. Then he played 5 matches against team B with an average of 38 runs. What will be his average in all 8 matches? Write your answer in the answer box.

    [   ]

13. A salesman's income was divided between commission and regular salary. His salary, therefore, varied from week to week. His weekly salaries over a 5-week period were $406.20, $413.50, $420, $425 and $395.30. What was his average weekly salary over the 5-week period?

    A. $400.40
    B. $408.90
    C. $410.40
    D. $412
    E. $2060

14. The AM(Arithmetic Mean) of 6 numbers is 24. Find the AM of 2 numbers, if the sum of the other 4 numbers is 96.

    A. 12
    B. 24
    C. 48
    D. 72
    E. 96

15. The AM(Arithmetic Mean) of 3 successive numbers is M. Which of the following statements could be true to fulfill the previous statement?

    I   One of the three numbers must be M

    II The AM of two numbers is M

    III M is an integer

    Select all that apply.

    A I
    B II
    C III
    D I & II only
    E I & III only
    F None of the above

16. Stella has some coins with her. She can bundle the coins equally into 6 bags with no coins left over. She can also pack the coins equally into 4 bags with no coins left over. However, when she bundles them into 7 bags, she has one coin left over. What is the least number of coins Stella could have?

    A 36
    B 29
    C 25
    D 12
    E 48

17. Sequence S is defined as $S_n = 3S_{n-1} - 3$. If $S_1 = 3$ then $S_5 - S_4 =$

    A 79
    B 80
    C 81
    D 82
    E 83

18. If a and b are positive integers and $a^{-3}b^{-2} = \dfrac{1}{36}$, what is the value of $a^{-2}b^{-3}$?

    (A) $\dfrac{1}{6}$

    (B) $\dfrac{1}{36}$

    (C) $\dfrac{1}{216}$

    (D) 216

    (E) 36

19. The average laptop price today is $700. If the average laptop price 5 years ago was 75% of the average laptop price today, what was the percentage increase in the average laptop price over the past 5 years?

    (A) 15%

    (B) 20%

    (C) $33\dfrac{1}{3}\%$

    (D) 50%

    (E) 36%

20. Simplify the expression: $17 - 3\left[5 - 6 \div 3 \times 2 + 3^2 - (4-2)^3\right]$

    (A) -4

    (B) 2

    (C) 11

    (D) 14

    (E) 20

21. In a bag of candy, there are 19 red candies, 25 blue candies, 18 green candies, 21 brown candies, and 6 yellow candies. What percent of the candies are green, blue, or yellow?

    (A) 27%

    (B) 48%

    (C) 49%

    (D) 55%

    (E) 72%

22.

It is given that n is a positive integer and $p = 4 \times 5 \times 6 \times 11 \times n$

Quantity A

Remainder when p is divided by 88

Quantity B

Remainder when p is divided by 40

- (A) Quantity A is greater.
- (B) Quantity B is greater.
- (C) The two quantities are equal.
- (D) The relationship cannot be determined from the information given.

23. 60% of the trees in a section of forest are maple and birch in a ratio of 3 :5. If there are a total of 440 trees in this section of forest, how many are birch?

- (A) 33
- (B) 99
- (C) 165
- (D) 264
- (E) 275

24. What is the value of the expression $\sqrt{\dfrac{4m^{10}z^6}{25}}$?

- (A) $\dfrac{2m^5z^3}{5}$
- (B) $\dfrac{2m^9z^4}{12.5}$
- (C) $\dfrac{4m^{10}z^6}{25}$
- (D) $\dfrac{2m^{10}z^6}{5}$
- (E) $\dfrac{2m^9z^4}{5}$

25.

Quantity A	**Quantity B**
The least positive integer that has 3 prime factors.	The least positive integer that is a perfect square.

- Ⓐ   Quantity A is greater.
- Ⓑ   Quantity B is greater.
- Ⓒ   The two quantities are equal.
- Ⓓ   The relationship cannot be determined from the information given.

Level: Medium

26. If we divide 5000 into $(k^2 - 16)$ equal parts where $\left(\dfrac{k+4}{25}\right)\%$ of each part is equal to 1, what is k?

    ☐

27. A survey of 100 individuals revealed that 96% are actively using Instagram and 85% are active on their Pinterest accounts. If 83% of the surveyed individuals have both Instagram and Pinterest accounts, what percent of these individuals do not use Instagram or Pinterest?

    ☐ %

28. $(2 + 2 \times 2) + \left(\dfrac{3}{5} + \dfrac{9}{7}\right) \times \dfrac{5}{6} = ?$ Write your answer in the answer box as a reduced improper fraction.

    ☐/☐

29. A woman drives 200 miles in a week. She drove 80 miles as "stop and go driving" and her mileage was 18 mile/gallon. She drove the remaining 120 miles on the highway and her mileage was 24 miles/gallon. Determine her average miles/gallon for the week to one decimal-place.

    ☐ mi/gal

30. A man travels 200 miles on 8 gallons of gas if his average traveling speed is 55 miles/hour. If he travels at 65 miles/hour, his gas consumption rate is 18 miles/gallon, and if he travels at 45 miles/hour, his gas consumption rate is 28 miles/gallon.

    He travels 300 miles in the following manner:

    (i)   100 miles at 55 miles/hour,

    (ii) 150 miles at 65 miles/hour, and

    (iii) the remaining distance at 45 miles/hour.

    Determine the gallons required (to 1 decimal place) for the trip.

    [   ] gal

31. $17^3 + 17^4 = ?$

    Select *all* that apply.

    - [A] 17^7
    - [B] $17^3(18)$
    - [C] $17^6(18)$
    - [D] $2(17^3) + 17$
    - [E] $2(17^3) - 17$
    - [F] $2(17^3)(3^2)$
    - [G] $2(17^4) + 17$
    - [H] $2(17^4) - 17$
    - [I] $3(17^3)(6)$

32. What is the value of $\dfrac{\sqrt[3]{64}+3^3}{(16)^{\frac{1}{4}}}$?

    (A) $\dfrac{17}{4}$

    (B) $\dfrac{31}{4}$

    (C) $\dfrac{17}{2}$

    (D) $\dfrac{35}{4}$

    (E) $\dfrac{31}{2}$

33. What is the value of the expression $\dfrac{2\frac{2}{3}+1\frac{5}{6}}{4\frac{4}{5}}$?

    (A) $\dfrac{85}{108}$

    (B) $\dfrac{125}{144}$

    (C) $\dfrac{15}{16}$

    (D) $1\dfrac{1}{16}$

    (E) $21\dfrac{3}{5}$

34. Which of the following are smaller than $\frac{2}{3}$?

    Select *all* that apply.

    A. $\frac{33}{50}$

    B. $\frac{8}{11}$

    C. $\frac{3}{5}$

    D. $\frac{13}{27}$

    E. $\frac{5}{8}$

    F. $\frac{11}{8}$

35. Tony and John started a business. Tony invested $50,000 and John invested $36,000. After one month, they had a profit of $20,000. How much of the profit did John and Tony receive according to their investments?

    Select *all* that apply.

    A. $8,372

    B. $9,232

    C. $10,000

    D. $11,628

36. If $8^x = 128^3$, what will the value of *x* be?

    Select *all* that apply.

    A. $\frac{21}{3}$

    B. $\frac{5}{3}$

    C. 5

    D. 7

    E. 21

    F. $\frac{3}{7}$

37.

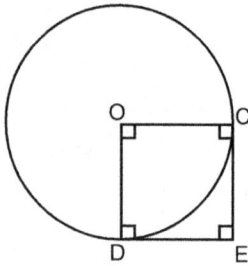

Circumference of the circle O is 12π. What is the ratio of the area bounded by the circle, CE, and DE to the area of the square?

- Ⓐ $4\pi - 1$
- Ⓑ $1 - \dfrac{\pi}{4}$
- Ⓒ $\dfrac{\pi}{4} - 1$
- Ⓓ $\dfrac{1}{4} + 1$
- Ⓔ $4\pi + 1$

38. One milk distributor visits Harry's local stores in every 3 days and another milk distributor visits his local stores in every 7 days. If both milk distributors visited today, when is the next time both milk distributor will visit on the same day?

- Ⓐ 4th day from today
- Ⓑ 5th day from today
- Ⓒ 10th day from today
- Ⓓ 21st day from today
- Ⓔ Can't be determined

39. A prize of $600 is to be distributed among 20 winners, each of whom must be awarded at least $20. If $\dfrac{2}{5}$ of the prize will be distributed to $\dfrac{3}{5}$ of the winners, what is the greatest possible individual award?

- Ⓐ $20
- Ⓑ $25
- Ⓒ $200
- Ⓓ $220
- Ⓔ $300

Arithmetic Practice Questions

40. Select all the alternate equivalents of $\frac{\sqrt{x}}{x^2}$.

    Select *all* that apply.

    - [A] $x^{\frac{-3}{2}}$
    - [B] $\frac{1}{\sqrt{x^3}}$
    - [C] $\frac{1}{x\sqrt{x}}$
    - [D] $\sqrt[3]{x}$
    - [E] $\frac{x^{-2}}{-\sqrt{x}}$
    - [F] $\frac{x^{-2}}{\sqrt{x}}$

41.

    If $A = (22)^5 + (33)^5$, $B = (33)^5 + (44)^5$, $C = (44)^5 + (22)^5$, and $M = (2.2)^5 + (3.3)^5 + (2.2)^5$.

    Quantity A

    $(10^5) M$

    Quantity B

    $(A + B + C)$

    - (A) Quantity A is greater.
    - (B) Quantity B is greater.
    - (C) The two quantities are equal.
    - (D) The relationship cannot be determined from the information given.

42. Richmond Publishing Company is planning to look for some simple interest loan between $120,000 and $150,000 at an annual interest rate of 6% for three years. What will be the range of the interest I of this loan?

    - (A) $21,800 < I < $27,000
    - (B) $21,600 < I < $27,000
    - (C) $21,600 < I < $29,000
    - (D) $22,800 < I < $29,200
    - (E) $23,600 < I < $31,000

43. A car travels 140 miles in 4 hours, while the return trip takes $3\frac{1}{2}$ hours. What is the average speed in miles per hour for the entire trip?

    Ⓐ 35

    Ⓑ $37\frac{1}{3}$

    Ⓒ $37\frac{1}{2}$

    Ⓓ 40

    Ⓔ 75

44. 30 liters of a certain drink is to be divided between the students of 5th and 10th class. A school teacher is appointed on that duty. He gave $\frac{3}{7}$ liter drink to each of 5th class student and then the remaining drink with $\frac{3}{2}$ liters to each of 10th class student. If there are 21 students of 5th class, then what will be the number of students of 10th class and what will be their percentage to the total number of students?

    Select all that apply.

    Ⓐ 12 students

    Ⓑ 14 students

    Ⓒ 16 students

    Ⓓ 40%

    Ⓔ 50%

    Ⓕ 60%

45.
    Integers m and n when individually divided by the number 5, their remainders are 2 and 1 respectively.

Quantity A	**Quantity B**
Remainder obtained when sum of m and n is divided by 5	Remainder obtained when product of m and n is divided by 5

    Ⓐ Quantity A is greater.

    Ⓑ Quantity B is greater.

    Ⓒ The two quantities are equal.

    Ⓓ The relationship cannot be determined from the information given.

46.

Quantity A	Quantity B
$1 + \dfrac{1}{2} + \dfrac{1}{4} + \dfrac{1}{16} + \dfrac{1}{32} + \dfrac{1}{64}$	2

- (A) Quantity A is greater.
- (B) Quantity B is greater.
- (C) The two quantities are equal.
- (D) The relationship cannot be determined from the information given.

47. The average of $\dfrac{5}{6}, \dfrac{3}{4}, \dfrac{2}{7}, \dfrac{5}{3}$ and $\dfrac{7}{2}$ is? Write your answer in the answer box up to two significant digits.

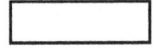

48.

Given: $A = \dfrac{3}{4} - \dfrac{5}{4} + \dfrac{9}{4}$, $B = \dfrac{3}{6} - \dfrac{5}{12} + \dfrac{7}{24}$, and $C = \dfrac{3}{8} + \dfrac{1}{8}$.

Quantity A	Quantity B
C% of (A + B)	$\dfrac{17}{160}$

- (A) Quantity A is greater.
- (B) Quantity B is greater.
- (C) The two quantities are equal.
- (D) The relationship cannot be determined from the information given.

49. Which of the following is between 5 and 5000?

- (A) 0.5×10^{-3}
- (B) $50000(0.00005)$
- (C) $0.05 \div 10^{-6}$
- (D) 5×10^{3}
- (E) $10^{-5} \div 10^{-7}$

50.

Variables *x* and *y* are all positive integers.

Quantity A $\qquad$ **Quantity B**

$\sqrt{\dfrac{x^{12}y^2}{9x^2y^{-4}}}$ $\qquad$ $\sqrt[3]{27x^4x^{11}y^{-7}y^{16}}$

- Ⓐ Quantity A is greater
- Ⓑ Quantity B is greater
- Ⓒ The quantities are equal.
- Ⓓ The relationship cannot be determined from the information given.

51.

Quantity A $\qquad$ **Quantity B**

$\sqrt{\dfrac{9^4 - 3^4}{3^8}}$ $\qquad$ $\sqrt[2]{(3^5 + 9^2)(3^5 - 9^2)}$

- Ⓐ Quantity A is greater
- Ⓑ Quantity B is greater
- Ⓒ The quantities are equal.
- Ⓓ The relationship cannot be determined from the information given.

52. What is the sum of all the odd factors of 45?
- Ⓐ 45
- Ⓑ 77
- Ⓒ 78
- Ⓓ 2025
- Ⓔ 46

53. Which is a multiple of the expression $-14 \div (114 - (-11)^2)$?
- Ⓐ 10
- Ⓑ 3
- Ⓒ 7
- Ⓓ 1
- Ⓔ −1

54. Max is traveling at 25 miles per hour during his trip. He travels for 14 hours to get to his destination. Gas costs $3.76 per gallon and his car averages 10 miles per gallon. If he starts off with $175.00, how much money does he have remaining when he reaches his destination?

    [ ]

55. Jordan works 21 miles from home. On his commute to work, he averages a speed of 12 miles per hour, and on his way back home, he averages a speed of 7 miles per hour. How many minutes total is Jordan's commute to and from work?

    [ ]

56.

Quantity A	**Quantity B**
The number of girls in a class of 272 with a boy to class ratio of 7:16	The number of bananas at the fruit stand if there are 100 peaches. The ratio of peaches to papayas is 5:7, and the ratio of papayas to bananas is 2:5.

   Ⓐ Quantity A is greater

   Ⓑ Quantity B is greater

   Ⓒ The quantities are equal.

   Ⓓ The relationship cannot be determined from the information given.

57. If the ratio of Patriots fans to Jets fans at a sports game is 6:5. Which of the following statements could be true?

    Select all that apply.

    [A] More than half of the fans at the game are Patriots fans.

    [B] If there are 72 Patriots fans at the game, there are 132 total fans (for both teams) in attendance.

    [C] If there are 110 total fans at the game, there are 10 more Patriots fans than Jets fans in attendance.

    [D] There are more Jets fans at the game than Patriots fans.

58. What is the value of $\dfrac{c}{d}$ when $\dfrac{4}{\dfrac{2}{c}+\dfrac{5}{c}} = \dfrac{6}{\dfrac{9}{3d}+\dfrac{16}{4d}}$

    (A) $\dfrac{2}{3}$

    (B) $\dfrac{3}{2}$

    (C) $\dfrac{4}{7}$

    (D) $\dfrac{4}{7}$

    (E) $\dfrac{7}{6}$

59. If Barbara has a ribbon that is $6\dfrac{2}{9}$ long and wants to cut it into at least 4 equal pieces with no leftover ribbon. Which of the following are possible values for the new cut pieces?

    (A) $1\dfrac{4}{9}$

    (B) $\dfrac{2}{3}$

    (C) $\dfrac{4}{9}$

    (D) $1\dfrac{1}{27}$

    (E) $1\dfrac{5}{9}$

60.

Quantity A	**Quantity B**
$\dfrac{11!}{5!}$	The sum of the smallest 3 digit prime numbers.

   (A) Quantity A is greater
   (B) Quantity B is greater
   (C) The quantities are equal.
   (D) The relationship cannot be determined from the information given.

61. What is the 12th digit in the following summation?

$$9.2\overline{74} + 2.\overline{36}$$

- (A) 2
- (B) 1
- (C) 4
- (D) 3
- (E) 8

62.

Use the expression $\sqrt{x^2 - 3x - 18}$

Quantity A

The minimum value of a positive solution for x to create a real number for the expression.

Quantity B

The absolute value of maximum value of a negative solution for x to create a real number for the expression.

- (A) Quantity A is greater
- (B) Quantity B is greater
- (C) The quantities are equal.
- (D) The relationship cannot be determined from the information given.

63. What is the correct order of the following real numbers? Multiple answers can be selected.

$$-\sqrt{13},\ -5\sqrt{2},\ -\frac{3}{7},\ 14.\overline{8},\ \pi$$

- (A) $-\sqrt{13} < -5\sqrt{2} < -\frac{3}{7} < 14.\overline{8} < \pi$
- (B) $-5\sqrt{2} < -\sqrt{13} < -\frac{3}{7} < 14.\overline{8} < \pi$
- (C) $|-5\sqrt{2}| < |-\sqrt{13}| < |-\frac{3}{7}| < 14.\overline{8} < \pi$
- (D) $-5\sqrt{2} < -\sqrt{13} < -\frac{3}{7} < \pi < 14.\overline{8}$
- (E) $|-\frac{3}{7}| < \pi < |-\sqrt{13}| < |-5\sqrt{2}| < 14.\overline{8}$
- (F) All of the above

Level: Difficult

64.

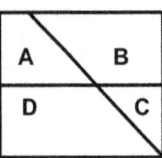

A and B form $\frac{1}{2}$ of the square, while C and D form the other $\frac{1}{2}$ of the square. The area of A is $\frac{1}{2}$ the area of B, while the area of C is $\frac{2}{5}$ the area of D. What fraction of the square is the area of C? Give the ratio in the simplest form.

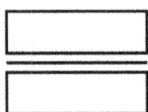

65. If n and m are even integers, which of the following are even integers?

   Select all that apply.

   A. $3mn$

   B. $(3m+2)(3n-2)$

   C. $3(2m-3)(3n-1)$

   D. $5(5m+2)(5n-6)$

   E. $\frac{1}{64}m^3n^3$

   F. m^2n^3

66. Sherry, Tom, Kim and Jolene invested $250, $100, $150 and $200 respectively to start a business. At the end of two months, they all shared half of the total profit in proportion with their contribution. If they earned a total amount of $1400 after two months, which partner(s) got less than a seventh of the total profit?

   Select all that apply.

   A. Jolene

   B. Tom

   C. Kim and Jolene

   D. Sherry and Jolene

   E. Kim

   F. None of them

Arithmetic Practice Questions

67. When $\frac{y}{x} > y$, which of the following statements could be true?

    Select all that apply.

    A y is infinite

    B x is infinite

    C $y < 0$ and $x < 0$

    D $y > 1$ and $x > 1$

    E $y > 0$ and $0 < x < 1$

    F   None of the above

68. A particular vehicle dealer sells only cars and trucks. The ratio of cars to trucks is 3:4, the ratio of four-wheel-drive trucks to two-wheel-drive trucks is 7:3, and the ratio of luxury cars to non-luxury cars is 3:2? If there are 108 luxury cars, what is the ratio of two-wheel-drive trucks to non-luxury cars?

    A   1:1

    B   1:2

    C   2:3

    D   3:2

    E   14:9

69. Two workers produce the same part. For the first worker it takes 5 minutes longer than second worker to complete the manufacturing of a part. Within 8 hours, the second worker produces 16 parts more than the number of parts the first worker makes. During this time period, how many parts two workers produce?

    A   28

    B   32

    C   33

    D   45

    E   48

70.

m is defined as the largest integer that is smaller than 12.022.

n is defined as the smallest integer that is greater than 23.032.

p is defined as the middle integer of the integers that lie between 34.43 and 43.34.

Quantity A	**Quantity B**
m^{n+p}	n^{n+p}

- Ⓐ Quantity A is greater.
- Ⓑ Quantity B is greater.
- Ⓒ The two quantities are equal.
- Ⓓ The relationship cannot be determined from the information given.

71. Which of the following statements could be true for $x = \dfrac{\left(\dfrac{1}{3} + \dfrac{1}{4} - \dfrac{2}{5}\right)}{4 - \left(\dfrac{1}{2} - \dfrac{3}{5} + \dfrac{1}{8}\right)}$?

   Select *all* that apply.

   - A $x < 0.04$
   - B $x < 0.02$
   - C $x > 0.03$
   - D $x > 0.04$

72. A water tank has 6m³ of water. The tank has one outlet drawing water at different rates based on the user's need. If the tap is allowed to supply water at a constant rate of flow for two days, identify the rates that would reduce the water by more than a third of the initial capacity within that period of time.

   Select *all* that apply.

   - A 16cm³/s
   - B 10cm³/s
   - C 12cm³/s
   - D 14cm³/s
   - E 9.5cm³/s
   - F 9cm³/s

73.

If P dollars borrowed or invested for t years at the interest rate r compounded n times per year, then the future value (A) will be $A = P\left(1 + \dfrac{r}{n}\right)^{nt}$

Two individuals, M and N invested P dollars with the following conditions and both gained the same future value at the end of the investment period:

M invested $P at the interest rate $\dfrac{r-5}{100}$ for 6 years compounded 4 times per year

N invested $P at the interest rate $\dfrac{r+5}{100}$ for 4 years compounded 6 times per year.

Quantity A	Quantity B
r	25

- (A) Quantity A is greater.
- (B) Quantity B is greater.
- (C) The two quantities are equal.
- (D) The relationship cannot be determined from the information given.

74.

Integers are related as follows, $a=2b$, $c=-3b$, and b is a negative integer.

Quantity A	Quantity B
$\dfrac{a^2 b^4}{c^3}$	$\dfrac{(-a)^2(-b)^4}{(-c)^3}$

- (A) Quantity A is greater
- (B) Quantity B is greater
- (C) The quantities are equal.
- (D) The relationship cannot be determined from the information given.

75. What is the least common multiple of the largest composite factors of 48 and 64 (excluding 48 and 64)?

- (A) 12
- (B) 96
- (C) 32
- (D) 512
- (E) 16

76. A chemist's secret solution is made by combining 5L of Substance A containing 20% of the Element X by volume with 3L of Substance B containing 45% of the Element X by volume. If the chemist wants to make 10L of his secret solution, how many liters of Substance A should he combine with a 40% Element X solution?

    (A) 8 L of Substance A

    (B) 5 L of Substance A

    (C) 5.3125 L of Substance A

    (D) 1.0625 L of Substance A

    (E) Not enough information given to determine the solution.

77. Which of the following could be the solution to the sum of a fraction and its multiplicative inverse?

    (A) $\dfrac{53}{14}$

    (B) $\dfrac{3}{2}$

    (C) $\dfrac{4}{7}$

    (D) $\dfrac{9}{13}$

    (E) $\dfrac{6}{7}$

78. A clothing company has changed their price of a popular pair of jeans twice in the last month. The current price is $54. If the jeans started at $64, which of the following are possible price changes?

    (A) 20% markup followed by a 15% discount

    (B) 12.5% markup followed by a 25% discount

    (C) 12.5% discount followed by 20% discount

    (D) 37.5% discount followed by a 35% markup

    (E) None of these options are possible price changes.

79. To make a pumpkin pie, Bart's recipe requires 25 oz of pumpkin puree all together. The pumpkin sauce contains 40% pumpkin puree, and he adds 12 oz. The pumpkin spread contains 22% of pumpkin puree, and he adds 6 oz. He then adds 40 oz of pumpkin seasoning to complete the requirements. When mixing he realizes he accidentally knocks 2 ounces of the pumpkin sauce into the mix. How many ounces of pumpkin seasoning (to the nearest hundredths place) should he add to make the ratio of pumpkin seasoning to total ingredients correct again?

- (A) 23.23
- (B) 18.88
- (C) 18.08
- (D) 40.00
- (E) 9.00

80. Simplify the expression: $\dfrac{3}{\sqrt{12}} + \dfrac{\sqrt{6}}{4} - \dfrac{2}{\pi}$

- (A) $\dfrac{3 + \sqrt{6} - 2}{\sqrt{12} + 4 - \pi}$

- (B) $\dfrac{-6\sqrt{6}}{\sqrt{12\pi}}$

- (C) $\dfrac{6\pi + 3\pi\sqrt{2} - 8\sqrt{3}}{4\pi\sqrt{3}}$

- (D) $\dfrac{6\pi + 3\pi\sqrt{2} - 8\sqrt{3}}{\sqrt{48\pi}}$

- (E) $\dfrac{6\sqrt{6}}{4\pi\sqrt{12}}$

Answers and Explanations

Level: Easy

1. **Sub topic: Percent**

   The correct answer is 3.99.

   To solve, convert the percent to its decimal form.

   21% ÷ 100 = 0.21

   Now multiply the 19 by the decimal form of the percent.

   19 × 0.21 = 3.99

2. **Sub topic: Decimals**

   The correct answers are (A), (C) and (F).

   First, we compare the value in the ones place. The numbers are between 5 and 6. Of the choices we have, they are all between 5 and 6.

   Now we compare numbers in the tenths place, which are 5.0 and 6.1. The choices we are given are A. 5.1, B 5.0, C. 5.7, D. 5.0, E. 6.1, and F. 6.0. 5.1 and 5.7 are between 5.0 and 6.1. A and C are between the two numbers.

   Now we compare numbers in the hundredths place. We want numbers between 5.04 and 6.10.

   Of the choices we have left, B 5.04, D 5.00, E.6.12 and F 6.04, D is less than 5.04 and E is greater than 6.10, but F is a solution because 6.04 is between 5.04 and 6.10.

3. **Sub topic: Exponents**

   The correct answer is (C).

   Since both bases on either side of the equation are different primes, we can set the exponents of each respective base equal to one another:

   $2x + 1 = 3x$, so $x = 1$

   $2y - 1 = 3y$, so $y = -1$

   Therefore, $x + y = 1 + (-1) = 0$.

   The correct answer is (C).

4. **Sub topic: Fractions**

   The correct answer is (D).

   This question has variables in it, so we should plug in. We simply have to obey the rules that $\frac{m}{n} = \frac{2}{3}$ and $n \neq 3$. Let's start with $m = 4$ and $n = 6$. In this case, Quantity A becomes $\frac{7}{9}$ which is less than $\frac{5}{6}$, so we can eliminate A and C. Now let's try some weird numbers. How about $m = -6$ and $n = -9$? These satisfy the condition that $\frac{m}{n} = \frac{2}{3}$. In this case Quantity A becomes $\frac{-3}{-6}$, which is equal to $\frac{1}{2}$. This is larger than Quantity B, so we can eliminate B and our answer must be D.

5. **Sub topic: Averages**

   The correct answer is (B).

   Use an Average Pie to solve this one. Write in the number of things, which is 4, and the average, which is 11.

   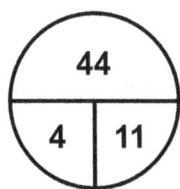

   Multiply to find the total, which is 44. Now you have to be careful with the vocabulary in the question. We know that the four distinct positive integers add up to 44. To find the greatest possible value of one of them, you need to figure out the smallest possible value of the other three. Since distinct means different, the other three numbers have to be the smallest positive integers: 1, 2, and 3. Those add up to 6, so the fourth number must be 44 – 6, or 38.

6. **Sub topic: Ratios**

   The correct answer is (A).

   Calling the number x and y, $\frac{x+y}{2} = x \frac{3}{5}$, that is $\frac{x+y}{2x} = \frac{3}{5}$

   Cross multiplying: $5x + 5y = 6x$, $5y = x$

   Hence, one number is five times as large as the other, so their ratio is 1 : 5.

   Alternatively, AM is 3 parts and One number is 5 parts. We know that 2 times AM = Sum of the two numbers. So, Sum = 6 parts, hence the smaller number is (6 – 5) parts = 1 part. Hence the ratio is 1 : 5

7. **Sub topic: Averages**

   The correct answer is $6,750.

   Total income of three = 4500 × 3 = $13,500

   Remaining income = 27000 – 13500 = $13,500

   Average of the two = $6,750

8. **Sub topic: Average**

   The correct answer is 11.67.

   Let the numbers be $x_1, x_2, \ldots, x_{10}$

   Without the loss of generality assume, $x_1 < x_2 < x_3 < \ldots < x_{10}$

   Therefore, the mean of the 10 numbers is

   $m = \frac{1}{10}(x_1 + x_2 + \ldots + x_{10}) = 7 \rightarrow x_1 + x_2 + \ldots x_{10} = 70$ (1)

   The mean value of the seven lowest numbers in the list is 5. Therefore

   $\frac{1}{7}(x_1 + x_2 + \ldots + x_7) = 5 \rightarrow x_1 + x_2 + \ldots x_7 = 35$ (2)

   Subtract equation (2) from equation (1):
   $x_8 + x_9 + x_{10} = 70 - 35 = 35$

   This is the sum of the highest three numbers.

   The mean of the highest three numbers = $\frac{1}{3}(x_8 + x_9 + x_{10}) = \frac{35}{3} = 11.67$ (2 decimal place accuracy)

   Answer: 11.67

9. **Sub topic: Progressions**

   The correct answer is (B).

   Analyzing the data given in the two tables, we can see that the costs charged by both the laundries are in arithmetic progression.

   At Laundry A, the cost progresses with weight as: $16, $18, $20, $22…

   First term a = $16

   Common difference d = $18 – $16 = $2

   The cost of washing 30 pounds of cloth at Laundry A = 30th term

   $= a + (n - 1) d$

   $= 16 + (30 - 1) \, 2$

   $= 16 + 29 \times 2$

   $= 16 + 58$

   $= \$74$

   At Laundry B, the cost progresses with weight as: $6, $10, $14, $18…

   First term a = $6

   Common difference d = 10 – 6 = $4

   The cost of washing 30 pounds of cloth at Laundry B = 30th term

   $= a + (n - 1) d$

   $= 6 + (30 - 1)4$

   $= 16 + 29 \times 4$

   $= 16 + 116$

   $= \$132$

   Laundry A charges $74 for washing 30 pounds of clothes, while laundry B charges $132 for the same weight.

   Hence, Laundry B charges more for washing 30 pounds of clothes.

10. **Sub topic: Integers**

    The correct answer is (B).

    All prime numbers- except for 2-are odd, but not vice-versa. Think of 9, 21, 35; all factors other than 1 and themselves. Consequently, there are more odd numbers than prime numbers.

11. **Sub topic: Fractions**

    The correct answer is 40%.

    1st group: Each person receives $\left(\dfrac{1}{2}\right)\left(\dfrac{1}{3}\right) = \dfrac{1}{6}$

    2nd group: Each person receives $\left(\dfrac{1}{4}\right)\left(\dfrac{1}{3}\right) = \dfrac{1}{12}$

    3rd group: Each person receives $\left(\dfrac{1}{5}\right)\left(\dfrac{1}{3}\right) = \dfrac{1}{15}$

    Ratio of smallest/largest serving = $\dfrac{\frac{1}{15}}{\frac{1}{6}} = \dfrac{2}{5} = 40\%$

    Answer: 40%

12. **Sub topic: Averages**

    The correct answer is 39.5.

    Total score in 3 matches against team A = 3 × 42 = 126 runs

    Total score in 5 matches against team B = 5 × 38 = 190 runs

    Total scores in 8 matches = 316 runs

    Average = $\dfrac{316}{8}$ = 39.5

13. **Sub topic: Averages**

    The correct answer is (D).

    Add up all the weekly wages: $406.20 + 413.50 + 420.00 + 425.00 + 395.30 = $2,060.00.

    Divide $2,060.00 by 5 to get the average weekly wage, $412.00.

14. **Sub topic: Averages**

    The correct answer is (B).

    This is an average problem, so use the average formula. If the average of 6 numbers is 24, we can solve for their sum: 6 × 24 = 144. If four of these numbers total 96, then by subtracting 96 from 144, we get the sum of the other two numbers, 48. To find the average of these two numbers, we divide their sum by their number: $\dfrac{48}{2} = 24$.

15. **Sub topic: Averages**

    The correct answers are (A), (B) and (C).

    Let the integers be $(x - 1), x, (x + 1)$.

    Then M = $\dfrac{x - 1 + x + x + 1}{3} = \dfrac{3x}{3} = x$.

    So, all I, II and III are true.

16. **Sub topic: Integers**

    The correct answer is (A).

    Since no coins were left over when she packed them into 4 or 6 bags, the number of coins should be a multiple of their LCM.

    LCM of 4 and 6 is 12.

    When she packs them into 7 bags, one coin is left over.

    Multiples of 12 are 12, 24, 36, 48,……..

    One less than these multiples should be a multiple of 7.

    The least number that fulfills this condition is 36 (as 36 – 1 = 35 is indeed a multiple of 7).

    Hence, the least number of coins Stella has is 36.

17. **Sub topic: Integers – Sequences**

    The correct answer is (C).

    We can use the formula to calculate the first 10 values of S:

    $S_1 = 3$

    $S_2 = 3(3) - 3 = 6$

    $S_3 = 3(6) - 3 = 15$

    $S_4 = 3(15) - 3 = 42$

    $S_5 = 3(42) - 3 = 123$

    $S_5 - S_4 = 123 - 42 = 81$.

Alternatively, we could solve this problem by noticing the following pattern in the sequence:

$S_2 - S_1 = 3$ or 3^1

$S_3 - S_2 = 9$ or 3^2

$S_4 - S_3 = 27$ or 3^3

We could extrapolate this pattern to see that $S_5 - S_4 = 3^4 = 81$.

The correct answer is (c).

18. **Sub topic: Exponents and Roots**

    The correct answer is (C).

    As per the question,

    $a^{-3}b^{-2} = \dfrac{1}{36}$

    $\dfrac{1}{(a^3 b^2)} = \dfrac{1}{36}$

    $a^3 b^2 = 36$

    The only positive integers that satisfy this expression are $a = 1$ and $b = 6$.

    Therefore, the value of

    $a^{-2}b^{-3} = \dfrac{1}{a^2 b^3} = \dfrac{1}{(1)^2 (6)^3} = \dfrac{1}{216}$.

    The correct answer is (C).

19. **Sub topic: Percent**

    The correct answer is (C).

    The formula for percentage change is change/original × 100.

    In this case, the average laptop price five years ago represents the original amount. The original amount = 75% of $700 or 75% × $700 = $525.

    The change is the difference between the original and new prices = $700 − $525 = $175.

    Thus, the percentage increase = $175/$525 × 100 = $33\dfrac{1}{3}\%$.

20. **Sub topic: Order of Operations**

    The correct answer is (C).

    To evaluate using order of operations, we need to use PEMDAS.

    P: Parenthesis

    E: Exponents

    M/D: Multiplication and Division done from Left to Right.

    A/S: Addition and Subtraction

    $17 - 3[5 - 6 \div 3 \times 2 + 3^2 - (4 - 2)^3]$

    $= 17 - 3[5 - 6 \div 3 \times 2 + 9 - (2)^3]$

    $= 17 - 3[5 - 6 \div 3 \times 2 + 9 - 8]$

    $= 17 - 3[5 - 2 \times 2 + 9 - 8]$

    $= 17 - 3[5 - 4 + 9 - 8]$

    $= 17 - 3[2]$

    $= 17 - 6$

    $= 11$

    Therefore, the correct answer is (C).

21. **Sub topic: Percent**

    The correct answer is (D).

    To begin this problem, we need to first find the total number of candies in the bag.

    19 Red + 25 Blue + 18 Green + 21 Brown + 6 Yellow = 89 Total

    Now we determine how many of the candies are green, blue or yellow.

    18 Green + 25 Blue + 6 Yellow = 49 Green, Blue or Yellow

    Now we can calculate the percentage of the candies that fit our description.

    $\% = \dfrac{Number\ That\ Fit\ Description}{Total\ Number} \times 100$

    $\% = \dfrac{49}{89} \times 100 = 0.55 \times 100 = 55\%$

    55% of the candies are Green, Blue, or Yellow. The correct answer is D.

22. **Sub topic: Percent**

    The correct answer is (C).

    $p = 4 \times 5 \times 6 \times 11 \times n \rightarrow p = 2 \times 2 \times 5 \times 2 \times 3 \times 11 \times n$.

    Therefore $p = 88 \times 15$ or $p = 40 \times 33$. So, p is divisible by both 88 and 40 and remainder will be zero in both the cases.

    Hence, the correct answer is (C)

23. **Sub topic: Percent and Ratios**

    The correct answer is (C).

    First determine how many trees are maple and birch by calculating 60% of 440, $0.6 \times 440 = 264$. The ratio of maple to birch is 3:5, which means $\frac{3}{8}$ are maple and $\frac{5}{8}$ are birch. $\frac{5}{8} \times 264 = 165$. There are 165 birch trees.

24. **Sub topic: Exponents and Roots**

    The correct answer is (A).

    The expression simplifies as follows:

    $\sqrt{\frac{4m^{10}z^6}{25}} = \frac{2m^5z^3}{5}$. This is because when you take the square root of a variable, you divide the variable's exponent by 2. When you take the square root of a constant, you find what value multiplies by itself to give you that constant. The solution is A.

25. **Sub topic: Prime Numbers**

    The correct answer is (A).

    Answer: The first three prime factors are 2, 3, and 5. Therefore, the least positive integer that has three prime factors would be $2 \times 3 \times 5 = 30$. The least positive integer that is a perfect square is 1, because the square root of 1 is 1. Therefore, Quantity A is greater.

Level: Medium

26. **Sub topic: Percent, Ratio, Rate**

    The correct answer is 6.

    Divide 5000 first into $(k^2 - 16)$ equal parts: $\frac{5000}{k^2 - 16}$

    Then, $\frac{k+4}{25}$% of $\frac{5000}{k^2 - 16} = 1$

    Write percent notation $\frac{k+4}{25}$% in a fraction form

    $\frac{\frac{k+4}{25}}{100} \times \frac{5000}{k^2 - 16} = 1$

    Simplify the first fraction and factor the denominator of the second fraction.

    $\frac{k+4}{2500} \times \frac{5000}{(k-4)(k+4)} = 1$

    Simplify

    $\frac{2}{k-4} = 1$

    $k - 4 = 2$

    $k = 6$

27. **Sub topic: Percent**

    The correct answer is 2%.

    Those who do not use Instagram nor Pinterest can be represented as $P(A \cup B)'$. First, let's solve for $P(A \cup B) = P(A) + P(B) - P(A \cap B)$

    Substituting the given values in decimal form,

    $P(A \cup B) = 0.96 + 0.85 - 0.83 = 0.98$

    $P(A \cup B)' = 1 - (A \cup B)$

    $P(A \cup B)' = 1 - 0.98 = 0.02$

    The percentage form of the answer is 2%.

28. **Sub topic: Order of Operations**

    The correct answer is $\frac{53}{7}$.

    Use order of operations to solve.

    $(2 + 2 \times 2) + \left(\frac{3}{9} + \frac{9}{7}\right) \times \frac{5}{6}$

$$= (2+4) + \left(\frac{3}{5} + \frac{9}{7}\right) \times \frac{5}{6}$$

$$= 6 + \left(\frac{66}{35}\right) \times \frac{5}{6}$$

$$= 6 + \frac{11}{7}$$

Find a common denominator.

$$= \frac{42}{7} + \frac{11}{7}$$

$$= \frac{53}{7}$$

29. **Sub topic: Time and Distance**

    The correct answer is 21.2mi/gal.

Math procedure	Strategy/ Explanation
80 miles / (18 miles/gal) $= (80mi)\left(\frac{1\,gal}{18\,mi}\right)$ $= 4.444$ gal	Calculate gallons required for 80 miles of "stop and go" driving.
120 miles / (24 miles/gal) $= (120mi)\left(\frac{1\,gal}{24\,mi}\right)$ $= 5.0$ gal	Calculate gallons required for 120 miles of highway driving.
Total gallons used $= 4.444 + 5.0$ $= 9.444$ gal Average miles/gallon $= \frac{200\,mi}{9.444\,gal}$ $= 21.177$ mi/gal.	9.444 gallons were used to drive 200 miles. Compute average miles per gallon for 200 miles. When rounded to 1 decimal place, we have 21.2 mi/gal.

30. **Sub topic: Time and Distance**

    The correct answer is 14.1gal.

    Strategy: Determine fuel consumption rate at the different traveling speeds.

    At 45 mi/hr, fuel consumption = 28 mi/gal

    At 55 mi/hr, fuel consumption = (200mi)/(8gal) = 25 mi/gal

    At 65 mi/hr, fuel consumption=18 mi/gal

    His trip:

    100 miles at 55 mi/hr consumes $(100mi)\frac{1\,gal}{25\,mi} = $ 4gal

    150 miles at 65 mi/hr consumes $(150mi)\frac{1\,gal}{18\,mi} = $ 8.333gal

    50 miles at 45 mi/hr consumes $(50mi)\frac{1\,gal}{28\,mi} = $ 1.786gal

    Total gallons consumed on trip = 4.0 + 8.333 + 1.786 = 14.119 gal = 14.1 (to 1 decimal place).

31. **Sub topic: Exponents and Roots**

    The correct answers are (B), (F) and (I).

    Since $17^3 = 17^3 \times 1$ and $17^4 = 17^3 \times 17$, then 17^3 may be factored out of each term. It follows that $17^3 + 17^4 = 17^3 (1 + 17) = 17^3 (18)$.

    (B) $17^3 (18)$

    (F) $2(17^3)(3^2) = 2(17^3)(9) = (17^3)(18)$

    (I) $3(17^3)(6) = 17^3 (18)$

    All other options are incorrect as they cannot be simplified to $17^3 (18)$ form.

32. **Sub topic: Exponents and Roots**

    The correct answer is (E).

    To determine the value of the expression, we need to simplify each part of the equation.

    $$\frac{\sqrt[3]{64} + 3^3}{(16)^{\frac{1}{4}}}$$

    - $\sqrt[3]{64}$ - This is the cube root of 64. In other words, what three numbers that are the same will multiply to 64. $4 \times 4 \times 4 = 64$, so $\sqrt[3]{64} = 4$.

    - 3^3 - We are raising 3 to the third power meaning we have $3 \times 3 \times 3$ or 27.

    - $(16)^{\frac{1}{4}}$ - To simplify a fractional power, use the following property $a^{m/n} = \sqrt[n]{a^m} = \left(\sqrt[n]{a}\right)^m$

$$(16)^{\frac{1}{4}} = \sqrt[4]{16} = 2$$

Now put the pieces together into one problem.

$$\frac{\sqrt[3]{64} + 3^3}{(16)^{\frac{1}{4}}} = \frac{4+27}{2} = \frac{31}{2}$$

33. **Sub topic: Fractions**

   The correct answer is (C).

   To simply the expression we need to follow these rules:

   - Adding/Subtracting Fractions: Get a common denominator for both fractions, combine the numerators, and simplify the fraction.
   - Multiplying Fractions: Multiply straight across the numerator and denominator to obtain your answer.
   - Dividing Fractions: Keep the first fraction. Change the division to multiplication and take the reciprocal of the second fraction. Simplify.

   First, we need to change each mixed number to an improper fraction.

   $$2\frac{2}{3} = \frac{3\times 2+2}{3} = \frac{8}{3}$$

   $$1\frac{5}{6} = \frac{6\times 1+5}{6} = \frac{11}{6}$$

   $$4\frac{4}{5} = \frac{5\times 4+4}{5} = \frac{24}{5}$$

   Second, simplify the numerator.

   $$\frac{8}{3} + \frac{11}{6} = \frac{8\times 2}{3\times 2} + \frac{11}{6} = \frac{16}{6} + \frac{11}{6} = \frac{27}{6}$$

   And last, we divide the resulting fraction

   $$\frac{\frac{27}{6}}{\frac{24}{5}} = \frac{\frac{27}{6}}{\frac{24}{5}} = \frac{27}{6} \times \frac{5}{24} = \frac{135}{144} = \frac{45}{48} = \frac{15}{16}$$

34. **Sub topic: Fractions**

   The correct answers are (A), (C), (D) and (E).

   Let $\frac{a}{b}$ be a fraction in which a and b are both positive. Then $\frac{a}{b} < \frac{2}{3}$ if and only if $3a < 2b$. Test each of the given fractions.

   (A) For $\frac{33}{50}$, since $3(33) = 99$, $2(50) = 100$, and $99 < 100$, then $\frac{33}{50} < \frac{2}{3}$

   (B) For $\frac{8}{11}$, since $3(8) = 24$, $2(11) = 22$, and $24 > 22$, then $\frac{8}{11} > \frac{2}{3}$

   (C) For $\frac{3}{5}$, since $3(3) = 9$, $2(5) = 10$, and $9 < 10$, then $\frac{3}{5} < \frac{2}{3}$

   (D) For $\frac{13}{27}$, since $3(13) = 39$, $2(27) = 54$, and $39 < 54$, then $\frac{13}{27} < \frac{2}{3}$

   (E) For $\frac{5}{8}$, since $3(5) = 15$, $2(8) = 16$, and $15 < 16$, then $\frac{5}{8} < \frac{2}{3}$

   So, except $\frac{8}{11}$ all other fractions are smaller than $\frac{2}{3}$

35. **Sub topic: Profit and Loss**

   The correct answers are (A) and (D).

   John's share according to his investment is

   $$(\text{profit}) \times \frac{\text{John's investment}}{\text{total investment}}$$
   $$= (20000) \times \frac{36,000}{86,000}$$
   $$= \$8,372$$

   Tony's share of the profit is = 20,000 - 8,372 = $11,628

36. **Sub topic: Exponents and Roots**

   The correct answers are (A) and (D).

   To solve, first convert $8^x = 2^{3x}$. Next, convert $128^3 = 2^{7\times 3} = 2^{21}$

   Now relate the two exponents and solve for x.

   $3x = 21$

   $x = 7$

37. **Sub topic: Ratios**

    The correct answer is (B).

    The circumference of a circle is the product of a radius and 2π. So, dividing the circumference by 2π gives the measure of a radius. Denote the length of a radius by r. Then

    $$r = \frac{12\pi}{2\pi}$$

    Reduce the fraction by 2π.

    $r = 6$

    Denoting by Q, find the area of one-quarter of the circle.

    $$Q = \frac{1}{4}\pi(6^2)$$
    $$= 9\pi$$

    A side of the square is same as a radius of the square. Denoting by S, find the area of the square.

    $S = 6^2$
    $= 36$

    The difference between S and Q is the area of the region bounded by the circle, CE, and DE.

    $S - Q = 36 - 9\pi$
    $= 9(4 - \pi)$

    We are asked to find the ratio of $S - Q$ to S. To do so, replace the known values in $\frac{S-Q}{S}$

    $$\frac{S-Q}{S} = \frac{9(4-\pi)}{36}$$

    Reduce the right fraction by 9.

    $$\frac{S-Q}{S} = \frac{(4-\pi)}{4}$$

    Decompose the right fraction.

    $$\frac{S-Q}{S} = \frac{4}{4} - \frac{\pi}{4}$$
    $$\frac{S-Q}{S} = 1 - \frac{\pi}{4}$$

38. **Sub topic: Real Numbers and Operations**

    The correct answer is (D).

    This problem simply asks you to find the LCM of the visits of the two milk distributors. Since both milk distributors visited today, the next time when they will visit together will be the LCM of their visiting frequency 3 and 7, which is 21. So, they will visit again on the 21st day from today.

39. **Sub topic: Percentages**

    The correct answer is (D).

    If $\frac{2}{5}$ of the prize ($\frac{2}{5}$ of $600 = $240) is distributed to $\frac{3}{5}$ of the winners ($\frac{3}{5}$ of 20 is 12 winners), this indicates that each of those 12 winners will receive a minimum of $20.

    That leaves $360 to be divided among 8 remaining winners. If 7 of those winners receive minimum $20 (total $140), then the eighth winner would receive all the remaining prize money, $360 − $ 140 = $220.

40. **Sub topic: Rules of Exponents**

    The correct answers are (A), (B) and (C).

    Let us rewrite the expression given in the question.

    $$\frac{\sqrt{x}}{x^2} = \frac{x^{\frac{1}{2}}}{x^2}$$
    $$= \frac{1}{x^{\frac{1}{2}} \times x^2}$$
    $$= \frac{1}{x^{\frac{1}{2}+2}}$$
    $$= \frac{1}{x^{\frac{-1+4}{2}}}$$
    $$= \frac{1}{x^{\frac{3}{2}}} = x^{-\frac{3}{2}}$$

    Let us now rewrite each option and compare with $x^{-\frac{3}{2}}$.

    Option A is $x^{-\frac{3}{2}}$. Hence, option A is correct.

Option B is $\dfrac{1}{\sqrt{x^3}}$

$\dfrac{1}{\sqrt{x^3}} = \dfrac{1}{\left(x^3\right)^{\frac{1}{2}}}$

$= \dfrac{1}{x^{\frac{3}{2}}} = x^{-\frac{3}{2}}$

Hence, option B is correct.

Option C is $\dfrac{1}{x\sqrt{x}}$

$\dfrac{1}{x\sqrt{x}} = \dfrac{1}{x \times x^{\frac{1}{2}}}$

$= \dfrac{1}{x^{1+\frac{1}{2}}}$

$= \dfrac{1}{x^{\frac{2+1}{2}}}$

$= \dfrac{1}{x^{\frac{3}{2}}} = x^{-\frac{3}{2}}$

Hence, option C is correct.

Option D is $\sqrt[3]{x}$.

$\sqrt[3]{x} = x^{\frac{1}{3}}$

$x^{\frac{1}{3}} \neq x^{-\frac{3}{2}}$

Hence, option D is incorrect.

Option E is $\dfrac{x^{-2}}{-\sqrt{x}}$

$\dfrac{x^{-2}}{-\sqrt{x}} = \dfrac{x^{-2}}{-1 \times \sqrt{x}}$

$= \dfrac{x^{-2}}{x^{\frac{1}{2}}}$

$= -x^{-2} \times x^{-\frac{1}{2}}$

$= -x^{-2 + \left(-\frac{1}{2}\right)}$

$= -x^{\frac{-4-1}{2}} = -x^{-\frac{5}{2}}$

Hence, option E is incorrect.

Option F is $\dfrac{x^{-2}}{\sqrt{x}}$

$\dfrac{x^{-2}}{\sqrt{x}} = \dfrac{x^{-2}}{x^{\frac{1}{2}}}$

$= x^{-2} \times x^{-\frac{1}{2}}$

$= x^{-2 + \left(-\frac{1}{2}\right)}$

$= x^{\frac{-4-1}{2}} = x^{-\frac{5}{2}}$

Hence, option F is incorrect.

41. **Sub topic: Exponents**

    The correct answer is (B).

    Start from Quantity B

    A + B + C

    $= (22^5 + 33^5) + (33^5 + 44^5) + (44^5 + 22^5)$

    $= 2 \times 22^5 + 2 \times 33^5 + 2 \times 44^5$

    $= 2(22^5 + 33^5 + 44^5)$

    $= 2[(2.2 \times 10)^5 + (3.3 \times 10)^5 + (4.4 \times 10)^5]$ (rewrite 22, 33, 44 as 2.2 × 10 etc. so that the numbers 2.2, 3.3, 4.4 found in M, show up)

    $= 2(2.2^5 \times 10^5 + 3.3^5 \times 10^5 + 4.4^5 \times 10^5)$

    $= 2 \times 10^5 (2.2^5 + 3.3^5 + 4.4^5)$

    $= 2 \times A$

    As Quantity B is 2 times Quantity A, Quantity B is greater.

    Therefore, the choice (B) is correct.

42. **Sub topic: Simple Interest**

    The correct answer is (B).

    We use the formula $I = P \times t \times r$, where I is the simple interest for principle P during t years at annual rate t.

    We are given $120{,}000 < P < 150{,}000$

    Multiplying all parts of this compound inequality by the product of rate $r = 6\%$ and the number of years $t = 3$ gives the following compound inequality:

    $(120{,}000)(6\%)(3) < P(3)(6\%) < (150{,}000)(6\%)(3)$

    Simplify this inequality.

    $21{,}600 < P(3)(6\%) < 27{,}000$

The middle expression represents the varying amount of the interest I.

Then,

$21,600 < I < $27,000

43. **Sub topic: Simple Interest**

    The correct answer is (B).

    The car travels a total distance of 280 miles $7\frac{1}{2}$ hours for the road trip. Its average speed in miles per hour is

    $280 \div 7\frac{1}{2} = \frac{280}{1} \div \frac{15}{2}$

    $= \frac{280}{1} \times \frac{2}{15} = \frac{560}{15} = \frac{112}{3} = 37\frac{1}{3}$ here and simply

    divided 280 by 7.5, getting 37.333, or $37\frac{1}{2}$

44. **Sub topic: Percent/Fraction**

    The correct answers are (B) and (D).

    Total drink drunk by 5th class students = $\left(\frac{3}{7}\right) \times 21 = 9$ liters

    Remaining drink = 30 − 9 = 21 liters

    As each student of 10th class is given $\frac{3}{2}$ liter

    of drink then 21 liters will be given to $\frac{21}{\frac{3}{2}} = 14$ students.

    Percentage will be $\left(\frac{14}{35}\right) \times 100 = 40\%$

45. **Sub topic: Integers**

    The correct answer is (A).

    The variable m can be any integer that ends in either a 2 or a 7. n can be any integer that ends in either a 1 or a 6. Plugging in will show that in any case, $m+n$ will leave a remainder of 3 when divided by 5, and mn will leave a remainder of 2 when divided by 5, so Quantity A is greater.

46. **Sub topic: Fractions**

    The correct answer is (B).

    The easiest method is by inspection (and/or addition). Quantity A is approaching 2 but will not get there. Mathematically getting a common denominator and adding gives

    $1 + \frac{1}{2} + \frac{1}{4} + \frac{1}{16} + \frac{1}{32} + \frac{1}{64}$

    $1 + \frac{32}{64} + \frac{16}{64} + \frac{4}{64} + \frac{2}{64} + \frac{1}{64}$

    $1 + \frac{55}{64}$

    $1 + \frac{55}{64} < 2$

47. **Sub topic: Fractions**

    The correct answer is 1.4.

    $\frac{5}{6} + \frac{3}{4} + \frac{2}{7} + \frac{5}{3} + \frac{7}{2} = \frac{591}{84}$

    Average $\frac{591}{84 \times 5} = \frac{591}{420} = 1.41$

    Up to 2 significant digits it will be 1.4

48. **Sub topic: Fractions and Percent**

    The correct answer is (B).

    Simplify all the given numerical statements A, B, and C first.

    Combine all the ratios in each expression.

    $A = \frac{3}{4} - \frac{5}{4} + \frac{9}{4}$

    $A = \frac{-2}{4} + \frac{9}{4}$

    $A = \frac{7}{4}$

    In (B), multiply the denominator and numerator of the first fraction by 4 and of the second fraction by 2 to make all the denominators the same, and then simplify.

    $B = \frac{12}{24} - \frac{10}{24} + \frac{7}{24}$

$B = \dfrac{3}{8}$

In (C), denominators are the same. Keep the same denominator and add the numerators.

$C = \dfrac{4}{8} = \dfrac{1}{2}$

Next, find A + B. Replace A and B with their values found above.

$A + B = \dfrac{7}{4} + \dfrac{3}{8}$

$A + B = \dfrac{17}{8}$

Replace the values of (A + B) and C found above in the expression below:

$C\% \text{ of } (A+B) = \left(\dfrac{1}{2}\%\right)\left(\dfrac{17}{8}\right)$

$= \left(\dfrac{1}{200}\right)\left(\dfrac{17}{8}\right)$

$= \dfrac{17}{1600}$

Since $= \dfrac{17}{1600} < \dfrac{17}{160}$, thus the choice (B) is correct.

49. **Sub topic: Percent**

    The correct answer is (E).

    Rewrite each answer choice in simplest form.

    (a) $0.5 \times 10^{-3} = 0.0005$

    (b) $50000(0.00005) = 2.5$

    (c) $0.05 \div 10^{-6} = 50000$

    (d) $5 \times 10^3 = 5000$

    (e) $10^{-5} \div 10^{-7} = 100$

    Only 100 is between 5 and 5000.

    The correct answer is (e).

50. **Sub topic: Exponents**

    The correct answer is (B).

    Quantity A simplifies to $\dfrac{x^5 y^3}{3}$, while Quantity B simplifies to $3x^5 y^3$. Therefore, Quantity B is greater because $x^5 y^3$ will be positive since both x and y are positive integers, and the coefficient is $9x$ the size of Quantity A's coefficient.

51. **Sub topic: Exponents**

    The correct answer is (B).

    Quantity A simplifies as follows:

    $\sqrt{\dfrac{9^4 - 3^4}{3^8}} = \sqrt{\dfrac{3^8 - 3^4}{3^8}} = \sqrt{\dfrac{3^4(3^4 - 1)}{3^8}} = \sqrt{\dfrac{(3^4 - 1)}{3^4}} = \dfrac{\sqrt{80}}{9}$

    Quantity B simplifies as follows:

    $\sqrt[2]{(3^5 + 9^2)(3^5 - 9^2)} = \sqrt[2]{3^{10} - 9^4} = \sqrt[2]{3^{10} - 3^6} =$

    $\sqrt{3^6(3^4 - 1)} = 27\sqrt{80}$

    So the answer is B. Quantity B is greater by a factor of 243.

52. **Sub topic: Factorization**

    The correct answer is (C).

    The odd factors of 45 are 1, 3, 5, 9, 15, and 45. When these values are added together, you get 78.

53. **Sub topic: Order of Operations**

    The correct answer is (A).

    First, simplify the expression.

    $-14 \div (114 - (-11)^2) = -14 \div (114 - 121) =$

    $-14 \div (-7) = 2$

    Then, look for a solution that is a multiple of 2. 10 is a multiple of 2 because $2 \times 5 = 10$. So the answer is A.

54. **Sub topic: Time Distance and Speed**

    The correct answer is 43.40.

    If Max travels 25 mph for 14 hours, he travels $25 \times 14 = 350$ miles in total. If his car averages 10 miles per gallon, he must use $350 / 10 = 35$ gallons to get to his destination. Gas costs

$3.76 per gallon, so the total he will spend on gas is $35 \times 3.76 = 131.60$. To find the amount he has remaining, you must subtract the total he spent on gas from the original amount he had. Therefore, 175 – 131.6 = 43.40.

55. **Sub topic: Time Distance and Speed**

    The correct answer is 285 minutes.

    Using $\frac{distance}{time} = speed$ equation, you can rearrange to get $\frac{distance}{speed} = time$, and plug in 21 for distance and 12 for speed, to get 21/12 = 1.75 hours. For his commute back home, his speed is 7, but his distance is still the same. Plugging distance as 21 and speed as 7 into the $\frac{distance}{speed} = time$ equation becomes 21/7 = 3 hours. 1.75 + 3 = 4.75 total hours. You then multiply by 60 to get the time in minutes, which is $4.75 \times 60 = 285$ minutes.

56. **Sub topic: Ratios / Proportions, Quantitative Comparison,**

    The correct answer is (B).

    To determine the value of Quantity A, set up a proportion. $\frac{7}{16} = \frac{x}{272}$. X represents the number of boys total in the class of 272 students. Use equivalent fractions to solve, where $16 \times 17 = 272$, so X must be $7 \times 17 = 119$. Because there are 119 boys, there must be 272 – 119 = 153 girls. For Quantity B, you must do two proportions. First find the number of papayas (p) by solving the proportion $\frac{5}{7} = \frac{1000}{p}$. Using equivalent fractions, $5 \times 20 = 100$, so $7 \times 20 = p$, $p = 140$. There are 140 papayas. Now use the number of papayas to find the number of bananas (b) by solving the proportion $\frac{2}{5} = \frac{140}{b}$. Use equivalent fractions to solve, where $2 \times 70 = 140$, so $5 \times 70 = b$, $b = 350$. Because $350 > 153$, The answer is B. Quantity B is greater.

57. **Sub topic: Ratios / Proportions**

    The correct answer is (B).

    To determine the value of Quantity A, set up a proportion. $\frac{7}{16} = \frac{x}{272}$. X represents the number of boys total in the class of 272 students. Use equivalent fractions to solve, where $16 \times 17 = 272$ so X must be $7 \times 17 = 119$. Because there are 119 boys, there must be 272 – 119 = 153 girls. For Quantity B, you must do two proportions. First find the number of papayas (p) by solving the proportion $\frac{5}{7} = \frac{100}{p}$. Using equivalent fractions, $5 \times 20 = 100$, so $7 \times 20 = p$, $p = 140$. There are 140 papayas. Now use the number of papayas to find the number of bananas (b) by solving the proportion $\frac{2}{5} = \frac{140}{b}$. Use equivalent fractions to solve, where $2 \times 70 = 140$, so $5 \times 70 = b$, $b = 350$. Because $350 > 153$, The answer is B. Quantity B is greater.

58. **Sub topic: Fractions**

    The correct answer is (B).

    Multiply the left side of the equation by $\frac{c}{c}$ and the right side by $\frac{d}{d}$.

    $$\frac{c}{c} \times \frac{4}{\frac{2}{c}+\frac{5}{c}} = \frac{6}{\frac{9}{3d}+\frac{16}{4d}} \times \frac{d}{d}$$

    Simplify.

    $$\frac{4c}{2+5} = \frac{6d}{3+4}$$

    $$\frac{4c}{7} = \frac{6d}{7}$$

    Multiply both sides by 7.

    $$4c = 6d$$

    Divide by 4d on both sides.

    $$\frac{c}{d} = \frac{6}{4}$$

    Simplify

    $$\frac{c}{d} = \frac{3}{2}$$

    The answer is B.

59. **Sub topic: Fractions**

    The correct answer is (E).

    Divide the total length of the ribbon $\left(6\frac{2}{9}\right)$ by all the answer choice to see if those ribbon lengths would give equal pieces. The correct answers are C, D, and E.

    For Answer Choice A: $6\frac{1}{9} \div 1\frac{4}{9}$, which becomes $\frac{56}{9} \div \frac{13}{9} = \frac{56}{9} \times \frac{9}{13} = \frac{56}{13}$, which does not simplify to a whole number value, meaning that cutting the ribbon into $1\frac{4}{9}$ pieces would not create equal sized ribbon with no leftovers.

    For Answer Choice B: $6\frac{2}{9} \div \frac{2}{3}$, which becomes $\frac{56}{9} \div \frac{2}{3} = \frac{56}{9} \times \frac{3}{2} = \frac{168}{18}$, which does not simplify to a whole number value, meaning that cutting the ribbon into $\frac{2}{3}$ pieces would not create equal sized ribbon with no leftovers.

    For Answer Choice C: $6\frac{2}{9} \div \frac{4}{9}$, which becomes $\frac{56}{9} \div \frac{4}{9} = \frac{56}{9} \times \frac{9}{4} = \frac{531}{36}$, which simplifies to 14. This means that using $\frac{4}{9}$ sized equal pieces would create 14 pieces of ribbon. Therefore, Answer Choice C is correct.

    For Answer Choice D: $6\frac{2}{9} \div 1\frac{1}{27}$, which becomes $\frac{56}{9} \div \frac{28}{27} = \frac{56}{9} \times \frac{27}{28} = 6$. This means that using $1\frac{2}{27}$ sized equal pieces would create 6 pieces of ribbon. Therefore, Answer Choice D is correct.

    For Answer Choice D: $6\frac{2}{9} \div 1\frac{5}{9}$, which becomes $\frac{56}{9} \div \frac{14}{9} = \frac{56}{9} \times \frac{9}{14} = \frac{56}{14} = 4$. This means that using $1\frac{5}{9}$ sized equal pieces would create 4 pieces of ribbon. Therefore, Answer Choice E is correct.

60. **Sub topic: Number properties**

    The correct answer is (A).

    Quantity A can be simplified by using factorial properties:

    $$\frac{11!}{5!} = (11-5)! = 6! = 6 \times 5 \times 4 \times 3 \times 2 \times 1 = 720$$

    Quantity B can be solved by finding the smallest 3 digit prime numbers. 101, 103, and 107. Their sum is 311.

    Therefore, Quantity A is bigger, and the solution is A.

61. **Sub topic: Decimals**

    The correct answer is (E).

    Write out the repeating decimals to the 13th digit for each and add them together.

    $$9.274747474747$$
    $$+2.363636363636$$
    $$11.638383838383$$

    The 12th digit is therefore an 8, and the correct answer choice is Choice E.

62. **Sub topic: Real numbers**

    The correct answer is (A).

    To be a real number, a square root cannot be zero. Therefore, $\sqrt{x^2 - 3x - 18} \geq 0$.

    Square both sides and factor the trinomial to obtain $(x-6)(x+3) > 0$. The solution is therefore $x \geq 6$ or $x \leq -3$. The minimum value of a positive solution would be 6. The maximum value of a negative solution would be -3, the absolute value is 3. Therefore, Quantity A is larger and the solution is Choice A.

63. **Sub topic: Real numbers**

    The correct solutions are (D) and (E).

    Convert all values into decimals and order from least to greatest.

    $$-5\sqrt{2} = -7.07$$
    $$-\sqrt{13} = -3.61$$
    $$-\frac{3}{7} = 0.43$$
    $$\pi = 3.14$$

When absolute value is applied, all the negative values become positive, so E is also correct.

Level: Difficult

64. **Sub topic: Ratios**

    The correct answer is $\frac{1}{7}$.

    Let the area of the square be s sq. units.

    Let the area of C be represented as c square units and the area of D be represented as d square units.

    It is given that area of C = $\frac{2}{5}$ area of D

    Hence, Area of D = $\frac{5}{2}$ area of C

    We also know that,

    Area of C + Area of D = $\frac{1}{2}$ area of the square

    Therefore,

    $c + \frac{5}{2}c = \frac{1}{2}s$

    $\frac{2c + 5c}{2} = \frac{s}{2}$

    $\frac{7c}{2} = \frac{s}{2}$

    $\frac{c}{s} = \frac{1}{2} \times \frac{2}{7}$

    $\frac{c}{s} = \frac{1}{7}$

65. **Sub topic: Integers**

    The correct answers are (A), (B), (D) and (F).

    Define the even integers m and n as follows, where a and b are some integers.

    (1) $m = 2a$

    (2) $n = 2b$

    Examine all the answer choices using the definitions (1) and (2).

    Choice (A): $3mn = [3(2a)(2b)]$: Replace m and I with their equivalents.

    = $12ab$: Multiply the numbers on the right.

    This is an even integer.

    Choice (B): $(3m + 2)(3n - 2) = [3(2a) + 2][3(2b) - 2]$: Replace m and n with their equivalents.

    = $[2(3a + 1)][2(3b - 1)]$: Factor 2 out within each bracket.

    The result is divisible by 4. So, the choice (B) is an even integer, as well.

    Choice (C): Using (1) and (2), we have $3(2m - 3)(3n - 1) = 3[2(2a) - 3][3(2b) - 1]$

    = $3(6a - 3)(6b - 1)$: Find the product inside each bracket.

    = $3[3(2a - 1)][3(2b - 1)]$: Factor 3 out within each parenthesis.

    = $27(2a - 1)(2b - 1)$: Multiply the factors 3.

    Since one less than an even number is an odd number, $(2a - 1)$ and $(2b - 1)$ are odd integers for all integers a and b. So, the product $27(2a - 1)(2b - 1)$ is an odd integer as a result. Therefore, this expression produces an odd integer for the integers m and n defined in the problem.

    Choice (D): Using (1) and (2), we have

    $5(5m + 2)(5n - 6) = 5[(5(2a) + 2][5(2b) - 6]$

    = $5(10a + 2)(10b - 6)$: Find the product inside each bracket.

    = $20(5a + 1)(5b - 3)$: Factor 2 out of each parenthesis.

    $(5a + 1)$ and $(5b - 3)$ are odd integers for all integers a and b.

    However, the product $20(2a - 1)(2b - 1)$ is an even integer due to the coefficient 20.

    Choice (E): Using (1) and (2), we have

    $\frac{1}{64}m^3n^3 = (2a)^3(2b)^3$: Replace m and n with their equivalents.

    = $\frac{1}{64}(8a^3)(8b^3)$: Raise inside each parenthesis to its power.

    = $a^3 b^3$: Multiply the coefficients.

    Since a and b can be odd numbers, then $a^3 b^3$ is not divisible by 2.

    Choice (F): Using (1) and (2), we have

$m^2 n^3 = (2a)^2 (2b)^3$: Replace m and n with their equivalents.

$= (4a^2)(8b^3)$: Raise inside each parenthesis to its power.

$= 32a^2 b^3$: Multiply the coefficients.

Since $32a^2 b^3$ is divisible by 2, $m^2 n^3$ is divisible by 2, and it is an even integer.

66. **Sub topic: Profit and loss**

    The correct answers are (B) and (E).

    The total capital = 250 + 100 + 150 + 200 = $700

    Total amount earned = $1,400

    Total profit = (400 – 700) = $700

    Half of total profit = $\frac{1}{2} \times (1400 - 700) = \$350$

    A seventh of the profit = $\frac{1}{7} \times 700 = \$100$

    Ratio of their contributions: 250:100:150:200 = 5:2:3:4

    Each received the following in profit:

    Sherry = $\frac{5}{14} \times 350 = \$125$

    Tom = $\frac{2}{14} \times 350 = \$50$

    Kim = $\frac{3}{14} \times 350 = \$75$

    Jolene = $\frac{4}{14} \times 350 = \$100$

    By observation, Tom and Kim got less than $100 $\left(\frac{1}{7} \text{ of the profit}\right)$

67. **Sub topic: Fractions**

    The correct answers are (C) and (E).

    In order for $\frac{y}{x} > y$, either both x and y should be negative numbers (as in answer C) or y is not negative and x must be a decimal number between 0 and 1.

68. **Sub topic: Ratios**

    The correct answer is (A).

    Begin with what you know.

    Cars:

    There are 108 luxury cars which is $\frac{3}{5}$ of all cars. The total number of cars is:

    $\frac{3}{5}x = 108$

    $x = 180$ – total cars

    This means there are $\frac{2}{5} \times 180$ or 72 non-luxury cars.

    Trucks:

    From above we know that there are a total of 180 cars which is $\frac{3}{7}$ of all vehicles. The total number of vehicles is $\frac{3}{7}x = 180 x = 420$ – total vehicles

    This means there are $\frac{4}{7} \times 420$ or 240 × trucks.

    Of these trucks $\frac{3}{10}$ are two-wheel drive or

    $240 \times \frac{3}{10} = 72$.

    The ratio of non-luxury cars to two-wheel drive trucks is 72:72 or 1:1.

69. **Sub topic: Time and Distance**

    The correct answer is (B).

    Let x be the number of minutes it takes the first worker to produce one part. Then, it takes the second worker (x – 5) minutes to produce one part.

    Eight hours is equal to 8 × 60 = 480 minutes. Within this period of time the number of parts two workers can produce are as follows:

    Number of parts the second worker can make within eight hours = $\frac{480}{x}$

    Number of parts the second worker can make within eight hours = $\frac{480}{x-5}$

Within eight hours also the first worker makes 16 parts less than the second workers. Therefore,

$$\frac{480}{x} + 16 = \frac{480}{x-5}$$

Multiply each side of this equation by $x(x-5)$ to eliminate fractions.

$480(x-5) + 16x(x-5) = 480x$

Divide each side by 16 and then solve.

$30(x-5) + x(x-5) = 30x$

$30x - 150 + x^2 - 5x - 30x = 0$

$x^2 - 5x - 150 = 0$

$(x-15)(x+10) = 0$

This equation gives $x = 15$ and $x = -1$, which only $x = 15$ is admissible since x represents the measure of time.

Thus, the first worker produces $\frac{480}{15} = 32$

70. **Sub topic: Integers and Exponents and Roots**

The correct answer is (B).

The largest integer that is smaller than 12.022 is 12 thus $m = 12$

The smallest integer that is greater than 23.032 is 24 thus $n = 24$

The middle integer of the integers that lie between 34.43 and 43.34 is the middle integer among the following integers: 35, 36, 37, 38, 39, 40, 41, 42, and 43. The middle number is 39. Thus $p = 39$

Next, find the given expressions:

$m^{n+p} = 12^{24+39} = 12^{63}$

$m^{m+p} = 24^{12+39} = 24^{51}$

Let's compare these two expressions by placing a question mark between them.

$12^{63} \boxed{?} 24^{51}$

Simplify both sides using the rules of exponents.

$12^{63} \boxed{?} (2 \times 12)^{51}$

$12^{63} \boxed{?} 2^{51} \times 12^{51}$

$12^{12} \boxed{?} 2^{51}$

$(2^2 \times 3)^{12} \boxed{?} 2^{51}$

$2^{24} \times 3^{12} \boxed{?} 2^{51}$

$3^{12} \boxed{?} 2^{27}$

Take logarithm of both sides.

12 log 3 $\boxed{?}$ 27 log 2

The difference between the log 3 and log 2 is a very small decimal. But the coefficient of log 2 is 15 more than the coefficient of log 3. Thus, the result of the right side will come out far more than the result of the left side.

71. **Sub topic: Fractions**

The correct answers are (C) and (D).

Add fraction in denominator and numerator separately.

$$x = \frac{\left(\frac{1}{3} + \frac{1}{4} - \frac{2}{5}\right)}{4 - \left(\frac{1}{2} - \frac{3}{5} + \frac{1}{8}\right)} + \frac{\left(\frac{20+15-24}{60}\right)}{4 - \left(\frac{20-24+5}{40}\right)} = \frac{\frac{11}{60}}{4 - \frac{1}{40}} =$$

$$\left(\frac{11}{60}\right)\left(\frac{40}{159}\right) = \frac{440}{9540} = 0.046$$

72. **Sub topic: Pipe & Cistern**

The correct answers are (A), (C) and (D).

Converting the given volume of the water in the tank to cm^3, we have

$6m^3 \times \frac{1000000 cm^3}{1 m^3} = 6,000,000 cm^3$.

2 days' time in seconds is 2 days × 24 hours/day × 3600 seconds/hour = 172,800 seconds

The rate of flow necessary to drain the tank by $\frac{1}{3}$ is $\frac{1}{3} \times \frac{6000000 cm^3}{172800 sec}$ = approximately 11.57.

The answer choices which are greater than 11.57 ($12 cm^3$, $14 cm^3$, $16 cm^3$) are all acceptable solutions.

The correct options are A, C, and D.

73. **Sub topic: Compound Interest**

The correct answer is (C).

The future values for M and N are as follows:

$$A_M = P\left(1 + \frac{r-5}{100 \times 4}\right)^{4 \times 6}$$

$$A_N = P\left(1 + \frac{r+5}{100 \times 6}\right)^{4 \times 6}$$

Set both future values equal and simplify.

$$P\left(1 + \frac{r-5}{400}\right)^{24} = \left(1 + \frac{r+5}{600}\right)^{24}$$

Divide both sides by P and take 24th root of each side.

$$\left(1 + \frac{r-5}{400}\right) = \left(1 + \frac{r+5}{600}\right)$$

$$\frac{r-5}{400} = \frac{r+5}{600}$$

$$\frac{r-5}{2} = \frac{r+5}{3}$$

$3r - 15 = 2r + 10$

$r = 10 + 15 = 25$

74. **Sub topic: Exponents**

The correct answer is (A).

When you substitute in the given values of a and c for Quantity A, you get the following expressions:

$$\frac{a^2 b^4}{c^3} = \frac{(2b)^2 b^4}{(-3b)^3} = \frac{4b^6}{-27b^3} = \frac{-4}{27}b^3$$

When you substitute in the given values of a and c for Quantity B, you get the following expressions:

$$\frac{(-a)^2(-b)^4}{(-c)^3} = \frac{(-2b)^2(-b)^4}{(3b)^3} = \frac{4b^2 b^4}{27b^3} = \frac{4b^3}{27}$$

Therefore, Quantity A is bigger since b is a negative integer (and thus, b^3 is a negative integer), so Quantity A is a positive and Quantity B is a negative. The solution is A.

75. **Sub topic: Factorization**

The correct answer is (B).

First, find the largest composite factors of 48 and 64. The factors of 48 are 1, 2, 3, 4, 6, 8, 12, 16, 24, and 48. The largest composite factor of 48 is 24. The factors of 64 are 1, 2, 4, 8, 16, 32, and 64. The largest composite factor of 64 is 32. The least common multiple of 24 and 32 is 96.

76. **Sub topic: Ratio, Proportion, Percent**

The correct answer is (C).

Use proportions to solve, where the numerator represents how much volume of Element X there is, and the denominator represents total volume. The left hand side represents the combination of Substance A and Substance B, and the right hand side represents the final solution. A represents the amount of Element X (in liters).

$$\frac{5(0.2) + 3(0.45)}{5 + 3} = \frac{A(0.2) + (10 - A)(0.4)}{10}$$

$$0.29375 = \frac{0.2A - 0.4A + 4}{10}$$

$$2.9375 = -0.2A + 4$$

$$2.9375 = -0.2A + 4$$

$$-1.0625 = -0.2A$$

$$5.3125 = A$$

So, the Solution is C. 5.3125 L of Substance A.

77. **Sub topic: Fractions**

The correct answer is (A).

A multiplicative inverse is the reciprocal of a fraction. We are looking for the solution to $\frac{a}{b} + \frac{b}{a}$. To simplify and combine these fractions, you would create a common denominator and equivalent fractions, then you would have $\frac{a^2 + b^2}{ab}$. You can then eliminate B, C, and D because there are not 2 values for a and b that would multiply to 2, 7, or 13 without one of the values being 1. A must be the solution, and a would need to be 2, and would need to be 7. Let's

check to make sure that works.
$\frac{2}{7}+\frac{7}{2}=\frac{4+49}{14}=\frac{53}{14}$. Therefore, A is the solution.

78. **Sub topic: Ratio, Proportion Percent**

The correct answers are (B) and (D).

Choice A: The jeans started at $64 and experienced a 20% markup. The new price would be $64 \times (1.2) = \$76.80$. A 15% discount would then be $76.80 \times (0.85) = \$65.28$. Choice A is incorrect.

Choice B: The jeans started at $64 and experienced a 12.5% markup. The new price would be $64 \times (1.125) = \$72$. A 25% discount would then be $72 \times (0.75) = \$54$. Choice B is correct.

Choice C: The jeans started at $64 and experienced a 25% discount. The new price would be $64 \times (0.875) = \$54$. A 20% discount would then be $54 \times (0.2) = \$43.20$. Choice C is incorrect.

Choice D: The jeans started at $64 and experienced a 37.5% discount. The new price would be $64 \times (0.625) = \$40$. A 35% mark up would then be $40 \times (1.35) = \$54$. Choice D is correct.

79. **Sub topic: Percent**

The correct answer is (A).

The total amount of ingredients is supposed to be 12+6+40=58. Therefore, the ratio of pumpkin puree to total ingredients should be $\frac{25}{58}$. However, now the total ingredients is 60 because of the additional 2 ounces added. The total amount of pumpkin puree is now $0.4 \times 14 + 0.22 \times 6 + 40P$, where P represents the percent of pumpkin puree in the pumpkin seasoning. Now, we will add an additional amount of pumpkin puree by adding AP, where A represents additional pumpkin seasoning added. The total amount of ingredients will now be 60 + A. To calculate A, we must set up a proportion of correct ratio of pumpkin puree to our current recipe.

$$\frac{25}{58} = \frac{0.4 \times 14 + 0.22 \times 6 + 40P + AP}{60 + A}$$

Cross multiply to get

$25 \times (60 + A) = 58 \times (0.4 \times 14 + 0.22 \times 6 + 40P + AP)$

Before we figure out A, we need to solve for P. We can find P by using the information about the total pumpkin puree requirement. It should be 25, which is the sum of $0.4 \times 12 + 0.22 \times 6 + 40P$. Solving for P would give us 0.472, or 47.2%. Now plug this in for P and solve for A.

$25 \times (60 + A) = 58 \times (0.4 \times 14 + 0.22 \times 6 +$
$40(0.472) + A(0.472))$

$1500 + 25A = 1444.8 = 27.376$

$55.2 = 2.376A$

$A = 23.23$ ounces

80. **Sub topic: Fractions / real numbers,**

The correct answer is (C).

First, simplify $\frac{3}{\sqrt{12}} = \frac{3}{2\sqrt{3}}$

Find a common denominator. The common denominator of the three fractions is $4\pi\sqrt{3}$. Now create equivalent fractions with the common denominator. Each fraction should look as follows:

$$\frac{3}{\sqrt{12}} = \frac{3}{2\sqrt{3}} = \frac{6\pi}{4\pi\sqrt{3}}$$

$$\frac{\sqrt{6}}{4} = \frac{\pi\sqrt{18}}{4\pi\sqrt{3}}$$

$$\frac{2}{\pi} = \frac{8\sqrt{3}}{4\pi\sqrt{3}}$$

To combine the fractions, add and subtract the numerators.

$$\frac{6\pi}{4\pi\sqrt{3}} + \frac{\pi\sqrt{18}}{4\pi\sqrt{3}} - \frac{8\sqrt{3}}{4\pi\sqrt{3}} = \frac{6\pi + \pi\sqrt{18} - 8\sqrt{3}}{4\pi\sqrt{3}}$$

$\sqrt{18}$ turns into $3\sqrt{2}$. This makes the final solution $\frac{6\pi + 3\pi\sqrt{2} - 8\sqrt{3}}{4\pi\sqrt{3}}$. The Answer is C.

This page is intentionally left blank

Chapter 4

Algebra Practice Questions

This chapter consists of *80 Algebra* practice questions. The questions cover all the question types as explained in Chapter 2 and are segregated into 3 levels of difficulty - Easy, Medium and Difficult. You may choose to start solving the Easy questions first and then move on to higher levels of difficulty or solve the questions in any random order. You will find answers and detailed explanations towards the end of this chapter.

Level: Easy

1. If $\frac{(x^2+7x+6)}{2}=3$, then x could equal:

   (A) −6
   (B) 0
   (C) −1
   (D) 1
   (E) 3

2.
It is given that $(x-5)(x+6) = 0$

Quantity A	Quantity B
$x - 6$	0

   (A) Quantity A is greater.
   (B) Quantity B is greater.
   (C) The two quantities are equal.
   (D) The relationship cannot be determined from the information given.

3.

It is given that $a @ b = a^2 + ab - 10$

Quantity A   **Quantity B**

2 @ 3   0

- Ⓐ Quantity A is greater.
- Ⓑ Quantity B is greater.
- Ⓒ The two quantities are equal.
- Ⓓ The relationship cannot be determined from the information given.

4.

It is given that $@x = x^2 - 11$ and $\#x = x^2 - x + 11$

Quantity A   **Quantity B**

$(@2)(\#3)$ $(\#2)(@3)$

- Ⓐ Quantity A is greater.
- Ⓑ Quantity B is greater.
- Ⓒ The two quantities are equal.
- Ⓓ The relationship cannot be determined from the information given.

5. For what value of k will the quadratic equation $x^2 - kx + 9 = 0$ have real and equal roots?

Select all that apply.

- A 6
- B 4
- C −4
- D −6
- E −3
- F All of the above

Algebra Practice Questions

6.

It is given that $4x - 10 \geq x + 8$

        Quantity A   **Quantity B**

              x 5

- Ⓐ Quantity A is greater.
- Ⓑ Quantity B is greater.
- Ⓒ The two quantities are equal.
- Ⓓ The relationship cannot be determined from the information given.

7.

It is given that $1.3 < w < 1.3101$ and $1.3033 < y$

        Quantity A   **Quantity B**

              w y

- Ⓐ Quantity A is greater.
- Ⓑ Quantity B is greater.
- Ⓒ The two quantities are equal.
- Ⓓ The relationship cannot be determined from the information given.

8. What is the value of $a - b + c - d - e$ if $a = 5$, $b = 2$, $c = 3$, $d = -8$, and $e = 10$?
   - Ⓐ −8
   - Ⓑ −4
   - Ⓒ −2
   - Ⓓ 4
   - Ⓔ 8

9. If $x^2 - 2x - 15 = 0$ and $x > 0$, which of the following must be equal to 0?

   Select <u>all</u> that apply.
   - ☐ A $x^2 - 6x + 9$
   - ☐ B $x^2 - 7x + 10$
   - ☐ C $x^2 - 10x + 25$
   - ☐ D $x^2 + 6x + 9$
   - ☐ E $x^2 + 7x + 10$
   - ☐ F $x^2 + 10x + 25$

10.

It is given that 0 < p < 1

Quantity A

$$\frac{1}{p^2}$$

Quantity B

$$\frac{1}{(p+1)^2}$$

- Ⓐ Quantity A is greater.
- Ⓑ Quantity B is greater.
- Ⓒ The two quantities are equal.
- Ⓓ The relationship cannot be determined from the information given.

11. A certain deck of cards contains r cards. After the cards are distributed evenly among s people, 8 cards are left over. In terms of r and s, how many cards did each person receive?

- Ⓐ $\frac{s}{8-r}$
- Ⓑ $\frac{r-s}{8}$
- Ⓒ $\frac{r-8}{s}$
- Ⓓ $s - 8r$
- Ⓔ $rs - 8$

12.

It is given that F > 0

Quantity A

$$\frac{2F-5}{2}$$

Quantity B

$$\frac{4F-1}{4}$$

- Ⓐ Quantity A is greater.
- Ⓑ Quantity B is greater.
- Ⓒ The two quantities are equal.
- Ⓓ The relationship cannot be determined from the information given.

13.

$$15 \text{ more than } 5x = 55$$

Quantity A	**Quantity B**
11	x

- (A) Quantity A is greater.
- (B) Quantity B is greater.
- (C) The two quantities are equal.
- (D) The relationship cannot be determined from the information given.

14.

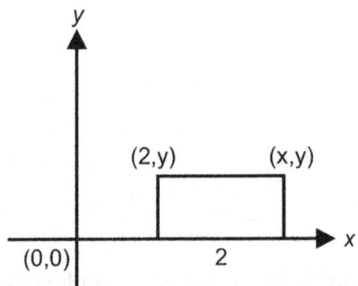

If the figure above is a rectangle, then what is the area of the figure, expressed in terms of x and y?

- (A) xy
- (B) $4x$
- (C) $8x$
- (D) $y(x-2)$
- (E) $x(y-2)$

15. Which of the statements below are equivalent to $y = \dfrac{1}{x} = \dfrac{1}{x+1}$?

    Select <u>all</u> that apply.

    A. $y = \dfrac{1}{x(x+1)}$

    B. $y = \dfrac{\frac{1}{x}}{x+1}$

    C. $y = \dfrac{\frac{1}{x^2}}{\frac{1+1}{x}}$

    D. $y = \dfrac{x}{x+1}$

    E. $y = \dfrac{x}{x-2}$

    F. All of the above

16. There are x employees in Company A. The number of employees in Company B is 85% of 20 less than thrice the employees in company A.

Quantity A	**Quantity B**
Employees in company B	$0.85(3x - 20)$

    A. Quantity A is greater.
    B. Quantity B is greater.
    C. The two quantities are equal.
    D. The relationship cannot be determined from the information given.

17.

$$a > 1$$
$$a - 1 = b$$

Quantity A	**Quantity B**
b^2	$a^2 - 1$

- Ⓐ   Quantity A is greater.
- Ⓑ   Quantity B is greater.
- Ⓒ   The two quantities are equal.
- Ⓓ   The relationship cannot be determined from the information given.

18. For all integers $n \neq 1$, let $<n> = \dfrac{n+1}{n-1}$. Which of the following has the greatest value?

- Ⓐ $< 0 >$
- Ⓑ $< 2 >$
- Ⓒ $< 3 >$
- Ⓓ $< 4 >$
- Ⓔ $< 5 >$

19.

$$x = -y$$

Quantity A	**Quantity B**
x	y

- Ⓐ   Quantity A is greater.
- Ⓑ   Quantity B is greater.
- Ⓒ   The two quantities are equal.
- Ⓓ   The relationship cannot be determined from the information given.

20.

$$3 > p > 1$$

Quantity A　　　　　　　　　　　　　　**Quantity B**

$\dfrac{p}{2}$　　　　　　　　　　　　　　　　$\dfrac{p+2}{4}$

- Ⓐ　Quantity A is greater.
- Ⓑ　Quantity B is greater.
- Ⓒ　The two quantities are equal.
- Ⓓ　The relationship cannot be determined from the information given.

21. Determine the positive value of y, where the graphs of $y = x^2 - 2$ and $y = 2x + 1$ intersect.

☐

22.

There are x books in a bookstore. After 1/4 of them were purchased by customers the bookstore received a shipment of 15 more books, bringing the total number of books on hand to 105.

Quantity A　　　　　　　　　　　　　　**Quantity B**

x　　　　　　　　　　　　　　　　　　　105

- Ⓐ　Quantity A is greater.
- Ⓑ　Quantity B is greater.
- Ⓒ　The two quantities are equal.
- Ⓓ　The relationship cannot be determined from the information given.

23.

$$n > 0$$

Quantity A　　　　　　　　　　　　　　**Quantity B**

$\dfrac{n^2 + 2}{n}$　　　　　　　　　　　　　　$n + \dfrac{1}{n}$

- Ⓐ　Quantity A is greater.
- Ⓑ　Quantity B is greater.
- Ⓒ　The two quantities are equal.
- Ⓓ　The relationship cannot be determined from the information given.

Algebra Practice Questions

24.

A man buys 16 shirts. Some of them cost $13 each, while the remainder cost $10 each.
The cost of all 16 shirts is $187.

Quantity A	Quantity B
The number of $13 shirts purchased	The number of $10 shirts purchased

- (A) Quantity A is greater.
- (B) Quantity B is greater.
- (C) The two quantities are equal.
- (D) The relationship cannot be determined from the information given.

25.

Quantity A	Quantity B
The slope of the line defined by $2y + 3x - 5 = 0$	$\dfrac{3}{2}$

- (A) Quantity A is greater.
- (B) Quantity B is greater.
- (C) The two quantities are equal.
- (D) The relationship cannot be determined from the information given.

26. If $|-2x + 7| > 5$, select all possible values for x:

- (A) 7
- (B) 4
- (C) 2
- (D) −6
- (E) 0

27. Car A was traveling at a speed of 20mph for 15 hours to get to Destination A. If Car B was driving 10mph faster than Car A, how long would it take Car B to get to the same destination?

☐

Level: Medium

28. If $f(x) = ax^4 - 5x^2 + ax - 5$, then $f(b) - f(-b)$ will equal:

    Ⓐ 0
    Ⓑ $2ab$
    Ⓒ $3ab^4 - 7b^2 - 8$
    Ⓓ $-3ab^4 + 7b^2 + 8$
    Ⓔ $3ab^4 - 4b^2 + 5ab - 6$

29. If $\dfrac{5x^2 + ax + b}{3x^2 + 7x + 5} = x$ and $3x^3 + 2x^2 - b = 0$, where $x \neq 0$, what is the value of a?

    ☐

30. What is $x + y - z$ if $x + y = 8$, $x + z = 11$, $y + z = 7$?

    Ⓐ 23
    Ⓑ 3
    Ⓒ 6
    Ⓓ 13
    Ⓔ 12

31. If $x > y$, $x < 9$, and $y > -4$, what is the largest prime number that could be equal to $x + y$?

    Ⓐ 17
    Ⓑ 11
    Ⓒ 13
    Ⓓ 7
    Ⓔ 5

32.

Quantity A	Quantity B
The number of real roots in the quadratic equation $f(x) = 2x^2 - 3x + 1$	The number of real roots in the quadratic equation $f(x) = x^2 - 7x - 8$

- (A) Quantity A is greater.
- (B) Quantity B is greater.
- (C) The two quantities are equal.
- (D) The relationship cannot be determined from the information given.

33. A company employs 150 persons who are 25 years or older. 30% of employees in the age group 25-35, and 63% of employees in the 35+ age group contribute to the defined benefits plan. If 52% of all employees contribute to the plan, how many employees are over 35 years of age?

    ☐

34. If $x^2 - 6x - 27 = 0$ and $y^2 - 6y - 40 = 0$, what is the maximum value of $2(x - y)$?
    - (A) 21
    - (B) 19
    - (C) 26
    - (D) 18
    - (E) 17

35. If $x^2 - 6x - 27 = 0$ and $y^2 - 6y - 40 = 0$, what is the minimum value of $x + y$?
    - (A) −4
    - (B) −5
    - (C) −7
    - (D) −6
    - (E) −3

36. If $b < 2$ and $2x - 3b = 0$, then which of the following can be values of x?

    Select all that apply.

    - [A] 4
    - [B] 3
    - [C] 2
    - [D] 1
    - [E] 0
    - [F] −1
    - [G] −2
    - [H] −3
    - [I] −4

37. Two functions are defined as $f(x) = 1 + x^3$, and $g(x) = \dfrac{x}{1+x}$ for all real and positive values of x. Compute $f[g(2)]$ to 2 decimal place accuracy.

    [   ]

38. If x, y and z are three non-zero numbers and $xy > 0$ and $yz < 0$, which of the following must be negative?

    Select all that apply.

    - [A] xyz
    - [B] xyz^2
    - [C] $xy^2 z$
    - [D] $xy^2 z^2$
    - [E] $x^2 y^2 z^2$
    - [F] $x^2 yz$
    - [G] $-(x^2 y^2 z^2)$
    - [H] $x^2 yz^2$
    - [I] $x(-y) z^2$
    - [J] $-(xyz^2)$

Algebra Practice Questions

39.
$$y = 3x^2 + 8x - 10$$

Quantity A	Quantity B
x	$y - 10$

- Ⓐ Quantity A is greater.
- Ⓑ Quantity B is greater.
- Ⓒ The two quantities are equal.
- Ⓓ The relationship cannot be determined from the information given.

40. James, John, and Austin divided $620 among them. James got $\frac{2}{5}$ of what John received and John received $\frac{2}{3}$ of what Austin got. What is the approximate amount that each received?

   Select all that apply.

   - ☐ A $86
   - ☐ B $168
   - ☐ C $213
   - ☐ D $283
   - ☐ E $321
   - ☐ F $366

41. If $-5x + 2y = 9$ and $3x - 4y = -4$, then what is the value of $7x + 10y$?

   - Ⓐ −19
   - Ⓑ −17
   - Ⓒ −9
   - Ⓓ 9
   - Ⓔ 19

42. Determine values of x that satisfy the equation $|x^2 - x + 1| = 2x - 1$

   Select all that apply.

   - ☐ A $x = -1$
   - ☐ B $x = 1$
   - ☐ C $x = 3$
   - ☐ D $x = 2$
   - ☐ E $x = -3$
   - ☐ F All of the above

43.

$$x > y$$
$$xy \neq 0$$

Quantity A   **Quantity B**

$\dfrac{x}{y}$ $\dfrac{y}{x}$

- Ⓐ Quantity A is greater.
- Ⓑ Quantity B is greater.
- Ⓒ The two quantities are equal.
- Ⓓ The relationship cannot be determined from the information given.

44. The function $f(x) = 2x^2 - 5x$ and $(x) = x^2 + x - 3$. What is the value of $(f \circ g)(-2) - [f(3) + g(2)]$?

   Select all that apply.

   - ☐ A   –6
   - ☐ B   –1
   - ☐ C   0
   - ☐ D   1
   - ☐ E   14
   - ☐ F   28

45.

$$x > 0$$
$$0 < x^2 < 1$$

Quantity A   **Quantity B**

$1 - x^2$ $1 - x$

- Ⓐ Quantity A is greater.
- Ⓑ Quantity B is greater.
- Ⓒ The two quantities are equal.
- Ⓓ The relationship cannot be determined from the information given.

Algebra Practice Questions

46. If $x + y = z$ and $x = y$, then of the following all are true EXCEPT

    (A) $2x + 2y = 2z$

    (B) $x - y = 0$

    (C) $x - z = y - z$

    (D) $x = \dfrac{z}{2}$

    (E) $z - y = 2x$

47.

$$x > 1$$
$$y > 0$$

Quantity A

y^x

Quantity B

$y^{(x+1)}$

(A) Quantity A is greater.

(B) Quantity B is greater.

(C) The two quantities are equal.

(D) The relationship cannot be determined from the information given.

48. A mathematical operation is defined as: $a\$b = \dfrac{\sqrt{a}}{\sqrt{a}+\sqrt{b}}$ for positive square root.

    Compute $1\$(4\$9)$ with 3 decimal place accuracy.

    ☐

49. If $\dfrac{(3a+2b)}{(7a+4b)} = \dfrac{15}{32}$, then what is $\dfrac{(3a+b)}{7b}$?

    (A) $\dfrac{1}{3}$

    (B) $\dfrac{1}{2}$

    (C) $\dfrac{2}{3}$

    (D) $\dfrac{3}{4}$

    (E) $\dfrac{4}{5}$

50.

$$c = d + 2$$

Quantity A　　　　　　　　　　　　　　　　　　　　**Quantity B**

$c^2 - d^2$　　　　　　　　　　　　　　　　　　　　　　$4d$

- Ⓐ Quantity A is greater.
- Ⓑ Quantity B is greater.
- Ⓒ The two quantities are equal.
- Ⓓ The relationship cannot be determined from the information given.

51. When the two curves $y = x^2 - x + 4$ and $y = 4x - 1$ intersect, the value of x satisfies which of the following conditions?

Select all that apply.

- [A] $x < 1$
- [B] $x > 1$
- [C] $x < 4$
- [D] x is undefined
- [E] $x = 0$
- [F] All of the above

52.

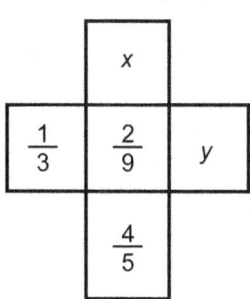

The sum of the numbers in the horizontal row of boxes equals the sum of the numbers in the vertical row of boxes.

Quantity A　　　　　　　　　　　　　　　　　　　　**Quantity B**

x　　　　　　　　　　　　　　　　　　　　　　　　　　y

- Ⓐ Quantity A is greater.
- Ⓑ Quantity B is greater.
- Ⓒ The two quantities are equal.
- Ⓓ The relationship cannot be determined from the information given.

Algebra Practice Questions

53.

$$x \geq 1$$

Quantity A   **Quantity B**

$x^{(x+2)}$ $(x+2)^x$

- Ⓐ Quantity A is greater.
- Ⓑ Quantity B is greater.
- Ⓒ The two quantities are equal.
- Ⓓ The relationship cannot be determined from the information given.

54. If $m - n = 1$, where $m \neq -n$, which of the following statements could be true?

- Ⓐ $m(m - 1) = n(n + 1)$
- Ⓑ $m(m + 1) = n(n - 1)$
- Ⓒ $n(m + 1) = m(n - 1)$
- Ⓓ $n(m - 1) = m(n + 1)$
- Ⓔ $m(m + n) = n(m - n)$

55.

Inequality 1: $4(x+2) \leq 2(x+5)+14$

Inequality 2: $\sqrt{16-8y+y^2} \leq 9$

Quantity A   **Quantity B**

x, where x is a solution of Inequality 1 y, where y is a solution of Inequality 2

- Ⓐ Quantity A is greater.
- Ⓑ Quantity B is greater.
- Ⓒ The two quantities are equal.
- Ⓓ The relationship cannot be determined from the information given.

56. Find the value of y given that $\dfrac{4y^2}{64} = 2^{-y}$ and $y < |y|$

57. If z is not equal to zero, and $z = \sqrt{(8zs - 16s^2)}$, then z equals:

   Ⓐ s

   Ⓑ $4s$

   Ⓒ $4s^2$

   Ⓓ $-\dfrac{4s^2}{3}$

   Ⓔ $-4s$

58. The following numerical expressions are given:

    $K = \left(\dfrac{2}{3}\right)$ of $\left(\dfrac{3}{2} + a\right)$

    $L = \left(\dfrac{3}{4}\right)$ of $\left(\dfrac{4}{3} + b\right)$

    $M = \left(\dfrac{a}{b}\right)$ of $\left(\dfrac{3}{5} + 3\right)$

    Which of the following statements could be true?

    Select all that apply.

    Ⓐ $12(K + L) = 8a + 9b + 24$

    Ⓑ $20(K + L) = \dfrac{2a + 3b + 7}{2}$

    Ⓒ $20(L + M) = \left(\dfrac{15b^2 + 20b + 72a}{b}\right)$

    Ⓓ $(L + M) = \left(\dfrac{15b^2 + 20b + 48a}{5b}\right)$

    Ⓔ $(K + M) = \left(\dfrac{10ab + 15b + 54a}{15b}\right)$

    Ⓕ $(K + M) = \left(\dfrac{10ab + 5b + 48a}{5b}\right)$

    Ⓖ $(L - K) = \left(\dfrac{2a + 3b - 1}{3}\right)$

Algebra Practice Questions

59.

Quantity A	**Quantity B**
The value of x where $2 - 3|x| < 4$	The value of y where $4y - 3 > 13$

- Ⓐ Quantity A is greater
- Ⓑ Quantity B is greater
- Ⓒ The quantities are equal.
- Ⓓ The relationship cannot be determined from the information given.

60.

$$\frac{9-5x}{7} \geq -3$$

Quantity A	**Quantity B**
The minimum value $10-x$	The minimum value of $\frac{-3x}{5} + 4$

- Ⓐ Quantity A is greater
- Ⓑ Quantity B is greater
- Ⓒ The quantities are equal.
- Ⓓ The relationship cannot be determined from the information given.

61.

$$f(x) = \frac{3x+4}{-2x-1}$$

Quantity A	**Quantity B**
The value of $f(4)$	The value of x when $f(x) = 16$

- Ⓐ Quantity A is greater
- Ⓑ Quantity B is greater
- Ⓒ The quantities are equal.
- Ⓓ The relationship cannot be determined from the information given.

62. If $m/z = \dfrac{2m-5z}{5m-z}$, then find the value of $\sqrt{9/-4}$

    A) $\sqrt{\dfrac{38}{7}}$

    B) $\dfrac{7}{\sqrt{38}}$

    C) $\sqrt{5}$

    D) $\sqrt{\dfrac{2}{37}}$

    E) $\sqrt{\dfrac{2}{37}}$

63. If $a \blacksquare b = 10 - (a-b)^{-2}$, select all the following values that are equal to $4 \blacksquare 5$

    A) $2 \blacksquare 3$

    B) $-4 \blacksquare -5$

    C) $(10 \blacksquare 8) + \dfrac{1}{4}$

    D) $(7 \blacksquare 5)$

    E) $1 \blacksquare 9$

64. If ▫ and ⊗ represent single digit positive values in the following subtraction problem, select all of the following answers that are equal to 5.

    $$\begin{array}{r} 2\,▫\,⊗ \\ -\,⊗\,5 \\ \hline 24\,▫ \end{array}$$

    A) $⊗ + ▫ - 1$

    B) $\dfrac{2 \otimes \times ▫ - 18}{6}$

    C) $▫ - ⊗$

    D) $4 \otimes + ▫$

    E) $⊗ - ▫$

Algebra Practice Questions

65.

Quantity A	Quantity B
The first integer in a set of 3 consecutive odd numbers that sum to 231	The value of x in the equation $9x - (-3x - 4x + 10) = -(15x + 2)$

- Ⓐ Quantity A is greater
- Ⓑ Quantity B is greater
- Ⓒ The quantities are equal.
- Ⓓ The relationship cannot be determined from the information given.

66. Maria went to buy a car, and the car was discounted in increments. For the first $7000 of the car's cost, it was taxed at 9%. For the next $10,000, it was taxed at 4%. The remaining amount was taxed at 2%. If the total tax on the car was $1,750, how much was the car in total?

- Ⓐ $34,000
- Ⓑ $53,000
- Ⓒ $45,760
- Ⓓ $53,600
- Ⓔ $17,000

67. Select all of the answer choices that could represent a piecewise function graph with the following requirements:

    - Function is increasing on the interval $1 < x < 3$

    - Function has 3 x intercepts

    - Function contains an absolute value piecewise function

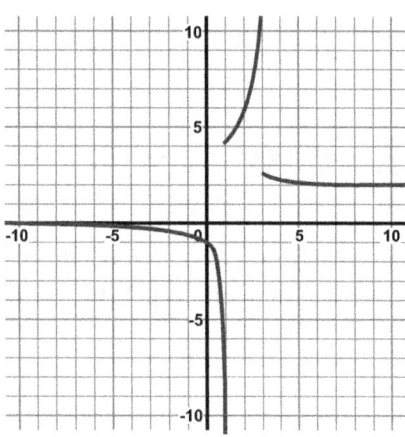

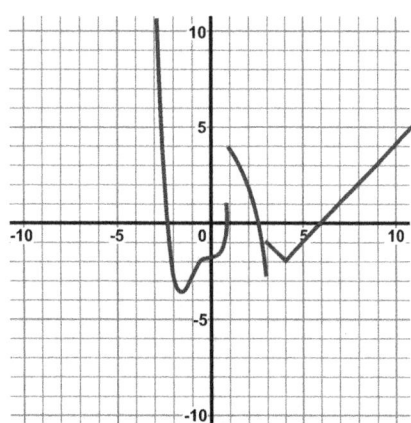

C

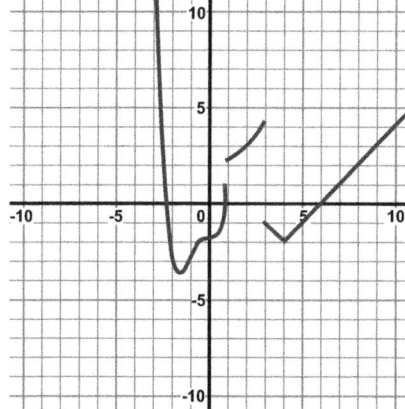

D

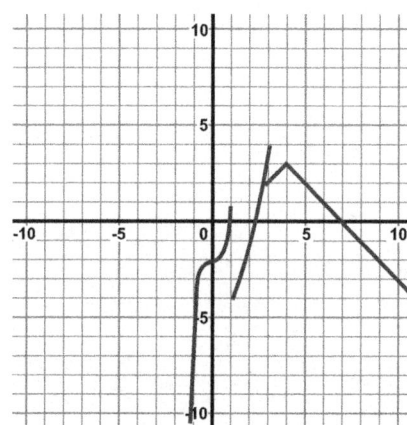

68. What is the value of k in the function $f(x) = x^2 + kx - 15$ if the graph of $f(x)$ is shown below?

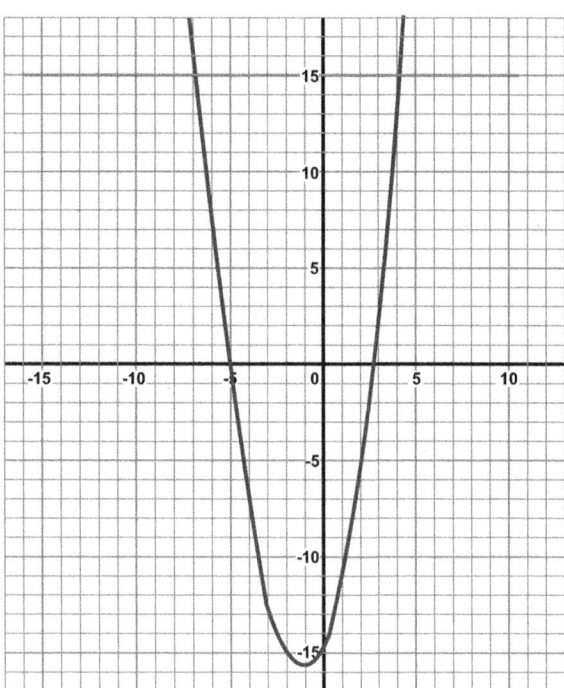

- Ⓐ 2
- Ⓑ −2
- Ⓒ −5
- Ⓓ 3
- Ⓔ −15

69. A manufacturing company produces radios at different rates depending on the total order size. The company charges $7 per radio for the first 70 radios, and then $5 for each additional radio. If x represents radios and y represents total costs, which of the following statements could be true?

   Select all that apply.

   - [A] The equation that represents this situation if there are 70 or more radios produced is $y = 7(70) + 5(x - 70)$
   - [B] The equation that represents this situation if there are 70 or more radios produced is $y = 7x + 5x$
   - [C] If there are 140 radios produced the total cost is $840.
   - [D] If there are 70 or less radios produced, the equation that represents this situation is $y = 7x$
   - [E] If there are 70 or less radios produced, the equation that represents this situation is $y = 5x$
   - [F] All of the above

Algebra Practice Questions

Level: Difficult

70.
$$-5x + 12y = 18$$
$$2x - 6y = -11$$

Quantity A	**Quantity B**
The value of the product of x and y	The value of the sum of x and y

- Ⓐ Quantity A is greater.
- Ⓑ Quantity B is greater.
- Ⓒ The two quantities are equal.
- Ⓓ The relationship cannot be determined from the information given.

71. A construction company purchased a total of 47 pieces of equipment for a total value of $2,730,000. The loaders cost $50,000 each, the dozers cost $60,000 each, and the scrapers cost $75,000 each.

    In addition, tires had to be purchased for the equipment. A total of 132 tires were purchased. The loaders require 4 tires each, the dozers require zero, and the scrapers require 6 tires each. How many dozers were purchased?

    - Ⓐ 18
    - Ⓑ 21
    - Ⓒ 6
    - Ⓓ 8
    - Ⓔ 14

72. Three pipes take 24 minutes, 6 minutes and 12 minutes respectively to fill a tank. If these pipes are turned on at the same time, find the most accurate range of time within which the pipes will fill the tank.

    - Ⓐ 7.1 to 9 minutes
    - Ⓑ 1 to 3 minutes
    - Ⓒ More than 9 minutes
    - Ⓓ 5.1 to 7 minutes
    - Ⓔ 3.1 to 5 minutes

73.

$$15 \text{ more than } 5x = 79 \text{ less } 3x$$

Quantity A

The quantity of twice *x* subtracted from the quotient of 12 and $\frac{1}{3}$, divided by 4

Quantity B

The quantity of *x* squared less the product of six and *x*, divided by 4

- Ⓐ Quantity A is greater.
- Ⓑ Quantity B is greater.
- Ⓒ The two quantities are equal.
- Ⓓ The relationship cannot be determined from the information given.

74. The following sets are given, where x is an integer greater than 1:

$$A = \{(-1 + x + x^2), (1 - x + x^2), (1 + x + x^2)\}$$
$$B = \{(-1 + x^2 + x^3), (1 - x^2 + x^3), (1 + x^2 + x^3)\}$$

Which of the following statements could be true?

Select all that apply.

- [A] The greatest element of A is less than the least element of B.
- [B] The greatest element of A is greater than the least element of B.
- [C] The greatest element of A is less than the greatest element of B.
- [D] The average of the elements of A is greater than the average of the elements of B.
- [E] The average of the elements of A is smaller than the average of the elements of B.
- [F] The average of the elements of A is equal to the average of the elements of B.
- [G] The average of the elements of A is twice the average of the elements of B.

Algebra Practice Questions

75. Jim has $50 in his piggy bank. His money consists of $31.50 in bills and 350 pennies. The remaining amount consists of nickels, dimes, and quarters. There are thrice as many nickels as quarters and three more dimes than nickels in the piggy bank.

    Select all that apply.

    A   He has 16 quarters.

    B   He has 66 dimes.

    C   He has 48 nickels.

    D   The sum of the dimes and nickels has a value greater than $7.00.

76.
    15 years ago, Mark's age was 6 times larger than Nick's age. Today, the sum of their ages is 65 years old.

    Quantity A   **Quantity B**

    Half of Mark's current age   5 more than Nick's current age

    A   Quantity A is greater

    B   Quantity B is greater

    C   The quantities are equal.

    D   The relationship cannot be determined from the information given.

77. If the graphs of $y = f(x)$ and $y = g(x)$ are given in the following diagram, which of the graphs represents $y = f(x + 6) + g(x + 6)$

$y = f(x)$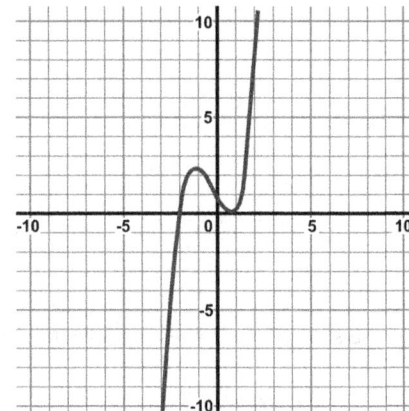

$y = g(x)$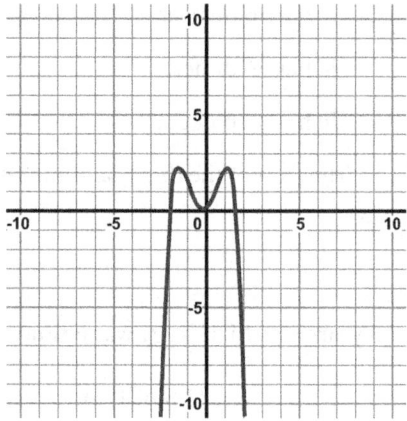

 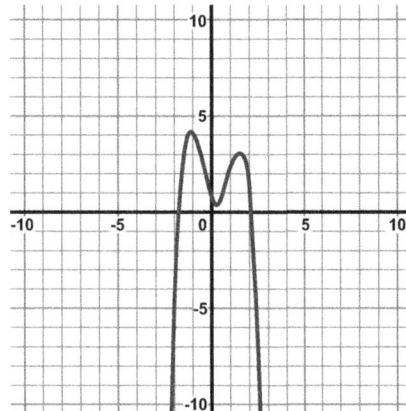

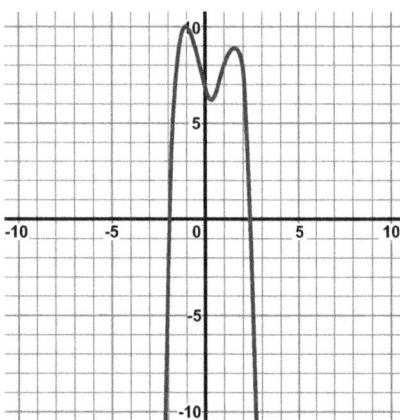

Algebra Practice Questions

(C)
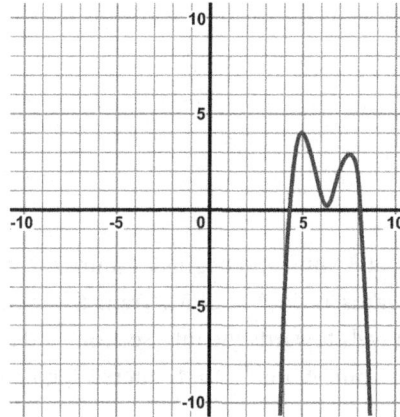

(D)
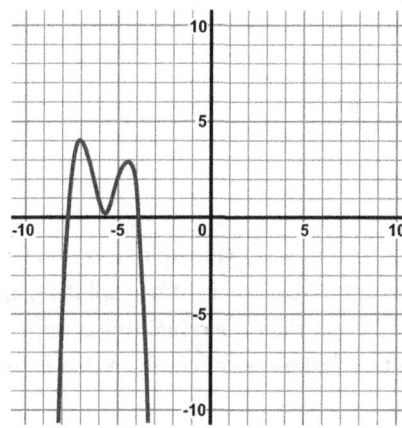

(E)
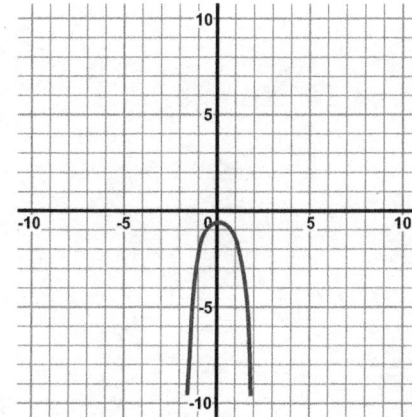

78. Select all of the following equations that are parallel and are 5 vertical units apart from $y = x - 5$

    - [A] $2x - 6y = 10$
    - [B] $3y - 9x = 12$
    - [C] $5x - 5y = 50$
    - [D] $10y = 10x$

79. Train A and B are at stations 560 miles away. Train A travels at 80mph and begins its journey towards Train B at noon. Train B travels at 40mph and beings its journey towards Train A at 3PM. Train C begins its journey 120 miles from where Train B and A cross each other and travels towards the intersection, and then toward Train B's start. Train C begins traveling at the exact moment Train A and Train B intersect, going 30mph. Which of the following statements could be true?

    Select all that apply.

    - [A] Train A and B intersect 240 miles from Train A's start.
    - [B] Train A and B intersect at 4 PM.
    - [C] Train C arrives at the Train A and B intersection at 8 PM.
    - [D] Train C and Train B intersect at 9 PM.

80. A group of children went trick-or-treating for Halloween. The group was made up of monsters and fairies. Each of the monsters got 4 treats each, and each of the fairies got 5 treats each. When splitting up candy, one group made up of one monster and 4 fairies shared their candy, and then the remaining groups were made up of 1 monster for every 2 fairies. The entire group had a total of 50 pieces of candy. What is the number of monsters in the trick or treating group?

    - (A) 2
    - (B) 3
    - (C) 4
    - (D) 5
    - (E) 11

Algebra Practice Questions

Answers and Explanations

Level: Easy

1. **Subtopic: Quadratic Equations**

   The correct answer is (B).

   If we multiply both sides of the equation by 2, we get $x^2 + 7x + 6 = 6$, which can be rearranged into standard quadratic form: $x^2 + 7x = 0$

   This can be factored as: $(x)(x + 7) = 0$, so $x = 0$ or -7.

   The correct answer is (B).

2. **Subtopic: Quadratic Equations**

   The correct answer is (B).

   $(x - 5)(x + 6) = 0 \rightarrow x = 5$ or $x = -6$

   If $x = 5$, then $x - 6 = 5 - 6 = -1$

   If $x = -6$, then $x - 6 = -6 - 6 = -12$

   In both the cases $x - 6$ is less than zero.

3. **Subtopic: Algebraic Expressions**

   The correct answer is (C).

   $a @ b = a^2 + ab - 10$. Therefore, $2 @ 3 = 2^2 + (2)(3) - 10 = 4 + 6 - 10 = 10 - 10 = 0$

4. **Sub topic: Quadratic Equations**

   The correct answer is (B).

   $@2 = 2^2 - 11 = 4 - 11 = -7$ and $\#3 = 3^2 - 3 + 11 = 9 - 3 + 11 = 17$.

   Therefore, $(@2)(\#3) = (-7)(17) = -119$

   $@3 = 3^2 - 11 = 9 - 11 = -2$ and $\#2 = 2^2 - 2 + 11 = 4 - 2 + 11 = 13$.

   Therefore, $(\#2)(@3) = (-2)(13) = -26$

   As $-26 > -119$ so, Quantity B is greater than Quantity A.

5. **Sub topic: Quadratic Equations**

   The correct answers are (A) and (D).

   Any quadratic equation of the form $ax^2 + bx + c = 0$ will have real and equal roots if its discriminant $b^2 - 4ac = 0$.

   In the given equation, $x^2 - kx + 9 = 0$, $a = 1$, $b = -k$ and $c = 9$.

   Therefore, $b^2 - 4ac = k^2 - 4(9)(1) = k^2 - 36$.

   For the roots of the given equation to be real and equal, $k^2 - 36 = 0$ or $k^2 = 36$ or $k = 6$ or $k = -6$.

6. **Sub topic: Inequalities**

   The correct answer is (A).

   $4x - 10 \geq x + 8$

   $3x \geq 18$

   $x \geq 6$

7. **Sub topic: Inequalities**

   The correct answer is (D).

   In order to answer the question, we must compare w and y.

   From the given conditions it is possible that w could be less than y. For example, w could be 1.305 and y could be 100. It is also possible that w could be greater than y. For example, w could be 1.310 and y could be 1.305. Thus, it is not possible to determine definitively whether w is lesser or greater than y.

8. **Sub topic: Operations on Algebraic Expressions**

   The correct answer is (D).

   To simplify the expression, we need to substitute a, b, c, d and e with the appropriate value and then simplify the expression.

   $a = 5, b = 2, c = 3, d = -8$, and $e = 10$

   $a - b + c - d - e$

   $= (5) - (2) + (3) - (-8) - (10) = 5 - 2 + 3 + 8 - 10$

   $= (5 + 3 + 8) - 2 - 10 = 16 - 12 = 4$

9. **Sub topic: Equations**

   The correct answers are (B) and (C).

   Since, $x^2 - 2x - 15 = 0$, then $(x - 5)(x + 3) = 0$, so $x = 5$ or $x = -3$. Since $x > 0$, then $x = 5$.

   (A) $5^2 - 6(5) + 9 = 25 - 30 + 9 = 4$ which is not 0.

   (B) $5^2 - 7(5) + 10 = 25 - 35 + 10 = 0$

   (C) $5^2 - 10(5) + 25 = 25 - 50 + 25 = 0$

   (D) $5^2 + 6(5) + 9 = 25 + 30 + 9 = 64$ which is not 0.

   (E) $5^2 + 7(5) + 10 = 25 + 35 + 10 = 70$ which is not 0.

   (F) $5^2 + 10(5) + 25 = 25 + 50 + 25 = 100$ which is not 0.

   So, the correct options are (B) and (C).

10. **Sub topic: Inequalities**

    The correct answer is (A).

    The best approach of solving such problems is picking a number. Since, p is a positive fraction less than 1 let's pick a value for it say $\frac{1}{9}$.

    $\frac{1}{9^2} = \frac{1}{81}$ and $\frac{1}{(9+1)^2} = \frac{1}{10^2} = \frac{1}{100}$.

    As, $\frac{1}{81}$ is greater than $\frac{1}{100}$ so clearly $\frac{1}{p^2}$ is greater than $\frac{1}{(p+1)^2}$.

11. **Sub topic: Algebraic Expressions**

    The correct answer is (C).

    When the r cards are distributed, there are 8 left over, so the number of cards distributed is $r - 8$. Divide the number of cards distributed by the number of people. Since there are s people, each will receive $\frac{r-8}{s}$ cards. Another approach is to pick numbers. Let $r = 58$ and $s = 10$; if $58 - 8$ or 50 cards were distributed evenly among 10 people, each would receive 5 cards. Plug the values you picked for r and s into the answer

    choices to see which ones give you 5:

    (A) $\frac{s}{8-r} = \frac{10}{8-58} = -\frac{1}{5}$, Eliminate

    (B) $\frac{r-s}{8} = \frac{58-10}{8} = 6$, Eliminate

    (C) $\frac{r-s}{s} = \frac{58-8}{10} = 5$, Works!

    (D) $s - 8r = 10 - (8 \times 58) = -454$, Eliminate.

    (E) $rs - 8 = (58 \times 10) - 8 = 572$. Eliminate.

    Since (C) is the only answer choice that gives you 5, it is the correct answer. But be sure to check all the answer choices when picking numbers.

12. **Sub topic: Algebraic Expressions**

    The correct answer is (B).

    $\frac{2F-5}{2} = F - \frac{5}{2}$ and $\frac{4F-1}{4} = F - \frac{1}{4}$.

    Now $\frac{5}{2} = 2.5$ and $\frac{1}{4} = 0.25$.

    Clearly $F - 2.5$ is smaller than $F - 0.25$ as $F > 0$.

13. **Sub topic: Linear Equations**

    The correct answer is (A).

    Write the expression in mathematical terms, solve for x and compare.

    15 more than $5x = 55$ is equivalent to $15 + 5x = 55$.

    $15 + 5x = 55$ Original equation

    $5x = 40$ Subtract 15

    $x = 8$ Divide by 5

    Quantity A: 11

    Quantity B: $x = 8$

    The quantity of A is greater than the quantity of B.

14. **Sub topic: Coordinate Geometry**

    The correct answer is (D).

    Here is question testing your understanding of

Algebra Practice Questions

the coordinate graph. To find the area of the rectangle, we must express the dimensions using x and y. The width of the rectangle is simply y, because the point (x, y) is located y units above the x-axis. The length of the rectangle is $x-2$ because it runs from point 2 to point x, parallel to the x-axis. Since width is y and length is $x-2$, the area is $y(x-2)$.

15. **Sub topic: Algebraic Expressions**

    The correct answers are (A), (B) and (C).

    $$y = \frac{1}{x} - \frac{1}{x+1} = \frac{x+1-x}{x(x+1)} = \frac{1}{x(x+1)}$$

    $$= \frac{\frac{1}{x}}{\left(\frac{x}{x}\right)(x+1)} = \frac{\frac{1}{x}}{x+1}$$

    $$= \frac{\frac{1}{x^2}}{\left(\frac{x}{x^2}\right)(x+1)} = \frac{\frac{1}{x^2}}{\frac{1}{x}(x+1)} = \frac{\frac{1}{x^2}}{1+\frac{1}{x}}$$

16. **Sub topic: Algebraic Expressions**

    The correct answer is (C).

    Try to write the information given in a mathematical statement.

    Employees in Company A = x.

    Thrice the employees in Company A = $3x$.

    20 less than thrice the employees in Company A = $3x - 20$.

    85% of 20 less than thrice the employees in Company A = $\left(\frac{85}{100}\right)(3x - 20) = 0.85 (3x - 20)$

    Therefore, employees in Company B = 0.85 (3x − 20)

17. **Sub topic: Algebraic Expressions**

    The correct answer is (B).

    You are given $a - 1 = b$, so Quantity A can be rewritten as $(a - 1)^2$. Don't assume that the quantities are equal though. In fact, $(a - 1)^2$ is not equal to $a^2 - 1$.

$a^2 - 1$ factors to $(a + 1)(a - 1)$. Quantity A can be expressed as $(a - 1)(a - 1)$. Since you know that a $a > 1$, you can factor an $(a - 1)$ from each quantity. This gives you $(a - 1)$ in Quantity A and $(a + 1)$ in Quantity B, so Quantity B is greater.

18. **Sub topic: Algebraic Expressions**

    The correct answer is (B).

    For this question, the safest way –as usual– is to try choices rather than to reason algebraically. Plugging in the choices for n, we get the following results:

    (A) $<0> = \frac{0+1}{0-1} = \frac{1}{-1} = -1$

    (B) $<2> = \frac{2+1}{2-1} = \frac{3}{1} = 3$

    (C) $<3> = \frac{3+1}{3-1} = \frac{2}{2} = 2$

    (D) $<4> = \frac{4+1}{4-1} = \frac{5}{3} = 1\frac{2}{3}$

    (E) $<5> = \frac{5+1}{5-1} = \frac{6}{4} = \frac{3}{2} = 1\frac{2}{3}$

    Choice (B) has the greatest value, so that must be the correct answer.

19. **Sub topic: Inequalities and Linear Equations**

    The correct answer is (D).

    Since no information is given directly about x or y, we cannot determine the relationship. Do not assume that since $x = -y$, y will be greater than $-y$ and thus greater than x. It is possible that y is a negative number, in which case x is a positive number and greater than y. Also, x and y could both be equal to zero.

20. **Sub topic: Inequalities**

    The correct answer is (D).

    Always be sure to plug in twice for Quantitative Comparison questions. You need to plug in numbers for p that are between 3 and 1. If $p = 2$, then Quantity A is 1 and Quantity B is 1. Since the quantities can be equal, you can cross out choices A and B. Now plug in a weird number. If $p = 1.5$ then Quantity A is .75 and Quantity B is .875. The quantities are no longer equal, so you can get more than one result. That means the answer must be D.

21. **Sub topic: System of Equations**

    The correct answer is 7.

Math procedure	Strategy/Explanation
$x^2 - 2 = 2x + 1$ $x^2 - 2x - 3 = 0$	When two curves intersect, they will have a common value of *y*. Therefore, set the right sides of the two equations equal, and simplify.
$(x - 3)(x + 1) = 0$ $x = 3, x = -1$	Factorize and solve to obtain $x = 3$, $x = -1$.
$y(3) = 2(3) + 1 = 7$ $y(-1) = 2(-1) + 1 = -1$	Use the simpler equation to compute y-values for $x = 2$, and for $x = -1$. The positive value of $y = 7$

    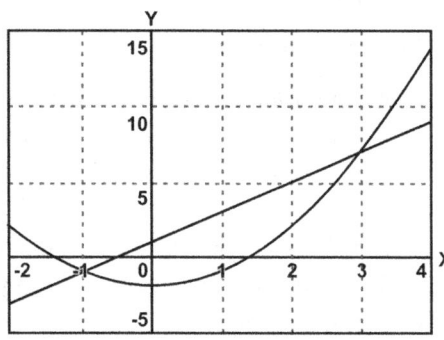

22. **Sub topic: Linear Equations**

    The correct answer is (A).

    Begin by finding the number of books that the bookstore started with, *x*.

    $x - \frac{1}{4}x + 15 = 105$

$\frac{3}{4}x + 15 = 105$

$\frac{3}{4}x = 90$

$x = 120$.

Since 120 is more than 105, Quantity A is bigger.

23. **Sub topic: Inequalities**

    The correct answer is (A).

    Rewriting the entry in Quantity A, we obtain $\frac{n^2 + 2}{n} = n + \frac{1}{n}$ thus, the problem becomes a comparison between $\frac{2}{n}$ in Quantity A and $\frac{1}{n}$ in Quantity B. Since $n > 0$, the entry in Column A is greater.

24. **Sub topic: Linear Equations**

    The correct answer is (A).

    The problem can be worked out using simultaneous equations, but that is not the most efficient way of solving it. For that reason, we will set up the equation (for the "aficionados"), but we will not actually solve for *x* and *y*. Let x be the number of shirts costing $13 and *y* the number costing $10.

    $x + y = 16$

    $13x + 10y = 187$

    Final solution: $x = 9$ and $y = 7$

    We have omitted the detailed calculations because there is a simpler method. Let us assume, for the sake of argument, that the two quantities are equal-that is, that the man bought equal numbers of both types of shirts. If we are correct in assuming that he bought eight $13 shirts and eight $10 shirts, then $(8 \times 13) + (8 \times 10)$ ought to equal $187. When we do the multiplication, we get the result $184. That tells us our original assumption of equal numbers was incorrect and, further, that the answer to the question is not (C). We should then make a second assumption, but should we assume that he bought more expensive shirts than we first guessed, or fewer? A moment of reflection will show that we should adjust our initial assumption to include a greater number of expensive shirts, for only by increasing that number will we add to the $184 which was the result of our original assumption. So, we would next assume-again for the purposes of argument-that the man bought nine $13 shirts and only seven $10 shirts. But at this point we have already solved the problem! We do not need to know the precise ratio, e.g., whether 9:7, 10:6, 11:5, 12:4, 13:3, 14:4, or 15:1; we have already determined that the ratio is one of those listed, and so it must be the case that Quantity A is greater.

25. **Sub topic: Coordinate Geometry**

    The correct answer is (B).

    We know that if a line is represented as $y = mx + c$ then m defines the slope of the line.

    Writing the given equation of the straight line in the similar format we get,

    $2y + 3x - 5 = 0$

    $2y = -3x + 5$

    $y = \left(-\frac{3}{2}\right)x + 5$

    So, the slope of the given line is $-\frac{3}{2}$ which is smaller than $\frac{3}{2}$

    The correct answer is (B).

26. **Sub topic: Linear inequalities**

    The correct solutions are (A), (D) and (E).

    To solve this absolute value inequality, separate the inequality into $-2x + 7 > 5$ and $-2x + 7 < -5$. For both inequalities, subtract 7 from both sides and then divide by –2 (make sure to switch the inequality sign when dividing by a negative). The first inequality then becomes $x < 1$ and the second becomes $x > 6$. Therefore, 7, –6, and 0 work. This makes the solutions A, D, and E.

27. **Sub topic: Time Distance and Speed**

    The correct answer is 10 hours.

    If Car A was traveling at a speed of 20mph for 15 hours, using speed × time = distance, $20 \times 15 = 300$ miles. If Car B was driving 10mph faster than Car A, it was traveling at 20 + 10 = 30mph. If they went to the same destination, Car B traveled 300 miles. Plugging this into the speed × time = distance equation becomes $30 \times t = 300$, where t is the time. Dividing by 30 on both sides gives t = 10. This means it took Car B 10 hours to drive to the same destination.

Level: Medium

28. **Sub topic: Functions**

    The correct answer is (B).

    Since $f(x) = ax^4 - 5x^2 + ax - 5$,

    $f(b) = ax^4 - 5x^2 + ax - 5$

    $= ab^4 - 5b^2 + ab - 5$

    $f(-b) = ax^4 - 5x^2 + ax - 5$

    $= a(-b)^4 - 5(-b)^2 + a(-b) - 5$

    $= ab^4 - 5b^2 - ab - 5$

    Therefore, $f(b) - f(-b) = ab^4 - 5b^2 + ab - 5 - (ab^4 - 5b^2 - ab - 5) = 2ab$

    Alternatively, we could have recognized that the only term of the function that will be different for $f(b)$ than for $f(-b)$ is "ax." The other three terms are all unaffected by the sign of the variable. More succinctly, $f(b)-f(-b)$ must equal $ab-(-ab) = 2ab$.

    The correct answer is (B).

29. **Sub topic: Linear Equation, Algebraic Expressions**

    The correct answer is 5.

    Place x over 1 to form a fraction on the right side.

    $\frac{5x^2 + ax + b}{3x^2 + 7x + 5} = \frac{x}{1}$

Cross multiply and simplify.

$x(3x^2 + 7x + 5) = 5x^2 + ax + b$

$3x^3 + 7x^2 + 5x = 5x^2 + ax + b$

Subtract $5x^2$, ax, and b from each side, and factor.

$3x^3 + 7x^2 + 5x - 5x^2 - ax - b = 5x^2 + ax + b - 5x^2 - ax - b$

$3x^3 + 2x^2 + 5x - ax - b = 0$

$3x^3 + 2x^2 + (5-a)x - b = 0$

$3x^3 + 2x^2 - b = 0$ (given in the problem)

$(5 - a)x = 0$

Divide each side by x knowing that we are given $x \neq 0$.

$5 - a = 0$

$a = 5$

30. **Sub topic: System of Equations**

    The correct answer is (B).

    $x + y = 8$ and $x + z = 11$. Therefore, $x + y - (x + z) = 8 - 11 = -3$ or $z - y = 3$

    $z - y = 3$ and $y + z = 7$. Therefore, $z - y + (y + z) = 3 + 7$ or, $2z = 10$ or $z = 5$.

    Checking $z - y = 3$ and $z = 5$. Therefore, $y = 2$.

    $x + y = 8$ and $y = 2$. Therefore, $x = 6$.

    So, $x + y - z = 6 + 2 - 5 = 3$.

31. **Sub topic: Inequalities**

    The correct answer is (A).

    Simplify the inequalities, so that all the inequality symbols point in the same direction. Then, line up the inequalities as shown. Finally, combine the inequalities.

    $y < x$, $x < 7$, and $-4 < y$ can be written together as $-4 < y < x < 9$.

    Now as x and y each cannot be equal to 9 and so the maximum value of $x + y < 18$. The largest prime number smaller than 18 is 17. Hence, the largest prime number that can be equal to $x + y$ is 17.

32. **Sub topic: Functions**

    The correct answer is (C).

    To determine the number of roots in the equation, set $f(x)=0$ and use the determinant ($b^2 - 4ac$) to determine the number of roots. If the determinant is negative, there are no real roots. If the determinant is zero, then there is exactly one real root, and if the determinant is positive, there are two real roots.

    Quantity A:

    $0 = 2x^2 - 3x + 1$

    $a = 2, b = -3, c = 1$

    Determinant = $b^2 - 4ac = (-3)^2 - 4(2)(1) = 1$

    2 real roots

    Quantity B:

    $0 = x^2 - 7x - 8$

    $a = 1, b = -7, c = -8$

    Determinant = $b^2 - 4ac = (-7)^2 - 4(1)(-8) = 81$

    2 real roots

    Both have two real roots, so the answer is C.

33. **Sub topic: Percent, Ratio, Rate**

    The correct answer is 100.

    52% of all employees or in other words 52% of 150 = 78 employees contribute to the plan.

    If S employees are in the 35 + age group, then 63% of S or 0.63S contribute.

    There are 150 – S employees in the 25-35 age group and 30% of these i.e. 0.3(150 - S) contribute. Thus $0.63S + 0.3(150 - S) = 78$. Solving we get S = 100.

34. **Sub topic: Quadratic Equations**

    The correct answer is (C).

    $x^2 - 6x - 27 = 0 \rightarrow (x + 3)(x - 9) = 0 \rightarrow x = -3$ or $x = 9$.

    $y^2 - 6y - 40 = 0 \rightarrow (y + 4)(y - 10) = 0 \rightarrow y = -4$ or $y = 10$.

    Therefore, the maximum value of $x - y = 9 - (-4)$

Algebra Practice Questions

= 13 and hence, maximum value of $2(x + y) = 2 \times 13 = 26$.

35. **Sub topic: System of Equations**

    The correct answer is (C).

    $x^2 - 6x - 27 = 0 \rightarrow (x + 3)(x - 9) = 0 \rightarrow x = -3$ or $x = 9$.

    $y^2 - 6y - 40 = 0 \rightarrow (y + 4)(y - 10) = 0 \rightarrow y = -4$ or $y = 10$.

    Therefore, the minimum value of $x + y = (-3) + (-4) = -7$.

36. **Sub topic: Linear inequalities**

    The correct answers are (C), (D), (E), (F), (G), (H) and (I).

    First solve the equation for b.

    $2x - 3b = 0$

    $2x = 3b$

    $\dfrac{2x}{3} = b$

    Then by substitution, the inequality $b < 2$ becomes

    $\dfrac{2x}{3} < 2$

    $x < \left(\dfrac{3}{2}\right)(2)$

    $x < 3$

    So, x is valid for all values less than 3.

37. **Sub topic: Functions**

    The correct answer is 1.30.

Math procedure	Strategy/Explanation
$g(2) = \dfrac{2}{1+2} = \dfrac{2}{3}$	Compute $g(2)$
$f\left(\dfrac{2}{3}\right) = 1 + \left(\dfrac{2}{3}\right)^3 = 1.2963$	Compute $f[g(2)] = f\left(\dfrac{2}{3}\right)$
$f\left(\dfrac{2}{3}\right) \approx 1.30$	Use 2 decimal place accuracy

38. **Sub topic: Relations**

    The correct answers are (C), (F), (G), (I) and (J).

    The table below shows all possibilities for the algebraic signs of x, y and z. Those satisfying $xy > 0$ are checked in the fourth column of the chart, and those satisfying $yz < 0$ are checked in the fifth column of the chart.

x	y	z	xy > 0	yz < 0
+	+	+	✓	
+	+	−	✓	✓
+	−	+		✓
+	−	−		
−	+	+		
−	+	−		✓
−	−	+	✓	✓
−	−	−	✓	

    The table below shows only the possibilities that satisfy both $xy > 0$ and $yz < 0$. Noting that the expression in answer choice (E) is the product of the squares of three non-zero numbers, which is always positive.

			(A)	(B)	(C)	(D)	(E)	(F)	(G)	(H)	(I)	(J)
x	y	z	xyz	xyz^2	xy^2z	xy^2z^2	$x^2y^2z^2$	x^2yz	$-x^2yz^2$	x^2yz	$x(-y)z^2$	$-(xyz^2)$
+	+	−	−	+	−	+	+	−	+	−	+	−
−	−	+	+	+	+	−	−	−	−	−	−	−

39. **Sub topic: Quadratic Equations**

    The correct answer is (D).

    Select choices for x and determine the value of $y - 10$ and compare. $y = 3x^2 + 8x - 10$

    When $x = 0$, $y = 3(0)^2 + 8(0) - 10 = -10$ and $y - 10 = -10 - 10 = -20$.

    In this case Quantity A is greater.

    When $x = 1$, $y = 3(1)^2 + 8(1) - 10 = 3 + 8 - 10 = 1$ and $y - 10 = 1 - 10 = -9$.

    In this case Quantity A is greater.

    When $x = 2$, $y = 3(2)^2 + 8(2) - 10 = 12 + 16 - 10 = 18$ and $y - 10 = 18 - 10 = 8$.

    In this case Quantity B is greater.

Since different results were obtained the correct answer is D, the relationship cannot be determined based on the information given.

40. **Sub topic: Applications**

    The correct answers are (A), (C) and (E).

    Let Austin be x then John will be $\frac{2x}{3}$ and James will be $\frac{4x}{15}$. This means that

    $\frac{4x}{15} + \frac{2x}{3} + x = 620x = 320.7$

    The share of James will be $4 \times \frac{320.7}{15} = 86$

    The share of John will be $2 \times \frac{320.7}{3} = 213$

    The share of Austin will be 321.

41. **Sub topic: System of Equation**

    The correct answer is (A).

    To determine the value of $7x + 10y$, we need to solve the system of equations for x and y using the linear combination or elimination method.

    $2(-5x + 2y = 9)$

    $1(3x - 4y = -4)$

    $-10x + 4y = 18$

    $3x - 4y = -4$

    $-7x = 14$

    $x = -2$

    Substituting $x = -2$ in the first equation i.e. $-5x + 2y = 9$, we get:

    $-5(-2) + 2y = 9$

    $10 + 2y = 9$

    $2y = -1$

    $y = -\frac{1}{2}$

    Therefore, $(x, y) = \left(-2, -\frac{1}{2}\right)$

    To solve for $7x + 10y$, plug the values of x and y into the equation.

    $7(-2) + 10\left(-\frac{1}{2}\right)$

    $= -14 - 5$

    $= -19$

    The answer is (A).

42. **Sub topic: Quadratic Equations**

    The correct answers are (A), (B) and (D).

    Case 1: Use positive value of $|x^2 - x + 1| = x^2 - x + 1$

    $x^2 - x + 1 = 2x - 1$

    $x^2 - 3x + 2 = 0 \to (x - 1)(x - 2) = 0$

    $x = 1, 2$

    Case 2: Use negative value of $|x^2 - x + 1| = -x^2 + x - 1$

    $-x^2 + x - 1 = 2x - 1$

    $x^2 + x = 0 \to x(x + 1) = 0$

    $x = 0, -1$

43. **Sub topic: Inequalities**

    The correct answer is (D).

    Try values for the variables.

    If $x = 2$ and $y = 1$, then 2 in Quantity A is greater than $\frac{1}{2}$ in Quantity B.

    But, if $x = -1$ and $y = -2$, then $\frac{1}{2}$ in Quantity A is less than 2 in Quantity B.

    Since more than one relationship is possible, choice (D) is correct.

44. **Sub topic: Quadratic Functions**

    The correct answer is (D).

    $f(x) = 2x^2 - 5x$ and $g(x) = x^2 + x - 3$

    Find the value of $(f \circ g)(-2) - [f(3) + g(2)]$

    $(f \circ g)(-2)$: means the same as $f(g(-2))$.

    First calculate $g(-2)$ then find f at that answer.

$g(-2) = (-2)^2 + (-2) - 3$

$g(-2) = 4 + (-2) - 3$

$g(-2) = 4 - 5$

$g(-2) = -1$

$f(-1) = 2(-1)^2 - 5(-1)$

$f(-1) = 2(1) - 5(-1)$

$f(-1) = 2 - (-5)$

$f(-1) = 7$

$f(3)$:

$f(3) = 2(3)^2 - 5(3)$

$f(3) = 2(9) - 5(3)$

$f(3) = 18 - (15)$

$f(3) = 3$

$g(2)$:

$g(2) = (2)^2 + (2) - 3$

$g(2) = 4 + (2) - 3$

$g(2) = 3$

$(f \circ g)(-2) - [f(3) + g(2)]$

$7 - (3 + 3) = 1$

45. **Sub topic: Inequalities**

The correct answer is (A).

Since x^2 is a positive fraction less than 1, its positive square root, x, must also be a fraction less than 1, which you are told is positive. When a positive fraction less than 1 is squared, the result is positive fraction smaller than the original. Therefore, $x^2 < x$. For example, $\left(\frac{1}{2}\right)^2 < \frac{1}{2}$, since $\left(\frac{1}{2}\right)^2 = \frac{1}{4}$, so in Quantity A you are subtracting a positive value from 1, and in Quantity B you are subtracting a larger positive value from 1, so Quantity A must be greater.

46. **Sub topic: System of Equation**

The correct answer is (E).

With algebraic answer choices, we should plug in numbers. Let $x = y = 2$, which makes $z = 4$. Plugging these values into the choices, we'd get the following:

[Yes] (A) $2(2) + 2(2) = 2(4)$

[Yes] (B) $2 - 2 = 0$

[Yes] (C) $2 - 4 = 2 - 4$

[Yes] (D) $2 = \frac{4}{2}$

[No] (E) $4 - 2 = 2(2)$

47. **Sub topic: Inequalities**

The correct answer is (D).

Try $x = y = 2$. Then Quantity A $= y^x = 2^2 = 4$. Quantity B $= y^{(x+1)} = 2^3 = 8$, making Quantity B greater. But if $x = 2$ and $y = \frac{1}{2}$, Quantity A $= \left(\frac{1}{2}\right)^2 = \frac{1}{4}$ and Quantity B $= \left(\frac{1}{2}\right)^3 = \frac{1}{8}$. In this case, Quantity A is greater than Quantity B, so the answer is (D).

48. **Sub topic:**

The correct answer is 0.613

Math Procedure	Strategy/Explanation
$4\$9 = \frac{\sqrt{4}}{\sqrt{4}+\sqrt{9}} = \frac{2}{5}$	Compute 4$9 and simplify.
$1\$\left(\frac{2}{5}\right) = \frac{\sqrt{1}}{\sqrt{1}+\sqrt{\frac{2}{5}}} = 0.6126$	Compute $1\$\left(\frac{2}{5}\right)$ and simplify
$1\$\left(\frac{2}{5}\right) \approx 0.613$	Use 3 decimal place accuracy.

49. **Sub topic: Linear Equations**

The correct answer is (A).

First, we solve the first equation for a in terms of b:

$\frac{(3a+2b)}{(7a+4b)} = \frac{15}{32}$; $(3a + 2b) \times 32 = 15 \times (7a + 4b)$ or

$96a + 64b = 105a + 60b$ or $4b = 9a$; $a = \dfrac{4b}{9}$

Now substitute the expression for a into the second equation:

$$\dfrac{(3a+b)}{7b} = \left(\dfrac{\dfrac{3\times 4b}{9}+b}{7b}\right) = \left(\dfrac{\dfrac{4b}{3}+b}{7b}\right) = \dfrac{7b}{(3\times 7b)} = \dfrac{1}{3}$$

50. **Sub topic: Inequalities**

    The correct answer is (A).

    It is given that $c = d + 2$. Quantity A asks for the value of $c^2 - d^2$, while Quantity B asks for the value of $4d$. Solve for the value in Quantity A first, in terms of d, by substituting the given information for c in $c^2 - d^2$. Then, $(d + 2)^2 - d^2 = (d^2 + 2d + 2d + 4) - d^2 = 4d + 4$. Now look again at Quantity B: $4d$. Is $4d + 4$ greater than $4d$? To compare, set up an inequality: $4d + 4 > 4d$. See if this inequality is true by solving for d. $4d + 4 - 4d > 4d - 4d$; so, $4 > 0$. Since this is true in every instance, $4d + 4$ must be greater than $4d$ no matter what value d takes on.

51. **Sub topic: Quadratic Equations**

    The correct answers are (B) and (C).

    The intercepts occur when the values of y are equal i.e. from the intersection of curves. (Geometry)

    $x^2 - x + 4 = 4x - 1$

    $x^2 - 5x + 5 = 0$

    $x = 5 \pm \dfrac{\sqrt{25-20}}{2} = \dfrac{5 \pm \sqrt{5}}{2}$

    $x = 3.62$, or $x = 1.38$

    Therefore (A) is false, (B) is true, (C) is true, (D) is false, (E) is false.

52. **Sub topic: Linear Equations**

    The correct answer is (B).

    There's one box that's in both rows -the one in the middle with value $\dfrac{2}{9}$.

    In fact, we have

    $\dfrac{1}{3} + \dfrac{2}{9} + y$ in the horizontal row,

    $x + \dfrac{2}{9} + \dfrac{4}{5}$ in the vertical row, and we are comparing x and y.

    Since $\dfrac{2}{9}$ is the part of both rows, we can throw it out.

    So, we have $\dfrac{1}{3} + y = \dfrac{4}{5} + x$.

    Since $\dfrac{4}{5}$ is greater, the number we add to $\dfrac{4}{5}$ has to be less than the number we add to $\dfrac{1}{3}$ for the sums to be the same.

    Hence, x must be less than y. The answer is (B).

53. **Sub topic: Exponents**

    The correct answer is (D).

    When in doubt, you must plug in at least twice for quantitative comparison questions. Since x can be 1, you should start by trying $x = 1$. In that case, Quantity A equals $1^{(1+2)}$, or 1^3, which is 1. Quantity B equals $(1+2)^1$, or 31, which is 3. Quantity B is greater. What if $x = 2$? In that case, Quantity A equals 2^{2+2} or 2^4, which is 16. Quantity B equals $(2+2)^2$, or 4^2, which is 16. So, the quantities can be equal. You can get more than one result, so the answer is D.

54. **Sub topic: Algebraic Expressions**

    The correct answer is (A).

    Multiply each side of the given equation by $(m + n)$.

    $(m + n)(m - n) = (m+n)$

    Find the product on the left using conjugate identity $a^2 - b^2 = (a + b)(a - b)$.

    $m^2 - n^2 = m + n$

    Subtract m from and add n^2 to each side.

    $m^2 - n^2 - m + n^2 = m + n - m + n^2$

    Combine the like terms.

    $m^2 - m = n + n^2$

Factor each side.

$m(m - 1) = n(n + 1)$

Thus, (A) is the correct answer.

55. **Subtopic: Inequalities and Roots**

The correct answer is (D).

First, we solve Inequality 1:

$4(x + 2) \leq 2(x + 5) + 14$

$4x + 8 \leq 2x + 10 + 14$

$2x \leq 16$

$x \leq 8$

Then we solve Inequality 2:

$\sqrt{16 - 8y + y^2} \leq 9$

$\sqrt{(4-y)^2} \leq 9$

The square root of a square expression will always be a positive number, so we can write this inequality as:

$|4 - y| \leq 9$

$-9 \leq 4 - y \leq 9$

$-13 \leq -y \leq 5$

We multiply with (−1) so the inequality sign changes:

$13 \geq y \geq -5$

Any number equal to, or less than, 8 is a solution of the first inequality, while for the second inequality the solutions are numbers equal to, or greater than, −5 and less than, or equal to, 13.

This means that 13 for instance is a solution for Inequality 2, which is greater than any solution of Inequality 1. However, in another example, 6 is a solution of Inequality 2, which is less than some solutions of Inequality 1 (8 for instance).

The relationship cannot be determined without further information and (D) is the correct answer.

56. **Subtopic: Exponential Equations and Quadratic Equations**

The correct answer is −2.

Multiplying by 64, we get $4^{y^2} = (64)2^{-y}$

Substituting $4 = 2^2$ and $64 = 2^6$ in the given equation results in

$(2^2)^{y^2} = (2^6)(2^{-y})$

Applying the law of Sequential Exponents, we have

$2^{2y^2} = 2^{6-y}$

Since the bases are equal and the numbers are equal, the indices must be the same.

Hence

$2y^2 = 6 - y$

$2y^2 + y - 6 = 0$

Expanding the middle term, we have

$2y^2 - 3y + 4y - 6 = 0$

$y(2y - 3) + 2(2y - 3) = (y + 2)(2y - 3) = 0$

$y + 2 = 0$ and $2y - 3 = 0$

Thus $y = -2$ and $y = \frac{3}{2} = 1\frac{1}{2}$

Since $y < |y|$, it implies that y must be negative, thus, $y = -2$

57. **Subtopic: Algebraic Expressions and Equations**

The correct answer is (B).

If we square both sides of the equation, we get $z^2 = 8zs - 16s^2$.

We can now put the quadratic in standard form $z^2 - 8zs + 16s^2 = 0$ and factor it as $(z - 4s)^2 = 0$.

Since $z - 4s = 0$, $z = 4s$.

58. **Sub topic: Operations on Algebraic Expressions**

The correct answers are (A), (C) and (E).

Simplify the given expressions:

$K = \left(\frac{2}{3}\right)\left(\frac{3}{2} + a\right)$

(1) $K = \left(\dfrac{2a+3}{3}\right)$

$L = \left(\dfrac{3}{4}\right)\left(\dfrac{4}{3}+b\right)$

(2) $L = \left(\dfrac{3b+4}{4}\right)$

$M = \left(\dfrac{a}{b}\right)\left(\dfrac{3}{5}+3\right)$

(3) $M = \left(\dfrac{18a}{5b}\right)$

$K + L = \left(\dfrac{2a+3}{3}\right) + \left(\dfrac{3b+4}{4}\right)$

$K + L = \left(\dfrac{8a+9b+24}{12}\right)$

$12(K + L) = 12\left(\dfrac{8a+9b+24}{12}\right)$

$= 8a + 9b + 24$

$L + M = \left(\dfrac{3b+4}{4}\right) + \left(\dfrac{18a}{5b}\right)$

$L + M = \left(\dfrac{15b^2 + 20b + 72a}{20b}\right)$

$K + M = \left(\dfrac{2a+3}{3}\right) + \left(\dfrac{18a}{5b}\right)$

$= \left(\dfrac{10ab + 15b + 54a}{15b}\right)$

$L - K = \left(\dfrac{3b+4}{4}\right) - \left(\dfrac{2a+3}{3}\right)$

$= \left(\dfrac{9a - 8b}{12}\right)$

59. **Subtopic: Absolute Value**

The correct answer is (D).

Quantity A is solved by first subtracting 2 from both sides to obtain $-3|x| < 2$, and then divide by -3 on both sides and switch the inequality. You then get $|x| > -2/3$. X can be any real number because any value's absolute value will give you a number greater than or equal to 0, which will always be greater than a negative value. Quantity B is solved by adding 3 to both sides to obtain $4y > 16$. Divide by 4 on both sides to get $y > 4$. Because we do not know the exact value of x or y, it is possible that either Quantity A or Quantity B could be larger, and therefore the solution is D. The relationship cannot be determined from the information given.

60. **Sub topic: Solving Linear Equations and Inequalities**

The correct answer is (A).

To solve here, first simplify the inequality given by multiplying 7 on both sides to get $9 - 5x \geq -21$. Then subtract 9 from both sides to get $-5x \geq -30$. Divide by -5, which flips the inequality sign to obtain $x \leq 6$. For Quantity A, the minimum value will be when $x = 6$, so $10 - 6 = 4$. Quantity A is 4. To find the minimum value for Quantity B, also choose 6, as this will give the largest negative value for the first term. Plugging in 6 turns the expression into $\dfrac{-3(6)}{5} + 4 = -3.6 + 4 = 0.4$. Therefore, $4 > 0.4$, and the answer is A, Quantity A is greater.

61. **Sub topic: Functions**

The correct answer is (B).

To find Quantity A, plug in 4 for x into $f(x)$ to obtain $\dfrac{3(4)+4}{-2(4)-1} = \dfrac{16}{-9}$. To find the value of x when $f(x) = 16$, plug in 16 for $f(x)$ and solve for x to obtain the following equation: $16 = \dfrac{3x+4}{-2x-1}$. Multiply both sides by $-2x - 1$ to get $16(-2x - 1) = 3x + 4$. Then distribute the $-2x - 1$ to get $-32x - 16 = 3x + 4$. Combine like terms by adding $32x$ and subtracting 4. Then, the equation becomes $-12 = 35x$. Divide by 35 to get $x = -12/35$. $-\dfrac{16}{9} < -\dfrac{12}{35}$, Quantity B is greater than Quantity A. The solution is B.

Algebra Practice Questions

62. **Sub topic: Exponential Operations**

The correct answer is (A).

The value of $\sqrt{9/-4}$ =

$$\sqrt{\frac{2(9)-5(-4)}{5(9)-(-4)}} = \sqrt{\frac{38}{49}} = \sqrt{\frac{38}{7}}$$

The solution is A.

63. **Sub topic: Functions**

The correct answers are (A), (B), and (C).

$4\blacksquare 5 = 10 - (4-5)^{-2} = 10 - (-1)^{-2} = 10 - 1 = 9$

Choice A: $2\blacksquare 3 = 10 - (2-3)^{-2} = 10 - (-1)^{-2} = 10 - 1 = 9$. This is equal to $4\blacksquare 5$ so Choice A is correct.

Choice B: $-4\blacksquare -5 =$
$10 - (-4-(-5))^{-2} = 10 - (1)^{-2}$
$= 10 - 1 = 9$. This is equal to $4\blacksquare 5$ so Choice B is correct.

Choice C: $(10\blacksquare 8) + \frac{1}{4} = 10 - (10-8)^{-2} + \frac{1}{4} = 10 - (2)^{-2} + \frac{1}{4} = 10 - \frac{1}{4} + \frac{1}{4} = 9$. This is equal to $4\blacksquare 5$ so Choice C is correct.

Choice D: $7\blacksquare 5 = 10 - (7-5)^{-2} = 10 - \frac{1}{4} = 9\frac{3}{4}$. This is not equal to $4\blacksquare 5$ so Choice D is incorrect.

Choice E: $1\blacksquare 9 = 10 - (1-9)^{-2} = 10 - (-8)^{-2}$
$= 10 - \frac{1}{64} = 9\frac{63}{64}$. This is not equal to $4\blacksquare 5$ so Choice E is incorrect.

64. **Sub topic: Functions**

The correct answers are (B) and (C).

First, find the values of $\square$ and $\otimes$. To do this, first look at the tens place. $\square - \otimes = 4$. Because there is no borrowing from the hundreds place (as seen from the 2 in the original subtraction step and a 2 in the solution). So, this means $\square > \otimes$. In the ones place, $\otimes - 5 = \square$. However,

a 1 must have been borrowed from the tens place because $\square > \otimes$. So, the first equation then becomes $\square - 1 - \otimes = 4$. So, $10 + \otimes - 5 = \square$. Now, test out values between 0 and 9, and you will find that $\square = 8$ and $\otimes = 3$

Choice A: $\otimes + \square - 1 = 3 + 8 - 1 = 10$. Choice A is not equal to 5 so this is incorrect.

Choice B: $\frac{2\otimes \times \square - 18}{6} = \frac{2 \times 3 \times 8 - 18}{6} = 5$. Choice B is equal to 5 so it is correct.

Choice C: $\otimes - \square = 8 - 3 = 5$. Choice C is equal to 5 so it is correct.

Choice D: $\otimes + \square = 4 \times 3 + 8 = 20$. Choice D is not equal to 5 so it is incorrect.

Choice E: $\otimes - \square = 3 - 8 = -5$. Choice E is not equal to 5 so it is incorrect.

The solutions are then Choice B and C.

65. **Sub topic: Integers**

The correct answer is (A).

Quantity A is found by setting up a consecutive integer equation. If the first integer is represented by x, the second will be $x + 2$, and the third will be $x + 4$. Because their sum is given as 231, the equation to solve for x is $x + x + 2 + x + 4 = 231$. To solve, add the like terms together to get $3x + 6 = 231$. Subtract 6 and divide by 3 to get 75 for x. This means the first integer in a set of 3 consecutive odd numbers is 75.

Next, find the value of x in the equation for Quantity B. Distribute the negative into both sets of parentheses: $9x + 3x + 4x - 10 = -15x - 2$. Combine like terms, and solve:

$16x - 10 = -15x - 2$

$31x = 8$

$x = \frac{8}{31}$

Since Quantity A is 75 and Quantity B is much less than 75, Quantity A is greater.

66. **Sub topic: Solving Linear Equations and Inequalities**

    The correct answer is (B).

    If x represents the cost of the car, the single variable linear equation that represents this situation is $7000 \times 0.09 + 0.04(10000) + 0.02(x - 17000) = 1750$. Simplifying and distributing gives $630 + 400 + 0.02x - 340 = 1750$. Combining like terms becomes $0.02x + 690 = 1750$. Subtracting 690 and dividing by 0.02 gives you $x = 53,000$. This is Choice B.

67. **Sub topic: Intercepts and Slopes of Lines**

    The correct answers are (C) and (D).

    Choice A: Choice A is increasing on the interval $1 < x < 3$, but does not have an absolute value piecewise function or any x intercepts. Therefore, Choice A is incorrect.

    Choice B: Choice B is decreasing on the interval $1 < x < 3$ and has 4 x intercepts. However, it does have an absolute value function. Choice B is incorrect.

    Choice C: Choice C has 3 x intercepts, is increasing from $1 < x < 3$, and has an absolute value function on the interval $x > 3$. Choice C is correct.

    Choice D: Choice D has 3 x intercepts, is increasing from $1 < x < 3$, and has an absolute value function on the interval $x > 3$. Choice E is correct.

    Therefore, Choices C and D are correct.

68. **Sub topic: Intercepts and Slopes of Lines**

    The correct answer is (D).

    The graph has x intercepts at $x = -5$ and $x = 3$, so the function must look like $f(x) = (x + 5)(x - 3)$ in factored form. When you foil this out, you get $f(x) = x^2 + 5x - 2x - 15$. Combining $5x$ and $-2x$ gives you $3x$, which means $k = 3$. The correct answer is D.

69. **Sub topic: Relations**

    The correct answers are (A), (C) and (D).

    Choice A: If there are 70 or more radios and x represents the total number of radios, then $7(70)$ represents the cost of the first 70 radios. The additional radios are represented by $x - 70$, and this value is multiplied by 5 to get the total cost of the additional radios. The sum of $7(70) + 5(x - 70)$ will give the total cost for the radios, y. Choice A is correct.

    Choice B: If there are 70 or more radios, it costs $5 for each additional radio, so we would need ($x - 70$) as in option A. Choice B is not correct.

    Choice C: If there are 140 radios produced, the total cost will be $7 \times 70 + 5 \times 70$, which is $490 + 350$, which is $840. Choice C is correct.

    Choice D: If there are less than 70 radios produced, the $5 per additional radio does not apply, so it will be $7 per radio, $y = 7x$. Choice D is correct.

    Choice E: If there are less than 70 radios, it will be $7 per radio rather than $5 per radio, so the equation will be $y = 7x$. Choice E is incorrect.

Level: Difficult

70. **Sub topic: System of Equations**

    The correct answer is (A).

    To determine which quantity is greater, we need to solve the equations for both x and y using linear combination or elimination methods.

    $1(-5x + 12y = 18)$ i.e. $-5x + 12y = 18$

    $2(2x - 6y = -11)$ i.e. $4x - 12y = -22$

    Add equations together to solve for x

    $-x = -4$ or $x = 4$

    Solve for y by plugging in 4 for x:

    $2(4) - 6y = -11$

    $8 - 6y = -11$

    $-6y = -19$

    $y = \dfrac{19}{6}$

Now to compare the two quantities:

Quantity A:

$(x)(y) = (4)\left(\frac{19}{6}\right) = \frac{38}{3}$

Quantity B:

$(x) + (y) = (4) + \left(\frac{19}{6}\right) = \frac{43}{6}$

The answer is A.

71. **Sub topic: System of Equations**

The correct answer is (A).

In order to solve the problem, three equations need to be constructed. The first involves the number of pieces of equipment, which is known to be 47.

Loaders = a, Dozers = b, and Scrapers = c:

$a + b + c = 47$

Next, an equation can be constructed based on the known total cost and known cost per item:

$\$50,000a + \$60,000b + \$75,000c = \$2,730,000$

Reduced is: $10a + 12b + 15c = 546$

Finally, an equation can be constructed based on the known tire quantities:

$4a + 0b + 6c = 132$

Now that we have three equations, we can solve for variables and substitute:

$4a + 0b + 6c = 132 \rightarrow 4a = 132 - 6c \rightarrow a = 33 - \frac{3}{2}c$

$a + b + c = 47 \rightarrow 33 - \frac{3}{2}c + b + c = 47 \rightarrow b$

$= 14 + \frac{1}{2}c$

$10a + 12b + 15c = 546 \rightarrow 10\left(33 - \frac{3}{2}c\right) +$

$12\left(14 + \frac{1}{2}c\right) + 15c = 546$

$330 - 15c + 168 + 6c + 15c = 546 \rightarrow 6c = 48 \rightarrow c = 8$

$4a + 0b + 48 = 132 \rightarrow 4a = 84 \rightarrow a = 21$

$b = 47 - 21 - 8 = 18$

The answer is (A).

72. **Sub topic: Applications**

The correct answer is (E).

The pipes can fill $\frac{1}{24}$, $\frac{1}{6}$ and $\frac{1}{12}$ of the tank individually, per minute.

If they are turned on at the same time, they take fill $\frac{1}{24} + \frac{1}{6} + \frac{1}{12} = \frac{1}{24}$ of the tank in one minute.

To be full, it takes $\frac{24}{7} = 3.43$ minutes, which falls within the range of 3.1 to 5 minutes.

73. **Sub topic: Inequalities**

The correct answer is (A).

Write the expression in mathematical terms, solve for x and compare.

15 more than $5x$ = 79 less $3x$ is equivalent to $15 + 5x = 79 - 3x$.

$15 + 5x = 79 - 3x$	Original equation
$5x = 64 - 3x$	Subtract 15.
$8x = 64$	Add $3x$.
$x = 8$	Divide by 8

Quantity A: The quantity of twice x subtracted from the quotient of 12 and $\frac{1}{3}$, divided by 4. ($x = 8$)

$\left\{\dfrac{12}{\frac{1}{3}} - 2(8)\right\} \div 4$	Original equation
$= \{36 - 2(8)\} \div 4$	Division in ( )
$= \{36 - 16\} \div 4$	Multiplication in ( )
$= \{20\} \div 4$	Subtraction in ( )
$= 5$	Division

Quantity B: The quantity of x squared less the product of six and x, divided by 4. ($x = 8$)

$= \dfrac{8^2 - (6)(8)}{4}$	Original equation
$= \dfrac{64 - (6)(8)}{4}$	Exponents in numerator

$$= \frac{64-48}{4}$$ Multiplication in numerator

$$= \frac{16}{4}$$ Subtraction in numerator

$$= 4$$ Division

Compare:

$5 > 4$

The quantity of A is greater than the quantity of B.

74. **Sub topic: Algebraic Expressions**

The correct answers are (B), (C) and (E).

Choose a number for x and determine the elements of each set. Let x= 3, for example. Then

A = {(−1 + 3 + 9), (1 − 3 + 9), (1 + 3 + 9)}

B = {(−1 + 9 + 27), (1 − 9 + 27), (1 + 9 − 27)}

Simplify the expressions in each set.

A = {11, 7, 13}

B = {35, 19, −17}

Now, check the statements one by one against these sets.

A. The greatest element of A is 13 and the least element of B is −17. Since 13 is not greater than −17, so (A) is false.

B. The greatest element of A, 13, is greater than the least element of B, −17; so (B) is true.

C. The greatest element of A, 13, is less than greatest element of B, 35. So, (C) is true.

D. Find the average of the elements of each set.

Average of A = M =

$$\frac{(-1+x+x^2)+(1-x+x^2)+(1+x+x^2)}{3}$$

$$= \frac{3x^2+x+1}{3}$$

Average of B = N =

$$\frac{(-1+x^2+x^3)+(1-x^2+x^3)+(1+x^2+x^3)}{3}$$

$$= \frac{3x^3+x^2+1}{3}$$

Next, compare two averages.

$$\frac{3x^2+x+1}{3} \boxed{?} \frac{3x^3+x^2+1}{3}$$

$3x^2 + x + 1 \boxed{?} 3x^3 + x^2 + 1$

$3x^2 + x \boxed{?} 3x^3 + x^2$

$x(3x + x) \boxed{?} x^2(3x − 1)$

$x \boxed{?} x^2$

Since the square of any real number greater than 1 is greater than the number itself, so we replace ? with <. That is, $x < x^2$. Thus, the statement (E) is true.

$x = x^2$ only when $x = 1$. So, answer (F) is incorrect.

Choice (G) cannot be true, since Option (E) disproves it.

75. **Sub topic: System of Equations**

The correct answers are (B) and (D)

The $31.50 in bills and $3.50 in pennies is subtracted from the total $50. The remaining amount = $15.00

Let q = number of quarters, d = number of dimes, n = number of nickels (3 unknowns).

$n = 3q$

$d = n + 3 \rightarrow d = 3q + 3$

$0.25q + 0.1d + 0.05n = 15$

$0.25q + 0.1(3q + 3) + 0.05(3q) = 15$

$0.7q + 0.3 = 15 \rightarrow q = 21$

$n = 63, d = 66$

Therefore, there are 63 nickels, 66 dimes, and 21 quarters, so (B) is correct and (A), (C), and (E) are incorrect.

To find the sum of dimes and nickels, do 66×0.10 + 63×0.05 = $9.75. Therefore, (D) is correct.

76. **Sub topic: Relations**

The correct answer is (B).

If Mark's current age is represented by x, then Nick's age is represented by $\frac{x-15}{6}+15$. Because the sum of their ages today is 65, we can write the equation $\frac{x-15}{6}+15+x=65$. Then, multiply the equation by 6 to clear the denominator to get $x - 15 + 90 + 6x = 390$. Combine x and $6x$, and -15 and 90 to obtain $7x + 75 = 390$. Subtract 75 from both sides and divide by 7 to get $x = 45$. Mark's current age is therefore 45, and Nick's current age is $\frac{45-15}{6}+15=20$. For Quantity A, half of Mark's current age is 22.5, and for Quantity B, 5 more than Nick's current age is 25. Therefore, 25 > 22.5 and Quantity B is greater. The correct answer is Choice B.

77. **Sub topic: Graphs of Functions, Equations, and Inequalities**

    The correct answer is (D).

    To combine two functions, you sum their y values. This will produce the graph of Choice A. However, when you transform a function by adding 6 to the x value, this represents a left shift of 6 in the x direction. Therefore, the answer choice would be D, where the summed graph is shifted 6 to the left.

78. **Sub topic: Intercepts and Slopes of Lines**

    The correct answers are (C) and (D).

    To be 5 vertical units apart, the y intercepts must be 5 units apart on the y axis.

    Choice A: Putting Choice A in slope-intercept form becomes $y=\frac{1}{3}x-\frac{5}{3}$. This y intercept of $-5/3$ is not 5 away from the original y intercept of -5, and the slopes are not the same so these are not parallel lines. Choice A is incorrect.

    Choice B: Putting Choice B into slope-intercept form becomes $y = 3x + 4$. This y intercept of 4 is not 5 away from the original y intercept of -5, and the slopes are not the same (3 is not the same as a slope of 1) so these are not parallel lines. Choice B is incorrect.

    Choice C: Putting Choice C into slope-intercept form becomes $y = x - 10$. This y intercept of -10 is 5 away from the original y intercept of -5, and the slopes are both 1, so these lines are parallel with a distance of 5 vertical units. Choice C is correct.

    Choice D: Putting Choice D into slope-intercept form becomes $y = x$. This y intercept of 0 is 5 away from the original y intercept of -5, and the slopes are both 1, so these lines are parallel with a distance of 5 vertical units. Choice D is correct.

    Choice E: Choice E does not have a parallel (equal) slope since 3 is not equal to 1, so Choice E is incorrect.

    The solutions are then both Choice C and D.

79. **Sub topic: Systems of Equations**

    The correct answers are (B) and (C).

    To set up an equation to find the intersection of Train A and B, set x = time passed since Train A began to move at noon. Train A's total distance toward Train B will be $80 \times x$. Train B starts 2 hours later, and it moves towards Train A. Train B's distance will be $560-\left(40\times\left(x-2\right)\right)$. Set these equal to find the time of intersection. This becomes $80x = 560-\left(40\times\left(x-2\right)\right)$. Distribute the 40 and the negative to get $80x = 560 - 40x - 80$. Combine like terms to obtain $120x = 480$. X is then 4, meaning 4 hours. The trains intersect at 4 hours after the start of Train A. Train A starts at 12, so 4 hours later it is 4PM. Therefore, Choice B is correct. At 4 hours, Train A and Train B are at $80 \times 4 = 320$ miles. Choice A is incorrect.

    Train C begins its journey 120 miles from 320 miles at the intersection. Since the Train is traveling toward Train B's origin, it will be at 200 miles to start from Train A. Train C starts moving at 4PM, and has to move 120 miles. Going 120 miles at a speed of 30mph will take 4 hours, making it 8PM when Train C passes the intersection. Choice C is correct.

    Train C is at 200 miles from Train A's start at

4PM, while Train B is at the intersection at 320 miles from Train A's start. Train C's location is expressed by 200 + 30y, where y is the number of hours past 4PM. Train B's location is expressed by 320 – 40y. Set them equal to find the time they intersect. 200 + 30y = 320 – 40y. Combine like terms across the equal sign to get 70y = 120. Y =12/7, or approximately 1.71 hours. This would mean they intersect at about 5:45 PM. Therefore, Answer D is incorrect and E is incorrect.

80. **Sub topic: Systems of Equations**

The correct answer is (B).

The number of monsters is represented by m, and the number of fairies is represented by f. When splitting up candy, there was one monster and 4 fairies that shared, making that $1 \times 4 + 4 \times 5 = 24$ pieces of candy. The remaining monsters were m-1 and then remaining fairies were $2 \times (m-1)$ because there were 2 fairies for every 1 monster. There were 26 pieces of candy left, and the total is represented by $26 = (m-1) + 5(2 \times (m-1))$ Simplify by distributing to get 26 = 4m – 4 + 10m – 10. Combine like terms to get 42 = 14m. Divide by 14, to get m = 3. This means there are 3 monsters.

Chapter 5

Geometry Practice Questions

This chapter consists of *81 Geometry* practice questions. The questions cover all the question types as explained in Chapter 2 and are segregated into 3 levels of difficulty - Easy, Medium and Difficult. You may choose to start solving the Easy questions first and then move on to higher levels of difficulty or solve the questions in any random order. You will find answers and detailed explanations towards the end of this chapter.

Level: Easy

1.

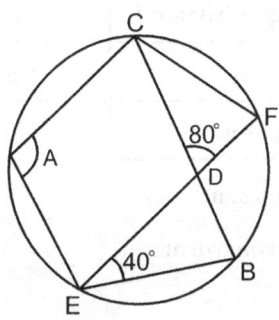

Select all the statements that best give the measure of ∠A.

Select all that apply.

A	between 80° and 100°
B	between 100° and 130°
C	between 50° and 80°
D	between 90° and 125°
E	between 130° and 150°
F	between 70° and 100°
G	between 91° and 115°

2.

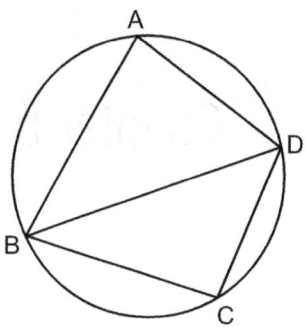

∠ABC = 80° and BD is the circle's diameter.

Quantity A

$m\angle BAD$

Quantity B

$m\angle ADC - 10°$

Ⓐ   Quantity A is greater.

Ⓑ   Quantity B is greater.

Ⓒ   The two quantities are equal.

Ⓓ   The relationship cannot be determined from the information given.

3. Which title best represents X in the table?

Name of quadrilateral	X	Four sides
Kites	Yes	Yes
Trapezoids	No	Yes

Ⓐ   Two pairs of consecutive congruent sides

Ⓑ   Two pairs of opposite angles congruent

Ⓒ   Four congruent sides

Ⓓ   Congruent diagonals

Ⓔ   Sum of all angles is 180°

Geometry Practice Questions

4.

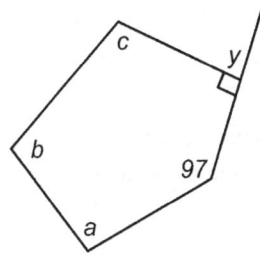

Determine the value of $a + b + c + y$.

☐ degrees

5. How many different pentagons can be drawn inside a hexagon?

Ⓐ 3

Ⓑ 4

Ⓒ 5

Ⓓ 6

Ⓔ 7

6.

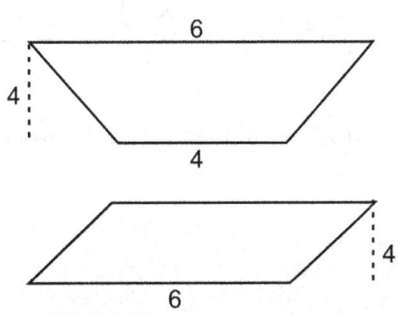

Quantity A

The area of the trapezoid

Quantity B

The area of the parallelogram

Ⓐ Quantity A is greater.

Ⓑ Quantity B is greater.

Ⓒ The two quantities are equal.

Ⓓ The relationship cannot be determined from the information given.

7. The diameter of a circle is 2√2m. The diameter of another circle having 8 times the area of the first circle is:

   [_____] m

8. A field is of a square shape. If total expense of building fence around it is $1600 at rate of $5 per meter. What will be the perimeter and length of one side of the field?

   Select *all* that apply.

   [A] 40m
   [B] 80m
   [C] 100m
   [D] 320m
   [E] 350m
   [F] 370m

9.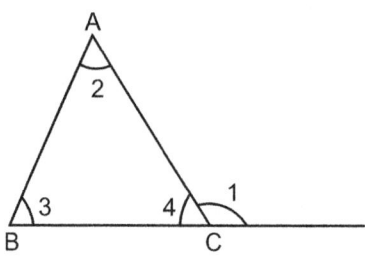

   ABC is a triangle and ∠1 is 124° and ∠2 is 46° then ∠3 & ∠4 will be?

   Select *all* that apply.

   [A] 46°
   [B] 56°
   [C] 78°
   [D] 124°
   [E] 132°
   [F] 136°

10.

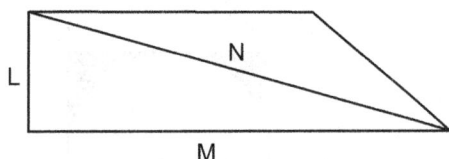

Quantity A	Quantity B
The length of line N	The sum of the lengths of lines M and L

- Ⓐ Quantity A is greater.
- Ⓑ Quantity B is greater.
- Ⓒ The two quantities are equal.
- Ⓓ The relationship cannot be determined from the information given.

11. In a regular polygon, the exterior angle has a measure of 12°. What type of polygon is it?

- Ⓐ Dodecagon
- Ⓑ 15-gon
- Ⓒ 20-gon
- Ⓓ 25-gon
- Ⓔ 30-gon

12. Five disks have circumferences $\pi, 10\pi, 12\pi, 20\pi$, and 50π. Label the disks A, B, C, D, E, respectively. Which disc(s) would fit into a hoop with area 470 units^2?

Select all that apply.

- ☐ A A
- ☐ B B
- ☐ C C
- ☐ D D
- ☐ E E
- ☐ F A, D and E

13.

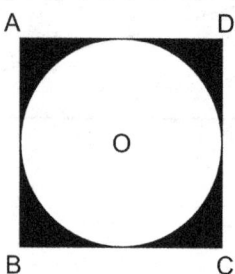

In the figure above ABCD is a square and a circle with center O touches its four sides internally. If radius of the circle is 5 meters, then what will be the area of shaded region? Provide the answer up to two significant digits in the answer box.

14. Length of a rectangle is 3cm less than the double of the width. If perimeter of the rectangle is 96cm then what will be its width and length?

    Select all that apply.

    | A | 15cm |
    | B | 17cm |
    | C | 27cm |
    | D | 31cm |
    | E | 34cm |
    | F | 37cm |

15. Point A is located at (-3, -11) and Point B is located at (4, 13). What is the length of line segment AB?

    Ⓐ 4√15
    Ⓑ 5
    Ⓒ 17
    Ⓓ 24
    Ⓔ 25

16.

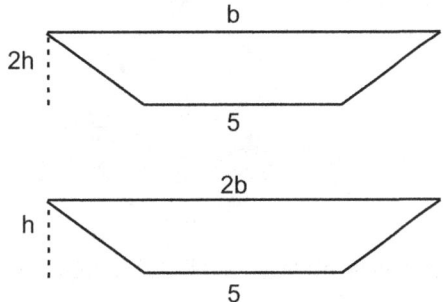

Quantity A	Quantity B
The area of the top trapezoid	The area of the bottom trapezoid

- Ⓐ Quantity A is greater.
- Ⓑ Quantity B is greater.
- Ⓒ The two quantities are equal.
- Ⓓ The relationship cannot be determined from the information given.

17. Let m_1 and m_2 be the slopes of two lines. The lines will be perpendicular to each other if one of the following is satisfied.

Select *all* that apply.

- [A] $m_1 m_2 = 1$
- [B] $m_1 = m_2$
- [C] $m_1 m_2 = -1$
- [D] $m_1 m_2 + 1 = 0$

18.

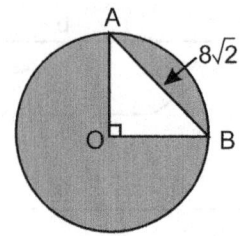

In the diagram above, if the hypotenuse of the right triangle is $8\sqrt{2}$, what is the area of the shaded region?

- Ⓐ $16\pi - 32$
- Ⓑ $16\pi - 32\sqrt{2}$
- Ⓒ 32π
- Ⓓ $64\pi - 32$
- Ⓔ $64\pi - 32\sqrt{2}$

19.

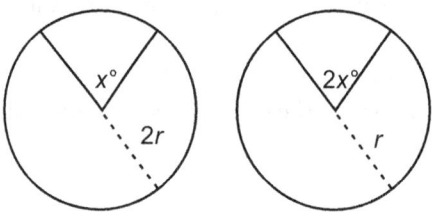

Quantity A	Quantity B
The area of the sector in the left circle	The area of the sector in the right circle

- Ⓐ Quantity A is greater.
- Ⓑ Quantity B is greater.
- Ⓒ The two quantities are equal.
- Ⓓ The relationship cannot be determined from the information given.

20. What is the surface area of a sphere with the same radius as the side of a square with a perimeter of 32?
$SA_{sphere} = 4\pi r^2$

- Ⓐ 16π
- Ⓑ 32π
- Ⓒ 64π
- Ⓓ 256π
- Ⓔ 1024π

21.

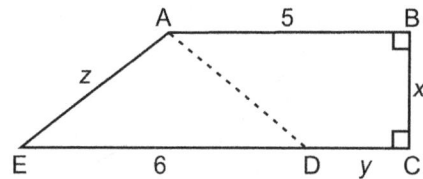

Which of the following statements could be true for the figure shown above?

Area of ΔAED = 12

y = 2

Select all that apply.

- [A] x = 4.5
- [B] x = 4
- [C] z = 5
- [D] z = 6

22.

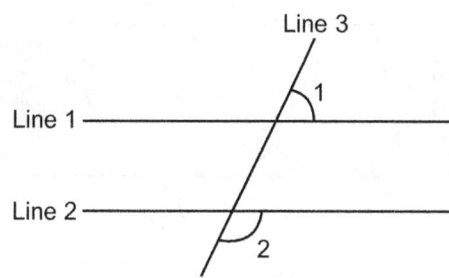

L_1 and L_2 are two lines parallel to each other and L_3 cuts through both these lines as shown in the figure above. If angle 1 is 45°, then what will the measure of angle 2 be in degrees? Write your answer in the answer box.

[   ]

23.

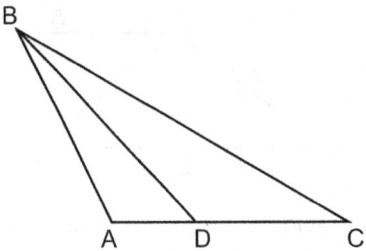

Note: Figure not drawn to scale.

In the preceding figure, AB = AD and BD = CD. If ∠C measures 19°, what is the measure of ∠A in degrees?

- Ⓐ 75
- Ⓑ 94
- Ⓒ 104
- Ⓓ 114
- Ⓔ 142

24. Find the area of the unshaded region of the parallelogram.

- Ⓐ $\frac{44}{9} in^2$
- Ⓑ $\frac{12}{7} in^2$
- Ⓒ $16 in^2$
- Ⓓ $11\frac{11}{63} in^2$
- Ⓔ $\frac{7}{12} in^2$

Geometry Practice Questions

25. What is the value of the length of the height in an equilateral triangle with a length of $2\sqrt{3}$?

    (A) $2\sqrt{3}$

    (B) $\sqrt{3}$

    (C)   3

    (D) $3\sqrt{3}$

    (E) $\dfrac{\sqrt{3}}{3}$

26. What is the area (in square meters) of an isosceles triangle with equal sides of 3 meters and base angles of 30⁰?

    (A) $\dfrac{3}{2}\sqrt{3}$

    (B) $\dfrac{9\sqrt{3}}{4}$

    (C) $\dfrac{9\sqrt{3}}{2}$

    (D) $\dfrac{3\sqrt{3}}{4}$

    (E) $\dfrac{2\sqrt{3}}{9}$

27.
The variable r is a positive whole number.

Quantity A	Quantity B
The area formed from a circle with $\dfrac{2}{3}r$ radius.	The circumference of a circle formed with $\dfrac{1}{5}r$ radius.

(A)   Quantity A is greater

(B)   Quantity B is greater

(C)   The quantities are equal.

(D)   The relationship cannot be determined from the information given.

Level: Medium

28.

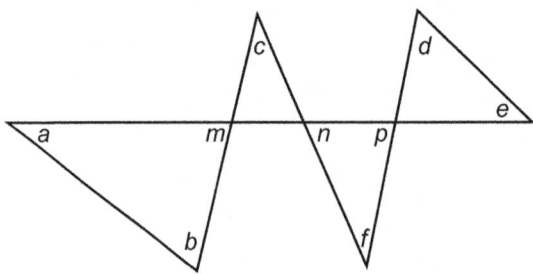

What will be the value of $a + b + c + f + d + e$, if $m + n + p$ is 200°?

- Ⓐ 420°
- Ⓑ 360°
- Ⓒ 340°
- Ⓓ 320°
- Ⓔ 280°

29. The points A(0, 0), B(0, 5p-2), and C(2p+2, 4p+6) form a triangle. If ∠ABC = 90°, what is the area of △ABC?

   Select all that apply.

- ☐ A Area of △ABC is < 250
- ☐ B Area of △ABC is < 300
- ☐ C Area of △ABC is > 300
- ☐ D Area of △ABC is < 350
- ☐ E Area of △ABC is > 380
- ☐ F Area of △ABC is > 420

30.

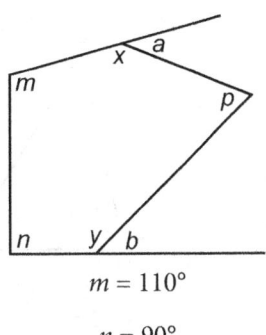

$m = 110°$

$n = 90°$

Quantity A	Quantity B
$a + b$	$90°$

Ⓐ Quantity A is greater.

Ⓑ Quantity B is greater.

Ⓒ The two quantities are equal.

Ⓓ The relationship cannot be determined from the information given.

31. If the number of diagonals in a polygon is 54, identify the statement that best gives the number of sides of the polygon.

Select <u>all</u> that apply.

A between 9 and 13

B between 8 and 10

C between 10 and 14

D between 13 and 15

E between 6 and 8

F between 7 and 11

G between 13 and 17

32.

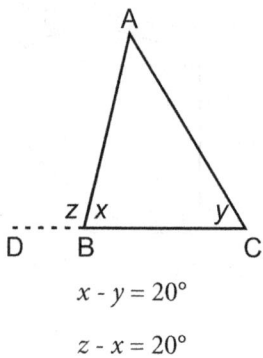

$x - y = 20°$

$z - x = 20°$

Quantity A	**Quantity B**
Measure of ∠BAC	40°

- Ⓐ Quantity A is greater.
- Ⓑ Quantity B is greater.
- Ⓒ The two quantities are equal.
- Ⓓ The relationship cannot be determined from the information given.

33.

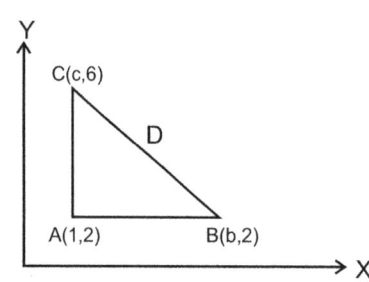

△ABC is an isosceles right triangle with hypotenuse BC. AD is perpendicular to BC. Points A, B and C are defined by their coordinates. What is the length of AD?

- Ⓐ $4\sqrt{2}$
- Ⓑ $2\sqrt{2}$
- Ⓒ $3\sqrt{2}$
- Ⓓ 2
- Ⓔ 3

Geometry Practice Questions

34. If each interior angle of a regular polygon is given to be 135° in measure, select the statements that best give the sum of all interior angles in the polygon.

    Select all that apply.

    - [A] between 900° and 1000°
    - [B] between 900° and 1240°
    - [C] between 810° and 900°
    - [D] between 1000° and 1240°
    - [E] between 1100° and 1240°
    - [F] between 700° and 1000°
    - [G] between 1200° and 1380°

35.

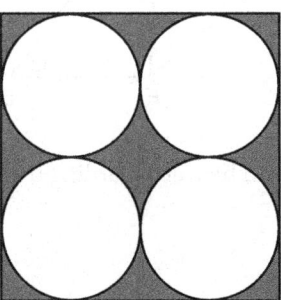

Figure not drawn to scale

In the figure above, four identical circles with equal diameters are enclosed in a square with an area of 256, each circle touches the edges of other circles and the square as shown.

Quantity A	Quantity B
The total area of the grey region	$300 - 50\pi$

- (A) Quantity A is greater.
- (B) Quantity B is greater.
- (C) The two quantities are equal.
- (D) The relationship cannot be determined from the information given.

36. A △ABC is defined by the points with the following coordinates: A(2, $2\sqrt{3}$), B(4,0) and C(0,0). What is the *m* ∠BAC?

    Ⓐ   30°

    Ⓑ   45°

    Ⓒ   60°

    Ⓓ   75°

    Ⓔ   90°

37.

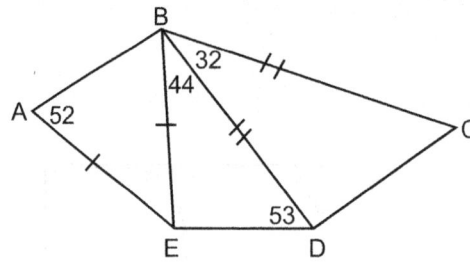

Which of the following statements could be true regarding the figure above?

Select all that apply.

A		AB is the longest side of △ABE.
B		BE is the shortest side of △EBD.
C		∠EBD =44°
D		△BED is an isosceles triangle.
E		∠BCD =78°
F		The sum of all interior angles of the pentagon is 720°
G		BD is the longest side of △BCD

38.

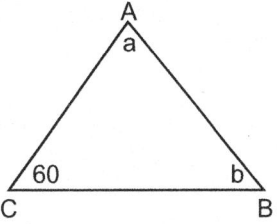

Figure not drawn to scale

In the △ABC above, AC > AB and ∠c = 60

Quantity A

Length of AB

Quantity B

Length of BC

- Ⓐ Quantity A is greater.
- Ⓑ Quantity B is greater.
- Ⓒ The two quantities are equal.
- Ⓓ The relationship cannot be determined from the information given.

39.

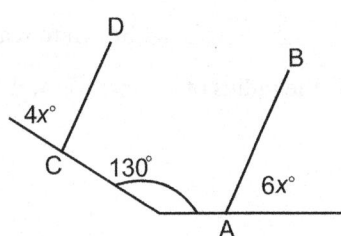

In the above figure given that AB ‖ CD, x is,

- Ⓐ 8.33
- Ⓑ 12.5
- Ⓒ 13
- Ⓓ 26
- Ⓔ 50

40. If area and perimeter of a rectangular region are 24cm² and 20cm respectively. Then length and width in cm will be?

    Select *all* that apply.

    [A] 2 cm
    [B] 3 cm
    [C] 4 cm
    [D] 6 cm
    [E] 8 cm
    [F] 12 cm

41.

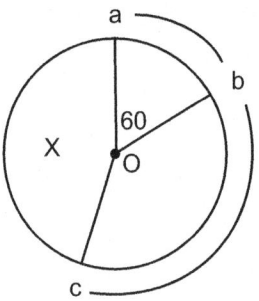

Figure not drawn to scale

In this figure, the radius of the circle is 4, the length of arc bc is 3π

Quantity A   **Quantity B**

Area X $\dfrac{21\pi}{3}$

- Ⓐ Quantity A is greater.
- Ⓑ Quantity B is greater.
- Ⓒ The two quantities are equal.
- Ⓓ The relationship cannot be determined from the information given.

42.

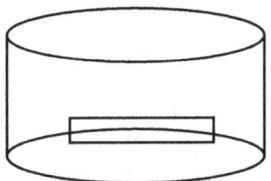

A cylinder container has a height of 4 cm and a radius of 3 cm; a metallic rectangular solid object has a length of 2 cm, width of 1 cm and height of 3 cm. This object rests on the bottom of the container and is completely covered by the cylinder as shown above (not drawn to scale). Now, you are trying to pour in 2 liters of orange juice into the cylinder from an old container. 1liter = (10cm)³ = 1000cm³

Quantity A

The total amount of juice fits into the cylinder

Quantity B

The total amount of juice remains in the old container

Ⓐ   Quantity A is greater.

Ⓑ   Quantity B is greater.

Ⓒ   The two quantities are equal.

Ⓓ   The relationship cannot be determined from the information given.

43.

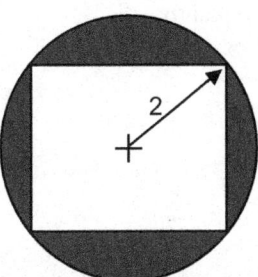

A square is inscribed inside a circle whose radius = 2, as shown in the figure. Determine, to 2 decimal places, the area of the shaded region.

44.

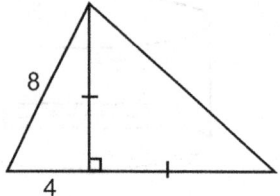

What is the area of the above triangle?

- Ⓐ   16 units²
- Ⓑ   22.5 units²
- Ⓒ   30 units²
- Ⓓ $8\sqrt{3} + 24$ units²
- Ⓔ $8\sqrt{3} + 6$ units²

45.

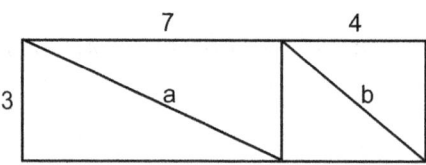

In the above diagram, the sum $a + b$ is equal to:

- Ⓐ $5 + \sqrt{58}$
- Ⓑ $16 + \sqrt{2}$
- Ⓒ   14
- Ⓓ $\dfrac{25}{3}$
- Ⓔ $17 + 3\sqrt{6}$

46.

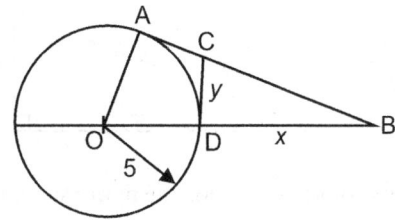

Which of the following statements could be true for the figure shown above?

AB is tangent to the circle at point A

CD is tangent to the circle at point D

Circle has radius = 5

Length of AB = 12

Select all that apply.

- [A] $x = 7$
- [B] $x = 8$
- [C] $y = 3$
- [D] $y = \dfrac{10}{3}$

47.

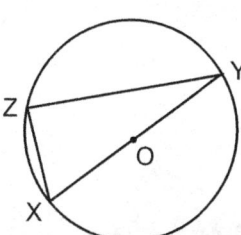

In circle O above, XY is a diameter, OX = 8.5, and YZ = 15. What is the area of △XYZ in square units?

- (A) 40
- (B) 60
- (C) 120
- (D) 127.5
- (E) 180

48.

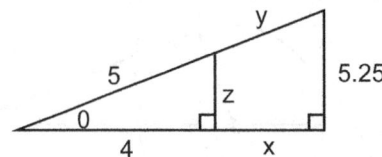

Which of the following statements could be true for the figure shown above?

Select *all* that apply.

[A] $x + y < 7$

[B] $x > 3$

[C] $y < 4$

[D] x and y cannot be determined

[E] The correct answers are (A), and (C)

49. What is the area of rhombus with a perimeter of 40 and a diagonal of 10?

Ⓐ $50\sqrt{3}$

Ⓑ 100

Ⓒ $100\sqrt{3}$

Ⓓ 200

Ⓔ 400

50.

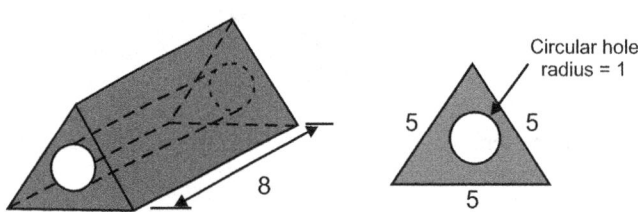

A circular hole that has a radius of 1 is bored through a triangular prism. Determine the percentage remaining from the original volume of the prism.

Ⓐ 65%

Ⓑ 68%

Ⓒ 71%

Ⓓ 75%

Ⓔ 78%

51.

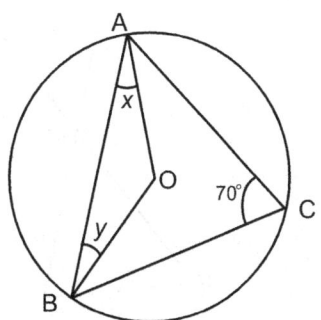

Select the statements that give the correct measure of $\angle x$.

Select all that apply.

- A between 25° and 30°
- B between 16° and 30°
- C between 22° and 42°
- D between 15° and 30°
- E between 25° and 30°
- F between 11° and 19°
- G between 21° and 27°

52.

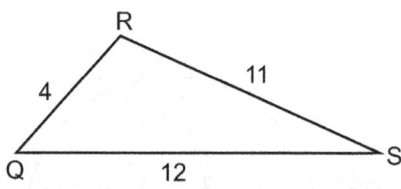

Quantity A	Quantity B
The area of triangle QRS	The perimeter of triangle QRS

- Ⓐ Quantity A is greater.
- Ⓑ Quantity B is greater.
- Ⓒ The two quantities are equal.
- Ⓓ The relationship cannot be determined from the information given.

53.

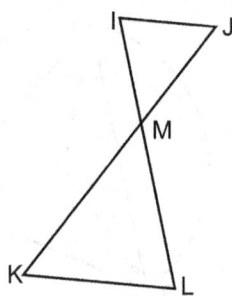

Which of the following statements could be true if IJ ∥ KL? ?

Select all that apply.

A	∠JIM ≅ ∠MKL
B	∠IMJ ≅ ∠LMK
C	$\dfrac{IM}{ML} = \dfrac{JM}{MK}$
D	△KLM ≅ △JIM
E	∠IJK ≅ ∠LKM
F	$\dfrac{KL}{IJ} = \dfrac{JM}{KM}$

54. What is the ratio of ∠1 to ∠2 if C is the center of the circle, the larger triangle is isosceles, and the radius is 15cm?

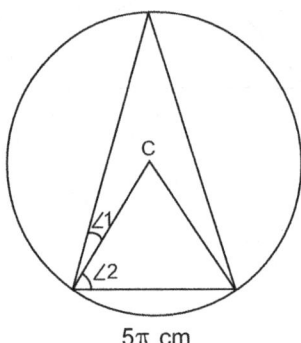

- A $\dfrac{4}{1}$
- B $\dfrac{1}{4}$
- C $\dfrac{5}{4}$
- D $\dfrac{4}{5}$
- E $\dfrac{3}{4}$

Geometry Practice Questions

55.

Compare Quantity A and Quantity B using the diagram of the cube below.

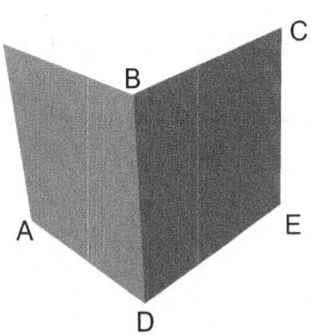

Quantity A

The value of $\dfrac{AB}{BC}$

Quantity B

The value of $\dfrac{AB}{AC}$

- (A) Quantity A is greater
- (B) Quantity B is greater
- (C) The quantities are equal.
- (D) The relationship cannot be determined from the information given.

56.

Use the diagram below. Rectangle ABFE : Rectangle GHEC with a ratio of 3:4, CDEF is a square, and EC = AC.

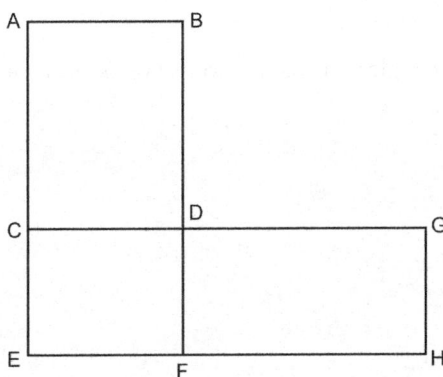

Quantity A

DH

Quantity B

AD+CF

- (A) Quantity A is greater
- (B) Quantity B is greater
- (C) The quantities are equal.
- (D) The relationship cannot be determined from the information given.

57. Use the diagram below. Rectangle ABFE ~ Rectangle GHEC with a ratio of 3:4, CDEF is a square, and EC = $\frac{1}{2}$ AC.

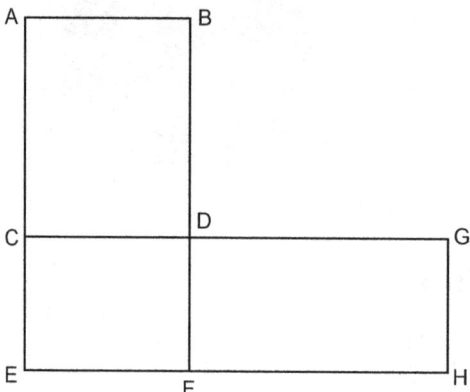

Quantity A

$\dfrac{AH}{BG}$

Quantity B

$\dfrac{BG}{CF}$

- Ⓐ Quantity A is greater
- Ⓑ Quantity B is greater
- Ⓒ The quantities are equal.
- Ⓓ The relationship cannot be determined from the information given.

58. What is measure of the smallest angle in a triangle whose vertices are at (5,4), (5,-5), and (-4,4)?

- Ⓐ 30
- Ⓑ 60
- Ⓒ 45
- Ⓓ 90
- Ⓔ 105

Geometry Practice Questions

59.

Compare Quantity A and Quantity B using the diagrams below. The hexagon is a regular polygon circumscribed about a rectangle.

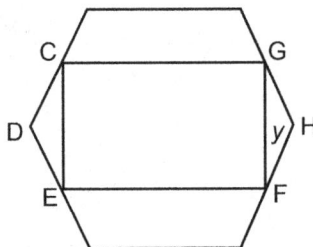

Quantity A

$\dfrac{CD}{y}$

Quantity B

$\dfrac{y}{CD}$

- Ⓐ Quantity A is greater
- Ⓑ Quantity B is greater
- Ⓒ The quantities are equal.
- Ⓓ The relationship cannot be determined from the information given.

Level: Difficult

60.

Given the segments MN, NP, and PD, only points M, D, and N are collinear.

D is the midpoint of MN.

Quantity A

DN - PM

Quantity B

PD

- Ⓐ Quantity A is greater.
- Ⓑ Quantity B is greater.
- Ⓒ The two quantities are equal.
- Ⓓ The relationship cannot be determined from the information given.

61.

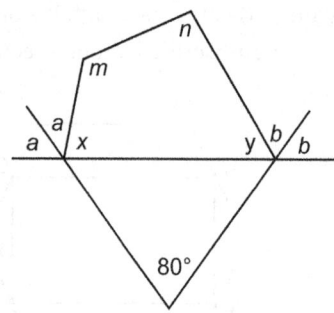

Quantity A	Quantity B
$m + n$	$180°$

(A) Quantity A is greater.

(B) Quantity B is greater.

(C) The two quantities are equal.

(D) The relationship cannot be determined from the information given.

62.

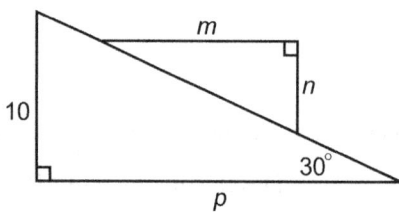

What will be the value of $p\left(\dfrac{m}{n}\right)$ in the figure above, if the horizontal legs of the triangles are parallel?

(A) 45

(B) 40

(C) 30

(D) 32

(E) 22

63.

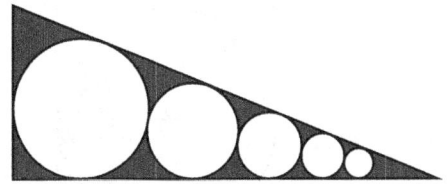

Figure NOT drawn to scale:

In this figure, five circles are fully encased in a triangle as shown above (they do not have to touch the sides of the triangle). The circles have radii of 16, 8, 4, 2, and 1 respectively. The grey regions measure a total of 679π, the base of the triangle measures 34π.

Quantity A	**Quantity B**
The height of this triangle	60

- Ⓐ Quantity A is greater.
- Ⓑ Quantity B is greater.
- Ⓒ The two quantities are equal.
- Ⓓ The relationship cannot be determined from the information given.

64.

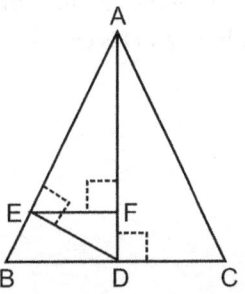

ABC is an equilateral triangle with side = 6.

Quantity A	**Quantity B**
EF	$\dfrac{5}{2}$

- Ⓐ Quantity A is greater.
- Ⓑ Quantity B is greater.
- Ⓒ The two quantities are equal.
- Ⓓ The relationship cannot be determined from the information given.

65.

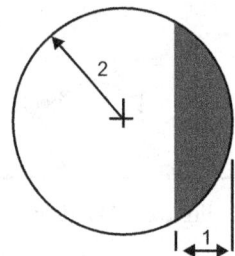

Determine the area of the shaded portion of the circle, with 1 decimal place accuracy.

66.

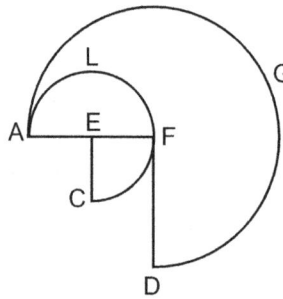

In the figure above, E and F are the centers of the circular curves (portions of circles). ALF is a semicircle, and EFC is a quadrant of a circle. Also, quadrant AFD is cut-out of the larger circle. If the arc CF measures 3π, what is the perimeter of the figure AGDFLA?

Ⓐ $20\pi + 8$

Ⓑ $12\pi + 8$

Ⓒ $16\pi + 6$

Ⓓ $22\pi + 12$

Ⓔ $24\pi + 12$

67. A metallic sheet of paper whose shape is a sector of 60° is extracted from a circle of diameter 18 inches. If the sector is used to make a cone, what would be the approximate volume of the cone?

Ⓐ   95 cubic inches

Ⓑ   191 cubic inches

Ⓒ   21 cubic inches

Ⓓ   185 cubic inches

Ⓔ   50 cubic inches

68. Find the value of ∆BAF if ∆ABC, ∆AEB, ∆BFK are isosceles, m∠FBK=30, and m∠AEF=90.

☐

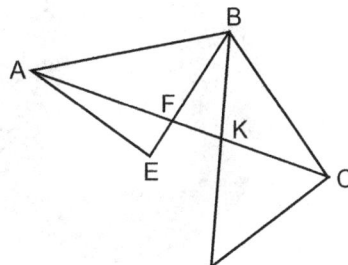

69.

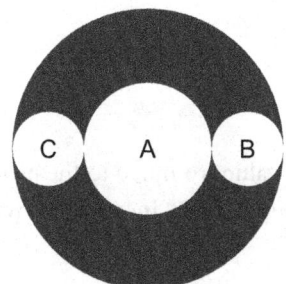

What is the ratio of new area to old area of the shaded region if Circle A's radius is cut in half, and Circle B and C remain congruent and increase to remain tangent to Circle A?

- Ⓐ $\dfrac{117}{58}$
- Ⓑ $\dfrac{1}{2}$
- Ⓒ $\dfrac{117}{116}$
- Ⓓ $\dfrac{2}{3}$
- Ⓔ $\dfrac{7}{8}$

70. Which of the following are true of an isosceles trapezoid inside a circle if the radius of the circle is 10 cm, the bases are 7cm and 5cm, and height of the isosceles trapezoid is 2π cm?

- Ⓐ The area of the trapezoid is 12π cm².
- Ⓑ The area of the trapezoid is 12 cm².
- Ⓒ The area of the circle is 10π cm².
- Ⓓ The shaded area is 2π cm².
- Ⓔ The area of the trapezoid is 6% the area of the circle.

71. What is the largest initial cube length value (rounded to the nearest thousandth) that would have a volume increase of 50% when increasing the length by 8, increase the width by 6, and decrease the depth by 50%.

☐

72. If Lines *a* and *b* are parallel, what is the value of *z*?

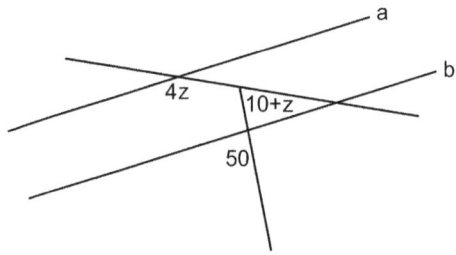

- Ⓐ 20
- Ⓑ -20
- Ⓒ 14
- Ⓓ 6
- Ⓔ 12

73. A circle is circumscribed about a regular polygon with each exterior angle measuring 60 degrees. The radius of the circle is 4cm. What is the area between the circle and the polygon?

- (A) $16\pi - 2\sqrt{3}$
- (B) 16π
- (C) $32\sqrt{3}\pi$
- (D) $16\pi - 12\sqrt{3}$
- (E) $2\sqrt{3}$

74. In the diagram below, the vertices of the angles of a regular hexagon are tangent to 6 congruent circles. The apothem, which is the value from the center of the hexagon to the midpoint of a side, is 4cm. If the circles take up 50% of the interior area of the hexagon, what is the radius of each circle?

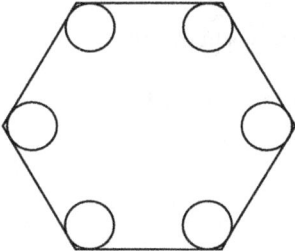

- (A) $4\sqrt{2}$
- (B) $8\sqrt{3}$
- (C) $\dfrac{2\sqrt{2}}{\sqrt[4]{3}}$
- (D) $4\sqrt{\dfrac{2}{3}}$
- (E) $\sqrt{\dfrac{8}{3}}$

75.

X is a positive value.

Quantity A

The area of a circle with a radius of x m.

Quantity B

The area of a hexagon made up of equilateral triangles of side length x m.

- (A) Quantity A is greater
- (B) Quantity B is greater
- (C) The quantities are equal.
- (D) The relationship cannot be determined from the information given.

76. Using the regular hexagon with a side length of 4cm intersecting isosceles right triangle as a mid segment, which of the following statements could be true?

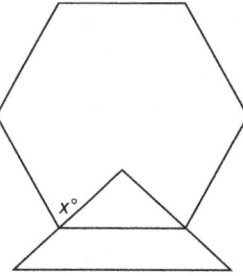

Select *all* that apply.

- [A] The area of the smaller triangle formed is 1 square cm.
- [B] The area of the larger triangle formed is 4 square cm.
- [C] The area of the hexagon is $24\sqrt{3}$ square cm.
- [D] The area of the hexagon is $4\sqrt{3}$ square cm
- [E] The value of *x* is 75.
- [F] None of the above

77.

Use the diagram of the isosceles triangle and the fact that $AB = 3b\sqrt{2}$.

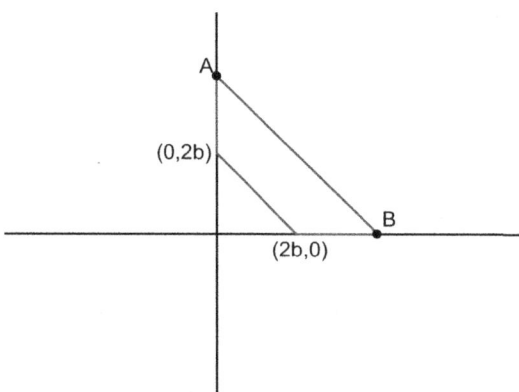

Quantity A	Quantity B
The height of the trapezoid	$\dfrac{b\sqrt{2}}{2}$

- Ⓐ Quantity A is greater
- Ⓑ Quantity B is greater
- Ⓒ The quantities are equal.
- Ⓓ The relationship cannot be determined from the information given.

Geometry Practice Questions

78. Two circles are on a coordinate plane, as shown below. One circle is tangent to the *x* and *y* axes, and the other circle is tangent to the first circle at Point P. If the circle to the left has a radius of 4, and the circle to the right has a radius of 5, what are possible slopes between the two centers of the circles?

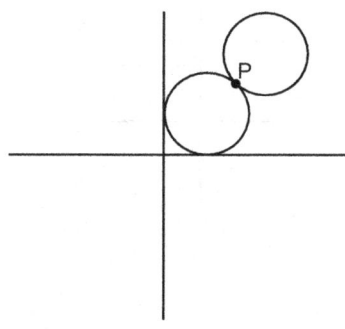

- (A) $\dfrac{7}{\sqrt{2}}$

- (B) $\dfrac{4\sqrt{2}}{7}$

- (C) $\dfrac{\sqrt{65}}{4}$

- (D) $\dfrac{5\sqrt{2}}{\sqrt{31}}$

- (E) $\dfrac{4}{7}$

79. What is the area of the purple shaded region if the radius of the circle is 10m and the arc length is $\dfrac{10\pi}{3}$?

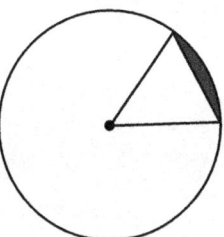

- (A) $\dfrac{50\pi}{3} - 25\sqrt{3}$ square meters

- (B) $\dfrac{10\pi}{3} - 5\sqrt{3}$ square meters

- (C) $25\sqrt{3}$ square meters

- (D) $\left(\dfrac{50\pi}{3}\right)25\sqrt{3}$ square meters

- (E) $\dfrac{5\pi}{2}$ square meters

80. What value does the variable *a* have to be if the area of the isosceles triangle is 12 square units, has a slope of $\frac{3}{4}$ for one of the legs, and a leg length of 5?

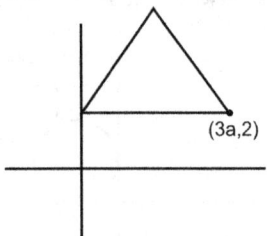

Answers and Explanations

Level: Easy

1. **Sub topic: Triangles**

    The correct answers are (B) and (D).

    In the figure, ∠CDF and ∠CDF are vertically opposite angles. Therefore, they are of equal measure.

    ∠CDF = ∠EDB = 80°

    Consider ΔDEB.

    ∠EDB = 80° and ∠DEB = 40°

    Since the three angles of a triangle add to give 180°,

    ∠DEB = 180°− 40°− 80°

    = 180° − 120°

    = 60°

    Consider the cyclic quadrilateral GEBC. Opposite angles of a quadrilateral add to 180°.

    ∠CGE + ∠CBE = 180°

    ∠A + ∠CBE = 180°

    ∠A = 180° − 60°= 120°

    Among the options, statements B and D give the measure of ∠A correctly.

2. **Sub topic: Circles**

    The correct answer is (C).

    The opposite angles in a quadrilateral inscribed in a circle are supplementary.

    That means that $m\angle ABC + m\angle ADC = 180°$

    $m\angle ADC = 180° - 80° = 100°$

    $m\angle ADC - 10° = 100° - 10° = 90°$

    If BD is the circle's diameter – ΔBAD and ΔBCD are both right angle triangles with the hypotenuse being BD – $m\angle BAD = 90°$

    $m\angle ADC - 10° = m\angle BAD = 90°$, hence the correct answer is (C).

3. **Sub topic: Quadrilaterals**

    The correct answer is (A).

    By definition, a quadrilateral is a kite if and only if it has two pairs of consecutive congruent sides. Further, only one pair of opposite angles is congruent, not both.

    A trapezoid may have exactly one pair of consecutive congruent sides. In the special case of an isosceles trapezoid, the base angles are congruent.

    Neither kites nor trapezoids have four congruent sides or congruent diagonals. The sum of all angle is not 180⁰ in kites and trapezoids.

    Hence, the title X can only be 'Two pairs of consecutive congruent sides'.

4. **Sub topic: Polygons**

    The correct answer is 443°.

    We know the formula to determine the sum of interior angles of a polygon is ($S = (n - 2)180$)

    Number of sides in a Pentagon = 5

    Sum of interior angles = (5 – 2) 180 = 3(180) = 540°

    Now we have the following equation:

    $a + b + c + 97 + 90 = 540$

    $a + b + c + 187 = 540$

    $a + b + c = 353$

    To calculate the value of y:

    $90 + y = 180$

    $y = 90$

    Now we can calculate the value of the expression.

    $a + b + c + y = 353 + 90 = 443°$

    The sum is 443°.

5. **Sub topic: Polygons**

    The correct answer is (C).

    Draw a hexagon and see how many pentagons can be drawn inside the hexagon.

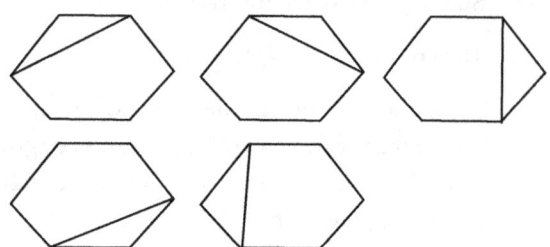

5 different pentagons can be made out of a hexagon.

The answer is C.

6. **Sub topic: Quadrilaterals**

   The correct answer is (B).

   The area of the trapezoid = $\frac{4(4+6)}{2} = 20$.

   The area of the parallelogram = $4 \times 6 = 24$.

7. **Sub topic: Circles**

   The correct answer is 8m.

   The area of a circle is πr^2. Area varies as the square of the radius. If the area becomes 8 times, the radius, and thus the diameter, becomes $\sqrt{8}$ times or $2\sqrt{2}$ times. The diameter of another circle having 8 times the area of the first circle becomes $2\sqrt{2} \times 2\sqrt{2} = 8m$.

8. **Sub topic: Polygons**

   The correct answers are (B) and (D).

   Total length of the fence will be $\frac{1600}{5} = 320$ meters.

   This will equal to the perimeter of the square field, so length of one side will be $\frac{320}{4} = 80$ meters.

9. **Sub topic: Triangles/Lines & Angles**

   The correct answers are (B) and (C).

   $\angle 1$ and $\angle 4$ are supplementary angles then $\angle 4$ will be 180° – 124° = 56°.

   As sum of all three angle of a triangle is 180° then $\angle 3$ will be 180° –(56° + 46°) = 78°

10. **Sub topic: Triangles**

    The correct answer is (B).

    The sum of any two sides must be greater than the third side to form a triangle. Since LMN forms a triangle, M + L > N.

11. **Sub topic: Polygons**

    The correct answer is (E).

    The sum of the exterior angles of a polygon is 360°. N represents the number of sides in the polygon. A

    represents the angle measure of one exterior angle.

    AN = 360

    (12)(N) = 360

    N = 30

    Therefore, the polygon is a 30-gon.

    The answer is (E).

12. **Sub topic: Circles**

    The correct answers are (A), (B), (C) and (D).

    Find the radius of each disc using the formula: C=2πr

    A: $\pi = 2\pi r \rightarrow r = \frac{1}{2}$

    B: $10\pi = 2\pi r \rightarrow r = 5$

    C; $12\pi = 2\pi r \rightarrow r = 6$

    D: $20\pi = 2\pi r \rightarrow r = 10$

    E: $50\pi = 2\pi r \rightarrow r = 25$

    Find the area of each disc using the formula: A = πr²

    A: $A = \pi \left(\frac{1}{2}\right)^2 = \pi/4 \approx 0.79$

    B: $A = \pi(5)^2 = 25\pi \approx 78.54$

    C: $A = \pi(6)^2 = 36\pi \approx 113.1$

    D: $A = \pi(10)^2 = 100\pi \approx 314.16$

E: $A = \pi(25)^2 = 625\pi \approx 1,963.46$

To save time, you can alternatively start with finding the area of disc C, since the options will increase. If C is too high to fit, D and E will be too high as well, and you only need to check A and B. Since C is small enough to fit, so are A and B, so you just need to check D and E.

The answers are A, B, C, D.

13. **Sub topic: Circles**

    The correct answer is $21 m^2$.

    Length of each side of the square is equal to the diameter of the radius that is

    Area of square will be $10 \times 10 = 100\ m^2$

    Area of the circle will be $3.142 \times 5^2 = 78.55\ m^2$

    Area of shaded region = Area of square - Area of the circle = $21.45\ m^2$, which in two significant digits is 21.

14. **Sub topic: Polygons**

    The correct answers are (B) and (D).

    Let width = x

    Then length = $2x - 3$

    Perimeter = $2(x + 2x - 3) = 6x - 6$

    According to the condition,

    $6x - 6 = 96$

    $x = 17 cm$

    Width = 17cm and length = 31cm

15. **Sub topic: Coordinate Geometry**

    The correct answer is (E).

    The distance formula, derived from the Pythagorean theorem, is

    $d = \sqrt{(x_1 - x_2)^2 + (y_1 - y_2)^2}$, where

    $x_1 - x_2$ and $y_1 - y_2$ are the lengths of the legs of the right triangle and d is the length of the hypotenuse.

The difference in x-values is $-3 - 4 = -7$

The difference in y-values is $-11 - 13 = -24$

At this point you may realize that 7 – 24 - 25 is a Pythagorean triple and d is thus equal to 25. Otherwise, substitute these values in the formula and solve for d.

$d = \sqrt{(-7)^2 + (-24)^2}$

$d = \sqrt{49 + 576}$

$d = \sqrt{625}$

$d = 25$

16. **Sub topic: Quadrilaterals**

    The correct answer is (A).

    The area of the top figure is $\frac{2h(b+5)}{2} = hb + 5h$.

    The area of the bottom figure is

    $\frac{h(2b+5)}{2} = hb + \left(\frac{5}{2}\right)h$.

    So, the correct answer is (A).

17. **Sub topic: Lines & Angles**

    The correct answers are (C) and (D).

    The slope of a line perpendicular to another line is the inverse reciprocal, so $m_2 = \frac{-1}{m_1}$.

    Option A: $m_1 m_2 = m_1 \left(\frac{-1}{m_1}\right) = -1 \neq 1$, so (A) is not correct.

    Option B: $m_1 \neq \frac{-1}{m_1}$, so (B) is not correct.

    Option C: $m_1 m_2 = m_1 \left(\frac{-1}{m_1}\right) = -1$, so (C) is correct.

    Option D: $m_1 m_2 + 1 = m_1 \left(\frac{-1}{m_1}\right) + 1 = -1 + 1 = 0$, so (D) is correct.

18. **Sub topic: Triangles/Circles**

    The correct answer is (D).

    Find the area of the triangle and subtract it from the area of the circle to find the area of the shaded region.

Area of the triangle:

Since leg OB and OA are also radii we know they are equal. An isosceles right triangle is a 45°–45°–90° triangle. The ratio of the sides of an isosceles triangle is $1:1:\sqrt{2}$, thus we know the length of the OB and OA are 8.

A_triangle = $\frac{bh}{2} = \frac{(8)(8)}{2} = \frac{64}{2} = 32$

The radius of the circle is the length of OB and OA: r = 8

A_circle = $\pi r^2 = \pi \times 8^2 = 64\pi$

Area of shaded region:

64π - 32

19. **Sub topic: Circles**

The correct answer is (A).

The area of the left sector is $\left(\frac{x}{2}\right)(2r)^2 = 2r^2 x$.

The area of the right one is $\left(\frac{2x}{2}\right)r^2 = r^2 x$

20. **Sub topic: Quadrilaterals/Three-Dimensional Figures**

The correct answer is (D).

Because the sides of a square are equal you can determine the length of the side by dividing the perimeter by 4, 32 ÷ 4 = 8. The SA of a sphere with a radius of 8 is:

$SA_{sphere} = 4\pi r^2$

$SA_{sphere} = 4\pi \times 8^2$

$SA_{sphere} = 4\pi(64)$

$SA_{sphere} = 256\pi$

21. **Sub topic: Triangles/Quadrilaterals**

The correct answers are (B) and (C).

Area of $\triangle AED = 12 = \frac{1}{2}(6)(x) \rightarrow x = 4$

$z^2 = 3^2 + 4^2 \rightarrow z = 5$

22. **Sub topic: Lines & Angles**

The correct answer is 135°.

Angles 1 and 2 are supplementary angles, if ∠1 is 45° then ∠2 = 180°- 45°= 135°

23. **Sub topic: Triangles**

The correct answer is (C).

BD = CD, ∠CBD = ∠C = 19°

Therefore, ∠BDC = 180° - (∠CBD + ∠C)

= 180° – (19° + 19°)

= 180° – 38° = 142°

Then ∠BDA = 180° – ∠BDC = 180° – 142° = 38°

Since AB = AD, ∠ABD = ∠BDA = 38°

Therefore, ∠A = 180° – (∠BDA + ∠ABD)

= 180° – (38° + 38°)

= 180° – 76° = 104°

The correct answer is C.

24. **Sub topic: Area, Perimeter, and Volum**

The correct answer is (D).

The area of the unshaded region is found by subtracting the area of the rectangle from the area of the parallelogram. The area of the parallelogram is found by multiplying the base $\left(7\frac{1}{4} \text{ in}\right)$ by the height $\left(1\frac{1}{9} \text{ in}\right)$. Multiplying these two values gives you $\frac{116}{9}$. We then want to find the area of the rectangle, which is base (2 in) multiplied by height $\left(\frac{6}{7} \text{ in}\right)$. Multiplying these gives you $\frac{12}{7}$. Subtract this from the area of the parallelogram $\frac{116}{9} - \frac{12}{7} = \frac{704}{63}, 11\frac{11}{63} \text{ in}^2$.

Therefore, the answer is D.

25. **Sub topic: Triangles**

The correct answer is (C).

If you split the equilateral triangle into two parts, the vertical part represents the height, which is the value we are solving for. This then creates a 30,60,90 triangle, with the value across from 30 being $\sqrt{3}$, which we will call x. Because 30,60,90 triangles have a x, $x\sqrt{3}$, $2x$ length pattern, respectively, the value across from 60 is going to be $x\sqrt{3}$, where x is $\sqrt{3}$, making the length across from 60 (the height) equal to $\sqrt{3}\sqrt{3} = 3$.

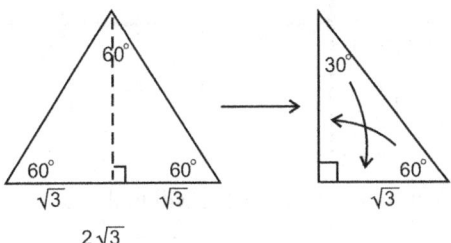

$\sqrt{3} = x$

$\sqrt{3}\sqrt{3} = x\sqrt{3}$

$3 = x\sqrt{3}$ length opp. 60°

26. **Sub topic: Triangles**

The correct answer is (B).

To find the height and base, split the triangle up into two 30, 60, 90 triangles. Then use the 30,60,90 relationship to find the missing height and base, and then multiply the base by 2 to get the original triangle's base. Then use the area formula of a triangle (A = b ∗ h / 2) to find the area.

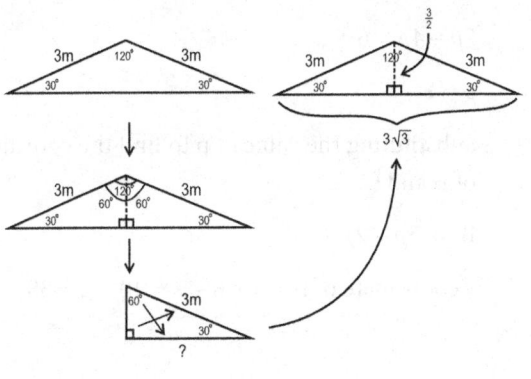

$x \to 30^0 \to \dfrac{3}{2}$

$x\sqrt{3} \to 60^0 \to \dfrac{3\sqrt{3}}{2}$

$2x \to 90^0 \to \dfrac{2x}{2} = \dfrac{3}{2} \to x = \dfrac{3}{2}$

$A = \dfrac{b \cdot h}{2}$

$A = \dfrac{\dfrac{3}{2} \cdot 3\sqrt{3}}{2}$

$A = \dfrac{9\sqrt{3}}{4} m^2$

27. **Sub topic: Area, Perimeter, and Volume**

The correct answer is (A).

To find Quantity A, use the area formula for a circle, $A = \pi r^2$, where $r = \dfrac{2}{3}r$. Plugging this in gives $A = \pi \left(\dfrac{2}{3}r\right)^2 = \dfrac{4\pi}{9}r^2$. Now find Quantity B using the circumference formula for a circle, $C = 2\pi r$, where $r = \dfrac{1}{5}r$. Plugging this in gives $C = 2\pi\left(\dfrac{1}{5}r\right) = \dfrac{2\pi}{5}r$. Because r is a positive whole number, the quantity $\dfrac{4\pi}{9}r^2$ will be larger than $\dfrac{2\pi}{5}r$ and therefore the answer is A: Quantity A is greater.

Level: Medium

28. **Sub topic: Angles/Triangles**

The correct answer is (D).

Apply the Angle Sum Postulate to each triangle.

(1) $a + m + b = 180°$

m and n are vertical angles with respect to two angles of the second triangle from left. So, we can replace the two unknown angles in the second triangle from the left with their vertical equivalents m, and n

(2) $c + m + n = 180°$

The sum of the interior angles in the third triangle from the left is expressed below:

(3) $n + p + f = 180°$

In the triangle to the right, one angle is vertical to p. Thus, the sum of the interior angles for this triangle will be as follows:

(4) $d + p + e = 180°$

Add (1) through (4).

$a + m + b + c + m + n + n + p + f + d + p + e = 180° + 180° + 180° + 180°$

(5) $a + b + c + d + e + f + 2(m + n + p) = 720°$

Replace the given value of $(m + n + p) = 200$ in this equation and simplify.

$a + b + c + d + e + f + 2(200) = 720°$

$a + b + c + d + e + f + 400 = 720°$

$a + b + c + d + e + f + 400 - 400 = 720° - 400°$

$a + b + c + d + e + f = 320°$

29. **Sub topic: Polygons**

The correct answers are (C) and (D).

Let us plot all the points on the coordinate plane.

The point A is the origin on the coordinate plane.

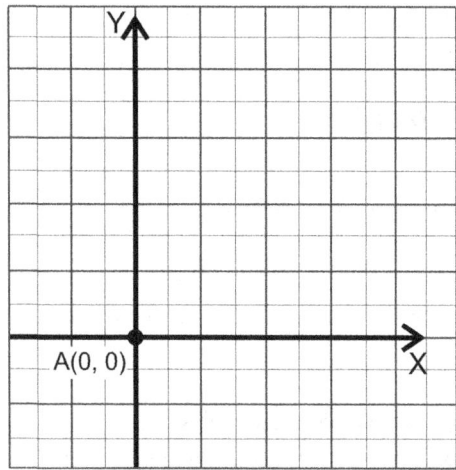

The point B has its x coordinate = 0, that shows it lies somewhere on the y-axis.

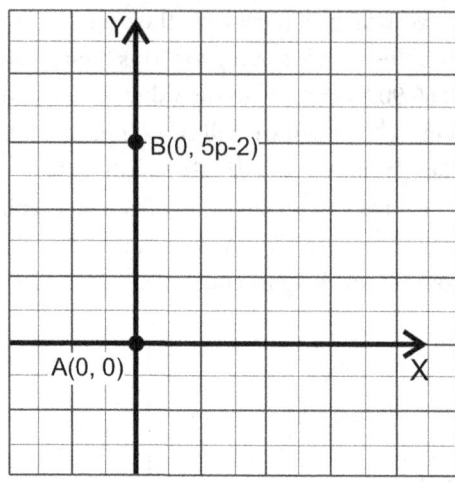

$\angle ABC = 90°$, then $\triangle ABC$ will look like:

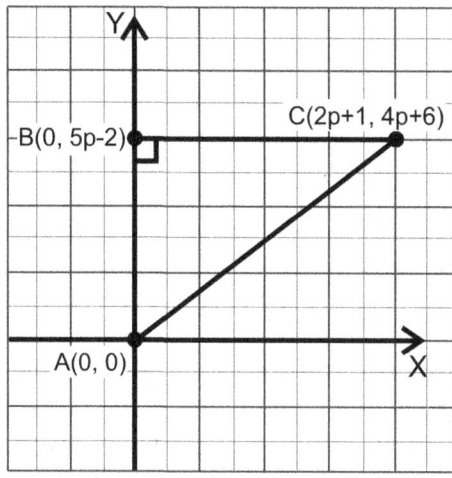

Since line BC is horizontal, the y coordinates of point B and C will be equal.

$5p - 2 = 4p + 6$

$5p - 4p = 6 + 2$

$p = 8$

Substituting the value of p to find the coordinates of B and C:

B $(0, 5p - 2)$

y coordinate of B $= 5 \times 8 - 2 = 40 - 2 = 38$

Geometry Practice Questions

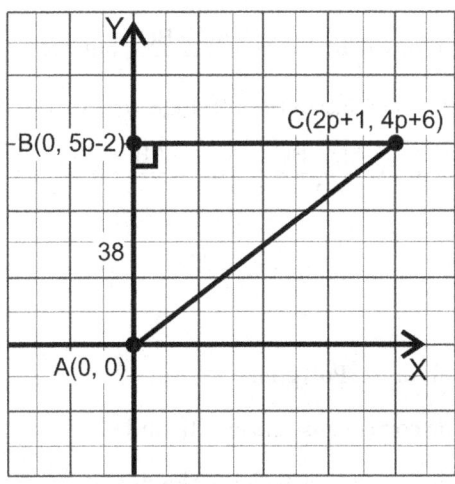

Similarly, C $(2p + 2, 4p + 6)$

x coordinate of C $= 2 \times 8 + 2 = 16 + 2 = 18$

y coordinate of C $= 4 \times 8 + 6 = 32 + 6 = 38$

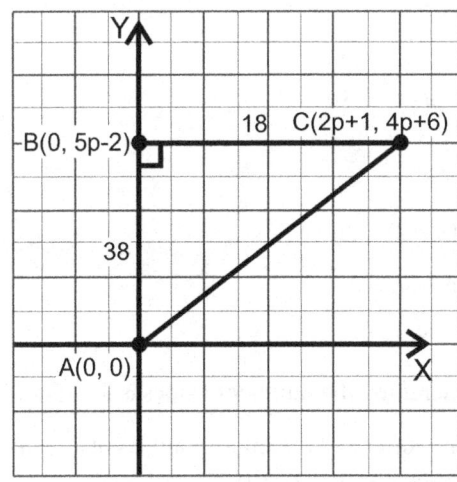

Area of Triangle $= \dfrac{\text{base} \times \text{height}}{2}$

Area of $\angle ABC = \dfrac{18 \times 38}{2} = 9 \times 38 = 342$

Options C and D are correct.

30. **Sub topic: Lines & Angles/Polygons**

The correct answer is (D).

In the figure

$x + a = 180°$

$y + b = 180°$

Adding these equations, we obtain

$x + y + a + b = 180° + 180° = 360°$

Having the value of $x + y$, then we can find $a + b$ using the equation above. To find $x + y$ as the sum of the measures of two interior angles of a pentagon, we need the sum of the measures of the other interior angles, m, n, and p. The given statements provide the values of m and n. The value of p is still unknown. Thus, to solve the problem, the given conditions are not sufficient. So, the correct answer choice is (D).

31. **Sub topic: Polygons**

The correct answers are (A) and (C).

In a polygon with 'n' vertices, the number of lines that can be drawn is given by

$n_{c_2} = \dfrac{n(n-1)}{2}$

In any polygon, a diagonal is a straight line which does not connect adjacent vertices. In a polygon with 'n' vertices, there are 'n' lines connecting adjacent vertices.

Hence, the number of diagonals in any polygon =

$\dfrac{n(n-1)}{2} - n$

$\dfrac{n^2 - 3n}{2} = 54$

$n - 3n = 108$

$n^2 - 3n - 108 = 0$

$(n - 12)(n + 9) = 0$

$n - 12 = 0$ or $n + 9 = 0$

$n = 12$ or $n = -9$

$n = -9$ is inadmissible. Hence, the polygon has 12 sides.

Among the options, statements A and C give the number of diagonals of the polygon.

32. **Sub topic: Lines & Angles/Triangles**

The correct answer is (C).

Let's use both statements. Here are the given statements:

$x - y = 20°$

$z - x = 20°$

Add the equations and cancel the opposite terms.

(1) $z - y = 40°$

From the figure, using the property of exterior angle in a triangle

(2) $z = m\angle A + y$

Subtract y from each side of (2).

(3) $m\angle A = z - y$

Replace the value of $z - y$ from (A1) in (3).

A = 40°

33. **Sub topic: Coordinate Geometry**

The correct answer is (B).

$\triangle ABC$ is an isosceles right triangle with hypotenuse BC → AC and AB are perpendicular

AB has a slope of 0 $\left(\text{slope} = \frac{(2-2)}{(b-1)} = \frac{0}{(b-1)} = 0\right)$

→ AB is parallel to x-axis

→ AC must be parallel to y-axis → C(c, 6) = C(1, 6) because c must be 1 to match with A(1,2)

$\triangle ABC$ is isosceles with hypotenuse BC → AC = AB

We use the coordinates of the points and the definition of the distance between the points, to rewrite the above as:

$\sqrt{(1-c)^2 + (2-6)^2} = \sqrt{(b-1)^2 + (2-2)^2}$ →

$\sqrt{(1-1)^2 + 16} = \sqrt{(b-1)^2}$

b − 1 = 4 → b = 5

AC = AB = 4

Using the same the definition of the distance between the points:

BC = $\sqrt{(b-c)^2 + (2-6)^2} = \sqrt{(5-1)^2 + 16}$

= $\sqrt{2 \times 16} = 4\sqrt{2}$

AD is perpendicular to BC → Area of $\triangle ABC$ can be calculated as $\frac{(AD \times BC)}{2}$ but because the triangle is also a right triangle the Area is also equal to $\frac{AD \times BC}{2} \rightarrow AD = \frac{AB \times AC}{BC}$

$AD = \frac{(4 \times 4)}{4\sqrt{2}} = \frac{4}{\sqrt{2}} = 2\sqrt{2}$

34. **Sub topic: Polygons**

The correct answers are (B) and (D).

The measure of each interior angle of a regular polygon = $\frac{(n-2) \times 180°}{n}$

Hence,

$\frac{(n-2) \times 180°}{n} = 135°$

$\frac{(n-2)}{n} = \frac{135°}{180°}$

$\frac{(n-2)}{n} = \frac{3}{4}$

$4(n - 2) = 3n$

$4n - 3n = 8$

$n = 8$

Therefore, the number of sides is 8.

The sum of all the interior angles of a regular polygon = $(n - 2) \times 180°$

We have n = 8

Hence, $(8 - 2) \times 180°$

= 6 × 180°

= 1080°

Among the options, statements B and D give the sum of all interior angles in the polygon.

35. **Sub topic: Circles**

The correct answer is (B).

First, we need to find the measurement of the four sides of the square. The side length is the square root of 256 is 16. Then, according to the figure, this is also the sum of the diameters of

Geometry Practice Questions

two circles, which means the diameter of each circle is $\frac{1}{2} \times 16 = 8$ and the radius is 4. Next, we find the area of each circle: $A = r^2\pi = 4^2\pi = 16\pi$. The total area of the four circles is $4 \times 16\pi = 64\pi$. Therefore, the area of the grey regions is the difference between the area of the square and the areas of the circles: $256 - 64\pi \approx 54.94$. This is smaller than $300 - 50\pi, \approx 142.92$.

This means B is the correct answer.

36. **Sub topic: Coordinate Geometry**

    The correct answer is (C).

    One approach would be to calculate the slopes of lines AB and AC to see if their product equals -1 in which case the lines would be perpendicular

    The slope of AB is $\frac{2\sqrt{3}-0}{2-4} = -\sqrt{3}$

    The slope of AC is $\frac{2\sqrt{3}-0}{2-0} = -\sqrt{3}$

    The product of the slopes is -3, which means the lines cannot be perpendicular. Option E is definitely wrong.

    Next, we can calculate the length of the triangle sides to see if that gives a helpful indication.

    $AB = \sqrt{(4-2)^2 + (0-2\sqrt{3})^2} = \sqrt{4+12} = 4$

    $AC = \sqrt{(0-2)^2 + (0-2\sqrt{3})^2} = \sqrt{4+12} = 4$

    $BC = \sqrt{(4-0)^2 + (0-0)^2} = \sqrt{16+0} = 4$

    $AB = AC = BC$

    $\triangle ABC$ is equilateral; all angles in $\triangle ABC = 60°$, including $\angle BAC$, which is answer (C).

37. **Sub topic: Triangles/Polygons**

    The correct answers are (A), (C) and (G).

    In the polygon ABCDE, we have a pentagon. The sum of the interior angles in a polygon is dictated by the following equation. $S=(n-2)180$

    Number of sides in a Pentagon $=5$

Sum of interior angles $=(5-2)180=3(180)=540°$

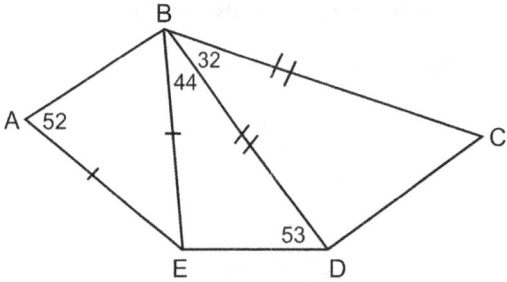

To determine if the statements are true, we need to first find the missing angles.

$\triangle ABE$ is an isosceles triangle, so therefore $\angle ABE$ is also 52°. The sum of the interior angles in the triangle should equal 180°. Now we can calculate $m\angle BEA$.

$\angle EAB + \angle ABE + \angle BEA = 180°$

$52° + 52° + \angle BEA = 180°$

$104° + \angle BEA = 180°$

$\angle BEA = 76°$

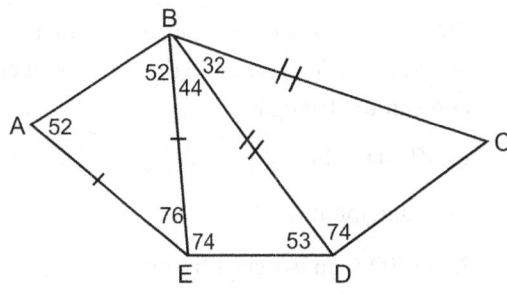

$\triangle BCD$ is also an isosceles triangle. Therefore $\angle BCD$ and $\angle BDC$ are congruent.

$\angle DBC + \angle BDC + \angle BCD = 180°$

$32° + \angle BDC + \angle BCD = 180°$

$\angle BDC + \angle BCD = 148°$

$\angle BDC = 74°$

$\angle BCD = 74°$

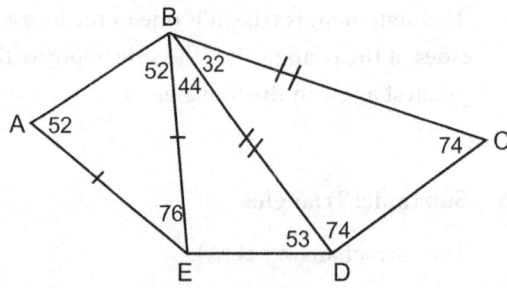

Now we can find the missing angle: ∠BED

∠BED + ∠EDB + ∠DBE = 180°

∠BED + 53° + 44° = 180°

∠BED + 97° = 180°

∠BED = 83°

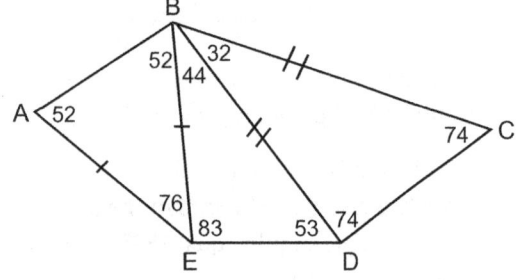

Now we can address the statements:

A. AB is the longest side of ΔABE.

This statement is true because the angle opposite is the largest angle in the triangle.

B. BE is the shortest side of ΔEBD.

This statement is false because this side is opposite the 53°angle, and there is a smaller angle in the triangle.

C. ∠EBD = 44°

This statement is true.

D. ΔBED is an isosceles triangle.

ΔBED is not an isosceles triangle because all three sides are different lengths.

E. ∠BCD = 44°

This statement has been proven false.

F. The sum of all interior angles of the pentagon is 720°.

This statement is false.

G. BD is the longest side of ΔBCD.

This statement is true. It is one of the longest sides of the triangle. It is the side opposite the greatest angle in the triangle.

38. **Sub topic: Triangles**

The correct answer is (A).

In order to solve this question, you would need to know some rules of triangles and use logical reasoning. First, we know right way ∠a + ∠b + 60 = 180. We also know the triangles is not an equilateral or an isosceles triangle since AC>AB, and c=60. This means that ∠b must be greater than ∠c =60.So, we can eliminate choice (C). Since ∠b >60 angle a must be less than 60. The rule of triangles states that, the side opposite the largest angle is the longest side, and the side opposite the smallest angle is the shortest side. Therefore BC, AB, AC are the sides of the triangle in order of smallest to largest and the correct answer is A.

39. **Sub topic: Lines & Angles**

The correct answer is (C).

As a rule, for all geometry questions it may be necessary to either redraw the diagram/ add lines/labels etc. We are aware of rules for parallel & transverse lines. Thus, we will have to create a similar situation. This is achieved by drawing a line EF which is parallel to both AB & CD as shown. Now ∠CEF = 4x°(Corresponding angles, CD || EF, CE is the transverse) and ∠AEF = 6x°. Thus 130°= 10x° and x = 13

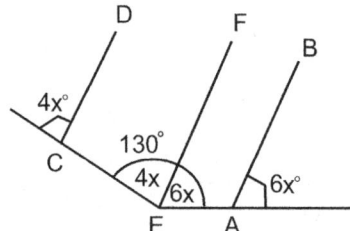

Note: If we do not pay close attention to the fact that AEC is NOT a straight line we may be tempted to say 6x° = 180 – 130, and x = 8.33 OR 4x° = 180 – 130, and x = 12.5. Once again it always helps to redraw the diagram provided to you. Remember it may not be the best representation of what you need.

40. **Sub topic: Polygons**

The correct answers are (C) and (D).

Let *x* be the width and *y* be the length

Perimeter = 2x + 2y = 20

x = 10 − y

Area = xy = 24

Putting the value of x

y(10 − y) = 24

10y − y² = 24

y² − 10y + 24 = 0

(y − 6)(y − 4) = 0

Length will be 6 cm and width will be 4 cm.

41. **Sub topic: Circles**

The correct answer is (A).

To solve this question, we need to know how to find the angle given the arc length and how to calculate area given the angle. Since the radius is 4, the diameter is 8 and the circumference of the circle is 8π. Therefore, ratio of arc $\frac{BOC}{Cir} = \frac{3\pi}{8\pi} = \frac{3}{8}$, which means $\frac{\angle BOC}{360°} = \frac{3}{8} \times 360 = \frac{3}{8} = 135°$. Therefore, $\angle AOB + \angle BOC = 135 + 60 = 195$, and $\angle AOC = 360 - 195 = 165°$. The ratio of X to the total area of the circle is $\frac{165}{360}$ or $\frac{11}{24}$. The total area of the circle is A = r²π = 4²π = 16π and the area of X = $\frac{11}{24} \times 16\pi = \frac{22\pi}{3}$, which is larger than $\frac{21\pi}{3}$.

Therefore, the correct answer is A.

42. **Sub topic: Three-Dimensional Figures**

The correct answer is (B).

To solve this problem, we need to find out the volume of the cylinder container and the volume of the rectangular object. To find the volume of the container, we use the given equation V = r²πh = 3² π(4) = 9π(4) = 36π cm³. The volume of the rectangular object is V = lwh = 2 × 1 × 3 = 6 cm³. This means the cylinder can now hold a maximum of 36π − 6 cm³ of juice, which is approximately 113.04 − 6 = 107.04 cm³. 2 liters = 2000 cm³. Since the cylinder can hold about 107.04 cm³, there will be 92.96 cm³ remaining in the old container. Therefore, (B) is the correct answer.

43. **Sub topic: Triangles**

The correct answer is 4.57.

From geometry, we know that the diagonals of an inscribed square are diameters of the circumscribed circle.

So, in the right ΔABC, AC = 2(2) = 4. Using the Pythagorean Theorem,

(AB)² + (BC)² = (AB)² + (AB)² = 4² = 16

2(AB)² = 16

AB = √8

The area of the square ABCD = $(\sqrt{8})^2$ = 8

On the other hand, Area of circle = π(2²) = 4π

Shaded area = 4π − 8 ≈ 4.57 (to 2 decimal places).

44. **Sub topic: Triangles**

The correct answer is (D).

In the figure we are going to use the ratios of the sides of a 30°- 60°- 90° triangle, which is $x : x\sqrt{3} : 2x$

The smaller triangle has a side length of 4 and a hypotenuse of 8.

4 : h : 8

$x : x\sqrt{3} : 2x$

The value of x is 4 in this triangle. Therefore, the height of the triangle is $4\sqrt{3}$. The length of the base is $4 + 4\sqrt{3}$

If we use the formula for the area of triangle, we can calculate the area of the triangle.

$A = \frac{1}{2}bh = \frac{1}{2}(4+4\sqrt{3})(4\sqrt{3})$

$A = \frac{1}{2}(16\sqrt{3} + 16\sqrt{9}) = \frac{1}{2}(16\sqrt{3} + 48)$

$A = 8\sqrt{3} + 24$

The answer is D.

45. **Sub topic: Triangles**

    The correct answer is (A).

    $b = \sqrt{4^2 + 3^2} = \sqrt{25} = 5$

    $a = \sqrt{7^2 + 3^2} = \sqrt{58}$

    The correct answer is (A), $5 + \sqrt{58}$

46. **Sub topic: Circles/Triangles**

    The correct answers are (B) and (D).

    Because AB is tangent to the circle, $\angle OAB = 90°$. Similarly, $\angle ODC = 90°$,

    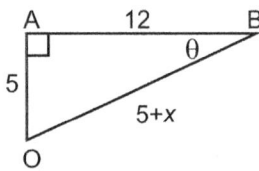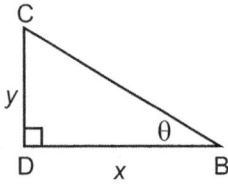

    $(5+x)^2 + 5^2 = 12^2 \rightarrow 5 + x\sqrt{169} = 13 \rightarrow x = 8$

    $\tan(\theta) = \dfrac{5}{12} = \dfrac{y}{8} \rightarrow y = \dfrac{10}{3}$

    Answers: (B), (D)

47. **Sub topic: Triangles/Circles**

    The correct answer is (B).

    $\angle XYZ$ is inscribed in a semicircle and is therefore a right angle.

    Therefore, ΔXYZ is a right triangle and the Pythagorean Theorem states

    $(XY)^2 = (XZ)^2 + (YZ)^2$

    $(17)^2 = (XZ)^2 + (15)^2$ (XY is a diameter)

    $289 = (XZ)^2 + 225$

    $289 - 225 = (XZ)^2$

    $(XZ)^2 = 64$

    $XZ = \sqrt{64}$

    $XZ = 8$

Area of $\Delta XYZ = \dfrac{1}{2}bh$

$= \dfrac{1}{2}(8)(15) = 60$

The correct answer is B.

48. **Sub topic: Triangles**

    The correct answers are (A), and (C).

    From the Pythagorean Theorem

    $z = \sqrt{5^2 - 4^2} = 3$

    Since the triangles are similar, we can calculate the variables using ratios:

    $\dfrac{5.25}{4+x} = \dfrac{3}{4} \rightarrow 3(4+x) = (4)(5.25) \rightarrow x = 3$

    $\dfrac{5.25}{5+x} = \dfrac{3}{5} \rightarrow 3(5+y) = (5)(5.25) \rightarrow y = 3.75$

    Answers: (A), (C)

49. **Sub topic: Quadrilaterals**

    The correct answer is (A).

    Because the perimeter of the rhombus is 40, each side has length 10. Because the diagonals of a rhombus are perpendicular and bisect each other.

    $x^2 + 5^2 = 10^2$

    $x^2 + 25 = 100$

    $x^2 = 75$

    $x = \sqrt{75}$, $x = 5\sqrt{3}$.

    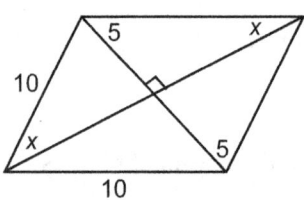

    The area of a quadrilateral with perpendicular diagonals d_1 and d_2 is

    $= \dfrac{1}{2} d_1 \cdot d_2$

    $= \dfrac{1}{2}(10)(10\sqrt{3})$

    $= 50\sqrt{3}$

Geometry Practice Questions

50. **Sub topic: Three-Dimensional Figures**

The correct answer is (C).

Math Procedure	Strategy
Height of equilateral triangular base = $\sqrt{5^2 - 2.5^2} = 4.33$	From Pythagorean Theorem, $\sqrt{(2a)^2 - a^2} = h$
Area of triangular base = $\frac{1}{2}(5)(4.33) = 10.825$	Area of triangle (Geometry)
Area of circular hole = π	Area of circle (Geometry)
Remaining area = $10.825 - \pi = 7.684$ % remaining area (or volume) = $100 \frac{7.684}{10.825} = 70.98\%$	*Note:* The lengths of the prism and the circular bore are the same and therefore the percentage of area and volume are the same.

The correct answer is C.

51. **Sub topic: Circles/Triangles**

The correct answers are (B) and (D).

By the property of circles, we know that the angle formed at the center is twice the angle formed at the circumference. Therefore $\angle AOB = 2 \times \angle ACB$

Hence, $\angle AOB = 2 \times 70° = 140°$

OB and OA are the radii of the circle.

OB = OA

Hence, ΔOAB is an isosceles triangle and $\angle OAB = \angle OBA$

By the triangle sum property,
$\angle OAB + \angle OBA + \angle AOB = 180°$

But, $\angle OBA = \angle OAB$

Hence, $\angle OAB + \angle OAB + 140° = 180°$

$2 \times \angle OAB = 180° - 140°$

$\angle OAB = 20° = \angle OBA$

Therefore, the value of the $\angle x$ is 20°.

Among the options, statements B and D give the current measure of $\angle x$.

52. **Sub topic: Area, Perimeter, and Volume**

The correct answer is (B).

B. First, draw a line segment from point R perpendicular to QS. This is the altitude of triangle QRS, and it must be less than 4. The formula for the area of a triangle is $\frac{1}{2} \times$ base $\times$ height. The base is 12, and if the height were 4, the area would be 24. Since the height is actually less than 4, the area must be less than 24. You don't have to find the actual value of area, though. Whatever the area is, the perimeter (the sum of all this sides) is 27. Quantity B is bigger regardless of the exact value of Quantity A.

53. **Sub topic: Triangles/Lines & Angles**

The correct answers are (B), (C) and (E).

If IJ || KL, then we have two similar triangles. To determine which angles are similar, we need to match the corresponding angles when we write the similarity statement.

Since the intersection of the two lines form a point of intersection at M, we know $\angle IMJ \cong \angle LMK$ because they are vertical angles. Statement B is true.

Since IJ || KL, we also know that the sets of alternate interior angles are also congruent.

The two pairs of alternate interior angles are: $\angle JIM \cong \angle KLM$ and. $\angle IJM \cong \angle LKM$ This means that statement A is false and statement E is true. Now we can write a similarity statement: $\Delta KLM \sim \Delta JIM$

Statement D is false because it states that the two triangles are congruent not similar.

Since two triangles are similar, we know the sides

are proportional between the two triangles.

If we compare the top triangle to the bottom triangle: $\frac{KL}{JI} = \frac{LM}{IM} = \frac{KM}{JM}$

If we compare the bottom triangle to the top triangle: $\frac{JI}{KL} = \frac{IM}{LM} = \frac{JM}{KM}$

Statement C is true and has a correctly written proportion. Statement F is false because the proportion is incorrectly written.

The true statements are B, C, E.

54. **Sub topic: Circles**

    The correct answer is (B).

    Because we are given the radius and the arc measure, we can find the central angle and the inscribed angle using the arc length equation

    Arc length = $2\pi r \times \frac{x}{360°}$, where I is the central angle. Plugging in the given values, we obtain $5\pi = 2\pi \times 15 \times \frac{x}{360°}$. Solving for x we get $x=60$, meaning the central angle is 60°. The inscribed angle is therefore 30°. The smaller triangle is therefore an equiangular and equilateral triangle, as the base angles must both be 60°, making $\angle 2$ =60°. Because the larger triangle is isosceles, the two base angles must be the same, so let's call them y. Then, $y + y + 30 = 180$, and $y = 75$. Therefore, $\angle 1 + \angle 2 = 75$. Since $\angle 2 = 60°$, $\angle 1 = 15°$, and the ratio is therefore $\frac{15}{60} = \frac{1}{4}$. The correct answer is Choice B.

55. **Sub topic: Three-Dimensional Figures**

    The correct answer is (B).

    To find Quantity A, find both values of AB and BC then write as a ratio. If the length of the cube is x, the value of AB would be $AB^2 = x^2 + x^2 = 2x^2$, so $AB = x\sqrt{2}$. The length of BC is x because it represents a length of the cube, which we had previously defined as x.

    Therefore, $\frac{AB}{BC} = \frac{x\sqrt{2}}{x} = \sqrt{2}$. To find Quantity B, find AB and BD. AB we found before to be $AB = x\sqrt{2}$. To find AC, use the triangle AEC. AE is the same length as AB, as it represents a diagonal on the face of the cube, so $AE = x\sqrt{2}$. EC= x because it represents a side length of the cube. Use Pythagorean theorem with AC as the hypotenuse to obtain $AC^2 = (x\sqrt{2})^2 + x^2 = 3x^2$, so then $AC = x\sqrt{3}$. Therefore, $\frac{AB}{AC} = \frac{x\sqrt{3}}{x} = \sqrt{3}$.

    Therefore, Quantity A is smaller than Quantity B. The answer is B.

56. **Sub topic: Congruent and Similar Figures**

    The correct answer is (B).

    Use the proportional relationship of the two rectangles to assign them side length values use x, which represents a relative scale factor. Because the side lengths of the square must be the same, and the square's side length is half Rectangle ABFE, you can assign these values x and $2x$. Then the other side length becomes x and $3x$. Then use distance formula to solve for the quantities compared. You then get Quantity $A = x\sqrt{10}$ and Quantity $B = x(\sqrt{10} + \sqrt{2})$. Because $\sqrt{5} + \sqrt{2} > \sqrt{10}$, Quantity B is larger. The correct answer is Choice B.

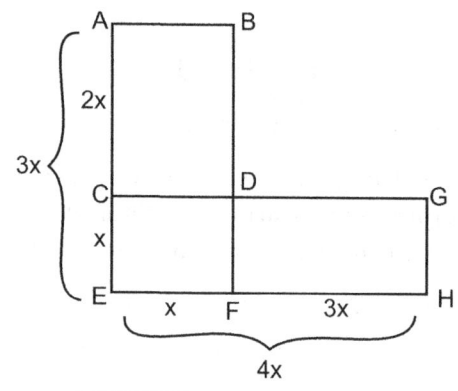

$DH = \sqrt{x^2 + (3x)^2} = \sqrt{10x^2} = x\sqrt{10}$

$AD = \sqrt{(2x)^2 + x^2} = \sqrt{5x^2} = x\sqrt{5}$

$CF = \sqrt{x^2 + x^2} = \sqrt{2x^2} = x\sqrt{2}$

$x\sqrt{5} + x\sqrt{2}$

$x(\sqrt{5} + \sqrt{2})$

$\sqrt{10} < \sqrt{5} + \sqrt{2}$

Geometry Practice Questions

57. **Sub topic: Congruent and Similar Figures**

    The correct answer is (B).

    By finding the distance of AH, BG, and CF using distance formula (as shown in the diagram below), you get AH= 5x, and $CF = x\sqrt{2}$. Setting up ratios for the specific quantities asked for, you get $\dfrac{AH}{BG} = \dfrac{5}{\sqrt{13}} = \sqrt{\dfrac{25}{13}}$ for Quantity A and

    Quantity B is $\dfrac{BG}{CF} = \dfrac{\sqrt{13}}{\sqrt{2}} = \sqrt{\dfrac{13}{2}}$. Because $\dfrac{13}{2}$ is larger than $\dfrac{25}{13}$, Quantity B is larger and the answer is B.

    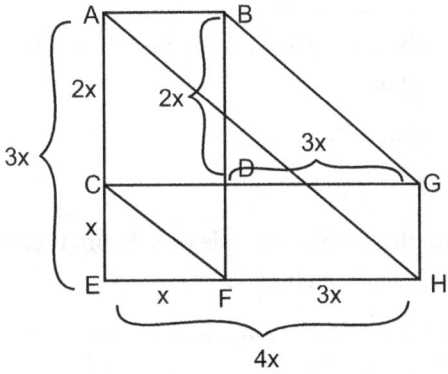

    $CF = \sqrt{x^2 + x^2} = x\sqrt{2}$

    $AH = \sqrt{(3x)^2 + (4x)^2} = 5x$

    $BG = \sqrt{(2x)^2 + (3x)^2} = x\sqrt{13}$

    $\dfrac{AH}{BG} = \dfrac{5\not{x}}{\not{x}\sqrt{13}} = \dfrac{5}{\sqrt{13}}$

    $\dfrac{BG}{CF} = \dfrac{x\sqrt{13}}{x\sqrt{2}} = \dfrac{\sqrt{13}}{\sqrt{2}}$

58. **Sub topic: Triangles**

    The correct answer is (C).

    Graphing this you can see that it creates a 45, 45, 90 triangle, and to check you can make sure the side lengths are $1:1:\sqrt{2}$, which is true here. Therefore, the smallest angle value is 45°.

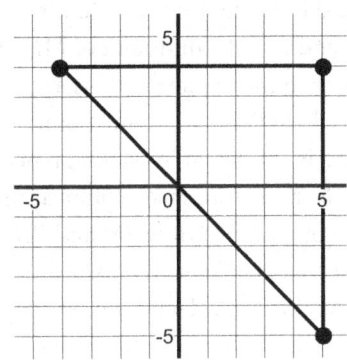

59. **Sub topic: Area, Perimeter, and Volume**

    The correct answer is (B).

    Because this is a regular hexagon, we can find the value of each angle in the hexagon by using the regular polygon angle formula: Angle Measure= $\dfrac{180(n-2)}{n}$, where n is the number of sides. Plugging in n=6 for the hexagon, we get Angle Measure= $\dfrac{180(6-2)}{6}$ =120°. Splitting Triangle CDE in half at the 120° angle gives two 30-60-90 triangles. Using the 30-60-90 properties, you find that across from the 60° is y/2, which represents $x\sqrt{2}$, and therefore $x = \dfrac{y}{2\sqrt{2}}$. CD is across from the 90°, which means it represents 2x, so we then get that

    $\dfrac{CD}{y} = \dfrac{2\left(\dfrac{y}{2\sqrt{2}}\right)}{y} = \dfrac{1}{\sqrt{2}} = \dfrac{\sqrt{2}}{2}$. This is less than

    Quantity B, which is $\dfrac{y}{CD} = \dfrac{\sqrt{2}}{1}$. Therefore, the answer is B.

Level: Difficult

60. **Sub topic: Lines & Angles/Polygons**

    The correct answer is (B).

    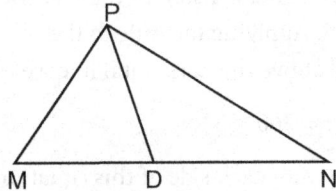

Since M, D, and N are collinear due to the statement (1) and D is the midpoint of MN by statement (2), then the segment MN is a straight-line segment, where D is an internal point between M and N, as shown in the graph below. Since only M, N, and D are given collinear in (1), therefore P is not on MN. Draw PM and PN. We know that in a triangle, the sum of two sides is greater than the third side. Hence, in ΔPDM,

(1) PD + PM > MD

Statement (2) indicates that

(2) DN = MD

Replacing DN for MD from (2) in (1), we get

DN < PD + PM or PD > DN − PM

Therefore, the proper answer choice is (B).

61. **Sub topic: Triangles/Polygons**

The correct answer is (A).

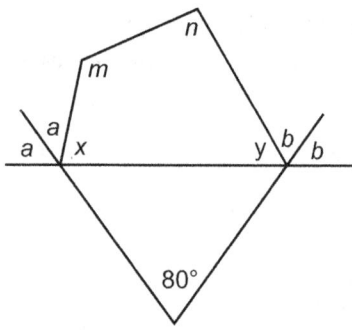

Angles a and b are vertical with two angles of the triangle. Using the angle sum postulate in a triangle, we obtain

$a + b + 80 = 180°$

Subtract 80 from each side of this equation and combine numbers on each side.

$a + b + 80 - 80 = 180° - 80°$

(1) $a + b = 100°$

In any quadrilateral, the sum of the interior angles is 360°. Applying this rule to the quadrilateral above the horizontal line we obtain

$m + n + x + y = 360°$

Subtract $x+y$ from each side of this equation and cancel out the opposite terms.

$m + n + x + y - (x + y) = 360° - (x + y)$

(2) $m + n = 360° - (x + y)$

The sum of the angles formed above the horizontal line around each point of intersection is 180. Thus,

(3) $x + a + a = 180°$

(4) $y + b + b = 180°$

Subtract $2a$ from each side of (3) and subtract $2b$ from each side of (4).

$x + a + a - 2a = 180° - 2a$

$y + b + b - 2b = 180° - 2b$

Combine the like terms on the left side of each equation.

$x = 180° - 2a$

$y = 180° - 2b$

Add these equations side by side and then factor out 2 on the right side.

(5) $x + y = 360° - 2(a + b)$

Replace (1) in (5).

(6) $x + y = 360 - 2(100) = 160°$

In any quadrilateral, the sum of the interior angles is 360°.

(7) $m + n + x + y = 360°$

Replace (6) in (7) and solve for $(m + n)$.

$m + n + 160° = 360°$

$m + n = 360° - 160°$

$= 200°$

Answer: (A).

62. **Sub topic: Triangles**

The correct answer is (C).

Since the horizontal angles of the triangles are parallel, therefore, the angle measures 30° in lower triangle and the corresponding angle in the upper triangle are alternate interior angles and are equal.

We know that two right triangles are similar if they have a pair of equal angles. Therefore, the two right triangles are similar. Write the proportion among the ratios of sides in the triangles.

(1) $\dfrac{m}{p} = \dfrac{n}{10}$

We know that if one of the angles is a right triangle is 30°, then the opposite leg is one-half the hypotenuse. So, in the larger triangle, the hypotenuse is $2 \times 10 = 20$. The other acute angle in each triangle is 60° since 30° + 60° + 90° = 180°.

In a right triangle, the leg opposite 60° angle is $\dfrac{\sqrt{3}}{2}$, times the hypotenuse. So, in the larger triangle

$p = \dfrac{\sqrt{3}}{2}(20) = 10\sqrt{3}$

Replace the value of p in (1).

(2) $\dfrac{m}{10\sqrt{3}} = \dfrac{n}{10}$

Multiply each side by $\dfrac{10\sqrt{3}}{n}$

$\left(\dfrac{10\sqrt{3}}{n}\right)\left(\dfrac{m}{10\sqrt{3}}\right) = \left(\dfrac{10\sqrt{3}}{n}\right)\left(\dfrac{n}{10}\right)$

Reduce the product of fractions on each side.

$\dfrac{m}{n} = \sqrt{3}$

Replace the known values in $p\dfrac{m}{n}$, and simplify.

$p\left(\dfrac{m}{n}\right) = 10\sqrt{3}(\sqrt{3}) = 10(3) = 30$

63. **Sub topic: Triangles/Circles**

The correct answer is (C).

We need to find the area of all the circles using the equation $A = \pi r^2$

Circle 1: $A = \pi(16^2) = 256\pi$

Circle 2: $A = \pi(8^2) = 64\pi$

Circle 3: $A = \pi(4^2) = 16\pi$

Circle 4: $A = \pi(2^2) = 4\pi$

Circle 5: $A = \pi^2$

Total area of circles: $(256 + 64 + 16 + 4 + 1)\pi = 341\pi$

Now, we can find the total area of the triangle, which is the total areas of the circle + the grey regions = $(341 + 679)\pi = 1020\pi$.

To find the height, we use the equation for area of triangle: $A = \left(\dfrac{1}{2}\right)bh \to 1020\pi = \left(\dfrac{1}{2}\right)34\pi h \to = 60$, so these quantities are equal, and the correct answer is C.

64. **Sub topic: Triangles**

The correct answer is (B).

ABC is an equilateral triangle and AD is perpendicular to BC.

AD is the height and it splits the ΔABC into two right angle triangles (ΔABD and ΔADC) with identical areas which are equal to half of the area of ΔABC.

As per the formula for the area of an equilateral triangle, the area of $\triangle ABC = AC^2 \times \dfrac{\sqrt{3}}{4}$

$= 6^2 \times \dfrac{\sqrt{3}}{4} = 9\sqrt{3}$

The area of $\triangle ABD = \dfrac{DE \times AB}{2} = \dfrac{DE \times 6}{2} = DE \times 3$

We established that the area of ΔABD is also half of the area of ΔABC.

$DE \times 3 = \dfrac{9\sqrt{3}}{2}$

$DE = \dfrac{9\sqrt{3}}{2 \times 3} = \dfrac{3\sqrt{3}}{2} = \dfrac{\sqrt{27}}{2}$

Alternatively, if you do not remember the formula for the area of an equilateral triangle, you can still arrive at the correct result by using the Pythagorean Theorem (as long as you remember the formula for the area of a triangle).

ΔADC has a right angle → you can apply the Pythagorean Theorem

$AC^2 = AD^2 + DC^2$

$AD^2 = AC^2 - DC^2 = 6^2 - 3^2 = 36 - 9 = 27$

AD = $\sqrt{27}$

From here you can calculate the area of ∆ABC as $\dfrac{AD \times AC}{2}$ and then follow the same steps as in the first solution.

Now that you know DE and AD, you can calculate AE applying Pythagoras' theorem in ∆ADE

$AD^2 = AE^2 + DE^2$

$AE^2 = AD^2 - DE^2 = 27 - \dfrac{27}{4} = \dfrac{81}{4}$

$AE = \dfrac{9}{2}$

We can see that ∆s ABD and AEF are similar. The ratio AE:AB is therefore equal to the ratio EF:BD.

The ratio is $\left(\dfrac{9}{2}\right) : 6 \rightarrow EF = \dfrac{9}{4}$ which is less than $\dfrac{5}{2} \rightarrow$ the right column is greater than the left column, hence (B) is the correct answer.

65. **Sub topic: Circles/Triangles**

The correct answer is 0.4.

From the geometry, we can determine that $\sin(\theta) = \dfrac{1}{2}$, or $\theta = 30°$.

The area of the triangle = $\left(\sqrt{3}\right)(1) = \sqrt{3}$

Area of entire circle (with 360° angle about the center) = $\pi(2^2) = 4\pi$

Area of arc of circle (with 300° angle about the center) = $\dfrac{300°}{360°}(4\pi) = \dfrac{10}{3}$

Area of shaded portion of circle = (Area of entire circle) - (Area of arc, shaded grey) - (Area of triangle, shaded white)

$= 4\pi - \dfrac{10}{3}\pi - \sqrt{3} = 0.3623 \approx 0.4$ (with 1 decimal place accuracy)

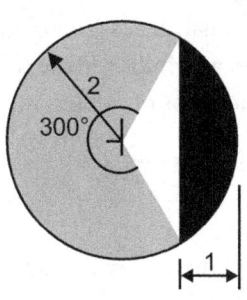
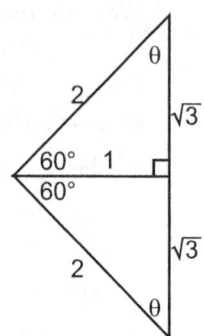

The correct answer is 0.4.

66. **Sub topic: Circles**

The correct answer is (E).

From the figure, we realize that CF is an arc from a circle whose diameter is AF and whose center is at E. The circumference of the circle E is four times the length of the arc CF according to the given fact. If we multiply the length of arc CF by 4, it gives us the circumference of the circle E.

Circumference of Circle E = 4[Length of arc (CF)]

$= 4(3\pi)$

$= 12\pi$

If we divide the circumference of the circle E by π, the result is the diameter of the circle.

Diameter of Circle E = $\dfrac{12\pi}{\pi}$

$= 12$

Now, we have a diameter of the circle E, then we can calculate the length of the semicircle ALF.

Length of Semicircle ALF = $\dfrac{\text{Circumference of Circle E}}{2}$

$= \dfrac{\pi(12)}{2}$

$= 6\pi$

The radius of the circle F is equal to the diameter of the circle E. Thus,

Radius of Circle F = AF

Doubling AF gives a diameter of the circle F.

Diameter of Circle F = 2(AF)

= 2(12)

= 24

Having a diameter of the circle F, calculate its circumference.

Circumference of Circle F = π(24)

= 24π

Length of the arc AGD is $\frac{3}{4}$ the circumference of the circle F.

Therefore, Length of arc AGD $= \frac{3}{4}(24\pi)$

= 18π

From the given figure,

Perimeter of the figure AGDFLA = Length of arc AGD + DF + Length of Semicircle ALF

Replace the measure of each arc in the equation above, knowing that DF is a radius of the circle F and is found to be 12.

Perimeter of the figure AGDFLA = 18π + 12 + 6π

= 24π + 12

67. **Sub topic: Three-Dimensional Figures**

The correct answer is (C).

Length of the arc of the sector = the circumference of the base of the cone

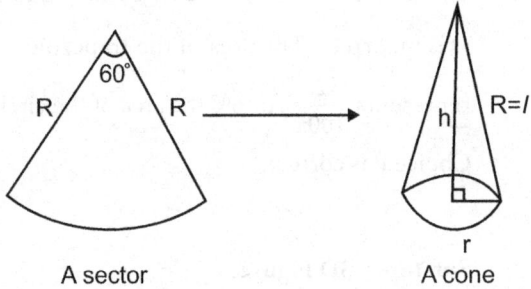

Taking R to be the radius of the circle where the sector is extracted and r to be the radius of the base of the cone, we have

Length of the arc of the sector = the circumference of the base of the cone

That is,

$\frac{60}{360} \times \pi \times 2R = \pi \times 2r$

Dividing both sides by 2π, we have

$r = \frac{60}{360} R = \frac{60}{360} \times 9 = \frac{3}{2}$ inches

The radius of the sector = the slant height of the cone

The perpendicular height h, slant height l, and the radius of the cone r forms a right-angle triangle where the slant height is the hypotenuse.

Using the Pythagorean Theorem, perpendicular height $= \sqrt{9^2 - 1.5^2} = \sqrt{78.75} = 8.874$

Volume $= \left(\frac{1}{3}\right) \times \pi \times \left(\frac{3}{2}\right)^2 \times 8.874 = 20.909 \approx 21$ cubic inches

68. **Sub topic: Triangles**

The correct answer is 37.5.

Assign *x*, *y*, and *z* variables for the indicated angles in the diagram. Use the triangle angle sum theorem, and the angle addition postulate to write equations for the variables. Use the given information that base angles of isosceles triangles are congruent, and solve for *x*. We obtain a solution of 30.

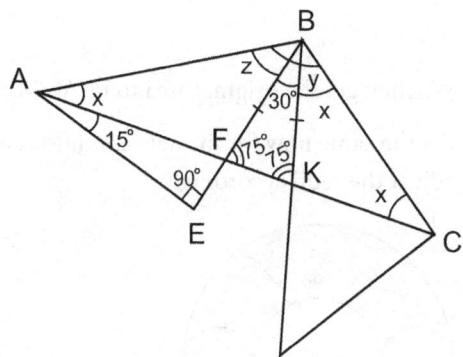

K = 105

z + 105 + x = 180

z = 75 - x

y = 30 + x + z

2z + y = 180

$2x + 30 + x + z = 180$

$3x + z = 150$

$3x + 75 - x = 150$

$2x = 75$

$x = 37.5$

$\angle BAF = 37.5$

69. **Sub topic: Circles**

    The correct answer is (C).

    To find the original shaded area, subtract the areas of Circles A, B, and C from the large circle's area, using x to represent the general relationship between the circles.

    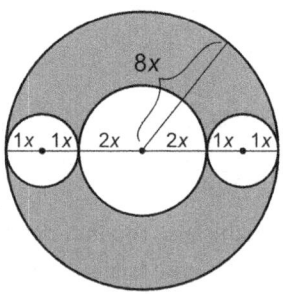

    Total A = $64x^2\pi$

    Circle A = $(2x)^2\pi = 4x^2\pi$

    Circle B/C = $x^2\pi = x^2\pi \cdot 2$

    $64x^2\pi - (6x^2\pi)$

    $= 58x^2\pi$

    We then get the original area to be $A=58x^2\pi$

    Do the same now for the new conditions and adjust the radii accordingly.

    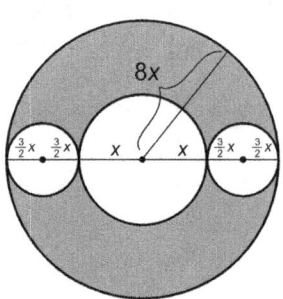

    A = $64x^2\pi$

    Circle A: $x^2\pi$

Circles B/C: $\left(\dfrac{3}{2}x\right)^2\pi = \dfrac{9}{4}x^2\pi \cdot 2 = \dfrac{9}{2}x^2\pi$

New area = $64x^2\pi - \left(x^2\pi + \dfrac{9}{2}x^2\pi\right)$

$= \dfrac{117}{2}x^2\pi$

The new shaded area is therefore $A = \dfrac{117}{2}x^2\pi$.

Therefore, $\dfrac{new\ area}{old\ area} = \dfrac{\dfrac{117}{2}x^2\pi}{58x^2\pi} = \dfrac{117}{116}$. The answer is Choice C.

70. **Sub topic: Quadrilaterals + Circles**

    The correct answers are (A), (D) and (E).

    The area of the circle is found by using the formula $A = \pi r^2$, where r=10cm.

    Therefore, the area of the circle is $A = \pi 10^2 = 100\pi$ cm². Therefore, Choice C is not correct. The area of the trapezoid is found using the formula $A = \dfrac{b_1 + b_2}{2} \times h$, where b_1 and b_2 are the bases and h is the height. Plugging in the given values, $A = \dfrac{7+5}{2} \times 2\pi = 12\pi$ cm². This means that answer Choice A is correct. The yellow area is the area of the circle subtracted by the area of the trapezoid. This is therefore $100\pi - 12\pi = 88$ cm². Choice D is incorrect. The area of the trapezoid represents $\dfrac{12\pi}{100\pi}$, or 6% the area of the circle. Choice E is correct.

71. **Sub topic: 3D Figures**

    The correct answer is 9.521.

    If the initial measure of each side of the cube is x, then the new length will be $(x + 8)$, the new width will be $(x + 6)$ and the new depth will be $(0.5x)$. Create an equation that compares the volumes, where the old volume is x^3, and the new volume is $(x + 8)(x + 6)(0.5x)$. Because the new volume is 50% larger than the old volume, the relationship between the new and old volume is as follows: $(x + 8)(x + 6)(0.5x)=1.5x^3$. FOIL out the left side to obtain $0.5x^3 + 7x^2 + 24x = 1.5x^3$. Move all terms over to the right side to get $0 = 1x^3 - 7x^2 - 24x$. Factor out x to get $0 = x(x^2 - 7x - 24)$. The factored-out x is not a solution, since it would be $x = 0$ and that would not create a 3D cube. Use the quadratic formula to solve for x for the trinomial inside the parentheses. You then get $x = \dfrac{7 \pm \sqrt{145}}{2}$. Use the positive solution to obtain $x = \dfrac{7 + \sqrt{145}}{2}$, which written as a decimal to the nearest thousandths is 9.521.

72. **Sub topic: Lines and Angles**

The correct answer is (A).

If lines a and b are parallel, then the corresponding angle to $4z$ on line b will also be $4z$. The linear pair to this (inside the triangle) will then be $180 - 4z$. The vertical angle to 50 will also be 50. We can then create a triangle and solve for the missing variable z. We therefore get $10 + I+ (180 - 4z) + 50 = 180$. Therefore, $z = 20$ and the answer is A.

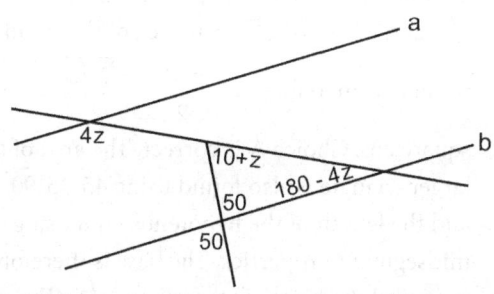

73. **Sub topic: Circles and Polygons**

The correct answer is (C).

If you have a regular polygon with exterior angles measuring 60 degrees, this means you have 6 angles and therefore 6 sides, making it a hexagon. This is because every polygon's exterior angles add up to 360, so if each exterior angle is 60, then 360/60=6 and there are 6 angles. Therefore, a hexagon is inscribed in the circle. The diagram will then look as follows:

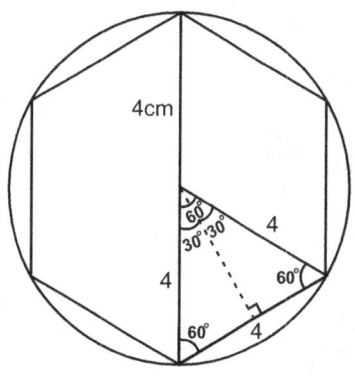

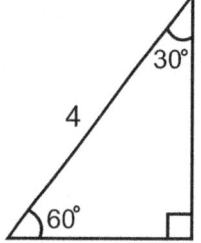

$4 = 2x \leftarrow 90°$
$2 = x \leftarrow 30°$
$2\sqrt{3} = x\sqrt{3} \leftarrow 60°$

By using the triangles formed inside the hexagon, and the 30-60-90 relationship, we find the height of one of the triangles to be $2\sqrt{3}$, and the base to be 2. The area of just one of the triangles is then $A = \dfrac{2\sqrt{3} * 2}{2} = 2\sqrt{3}$. Multiply this by 6 to form the entire hexagon to them obtain $12\sqrt{3}$. The area of the circle is $A=\pi r^2$, where r is 4. This becomes 16π. We then subtract the area of the hexagon from the area of the circle to get $16\pi - 12\sqrt{3}$, which is Answer Choice C.

74. **Sub topic: Circles and Polygons**

The correct answer is (C).

First, find the radius of the circle by finding the area of the hexagon, dividing it by 2, and then using the area formula of a circle to find the radius of each circle, as shown in the diagram below.

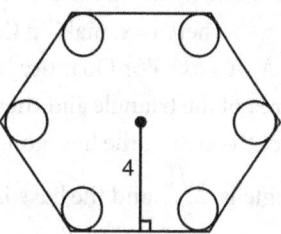

Area of circles: $\dfrac{96\sqrt{3}}{3} \div 2$

Area of circles: $\dfrac{48\sqrt{3}}{3} \div 6$

Area of circles: $\dfrac{8\sqrt{3}}{3}$

$A = \pi r^2 = \dfrac{8\sqrt{3}}{3} \qquad r = \sqrt{\dfrac{8\sqrt{3}}{3}}$

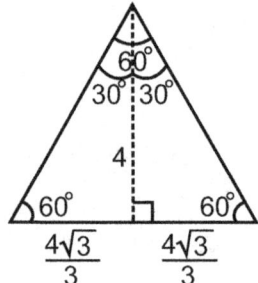

$x\sqrt{3} = 4 \rightarrow 60°$

$x = \dfrac{4\sqrt{3}}{3} \rightarrow 30°$

$A = \dfrac{1}{2} bh$

$A = \dfrac{1}{2}\left(\dfrac{8\sqrt{3}}{3}\right)(4)$

$A = \dfrac{16\sqrt{3}}{3} \cdot 6$

$6\triangle s$

$A = \dfrac{96\sqrt{3}}{3}$

The radius is then $\sqrt{\dfrac{8\sqrt{3}}{3}} = \sqrt{\dfrac{8}{\sqrt{3}}} = \dfrac{\sqrt{8}}{\sqrt[4]{3}} = \dfrac{2\sqrt{2}}{\sqrt[4]{3}}$, which is Answer Choice C.

75. **Sub topic: Circles and Triangles**

The correct answer is (A).

Quantity A can be found by using the area of a circle formula $A = \pi r^2$, where $r=x$, making the value of Quantity A, $A = \pi x^2$. For Quantity B, you need to find the area of the triangle and then multiply by 6 to get the area of the hexagon. The height of the triangle is $\dfrac{x\sqrt{3}}{2}$ and the base is x as

proven in the diagram. The area of the hexagon is therefore $A = 6 \times \dfrac{\dfrac{x\sqrt{3}}{2} \times x}{2} = \dfrac{3\sqrt{3}x^2}{2}$. Because $\dfrac{3\sqrt{3}}{2}$ Quantity A is larger. The answer is Choice A.

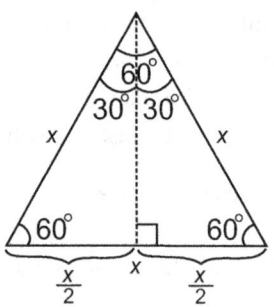

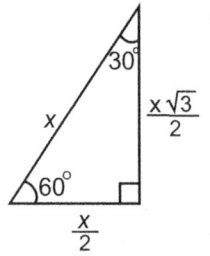

76. **Sub topic: Triangles and Polygons**

The correct answers are (A), (C) and (E).

The area of the small triangle is found by using 45-45-90 side relationships to get a height of $\sqrt{2}$ and a base of $\sqrt{2}$. The area of the small triangle is therefore $A = \dfrac{b \times h}{2} = \dfrac{\sqrt{2}\sqrt{2}}{2} = 1$ square cm. Choice A is correct. The area of the larger triangle is also found using 45-45-90, and the length of the hypotenuse is 8 using the midsegment properties. The base is therefore $4\sqrt{2}$ and the height is therefore $4\sqrt{2}$. The area is therefore $A = \dfrac{b \times h}{2} = \dfrac{4\sqrt{2} \times 4\sqrt{2}}{2} = 16$ square cm, not 4 square cm. B is incorrect. The area of the hexagon is found by creating 6 equilateral triangles, and using 30-60-90 relationships, you can find the heigh to be $2\sqrt{3}$ and the base is the length of the side of the hexagon, 4cm. The area of the triangle is then $A = \dfrac{b \times h}{2} = \dfrac{4 \times 2\sqrt{3}}{2} = 4\sqrt{3}$ Multiply this by 6 to get the total area of the hexagon, which is $24\sqrt{3}$ square cm. Choice

Geometry Practice Questions

C is therefore correct. Because the hexagon is regular, the value of each angle is Angle= $\frac{180\times(n-2)}{n}=\frac{180\times(6-2)}{6}$. The total angle is 120, made up of x and 45. Therefore, $x = 75$ and E is correct.

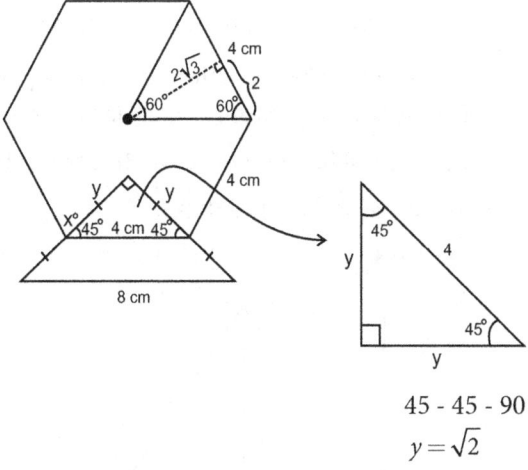

77. **Sub topic: Quadrilaterals (Trapezoids)**

The correct answer is (C).

Assign x to be the distance between $2b$ and the y value of A, and $2b$ and the x value of B. We know these are both x because this is an isosceles trapezoid with legs congruent. Using Pythagorean Theorem, you can find x to be b. This shows that the larger triangle is also isosceles, and that A is 45 degrees. Using 45-45-90 relationship, we can find the height of the trapezoid to be $\frac{b\sqrt{2}}{2}$, which would make Quantity A and B equal. Therefore, the answer is C.

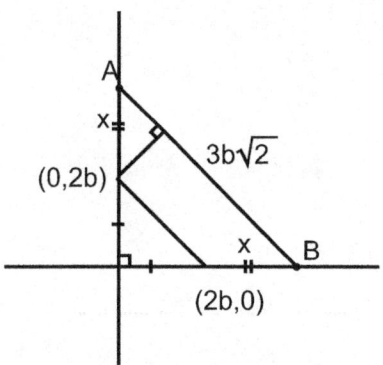

$a^2 + b^2 = c^2$
$(2b+x)^2 + (2b+x)^2 = (3b\sqrt{2})^2$
$\frac{2(2b+x)^2}{2} = \frac{9b^2 \cdot 2}{2}$
$\sqrt{(2b+x)^2} = \sqrt{9b^2}$
$2b + x = 3b$
$x = b$

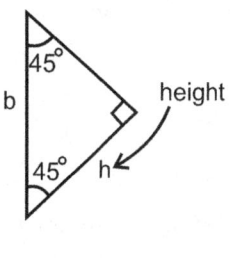

$\frac{b}{\sqrt{2}} = \frac{h\sqrt{2}}{\sqrt{2}}$

$\frac{b\sqrt{2}}{2} = h$

78. **Sub topic: Circles (Tangents)**

The correct answers are (B), (C) and (D).

For a solution to work, it must have a numerator that works for y in the Pythagorean theorem shown above, and a denominator that works for x in the equation.

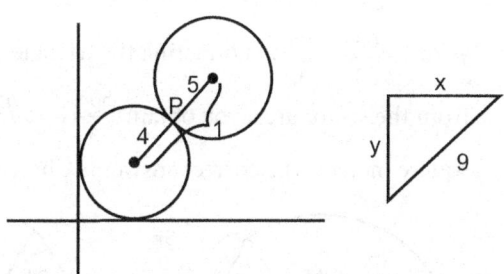

Choice A: $\sqrt{2}^2 = +7^2 = 9^2$ so for this to work, 51=81, which is not true so Choice A is incorrect.

Choice B. $(4\sqrt{2})^2 + 7^2 = 32 + 49 = 9^2 = 81$. This works because the x and y values given complete the Pythagorean theorem for a hypotenuse of 9. Choice B is correct.

Choice C. $(\sqrt{65})^2 + 4^2 = 65 + 16 = 9^2 = 81$. This

works because the *x* and *y* values given complete the Pythagorean theorem for a hypotenuse of 9. Choice C is correct.

Choice D. $\left(5\sqrt{2}\right)^2 + \sqrt{31}^2 = 50 + 31 = 9^2 = 81$. This works because the *x* and *y* values given complete the Pythagorean theorem for a hypotenuse of 9. Choice D is correct.

Choice E: $4^2 + 7^2 = 9^2$ so for this to work, 65=81, which is not true so Choice E is incorrect.

79. **Sub topic: Circles (Sector)**

The correct answer is (A).

To find the purple shaded region, subtract the area of the triangle from the area of the sector. If the arc length is is $\frac{10\pi}{3}$, you can solve for the central angle by using the equation $\frac{Angle}{360} \times 2\pi$ = *Arc length*. You will find that arc length is 60°.

Then create a 30, 60, 90 triangle by splitting the central angle in half. Using the 30,60,90 relationship, you get the height of the triangle is $5\sqrt{3}$, and the base is 10. The area of the triangle is therefore $A = \frac{5\sqrt{3} \times 10}{2} = 25\sqrt{3}$, To find the total sector area, using the formula Sector Area= $\pi r^2 \times \frac{Angle}{360}$. Plugging in, you get Sector Area= $\pi(10)^2 \times \frac{60}{60} = \frac{50\pi}{3}$. Subtracting the triangle area from the sector area, you obtain $\frac{50\pi}{3} - 25\sqrt{3}$ square meters. The correct answer is Choice A.

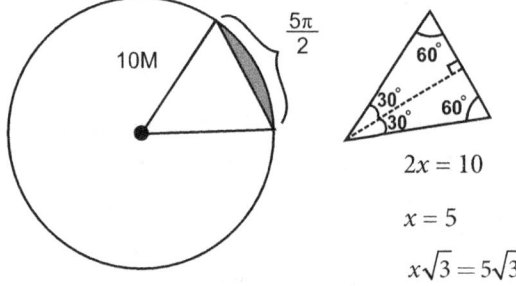

80. **Sub topic: Triangles in Coordinate Systems**

The correct answer is $\frac{8}{3}$.

Draw the height through the triangle perpendicular to the base. Use the area equation to write an expression for the height in terms of 8. $A = \frac{b \times h}{2}$ becomes $12 = \frac{3b \times h}{2}$. So, $h = \frac{8}{a}$

Use the slope of the line and the length of the leg to find the vertex at the top of the height. Because the slope is 3/4 and the length is 5, the height must be 3 and the base (3*a*/2) must be 4. Therefore, if $\frac{3a}{2} = 4$, *a*=8/3.

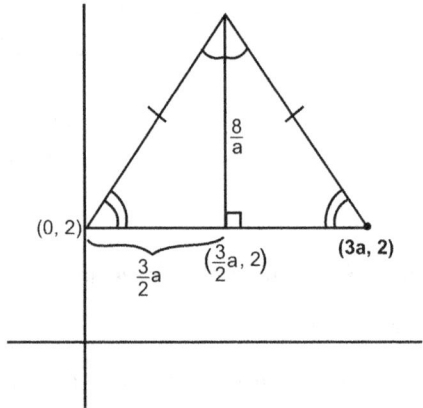

Chapter 6

Data Analysis Practice Questions

This chapter consists of *80 Data Analysis* practice questions. The questions cover all the question types as explained in Chapter 2 and are segregated into 3 levels of difficulty - Easy, Medium and Difficult. You may choose to start solving the Easy questions first and then move on to higher levels of difficulty or solve the questions in any random order. You will find answers and detailed explanations towards the end of this chapter.

Level: Easy

For Questions 1 to 3, refer to the bar graph below.

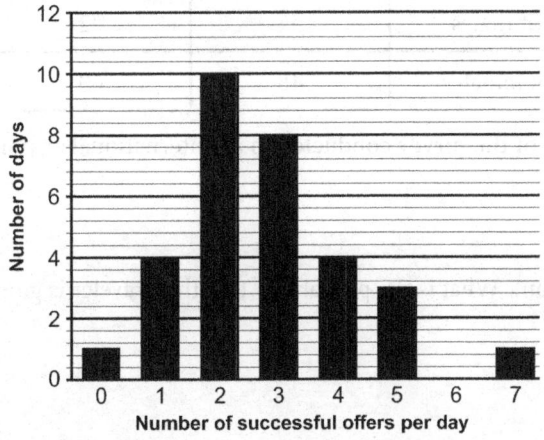

Michael keeps track of the number of successful product offers he makes per day. The graph above represents Michael's data for the past month.

1. What is the probability that Michael will make 7 successful offers in any given day? (Round off to 3 decimal places)

    - (A) 0.143
    - (B) 0.125
    - (C) 0.100
    - (D) 0.032
    - (E) 0.169

2. What is the probability that Michael will make 2 or 3 successful offers on a given day? (Round off to 3 decimal places)

   (A) 0.083

   (B) 0.323

   (C) 0.581

   (D) 0.600

   (E) 0.815

3. Find the probability that Michael makes at least 1 successful offer on a given day. (Round off to 3 decimal places)

   (A) 0.968

   (B) 0.677

   (C) 0.419

   (D) 0.032

   (E) 0.017

Questions 4 to 6 are based on the following table.

Destination	North America	Europe	Asia
Number of males	55	72	23
Number of females	48	60	17

The table above shows the results of the survey conducted in an international airport where travelers were asked of their flight destinations.

4. A traveler is chosen at random. What is the probability that this traveler is going to Asia? (Answer in fraction)

   ▭/▭

5. A traveler is selected at random. Find the probability that the traveler is a female going to Europe. (Answer in fraction)

   ▭/▭

Data Analysis Practice Questions

6. A traveler is selected at random. What is the probability that this traveler is a male, given that he is going to North America? (Answer in fraction)

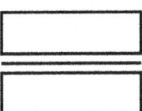

For Questions 7 and 8, refer to the following Venn diagram.

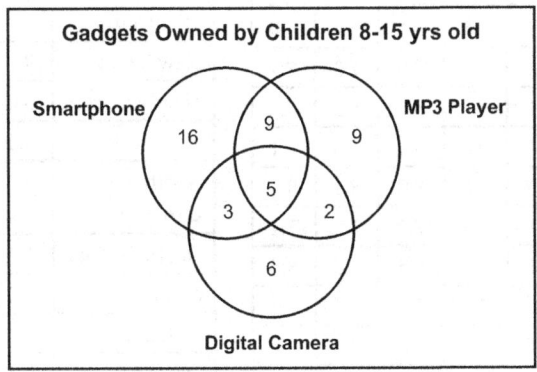

A group of 50 children aged 8 to 15 years old were interviewed and asked whether they own any smart phone, MP3 player or digital camera. The results of the survey were presented in a Venn Diagram as shown above.

7. If a child owns a smart phone, what is the probability that he also owns an MP3 player?

   (A) $\dfrac{9}{16}$

   (B) $\dfrac{7}{8}$

   (C) $\dfrac{14}{33}$

   (D) $\dfrac{9}{33}$

   (E) $\dfrac{1}{8}$

8. Two children are chosen at random. Find the probability that both of them own only a digital camera.

   (A) 0.012

   (B) 0.014

   (C) 0.098

   (D) 0.125

   (E) 0.001

Questions 9 and 10 are based on the following table.

The following table lists the unemployment rates for all states of the United States based on data from the Bureau of Labor Statistics. Answer the following questions regarding the table:

2013 State Unemployment Rates *

State	Jan	Feb	Mar	Apr	May	Jun	Jul
Alabama	6.9	7.2	7.2	6.9	6.8	6.5	6.3
Alaska	6.7	6.5	6.2	6.0	5.9	6.1	6.3
Arizona	8.0	7.9	7.9	7.9	7.8	8.0	8.0
Arkansas	7.2	7.2	7.2	7.1	7.3	7.3	7.4
California	9.8	9.6	9.4	9.0	8.6	8.5	8.7
Colorado	7.3	7.2	7.1	6.9	6.9	7.0	7.1
Connecticut	8.1	8.0	8.0	8.0	8.0	8.1	8.1
Delaware	7.2	7.2	7.3	7.2	7.2	7.3	7.4
D.C.	8.6	8.6	8.5	8.5	8.5	8.5	8.6
Florida	7.8	7.7	7.5	7.2	7.1	7.1	7.1
Georgia	8.7	8.6	8.4	8.2	8.3	8.6	8.8
Hawaii	5.2	5.2	5.1	4.9	4.7	4.6	4.5
Idaho	6.3	6.2	6.2	6.1	6.2	6.4	6.6
Illinois	9.0	9.5	9.5	9.3	9.1	9.2	9.2
Indiana	8.6	8.7	8.7	8.5	8.3	8.4	8.4
Iowa	5.0	5.0	4.9	4.7	4.6	4.6	4.8
Kansas	5.5	5.5	5.6	5.5	5.7	5.8	5.9
Kentucky	7.9	7.9	8.0	7.9	8.1	8.4	8.5
Louisiana	5.9	6.0	6.2	6.5	6.8	7.0	7.0
Maine	7.3	7.3	7.1	6.9	6.8	6.8	6.9
Maryland	6.7	6.6	6.6	6.5	6.7	7.0	7.1
Massachu-setts	6.7	6.5	6.4	6.4	6.6	7.0	7.2
Michigan	8.9	8.8	8.5	8.4	8.4	8.7	8.8
Minnesota	5.6	5.5	5.4	5.3	5.3	5.2	5.2
Mississippi	9.3	9.6	9.4	9.1	9.1	9.0	8.5
Missouri	6.5	6.7	6.7	6.6	6.8	6.9	7.1
Montana	5.7	5.6	5.6	5.5	5.4	5.4	5.3

State	Jan	Feb	Mar	Apr	May	Jun	Jul
Nevada	9.7	9.6	9.7	9.6	9.5	9.6	9.5
New Hampshire	5.8	5.8	5.7	5.5	5.3	5.2	5.1
New Jersey	9.5	9.3	9.0	8.7	8.6	8.7	8.6
New Mexico	6.6	6.8	6.9	6.7	6.7	6.8	6.9
New York	8.4	8.4	8.2	7.8	7.6	7.5	7.5
North Carolina	9.5	9.4	9.2	8.9	8.8	8.8	8.9
North Dakota	3.3	3.3	3.3	3.3	3.2	3.1	3.0
Ohio	7.0	7.0	7.1	7.0	7.0	7.2	7.2
Oklahoma	5.1	5.0	5.0	4.9	5.0	5.2	5.3
Oregon	8.4	8.4	8.2	8.0	7.8	7.9	8.0
Pennsyl-vania	8.2	8.1	7.9	7.6	7.5	7.5	7.5
Puerto Rico	14.6	14.5	14.2	13.7	13.4	13.2	13.5
Rhode Island	9.8	9.4	9.1	8.8	8.9	8.9	8.9
South Carolina	8.7	8.6	8.4	8.0	8.0	8.1	8.1
South Dakota	4.4	4.4	4.3	4.1	4.0	3.9	3.9
Tennessee	7.7	7.8	7.9	8.0	8.3	8.5	8.5
Texas	6.3	6.4	6.4	6.4	6.5	6.5	6.5
Utah	5.4	5.2	4.9	4.7	4.6	4.7	4.6
Vermont	4.7	4.4	4.1	4.0	4.1	4.4	4.6
Virginia	5.6	5.6	5.3	5.2	5.3	5.5	5.7
Washington	7.5	7.5	7.3	7.0	6.8	6.8	6.9
West Virginia	7.4	7.3	7.0	6.6	6.2	6.1	6.2
Wisconsin	7.0	7.2	7.1	7.1	7.0	6.8	6.8
Wyoming	4.9	4.9	4.9	4.8	4.6	4.6	4.6

Source: Bureau of Labor Statistics

* Preliminary figures provided by BLS in its monthly updates

9. Based on the data presented in the table, what percentage of the states and other locations saw a decline of 0.8% or greater (in percentage points) between January 2013 to July 2013?

- Ⓐ 3%
- Ⓑ 6%
- Ⓒ 9%
- Ⓓ 12%
- Ⓔ 15%

10. Florida has a population of 19.32 million. How many people are unemployed in May 2013 assuming only 65% of the population can legally work?

    (A) 0.89 million people

    (B) 1.32 million people

    (C) 3.56 million people

    (D) 8.91 million people

    (E) 12.5 million people

Questions 11 and 12 are based on the following chart.

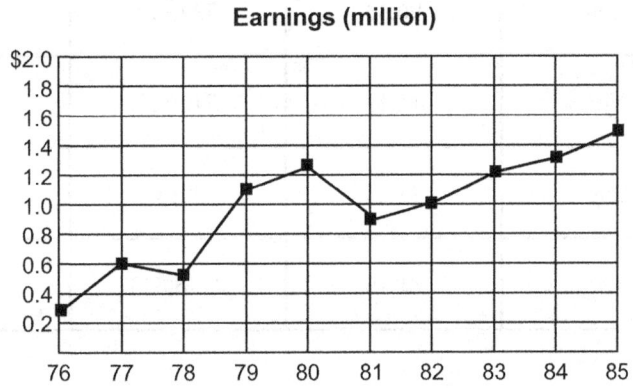

11. From 1977 to 1983, inclusive, what was the amount of the greatest increase in earnings from one year to the next?

    (A) $1,000,000

    (B) $1,200,000

    (C) $300,000

    (D) $600,000

    (E) $750,000

12. For years 1981 to 1985, inclusive, average earnings of Company K were approximately

    (A) $1,180,000

    (B) $720,000

    (C) $880,000

    (D) $920,000

    (E) $998,000

Questions 13 and 14 are based on the following data.

One Day Summary of Activity			
Stock symbol	Closing Price($)	Volume (1,000's)	Change in Price
Arx	53.25	869.45	$2\frac{3}{4}$
Bim	41.4	4110.392	$2\frac{11}{16}$
Csf	27.84	36.411	$-1\frac{1}{8}$
Mbd	96.33	599.994	$-3\frac{1}{2}$
Nys	11.11	546.362	$\frac{1}{4}$
Qug	22.28	8.13	$1\frac{7}{16}$
Tvk	81.15	3146.633	$\frac{3}{8}$

13. What was the opening price for *Mbd*?

    (A) $27.52
    (B) $92.83
    (C) $96.33
    (D) $99.70
    (E) $99.83

14. How many stocks closed at a higher price than the stock with the greatest amount of activity for the day?

    (A) 1
    (B) 2
    (C) 3
    (D) 4
    (E) 5

Questions 15 and 16 are based on the following diagram.

BUDGET INFORMATION FOR COLLEGE M IN A YEAR

OUTLAYS*

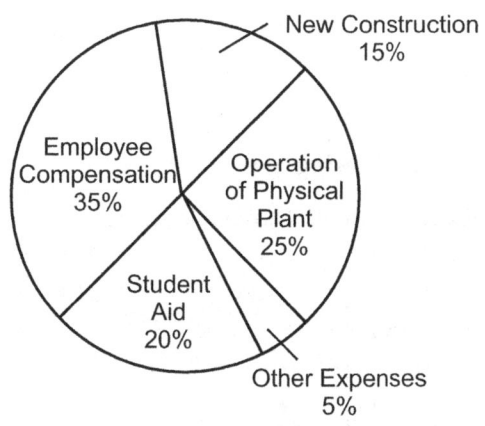

INCOME*
(Millions of Dollars)

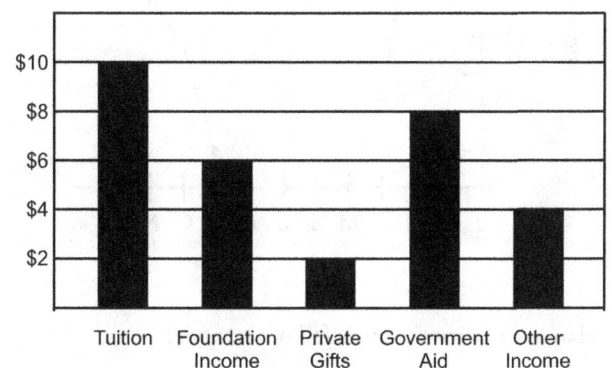

*Includes all expenditure
**Includes all Source of Income
NOTE: Outlays (Expenditures) must equal Income

15. For the year shown, College M spent how much money on the operation of its physical plant?

- (A) $2,500,000
- (B) $4,000,000
- (C) $7,500,000
- (D) $8,000,000
- (E) $9,500,000

16. For the year shown, what percentage of College M's income came from foundation income?

    A) 6%
    B) 20%
    C) 25%
    D) 33%
    E) 60%

Questions 17 to 20 are based on the following chart.

Average snowfall during previous year at South Haven's ski resort

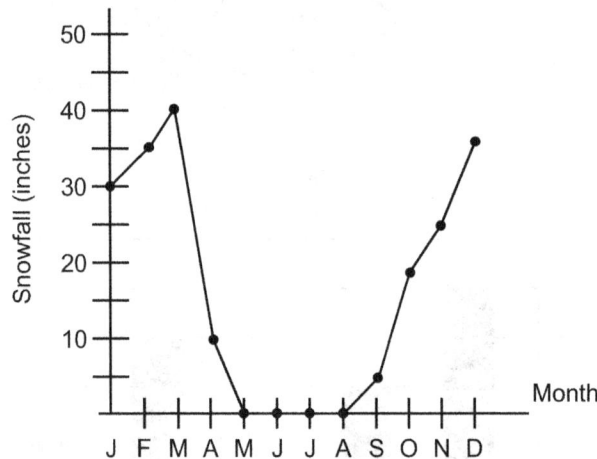

17. How many months averaged at least twice the snowfall of October?

    A) 1
    B) 2
    C) 3
    D) 4
    E) 5

18. Which month had $\frac{2}{3}$ less snowfall than December?

    A) March
    B) April
    C) September
    D) October
    E) November

19. What percentage drop in snowfall occurred between March and April?

    (A) 300%

    (B) 30%

    (C) 400%

    (D) 25%

    (E) 75%

20. What was the average amount of snowfall from January through May?

    (A) 24 inches

    (B) 30 inches

    (C) 23 inches

    (D) 28 inches

    (E) 15 inches

Questions 21 to 24 are based on the following diagram.

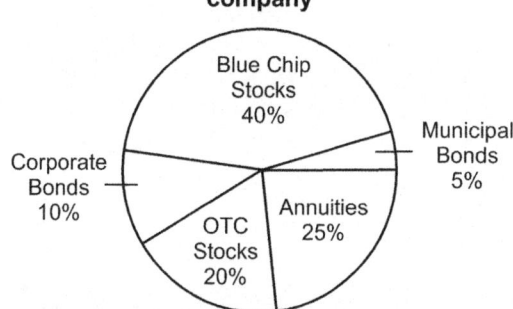

21. What percentage of earning is not invested in stocks?

    (A) 20%

    (B) 40%

    (C) 60%

    (D) 80%

    (E) 85%

22. If $3,000 was invested last month, what amount went into annuities?

    (A) $2,250
    (B) $1,500
    (C) $1,200
    (D) $750
    (E) $600

23. How much more money was invested in annuities than in corporate bonds if a total of $10,000 was invested?

    (A) $1,500
    (B) $2,500
    (C) $1,000
    (D) $8,500
    (E) $3,500

24. Which sector had $800 invested in it from $4,000 earnings?

    (A) OTC Stocks
    (B) Corporate Bonds
    (C) Blue Chip Stocks
    (D) Municipal Bonds
    (E) Annuities

Data Analysis Practice Questions 179

Questions 25 to 26 are based on the following bar chart.

The bar graph below shows the gender wise percentage of population that is employed in five different countries.

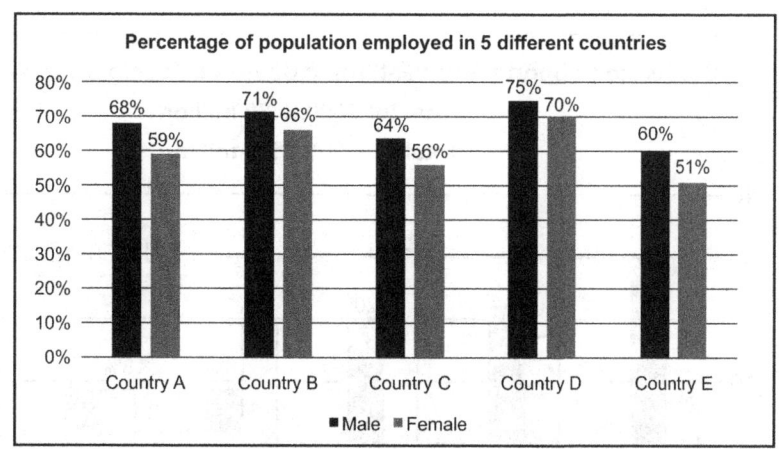

25. Which country has the smallest difference in the percentage of males and females employed?

    Ⓐ   Country A and E
    Ⓑ   Country B and D
    Ⓒ   Country C
    Ⓓ   Country A and D
    Ⓔ   Country B and E

26. If the female population of Country C is 1.5 million, how many females in Country C are unemployed?

    Ⓐ   0.25 million
    Ⓑ   0.39 million
    Ⓒ   0.66 million
    Ⓓ   0.85 million
    Ⓔ   0.91 million

Level: Medium

Questions 27 to 30 are based on the following graph.

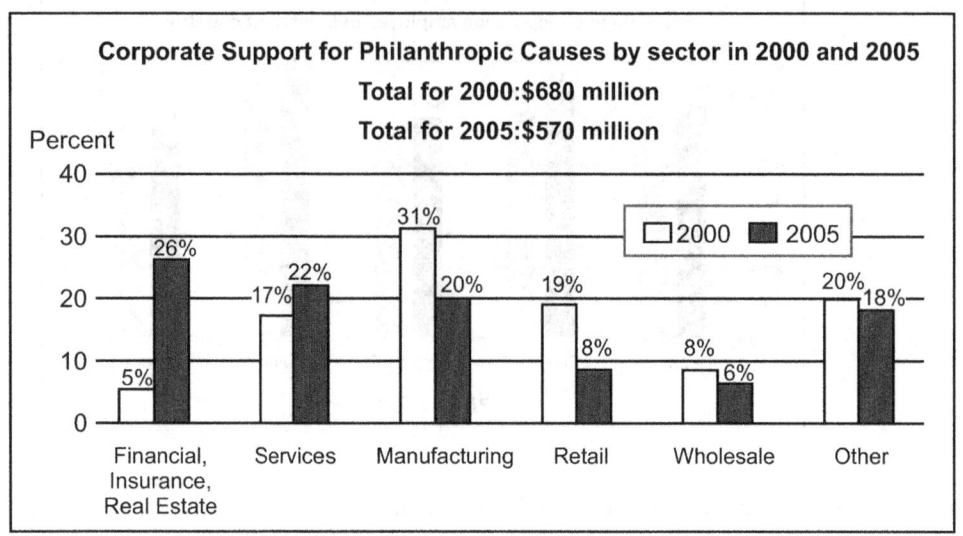

27. What was the total contribution in 2005 (approx. in million dollars) by the corporate sectors that decreased their support for Philanthropic causes from 2000 to 2005?

    (A) 150 million dollars
    (B) 200 million dollars
    (C) 250 million dollars
    (D) 300 million dollars
    (E) 350 million dollars

28. What is the average amount contributed by those sectors who contributed more than $100 million each to the Philanthropic Causes in both 2000 and 2005?

    (A) $114 million
    (B) $238.6 million
    (C) $263.13 million
    (D) $324.8 million
    (E) $342.6 million

Data Analysis Practice Questions   181

29. Of the Financial, Insurance and Real Estate Sector's 2005 contribution to Philanthropic Causes, one-third went for rebuilding homes lost due to Hurricane Katrina and one fourth of the remainder went to providing medical aid to the injured. Approximately how many million dollars more did the Financial, Insurance and Real Estate Sector contribute towards rebuilding homes that year than to providing medical aid?

    (A) $20 million
    (B) $25 million
    (C) $30 million
    (D) $35 million
    (E) $40 million

30. Financial, Insurance and Real Estate Sector showed a steep increase in contribution for philanthropic causes between 2000 and 2005. If the government excluded this industry and calculated, what would be the average change in contribution of all the other industries, calculated to the nearest integer?

    (A) −30%
    (B) −31%
    (C) −32%
    (D) −33%
    (E) −34%

Questions 31 and 32 are based on the following diagram.

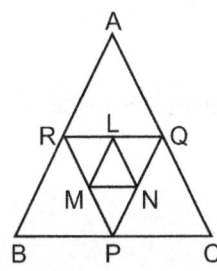

The midpoints of the sides of a △ABC are joined to form a new △PQR. The midpoints of the △PQR so formed are joined to form another △LMN.

31. Which of these is the ratio of the perimeter of △ABC to the perimeter of △LMN?

    (A) 1 : 3
    (B) 3 : 1
    (C) 1 : 4
    (D) 4 : 1
    (E) 1 : 16

32. If △ABC were a right-angled triangle right angled at B such that AB = x and BC = y, then which of these would have been the area of △LMN?

    Ⓐ $\frac{1}{2}xy$

    Ⓑ $\frac{1}{4}xy$

    Ⓒ $\frac{1}{8}xy$

    Ⓓ $\frac{1}{16}xy$

    Ⓔ $\frac{1}{32}xy$

For Questions 33 and 34, refer to the figure below.

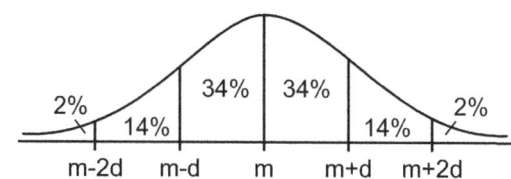

The figure above shows the bell curve or normal distribution curve with mean, m, and standard deviation, d. The percentages given refer to the approximate probability under the specified area. For example, the probability of an event occurring that is between the mean (m) and +1 standard deviation away from the mean ($m + d$) is 34%.

In a certain district, the heights of 1,000 high school students are normally distributed with a mean of 165 cm and standard deviation of 3 cm.

33. If a high school student is selected at random, what is, approximately, the probability that the student's height is less than 162 cm?

    Ⓐ 14%

    Ⓑ 16%

    Ⓒ 34%

    Ⓓ 56%

    Ⓔ 84%

34. A high school student selected at random will have any of the following heights:

   I.   Less than 159 cm
   II. Between 159 cm and 162 cm
   III. Between 162 cm and 165 cm
   IV   Between 165 cm and 168 cm
   V.   Between 168 cm and 171 cm
   VI. More than 171 cm

   Which of the following pairs have equal probabilities?

   Select *all* that apply.

   [A]   I and VI
   [B]   II and V
   [C]   III and IV
   [D]   II and IV

Questions 35 to 38 are based on the following chart.

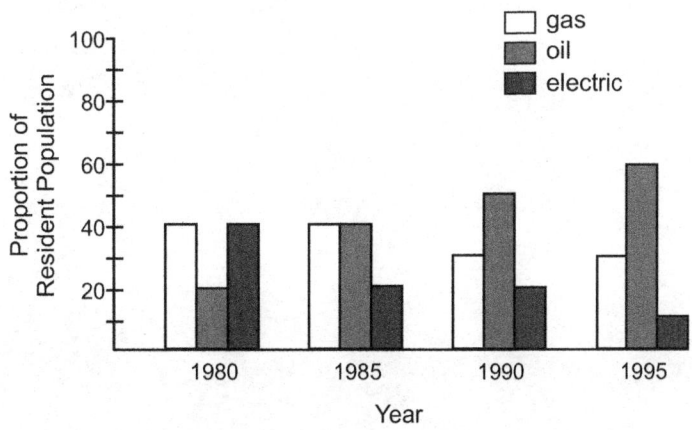

Heating Methods utilized by residents of Region X

35. What year or years had the greatest increase in oil usage by residents from one set of years to the next?

   (A) 1980
   (B) 1985
   (C) 1990
   (D) 1995
   (E) 1990 and 1995

36. What is the mean percent of residents who use oil as their main heating source?

    - Ⓐ 42.5%
    - Ⓑ 35%
    - Ⓒ 22.5%
    - Ⓓ 50%
    - Ⓔ 37.5%

37. If 50,000 residents make up Region X, how many more residents chose oil heat over electric heat in 1995?

    - Ⓐ 5,000
    - Ⓑ 15,000
    - Ⓒ 25,000
    - Ⓓ 30,000
    - Ⓔ 55,000

38. What percentage of gas consumers from 1985 switched to alternative heating method in 1990?

    - Ⓐ 10%
    - Ⓑ 25%
    - Ⓒ 50%
    - Ⓓ 75%
    - Ⓔ 100%

Data Analysis Practice Questions

Questions 39 to 42 are based on the following chart.

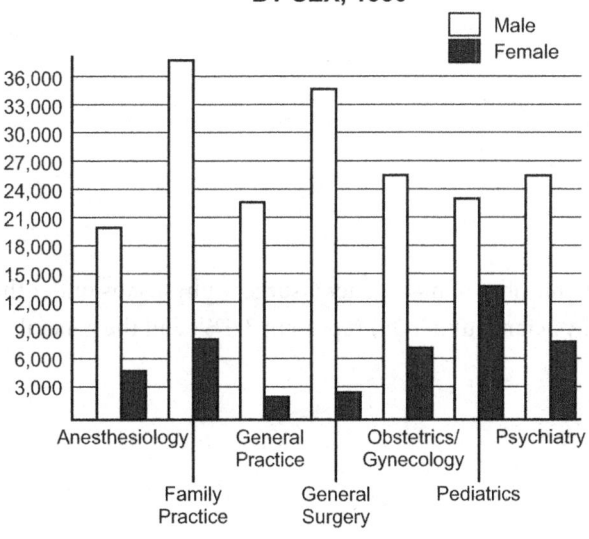

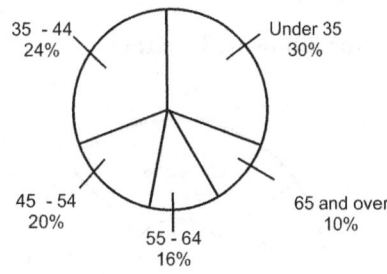

39. In 1986, the lowest ratio of males to females was observed in which speciality of physicians?

    (A) Family practice
    (B) General surgery
    (C) Obstetrics/gynecology
    (D) Pediatrics
    (E) Psychiatry

40. In 1986, approximately how many general surgery physicians were between the ages of 45 and 54, inclusive?

    (A) 5,440
    (B) 6,300
    (C) 7,350
    (D) 7,800
    (E) 8,900

41. If in 1986 all the family practice physicians represented 7.5 percent of all the physicians in the United States, approximately how many physicians were there total?

    (A) 300,000
    (B) 360,000
    (C) 430,000
    (D) 485,000
    (E) 570,000

42. Calculate the approximate number of male general surgery physicians under the age of 35, considering the female general surgery physicians (under 35) represent 3.5% of all the general surgery physicians.

    (A) 9,200
    (B) 9,800
    (C) 10,750
    (D) 11,260
    (E) 11,980

Questions 43 and 44 are based on the following Diagram.

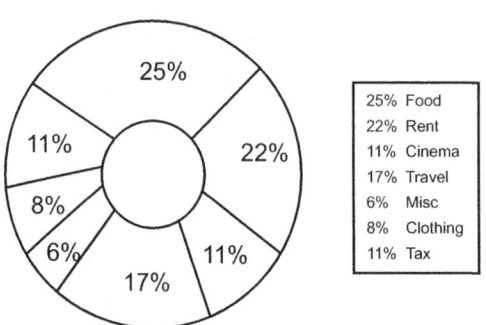

Distribution of expenses

43. Which of the following items amounts to the same expenditure as on food?

    (A) Tax, clothing and miscellaneous
    (B) Travel, cinema and miscellaneous
    (C) Cinema and travel
    (D) Rent and miscellaneous
    (E) Rent and cinema

44. A reduction of 2% in taxation enables him to increase his expenditure by one per cent on each of the items, cinema and travel. Then a ratio of 1:2:3 is maintained on the expenditures incurred on which of the following items.

   (A) Travel, miscellaneous and cinema
   (B) Miscellaneous, cinema and travel
   (C) Miscellaneous, tax and clothing
   (D) Miscellaneous, travel and cinema
   (E) None of the above

45. If there are 5.4 million males and 4.8 million females residing in Country E, which of the following is closest to the overall percentage of the population in Country E that is employed?

   (A) 52%
   (B) 54%
   (C) 55%
   (D) 56%
   (E) 59%

46. The ratio of male population in Country A to that in Country B is 6:5. What percent of the male population in Countries A and B (combined) are employed, rounded to the nearest tenth of a percent?

   (A) 68.5
   (B) 69.1
   (C) 69.4
   (D) 70.2
   (E) 70.9

47.

Advertising Budget for company D by Expenditure in 2020	
Expenditure	Percentage of Budget
Television	46%
Internet	25%
Print	8%
Other	21%
Total: $950,000	

Of the money Company D spent on print advertising in 2020, 2/5 was spent on newspapers and 3/5 of the remainder was spent on flyers. Approximately, how many more thousands of dollars was spent on newspaper advertisements than on flyers?

- Ⓐ 3.04
- Ⓑ 12.16
- Ⓒ 18.24
- Ⓓ 45.50
- Ⓔ 47.16

48. Sahana asked some people in her neighborhood how many times they visited the mall last month.

Trips to the mall last month	
Number of trips	Frequency
0	18
1	11
2	15
3	8
4	6

What was the median number of trips to the mall last month made by the people surveyed?

- Ⓐ 0.5
- Ⓑ 1.5
- Ⓒ 2
- Ⓓ 2.5
- Ⓔ 3

49. A computer store offers a discount of 10% on any item that costs above $50. The table below shows the items and their corresponding prices before discount that Lisa bought from the store.

Item	Price in dollars
LED Monitor	140
Keyboard	14
Digital Pen Tablet	42
External Hard Drive	58
Laptop Case	32

If a sales tax of 5.5% was applied on the amount after the discounts were applied, how much did Lisa pay overall?

- (A) $266.20
- (B) $271.56
- (C) $280.84
- (D) $295.45
- (E) $300.33

50. A group of scientists were studying some common metals. The following table shows the metals they studied, their densities and the mass of each sample of metal studied. If density = mass divided by volume, what is the total volume of all the samples studied?

Metal	Density (grams per cubic cm)	Mass of sample studied (grams)
Silver	10.5	4.0
Copper	9.0	6.2
Aluminum	1.7	9.5
Lead	11.4	5.5
Iron	7.9	8.2

- (A) 8.18 cubic cm
- (B) 9.32 cubic cm
- (C) 10.56 cubic cm
- (D) 12.48 cubic cm
- (E) 15.75 cubic cm

51. The table below shows the revenue generated and the number of customers in three different store locations of a certain business over the last week.

Store Location	Revenue ($)	Number of customers
Princeton Street	31,144	458
St Agnes Road	58,320	720
Hayat Street	34,336	592

    What is the average of the revenues generated per customer at the three locations?

    - (A) 55
    - (B) 58
    - (C) 68
    - (D) 69
    - (E) 81

52. Kabir is hosting a contest attended by 200 people, 80 of whom are males and the rest females. At the end of the contest, one of the contestants will be chosen at random to win a prize. If 1/5 of male contestants and 1/6 of female contestants arrived late, what is the probability that the prize will be won by a contestant who arrived late?

    - (A) 4/25
    - (B) 6/35
    - (C) 9/50
    - (D) 9/80
    - (E) 1/9

53. Adam's grandmother wants to display photos of her grandchildren on her mantel. She has one photo of each of her 12 grandchildren, but she can fit only five photos on the mantel. Adam requests her to keep his photo center. How many different arrangements of photos are possible?

    - (A) 330
    - (B) 495
    - (C) 7,920
    - (D) 11,880
    - (E) 95,040

Level: Difficult

Questions 54 to 58 are based on the following data.

Average Undergraduate Budgets, 1998-99						
Sector	Tuition & Fees	Books & Supplies	Room & Board	Transport-ation	Other Expenses	Total Expenses
2-year Public Resident	1600	620	*	*	*	N/A
Commuter	1,600	620	2,000	1,000	1,200	6,420
2-year Private Resident	7,300	660	4,600	550	1,000	14,110
Commuter	7,300	660	2,200	880	1,200	12,240
4-year Public Resident	3,250	660	4,500	600	1,400	10,140
Commuter	3,250	660	2,100	1,000	1,500	8,510
Out-of-State	8,400	6600	4,500	600	1,400	15,560
4-year Private Resident	14,500	670	5,800	550	1,000	22,520
Commuter	14,500	670	2,100	860	1,200	19,330

54. If a commuter decides to attend a two-year private college instead of a two-year public college, she can expect her total expenses to be

- (A) Approximately the same
- (B) Almost twice as much
- (C) Almost thrice as much
- (D) Slightly less
- (E) There is not enough information to determine the amount

55. How much more does a resident attending a two-year private college pay for room and board than a commuter does?

- (A) $330
- (B) $2,200
- (C) $2,400
- (D) $3,700
- (E) $6,800

56. Approximately what percent of a four-year public college commuter's total expenses are for transportation?

    Ⓐ 4%
    Ⓑ 6%
    Ⓒ 8%
    Ⓓ 12%
    Ⓔ 15%

57. Approximately what percent of a four-year private resident's college budget is used to pay non-tuition and fee expenses?

    Ⓐ 16%
    Ⓑ 20%
    Ⓒ 24%
    Ⓓ 28%
    Ⓔ 36%

58. Tuition and fees and room and board account for approximately what percent of two-year public college commuters' expenses?

    Ⓐ 44%
    Ⓑ 52%
    Ⓒ 56%
    Ⓓ 62%
    Ⓔ 68%

Question 59 is based on the following table.

Diameter of heart (in mm)	120	121	122	123	124	125
Number of persons	5	9	14	8	5	9

59. The median of the given frequency distribution is:

    Ⓐ 122 mm
    Ⓑ 122.25 mm
    Ⓒ 123 mm
    Ⓓ 122.5 mm
    Ⓔ 122.75 mm

Data Analysis Practice Questions

60. In a certain museum exhibit, 2/5 of the artifacts are Palaeolithic, and the remaining 45 are Neolithic. Of the Palaeolithic artifacts, 2/3 are Mediterranean. If 40 the artifacts are Mediterranean, how many Neolithic artifacts are not Mediterranean?

    ☐

61. Set A comprises all 3-digit numbers that are multiples of 9. Set B comprises all 3-digit numbers that are multiples of 3 but are not multiples of 6. How many elements does (A∪B) have?

    ☐

62. Set P consists of positive distinct integers $[a, b, c, d, e, f, g]$, such that $a < b < c < d < e < f < g$. The median of set P is 8. The minimum possible value of $a + b + c + d + e + f + g$ is P. Set Q consists of positive integers $[m, n, o, p, q, r, s]$, such that $m < n < o < p < q < r < s$. The median of set Q is also 8. If the minimum possible value of $m + n + o + p + q + r + s$ is Q, what is the sum of P and Q?

    ☐

63. There are 24 members in a music club, who play any one or more of the instruments piano, violin and trumpet. 15 members play the piano, 11 play the violin and 7 play the trumpet. If it is known that 6 of the members who play the piano also play the violin, how many of the trumpet players play another instrument?

    ☐

64. Of the 200 employees at PPP Appliances, one half works in both the Marketing and the Sales department. If 160 employees work in the Marketing department, and the number of employees in Sales department is 3 times the number of employees that are neither in Marketing nor in Sales, how many of the employees work in the Sales department?

    Ⓐ 35
    Ⓑ 105
    Ⓒ 140
    Ⓓ 160
    Ⓔ 180

65. A group of 180 high school science students was asked to opt for one or more of the subjects Physics, Chemistry and Biology. The number of students opting for each of the subjects is shown in the incomplete Venn Diagram below. If 99 students opted for Chemistry and 90 students opted for Biology, how many students opted for both Chemistry and Biology?

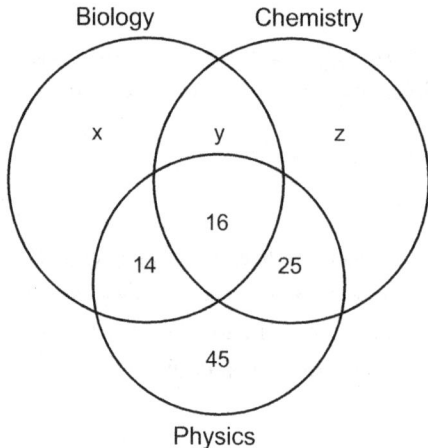

- A) 38
- B) 54
- C) 78
- D) 80
- E) 95

66.

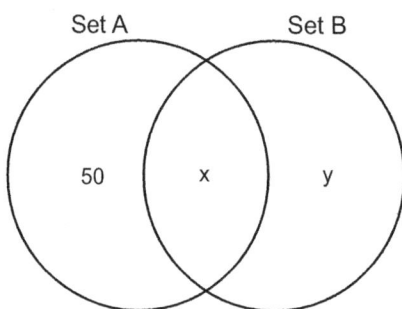

In the figure above, the total number of elements in sets A and B is 100. If an element is selected at random from set B, the probability that it is also in set A is 3/5. How many elements are in set A?

- A) 30
- B) 50
- C) 70
- D) 80
- E) 90

The graphs below show the variation of population and the percentage of population who got married in country X over the period 2010-2015.

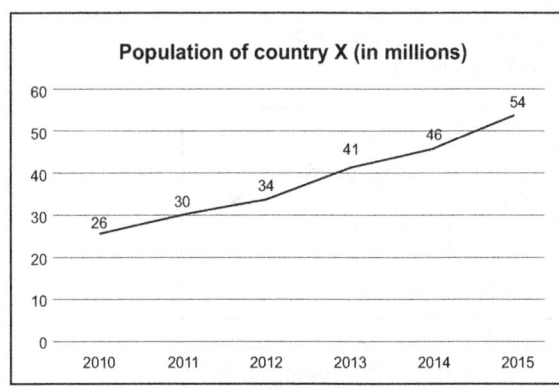
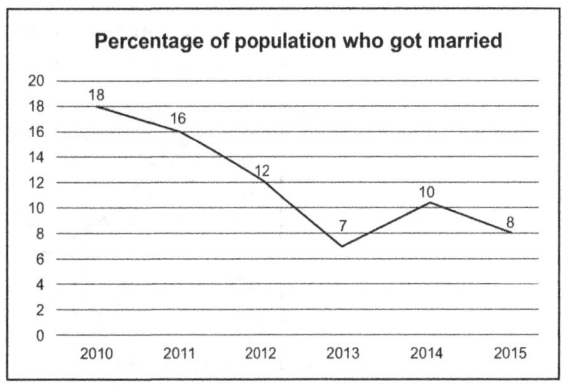

67. In which of the following years did the most number of people marry?

    Ⓐ 2011
    Ⓑ 2012
    Ⓒ 2013
    Ⓓ 2014
    Ⓔ 2015

68. During the year in which the least percentage of people got married in country X, which of the following is closest to the difference between the number of people who did not get married to the number of people who got married?

    Ⓐ 25.50 million
    Ⓑ 28.94 million
    Ⓒ 32.48 million
    Ⓓ 35.26 million
    Ⓔ 38.13 million

For the following two questions, refer to the following graph.

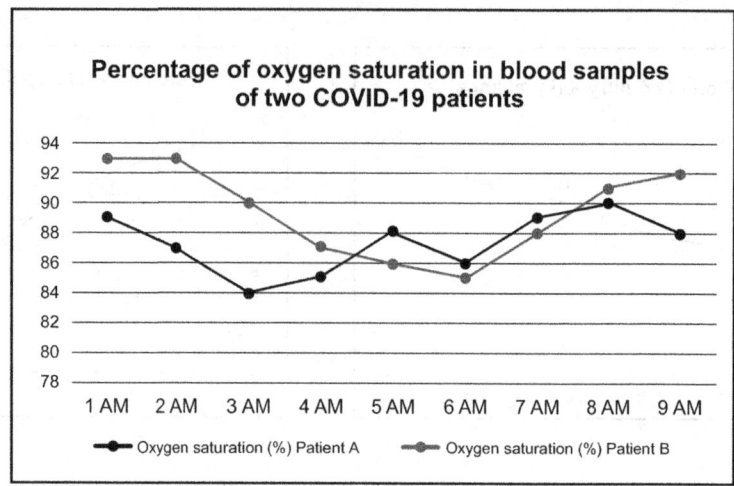

69. What was the average of the recorded oxygen saturation levels in the blood sample of patient A, during the period in which the oxygen saturation of patient B was less than the oxygen saturation of patient A?

   (A) 86.33
   (B) 86.67
   (C) 87.67
   (D) 88.25
   (E) 89.50

70. Between which two hours did the greatest percentage change in the oxygen saturation of patient B happen?

   (A) 2 AM – 3 AM
   (B) 3 AM – 4 AM
   (C) 5 AM – 6 AM
   (D) 6 AM – 7 AM
   (E) 7 AM – 8 AM

Data Analysis Practice Questions

The graphs below show the variation of price of a particular brand of smart watch for a store and revenues generated from the sale of all watches by the store during the period 2011 - 2020.

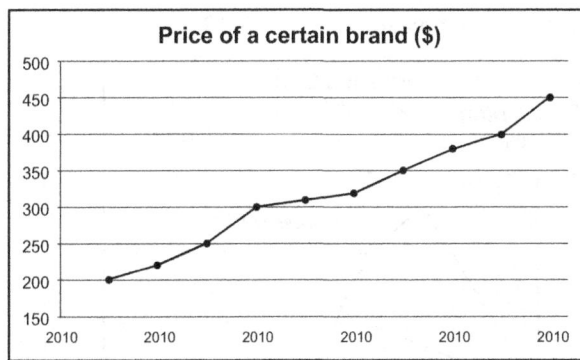
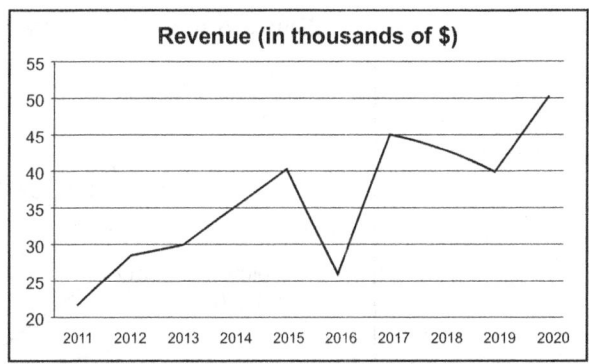

71. During which of the following periods was the percentage increase in the price between 60% and 100%, inclusive?

    Select all that apply.

    A 2012 to 2014
    B 2011 to 2016
    C 2013 to 2018
    D 2011 to 2019
    E 2012 to 2020
    F 2015 to 2019

72. If it is known that the revenue generated from the sale of this brand of smart watches was more than 50% of the total revenue generated by the store in 2019, which of the following could be the number of watches of the given brand sold by the store in that year?

    Indicate all such numbers.

    A 38
    B 45
    C 50
    D 62
    E 88
    F 100
    G 105
    H 110

The graphs below show the distribution of the favourite potato chips flavours of Mr. Prasad's class and the number of students in his class over the period 2015 – 2020.

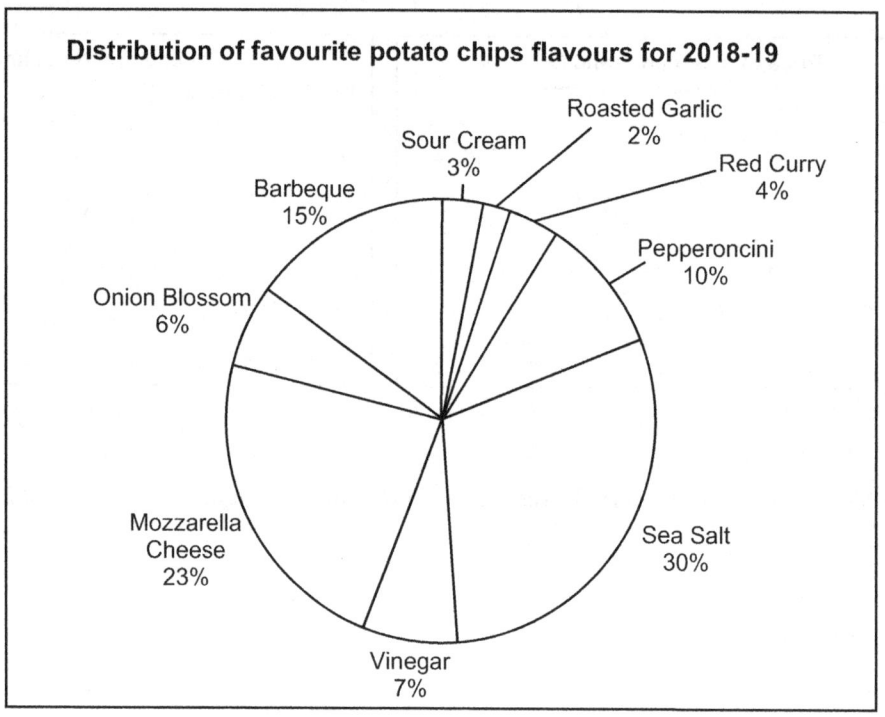

Number of students in Mr. Prasad's class

Year	Number of students
2015-16	120
2016-17	150
2017-18	170
2018-19	200
2019-20	240

73. If the number of students preferring Sea Salt flavour in 2018-19 was double the number of students preferring that flavour in 2019-20, what is the difference between the percentage of students preferring that flavour in 2018-19 and the percentage of students preferring that flavour in 2019-20?

Ⓐ 6%

Ⓑ 12.5%

Ⓒ 15%

Ⓓ 17.5%

Ⓔ 50%

Data Analysis Practice Questions

74. If m stands for the mean number of students per year and if M stands for the median number of students in Mr. Prasad's class over the given period, what percent of M is m?

- (A) 3.4%
- (B) 3.5%
- (C) 28.9%
- (D) 96.6%
- (E) 103.5%

The graphs below show the percentage distribution of college majors in city A and college X in city A, respectively.

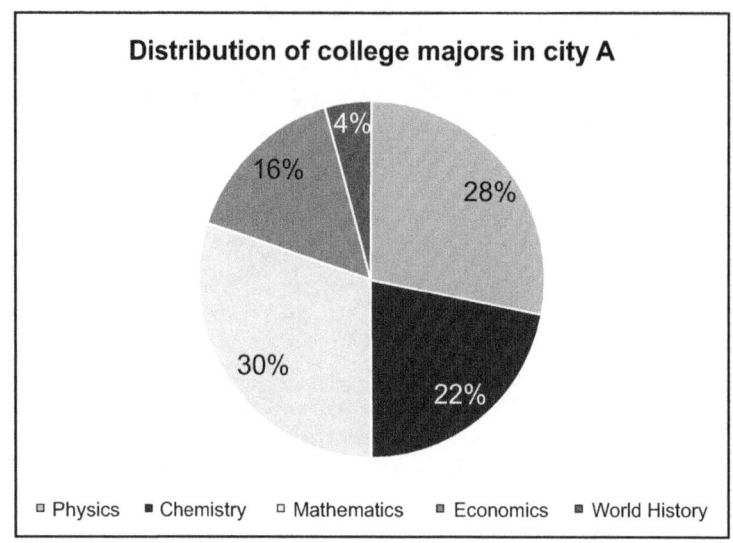

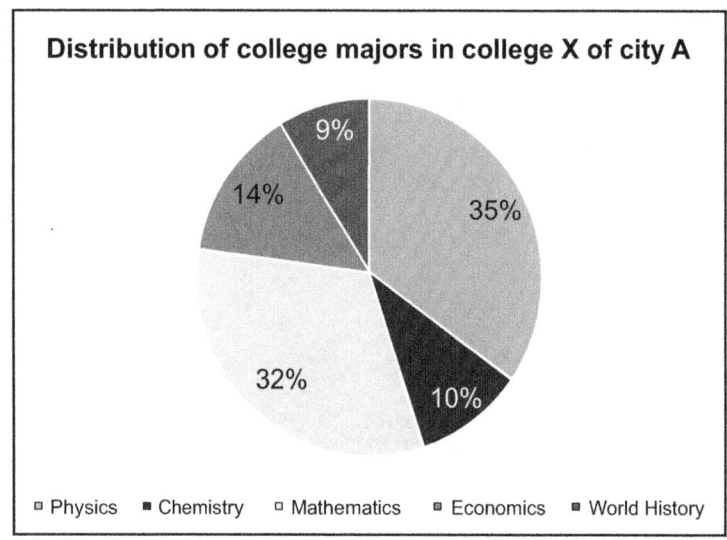

75. If the Physics majors in college X represents 50% of all Physics majors in city A, what is the ratio of the total number of students in college X to the total number of college students in city A?

    (A) 1/4
    (B) 1/3
    (C) 2/5
    (D) 2/3
    (E) 3/4

76. By what percent is the central angle represented by Mathematics majors in city A greater than the central angle represented by Economics majors in college X?

   - (A) 53.3%
   - (B) 66.7%
   - (C) 87.5%
   - (D) 114.3%
   - (E) 125%

The scatter plot below shows the goals scored and goals conceded by a football team in the first 10 of its league matches.

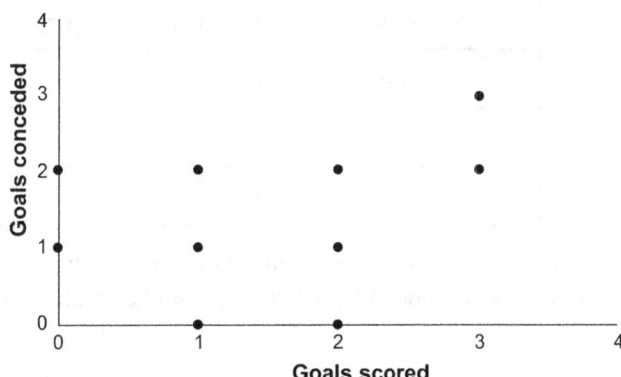

77. What is the ratio of the mean number of goals scored to the mean number of goals conceded by the team for the matches in which it won?

   - (A) 8:3
   - (B) 5:3
   - (C) 2:1
   - (D) 5:1
   - (E) 3:2

78. What is the difference between the total number of goals scored and the total number of goals conceded by the team across all ten matches?

   - (A) 0
   - (B) 1
   - (C) 2
   - (D) 3
   - (F) 4

79. The goal difference in any match is given as number of goals scored minus number of goals conceded. What is the median of the goal differences across the ten matches the team played?

    (A) 0
    (B) 1
    (C) 2
    (D) 3
    (E) 4

80. Sharvari takes a survey of some people in her neighbourhood about their dietary habits and records the results in the table below. She divides the dietary habits as Vegetarian, Vegan or Others only.

Dietary habits	Relative Frequency
Vegetarian	?
Vegan	?
Others	0.375

    If the ratio of the number of people who are vegetarians to the number of people who are vegans is 4:1, and if the total number of people surveyed is 400, how many people said they are vegetarians?

    (A) 50
    (B) 80
    (C) 200
    (D) 250
    (E) 300

Answers and Explanations

Level: Easy

1. **Sub topic: Data Interpretation with Probability**

   The correct answer is (D).

   First, identify the total number of days Michael recorded his successful offers. Adding the number of days represented by the bars from the graph, the total number of days is 31. Michael makes 7 successful offers on 1 out of 31 days. Hence, the probability is $\frac{1}{31} = 0.032258 \cong 0.032$.

2. **Sub topic: Data Interpretation with Probability**

   The correct answer is (C).

   The event of making 2 successful offers is mutually exclusive from the event of making 3 successful offers. The bars on the graph represent 31 days. Therefore, the number of days for each event can be read from the bar graph, and the probabilities can be added together.

   P(2 offers) + P(3 offers) $= \frac{10}{31} + \frac{8}{31} = \frac{18}{31} = 0.58065$
   $\cong 0.581$.

3. **Sub topic: Data Interpretation with Probability**

   The correct answer is (A).

   The probability of having at least 1 successful offer is the complement (or opposite) of having 0 offers on a day. Therefore, the equation for this is:

   P(at least 1 offer) = 1 - P(no offer)

   P(at least 1 offer) = $1 - \frac{1}{31} = 1 - 0.032 = 0.968$

4. **Sub topic: Probability**

   The correct answer is $\frac{8}{55}$.

   There is a total of 275 travelers who participated in the survey. There are 40 people traveling to Asia (23+17). Hence, the probability is $\frac{40}{275} = \frac{8}{55}$.

5. **Sub topic: Probability**

   The correct answer is $\frac{12}{55}$.

   There is a total of 275 travelers who participated in the survey. The number of females going to Europe is 60. Hence, the probability is $\frac{60}{275} = \frac{12}{55}$.

6. **Sub topic: Probability**

   The correct answer is $\frac{55}{103}$.

   This is a conditional probability question. There are 55 males going to North America, and there are a total of (55 + 48 = 103) people going to North America. Since the condition is that the traveler is going to North America, the probability that the traveler is a male is 55 out of 103, or $\frac{55}{103}$.

7. **Sub topic: Probability**

   The correct answer is (C).

   This is a conditional probability question. The total number of children who own a smart phone is 16 + 9 + 5 + 3 = 33 children. Out of the 33 children, those who also own an MP3 player are 9 + 5 = 14 children. Hence, the probability is $\frac{14}{33}$.

8. **Sub topic: Probability**

   The correct answer is (A).

   There are 6 children who own only a digital camera. Choosing two children is a simultaneous event without replacement. Hence, the probability can be solved as follows:

   P(2 children with only digital camera) =
   $\frac{6}{50} \times \frac{5}{49} = \frac{30}{2450} = 0.01224 \cong 0.012$.

9. **Sub topic: Numerical Methods**

   The correct answer is (E).

   There is a total of 52 locations in the table. We need to calculate the number of areas that saw a decline of 0.8% or greater from the list of areas by calculating the difference in the unemployment rates.

The following locations had a decline of 0.8% or more:

California	9.8	9.6	9.4	9.0	8.6	8.5	8.7
Mississippi	9.3	9.6	9.4	9.1	9.1	9.0	8.5
New Jersey	9.5	9.3	9.0	8.7	8.6	8.7	8.6
New York	8.4	8.4	8.2	7.8	7.6	7.5	7.5
Puerto Rico	14.6	14.5	14.2	13.7	13.4	13.2	13.5
Rhode Island	9.8	9.4	9.1	8.8	8.9	8.9	8.9
Utah	5.4	5.2	4.9	4.7	4.6	4.7	4.6
West Virginia	7.4	7.3	7.0	6.6	6.2	6.1	6.2

There are 8 locations that fit this description. The percentage of locations that had a change of 0.8% is:

$\frac{8}{52} \times 100 = 0.15 \times 100 = 15\%$

Therefore, the answer is E.

10. **Sub topic: Numerical Methods**

    The correct answer is (A).

    Florida has a population of 19.32 million, but only 65% of those are allowed to legally work. So, to determine the number of people that can legally work,

    $(19.32 \times 10^6)(0.65) = 12.56 \times 10^6 = 12.56$ million

    Based on the chart, the unemployment rate is 7.1% for Florida during the month of May.

    So, we multiply 12.56 million by 7.1% to get the number of unemployed in Florida.

    $(12.56 \times 10^6)(0.071) = 0.892 \times 10^6 = 0.89$ million

11. **Sub topic: Graphical Methods**

    The correct answer is (D).

    Based on the slope of the line segments, the greatest increase occurred from 1978 to 1979. Estimate the earnings from the graph to find the increase:

    1979 Earnings – 1978 Earnings = 1.1 – 0.5 = 0.6 million = $600,000.

12. **Sub topic: Graphical Methods**

    The correct answer is (A).

    Calculate the average: $(0.9 + 1.0 + 1.2 + 1.3 + 1.5) \div 5 = 5.9 \div 5 = 1.18 = \$1,180,000$.

13. **Sub topic: Numerical Data Description**

    The correct answer is (D).

    The opening price is found by subtracting the change in price from the closing price of stock.

    The change in price for *Mbd* stock is $-3\frac{1}{2}$ or -$3.50.

    The closing price for *Mbd* stock is $96.33.

    The opening price, then is 96.33 – (–3.50) = 96.33 + 3.50 = $99.83.

14. **Sub topic: Numerical Data Description**

    The correct answer is (C).

    The stock with the greatest amount of activity is the stock with the greatest volume. *BIm* stock had the greatest amount of activity on this particular day. Its closing price is $41.40. Three stocks have closing prices greater than $41.40 (*Arx*, *Mbd*, and *Tvk*).

15. **Sub topic: Graphical Data Description**

    The correct answer is (C).

    To answer this question, you must first determine the total number of dollars in the budget. This can be done by adding together the various sources of income shown in the bar graph:

    $10 + $6 + $2 + $8 + $4 = $30 (millions of dollars).

    From the pie chart, we learn that 25%, $\frac{1}{4}$ or of this $30 million was allocated to operation of the physical plant, $\frac{1}{4}$ of $30 million is $7,500,000.

16. **Sub topic: Graphical Data Description**

    The correct answer is (B).

    Income from the foundation accounted for $6 million of the total of $30 million, and $\frac{6}{30} = \frac{1}{5} = 20\%$.

17. **Sub topic: Graphical Description**

    The correct answer is (D).

    The snowfall that accumulated in October was approximately 15 inches. Twice that amount is 30 inches, the months that averaged at least 30 inches, including 30 inches, were January, February, March, and December, for a total of 4 months.

18. **Sub topic: Graphical Description**

    The correct answer is (B).

    December had about 30 inches of snow. Two-thirds of this amount is $30 \times \frac{2}{3} = 20$ inches.

    The month that had two-thirds less or 20 inches less snow than December's 30 inches must have had 10 inches of snow. Find the mark on the graph corresponding to 10 inches. Looking across that point in the horizontal direction, only month April had that amount.

19. **Sub topic: Graphical Description**

    The correct answer is (E).

    The amount of snow that fell in March was about 40 inches. The amount of snow that fell in April was about 10 inches. From March to April, the drop-in snowfall is 40 − 10 = 30 inches. The drop-in snowfall divided by the original amount of snowfall gives the percentage drop between the two months. So, (30 inch drop)/(40 inches originally) = $\frac{3}{4}$ = 75 percent

20. **Sub topic: Graphical Description**

    The correct answer is (C).

    To find the average amount of snowfall, add up the amount of snowfall for each month in the given range, and divide that sum by the total number of months. From January to May, the amount of snowfall, respectively, was 30 + 35 + 40 + 10 + 0 = 115 inches. Since the range includes a total of 5 months, the average snowfall is $\frac{115}{5} = 23$ inches.

21. **Sub topic: Graphical Data Description**

    The correct answer is (B).

    Stocks include Blue Chip and OTC. Together, these make up 40 + 20 = 60 percent of the distribution. Be careful when answering this question. What is being asked for is the amount not being invested in stocks. 100 − 60 = 40 percent of investments are not put into stocks.

22. **Sub topic: Graphical Data Description**

    The correct answer is (D).

    The percentage of earnings going towards Annuities is 25 percent. The dollar amount is $3000 × 25% = $750, which is choice (D).

23. **Sub topic: Graphical Data Description**

    The correct answer is (A).

    If a total of $10,000 is invested, 25 percent or $2,500 is put into Annuities and 10 percent or $1,000 is put into Corporate Bonds. The difference between these two amounts is $2,500 − $1,000 = $1,500.

24. **Sub topic: Graphical Data Description**

    The correct answer is (A).

    To find the sector with $800 from a $4,000 investment, find the percentage 800 is of 4,000. The correct answer is 0.2 or 20 percent. From the pie chart, only OTC Stocks make up 20 percent of the distribution.

25. **Sub topic: Interpreting data in tables and graphs**

    The correct answer is (B).

    Differences in the percentage of males and females employed are as follows:

    Country A: 68% − 59% = 9%

    Country B: 71% − 66% = 5%

    Country C: 64% − 56% = 8%

    Country D: 75% − 70% = 5%

    Country E: 60% − 51% = 9%

    So the smallest differences are for both Country B and Country D (5%).

26. **Sub topic: Interpreting data in tables and graphs**

    The correct answer is (C).

    Percentage of females in Country C that are employed = 56

    Therefore, percentage of females in Country C that are unemployed = 100 − 56 = 44

    Female population of Country C = 1.5 million

    Therefore, number of females in Country C that are unemployed = 44% of 1.5 million = 0.44 × 1.5 million = 0.66 million

Level: Medium

27. **Sub topic: Graphical Methods**

    The correct answer is (D).

    The corporate sectors that decreased their support for Philanthropic causes from 2000 to 2005 are: Manufacturing, Retail, Wholesale and Others.

    The total contribution by the Corporate Sectors towards Philanthropic Causes in the year 2005 was $570 million.

    Amount contributed by the Manufacturing Sector in 2005 = 20% of 570 million

    $= \dfrac{20}{100} \times 570 = \$114$ million

    Amount contributed by the Retail Sector in 2005 = 8% of 570 million

    $= \dfrac{8}{100} \times 570 = \$45.6$ million

    Amount contributed by the Wholesale Sector in 2005 = 6% of 570 million

    $= \dfrac{6}{100} \times 570 = \$34.2$ million

    Amount contributed by the Other Sectors in 2005 = 18% of 570 million

    $= \dfrac{18}{100} \times 570 = \$102.6$ million

    The total amount contributed by these four sectors towards Philanthropic Causes in the year 2005 = 114 + 45.6 + 34.2 + 102.6 = $296.4 million = $300 million approximately.

    Option D is correct.

28. **Sub topic: Graphical Methods**

    The correct answer is (C).

    Amount contributed by the Finance, Insurance and Real Estate Sector in:

    Year 2000 $= \dfrac{5}{100} \times 680 = \$34$ million

    Year 2005 $= \dfrac{26}{100} \times 570 = \$148.2$ million

    Amount contributed by the Service Sector in:

    Year 2000 $= \dfrac{17}{100} \times 680 = \$115.6$ million

    Year 2005 $= \dfrac{22}{100} \times 570 = \$125.4$ million

    Amount contributed by the Manufacturing Sector in:

    Year 2000 $= \dfrac{31}{100} \times 680 = \$210.8$ million

    Year 2005 $= \dfrac{20}{100} \times 570 = \$114$ million

    Amount contributed by the Retail Sector in:

    Year 2000 $= \dfrac{19}{100} \times 680 = \$129.2$ million

    Year 2005 $= \dfrac{8}{100} \times 570 = \$45.6$ million

Amount contributed by the Wholesale Sector in:

Year 2000 $= \frac{8}{100} \times 680 = \$54.4$ million

Year 2005 $= \frac{6}{100} \times 570 = \$34.2$ million

Amount contributed by the Other Sectors in:

Year 2000 $= \frac{20}{100} \times 680 = \$136$ million

Year 2005 $= \frac{18}{100} \times 570 = \$102.6$ million

We see that three sectors (Service, Manufacturing and Other) contributed more than $100 million in both 2000 and 2005.

Total amount contributed by the Service Sector in both years = 115.6 + 125.4 = $241 million

Total amount contributed by the Manufacturing Sector in both years = 210.8 + 114 = $324.8 million

Total amount contributed by the Other Sectors in both years = 136 + 102.6 = $238.6 million

Average amount contributed by these three sectors $= \frac{241 + 324.8 + 238.6}{3} = \$263.13$ million

29. **Sub topic: Graphical Methods**

The correct answer is (B).

Financial, Insurance and Real Estate Sector's 2005 contribution to Philanthropic Causes

$= \frac{26}{100} \times 570 = \$148.2$ million

Amount given for re-building homes

$= \frac{1}{3} \times 148.2 = \$49.4($ million

Amount remaining = 148.2 − 49.40 = $98.80 million

Amount given for providing medical aid

$= \frac{1}{4} \times 98.8 = \$24.7$ million

Amount spent on rebuilding homes− Amount spent on medical aid

= 49.40 − 24.70 = $24.7 million = $25 million approximately.

Option B is correct.

30. **Sub topic: Graphical Methods**

The correct answer is (D).

Draw a table of the figures.

	Year	Financial, Insurance and Real Estate	Services	Manufacturing	Retail	Wholesale	Others
680	2000	34	115.6	210.8	129.2	54.4	136
570	2005	148.2	125.4	114	45.6	34.2	102.6
Increase/Decrease		335.88 %	8.48 %	-45.92 %	-64.71 %	-37.13 %	-24.56 %

Excluding the Financial, Insurance, and Real Estate industries, the average change in contribution works out to −33%.

31. **Sub topic: Area, Perimeter, and Volume**

The correct answer is (D).

Perimeter of $\triangle ABC = AB + BC + CA = P_1$ (Say)

Given that the points P, Q and R are the midpoints of the sides of the $\triangle ABC$.

Remember, in a triangle, the line joining the centers of the 2-sides of a $\triangle$ is parallel to the 3rd side.

So, $PQ = \frac{1}{2} AB$

$QR = \frac{1}{2} BC$

$RP = \frac{1}{2} CA$

So, the perimeter of $\triangle PQR = PQ + QR + RP = P_2$ (Say)

$P_2 = \frac{1}{2}(AB + BC + CA)$

$P_2 = \frac{1}{2} P_1 \ldots (1)$

Similarly, the points L, M and N are the mid points of the sides of the $\triangle PQR$.

So, in the same way as above we can obtain that,

Perimeter of $\triangle LMN$, $P_3 = \frac{1}{2}$ (Perimeter of $\triangle PQR$)

$P_3 = \frac{1}{2} P_2 \ldots (2)$

Substituting the value of P_2 from the equation (1) in equation (2), we get

$$P_3 = \frac{1}{2}\left(\frac{1}{2}P_1\right)$$

$$P_3 = \frac{1}{4}P_1$$

$$\frac{P_1}{P_3} = \frac{4}{1}$$

So, the ratio of the perimeter of the $\triangle ABC$ to the perimeter of $\triangle LMN$ is 4:1.

Hence option D is correct.

32. **Sub topic: Congruent and Similar Figures**

The correct answer is (E).

Given that $\triangle ABC$ is a right-angled triangle and the points P, Q and R are the midpoints of the sides of the $\triangle ABC$.

$ar\triangle ABC = \frac{1}{2}xy$ .... (1)

Remember, in a triangle, the line joining the centers of the 2- sides of a $\triangle$ is parallel to the 3rd side and half of it.

So, $PQ = \frac{1}{2}AB$

$$\frac{PQ}{AB} = \frac{1}{2}$$

$$QR = \frac{1}{2}BC$$

$$\frac{QR}{BC} = \frac{1}{2}$$

$$RP = \frac{1}{2}CA$$

$$\frac{RP}{CA} = \frac{1}{2}$$

Thus, $\frac{PQ}{AB} = \frac{QR}{BC} = \frac{RP}{CA} = \frac{1}{2}$

So, by SSS Similarity Criteria, $\triangle ABC \sim \triangle PQR$.

The ratio of the areas of two similar triangles is equal to the square of the ratio of their corresponding sides.

$$\frac{ar\triangle PQR}{ar\triangle ABC} = \left(\frac{1}{2}\right)^2$$

$$\frac{ar\triangle PQR}{ar\triangle ABC} = \frac{1}{4}$$

$$ar\triangle PQR = \frac{1}{4}ar\triangle ABC$$

$ar\triangle PQR = \frac{1}{4}\left(\frac{1}{2}xy\right)$ [From equation (1)]

$ar\triangle PQR = \frac{1}{8}xy$ ....(2)

Similarly, in $\triangle PQR$, L, M and N are the mid points of the sides RQ, RP and PQ respectively.

So, as above, we may get,

$$ar\triangle LMN = \frac{1}{4}ar\triangle PQR$$

$ar\triangle LMN = \frac{1}{4}\left(\frac{1}{8}xy\right)$ [From equation (2)]

$$ar\triangle LMN = \frac{1}{32}xy$$

Hence option E is correct.

33. **Sub topic: Data Interpretation with Statistics**

The correct answer is (B).

Given that $m = 165$ and $d = 3$, 162cm = 165 – 3 = $m - d$. Looking at the graph above, the sections on the bell curve to the left of $m - d$ represent the probabilities of 14% and 2%, which add up to 16%.

34. **Sub topic: Data Interpretation with Statistics**

The correct answers are (A), (B), and (C).

Each event above has the following probabilities:

I. Less than 159 = 2%

II. Between 159 and 162 = 14%

III. Between 162 and 165 = 34%

IV. Between 165 and 168 = 34%

V. Between 168 and 171 = 14%

VI. More than 171 = 2%

By observation, I and VI are equal, II and V are equal, and III and IV are equal.

35. **Sub topic: Graphical Methods**

    The correct answer is (B).

    Find the proportion of oil usage by residents for each of the given years. In 1980, 20% used oil; in 1985, 40% used oil; in 1990, 50% used oil; and in 1995, 60% used oil. The greatest increase was from 20% to 40%, which occurred in 1985.

36. **Sub topic: Graphical Methods**

    The correct answer is (A).

    Mean refers to the average. To find the average sum all percentage of oil usage from the given years and divide by the number of given years. The average is
    $\frac{20+40+50+60}{4} = \frac{170}{4} = 42.5\%$.

37. **Sub topic: Graphical Methods**

    The correct answer is (C).

    The proportion of residents who used oil heat in 1995 was 60%. The proportion that used electric heat that year was 10%. The percentage difference between these two types of heating methods is 50%; 50% of 50,000 is 25,000.

38. **Sub topic: Graphical Methods**

    The correct answer is (B).

    The percentage of gas consumers in 1985 was 40%. In 1990, gas consumers made up 30% of the population. So 10% of the gas users from 1985 changed to alternative heating methods in the following time frame.

39. **Sub topic: Graphical Methods**

    The correct answer is (D).

    We're looking for the lowest ratio of males to females, so we have to get the smallest number of males and the largest number of females. Skimming the bar graphs, we can see that in pediatrics the female graph and the male graph are closer than any of the others. Pediatrics is (D), the correct answer.

40. **Sub topic: Graphical Methods**

    The correct answer is (C).

    To refer to ages of physicians, find the slice of the pie that goes from 45 to 54, which is 20%. Since the question is looking for a number of doctors, find the total number of general surgery physicians, which is 35,000 + 2,000 = 37,000 people. Finally, find 20% of 37,0000: .2 × 37,000 = 7,400. Answer (C) is the closest, and is the correct answer due to estimation.

41. **Sub topic: Graphical Methods**

    The correct answer is (E).

    To find the total number of physicians, first estimate the total number of family practice physicians. The male bar is slightly over 36,000 and the female bar is slightly over 6,000, so the total number is slightly over 43,000 people. Since 7.5% of all physicians is 43,000 people, we can set up a proportion:

    $\frac{7.5}{100} = \frac{43000}{n}$

    7.5n = 100 × 43000

    7.5n = 4300000

    n = 573,333 physicians. The correct answer is (E).

42. **Sub topic: Graphical Methods**

    The correct answer is (B).

    To find the number of male general surgery physicians younger than 35, we first need to find the number of females in the same group. The pie chart shows that 30% of all general surgery physicians are under 35, and we know that the females in that group represent 3.5% of all general surgery physicians, so the males must represent 30% - 3.5%, or 26.5%. The total general surgery physicians is slightly over 37,000, so the number of males is:

    $\frac{26.5}{100} = \frac{m}{37000}$

100m = 26.5 × 37000

100m = 980500

m = 9,805 people, which is closest to answer (B)

43. **Sub topic: Graphical Methods**

    The correct answer is (A).

    Tax, Clothing and miscellaneous = 11 + 8 + 6 = 25% = $\frac{1}{4}$ th of his income which is the expenses on food.

44. **Sub topic: Graphical Methods**

    The correct answer is (B).

    After reduction of 2% in tax: 11% – 2% = 9%. Increase of 1% each on cinema and travel amount to 12% on cinema and 18% on travel.

45. **Sub topic: Sub topic: Percent, Ratio, Rate**

    The correct answer is (D).

    Total population of Country E = 5.4 million + 4.8 million = 10.2 million

    Number of employed males in Country E = 60% of 5.4 million = 0.60 × 5.4 million = 3.24 million

    Number of employed females in Country E = 51% of 4.8 million = 0.51 v 4.8 million = 2.448 million

    Total number of people employed in Country E = 3.24 million + 2.448 million = 5.688 million

46. **Sub topic: Sub topic: Percent, Ratio, Rate**

    The correct answer is (C).

    Let the number of males in Country A be $6x$ and that in Country B be $5x$ (so the ratio is 6:5)

    Number of males employed in Country A = 68% of $6x = 0.68(6x) = 4.08x$

    Number of males employed in Country B = 71% of $5x = 0.71(5x) = 3.55x$

Total number of males employed in Country A and B combined = $4.08x + 3.55x = 7.63x$

Total number of males in Country A and B combined = $6x + 5x = 11x$

Percentage of males employed in both countries combined = $(7.63x/11x) \times 100 = 69.36\% \approx 69.4\%$ (rounded to the nearest tenth of a percent).

47. **Sub topic: Interpreting data in tables and graphs**

    The correct answer is (A).

    Amount spent on print media = 8% of $950 thousands = 0.08 × $950 thousands.

    Amount spent on newspapers = 2/5 of 0.08 × 950 thousands = 2/5 × 0.08 × $950 thousands = $30.4 thousands.

    Remainder of print media expenses = 3/5 × 0.08 × $950 thousands.

    Expenses on flyers = 3/5 of the remainder = 3/5 × 3/5 × 0.08 × $950 thousands = $27.36 thousands.

    Difference between spendings on newspapers and flyers
    = $30.4 thousands - $27.36 thousands = $3.04 thousands

48. **Sub topic: Measures of Center**

    The correct answer is (B).

    Total number of people surveyed = 18 + 11 + 15 + 8 + 6 = 58

    So the median will be the mean (average) of the 29th and 30th data points in the sorted list containing

    18 – 0s, followed by 11 – 1s, followed by 15 – 2s, followed by 8 – 3s, followed by 6 – 4s.

    The 29th data point is 1 and the 30th data point is 2, therefore median = (1 + 2)/2 = 1.5

Data Analysis Practice Questions

49. **Sub topic: Interpreting data in tables and graphs**

    The correct answer is (C).

    Discounts would apply to LED monitor and external hard drive.

    Price after discounts ($):

LED Monitor	$140 \times 0.9 = 126$
Keyboard	14
Digital Pen Tablet	42
External Hard Drive	$58 \times 0.9 = 52.20$
Laptop Case	32

    Total price before tax = $126 + $14 + $42 + $52.20 + $32 = $266.20

    Add sales tax: 5.5% of $266.20 = 0.055 x $266.20 = $14.64

    Total amount paid = $266.20 + $14.64 = $280.84

50. **Sub topic: Interpreting data in tables and graphs**

    The correct answer is (A).

    As density = mass ÷ volume, we have volume = mass ÷ density

    So the volumes of the samples are as follows:

    Silver: 4 ÷ 10.5 = 0.38 cubic cm

    Copper: 6.2 ÷ 9 = 0.69 cubic cm

    Aluminum: 9.5 ÷ 1.7 = 5.59 cubic cm

    Lead: 5.5 ÷ 11.4 = 0.48

    Iron: 8.2 ÷ 7.9 = 1.04 cubic cm

    Total volume of all the metals = 8.18 cubic cm

51. **Sub topic: Measures of Center**

    The correct answer is (D).

    Revenue generated per customer is given as Revenue/Number of customers

    Revenue generated per customer at Princeton Street = $31,144/458 = $68

    Revenue generated per customer at St Agnes Road = $58,320/720 = $81

    Revenue generated per customer at Hayat Street = $34,336/592 = $58

    Average of all three = ($68 + $81 + $58)/3 = $69

52. **Sub topic: Elementary Probability**

    The correct answer is (C).

    Number of female contestants = 200 − 80 = 120

    Number of male contestants arriving late = 1/5 of 80 = 16

    Number of female contestants arriving late = 1/6 of 120 = 20

    Total number of contestants arriving late = 16 + 20 = 36

    Probability that the prize will be won by a contestant who arrived late

    = Number of people arriving late/Total number of contestants

    = 36/200 that simplifies to 9/50

53. **Sub topic: Counting Methods**

    The correct answer is (C).

    Start from the condition, Adam has to be at the center.

		Adam		

    There are four positions to be filled from the remaining 11 grandchildren, so the number of arrangements = $_{11}P_4$

    $= \dfrac{11!}{(11-4)!}$

    $= \dfrac{11!}{7!}$

    $= 8 \times 9 \times 10 \times 11$

    $= 7920$

Level: Difficult

54. **Sub topic: Interpreting data in tables and graphs**

    The correct answer is (B).

    The total expenses for a commuter at a two-year public college are $6,420, while the total expenses for a commuter at a two-year private college are $12,240. The best answer is, thus, "almost twice as much."

55. **Sub topic: Interpreting data in tables and graphs**

    The correct answer is (C).

    A resident attending a two-year private college pays $4,600, while a commuter pays $2,200. The difference is $4,600 – $2,200 = $2,400.

56. **Sub topic: Interpreting data in tables and graphs**

    The correct answer is (D).

    The transportation expenses are $1,000 out of a total of $8,510 to $8,500 gives us an approximate answer of
    $$\frac{1000}{8500} \times 100\% = \frac{10}{85} \times 100\% \approx 11.7\% \approx 12\%$$

57. **Sub topic: Interpreting data in tables and graphs**

    The correct answer is (E).

    The easiest way to do this problem is to find what percent tuition and fees represent and subtract this percentage from 100%.
    $$\frac{14,500}{22,520} \times 100\% \approx 64\%$$

    Therefore, the percent spent on non-tuition and fee expenses is 100% – 64% = 36%.

58. **Sub topic: Interpreting data in tables and graphs**

    The correct answer is (C).

    The total tuition and fees and room and board expenses are $1,600 + $2,000 = $3,600. The total expenses are $6,420 ≈ $6,400. Thus, the percent is
    $$\frac{3,600}{6,400} \times 100\% = \frac{9}{16} \times 100\% \approx 56\%$$

59. **Sub topic: Measures of Center**

    The correct answer is (A).

    The given table may be presented as:

Diameter of heart (in mm)	Number of persons	Cumulative frequency
120	5	5
121	9	14
122	14	28
123	8	36
124	5	41
125	9	50

    Here $n = 50$.

    So $\frac{n}{2} = 25$ & $\frac{n}{2} + 1 = 26$.

    Median = $\frac{1}{2}$ (25th term + 26th term) = $\frac{(122 + 122)}{2}$
    = 122. [Because both lie in that row whose c.f. is 28]

60. **Sub topic: Elementary Probability**

    The correct answer is 25.

    The total number of artifacts are divided as either Palaeolithic or Neolithic. As 2/5 of the artifacts are Palaeolithic, 3/5 of them are Neolithic.

    As there are 45 Neolithic artifacts, we have 3/5 of the total = 45

    Therefore, the total = 45 × 5/3 = 75

Now let's create a table, enter the values and fill up the empty cells:

	Mediterranean	Not Mediterranean	Total
Palaeolithic	2/3 of 2/5 of 75 = 20	30 – 20 = 10	2/5 of 75 = 30
Neolithic	40 – 20 = 20	45 – 20 = 25	3/5 of 75 = 45
Total	40	75 – 40 (or 10 + 25) = 35	75

61. **Sub topic: Conditional Probability**

The correct answer is 200.

Set A = the set of all 3-digit numbers that are multiples of 9 = {108, 117… 999}.

Set B = the set of all 3-digit numbers that are multiples of 3 but not multiples of 6 = {105, 111, 117… 999}.

The common elements from both Set A and Set B = {117, 135… 999}.

The formula to find the number of elements of a set is given by $n = \frac{last\ term - first\ term}{difference} + 1$.

The number of elements in Set A = (999 – 108)/9 + 1 = 99 + 1 = 100

The number of elements in Set B = (999 – 105)/6 + 1 = 149 + 1 = 150

The number of common elements in sets A and B = (999 – 117)/18 + 1 = 49 + 1 = 50

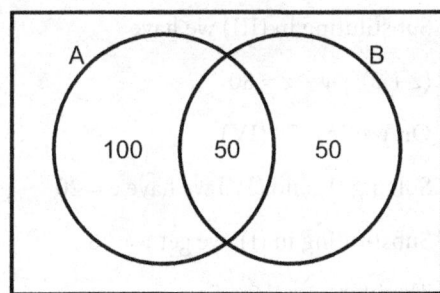

Hence A U B has 100 + 50 + 50 = 200 elements.

62. **Sub topic: Measures of Center**

The correct answer is 79.

Both sets P and Q are sorted, so the median of set P is (the middle number) d and the median of set Q is (the middle number) p.

Therefore, $d = p = 8$

As set P consists of distinct positive integers, to minimize the sum of the elements, we have

$a = 1, b = 2, c = 3, d = 8, e = 9, f = 10$ and $g = 11$

Then the minimum value of $a + b + c + d + e + f + g = P = 1 + 2 + 3 + 8 + 9 + 10 + 11 = 44$

The integers in set Q are not necessarily distinct.

Therefore, to minimize the sum of the elements, we have

$m = n = o = 1, p = q = r = s = 8$

Then the minimum value of $m + n + o + p + q + r + s = Q = 1 + 1 + 1 + 8 + 8 + 8 + 8 = 35$

Therefore, $P + Q = 44 + 35 = 79$

63. **Sub topic: Conditional Probability**

The correct answer is 3.

The situation is represented in the Venn Diagram shown below:

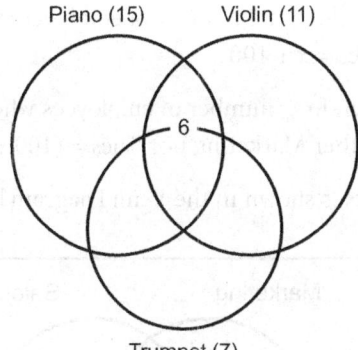

It follows that number of members who play only piano or piano + trumpet only = 15 – 6 = 9

Likewise, number of members who play only violin or violin + trumpet only = 11 – 6 = 5

This means the number of members who play only the trumpet must be 24 − (9 + 6 + 5) = 4, as shown in the figure below.

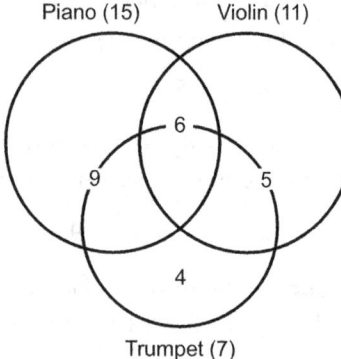

Now, as there are 7 members who play the trumpet and 4 of them play only the trumpet, 7 − 4 = 3 members who play the trumpet play another instrument.

64. **Sub topic: Conditional Probability**

The correct answer is (B).

Number of employees who work in both Marketing and Sales = 1/2 of 200 = 100

As 160 employees work in the Marketing department, number of employees who work in Marketing only = 160 − 100 = 60

If x is the number of employees who work only in Sales, total number of employees who work in Sales = x + 100

Therefore, number of employees who work in neither Marketing nor Sales = (100 + x)/3

This is shown in the Venn Diagram below:

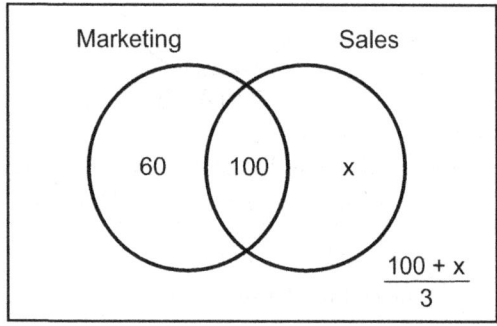

As the total number of employees = 200, we have

60 + 100 + x + (100 + x)/3 = 200

Or, 160 + x + (100 + x)/3 = 200

Or, x + (100 + x)/3 = 40

Multiplying throughout by 3 we have

$3x$ + 100 + x = 120

Or, $4x$ = 20

Or, x = 5

Therefore, number of employees working in the Sales department = 100 + 5 = 105

65. **Sub topic: Conditional Probability**

The correct answer is (B).

The number of students who opted for both Chemistry and Biology = y + 16.

So to answer the question, we need to find y.

As 99 students opted for Chemistry, we have

$y + z + 16 + 25 = 99$

Or, $y + z = 58$ (I)

As 90 students opted for Biology, we have

$x + y + 14 + 16 = 90$

Or, $x + y = 60$ (II)

Again, as the total number of students = 180, we have

$x + y + z + 14 + 16 + 25 + 45 = 180$

Or, $x + y + z = 80$ (III)

From (I) and (II) we have $x − z = 2$, or $x = z + 2$

Substituting in (III) we have

$(z + 2) + y + z = 80$

Or, $y + 2z = 78$ (IV)

Solving (I) and (IV) we have $z = 20$

Substituting in (I), we get $y = 38$

Therefore, $y + 16 = 54$

66. **Sub topic: Conditional Probability**

    The correct answer is (D).

    The answer to the question "how many elements are in set A?" is $50 + x$

    Therefore we need to find x.

    As the total number of elements in sets A and B is 100, we have

    $50 + x + y = 100$

    Or, $x + y = 50$ (I)

    Again, it is given that if an element is selected at random from set B, the probability that it is also in set A is 3/5.

    Number of elements in set B $= x + y$

    Number of elements in A and B both $= x$

    Therefore, $x/(x + y) = 3/5$

    Or, $5x = 3(x + y)$

    Or, $5x = 3x + 3y$

    Or, $2x = 3y$

    Or, $y = 2x/3$ (II)

    Substituting in (I) we have

    $x + 2x/3 = 50$

    Multiplying throughout by 3 we have

    $3x + 2x = 150$

    Or, $5x = 150$

    Or, $x = 30$

    Therefore there are $50 + 30 = 80$ elements in set A.

67. **Sub topic: Interpreting data in tables and graphs**

    The correct answer is (A).

    From the graphs we see that as the population increases the percentage of population who got married decreases (overall), so it is hard to eliminate the options by estimating.

    The quickest way to find the answer in this case is to use the calculator:

    Number of people (in millions) who got married in 2011
    = 16% of 30 = 4.80

    Number of people (in millions) who got married in 2012
    = 12% of 34 = 4.08

    Number of people (in millions) who got married in 2013
    = 7% of 41 = 2.87

    Number of people (in millions) who got married in 2014
    = 10% of 46 = 4.6

    Number of people (in millions) who got married in 2015
    = 8% of 54 = 4.32

    Therefore, the largest number of people who got married was in 2011.

68. **Sub topic: Interpreting data in tables and graphs**

    The correct answer is (D).

    The year in which the least percentage of people got married in country X is 2013.

    Number of people who married in 2013 = 7% of 41 million

    Number of people who did not marry in 2013 = (100 − 7)% of 41 million = 93% of 41 million.

    Difference = 93% of 41 million − 7% of 41 million = 86% of 41 million = 35.26 million

69. **Sub topic: Interpreting data in tables and graphs**

    The correct answer is (C).

    The oxygen saturation of patient B was less than the oxygen saturation of patient A during the period 4:30 AM – 7:30 AM (approximately).

    The recorded oxygen saturation levels in the blood sample of patient A during this period were 88% (at 5 AM), 86% (6 AM), 89% (7 AM)

    Average = $(88 + 86 + 89)/3 = 87.67$

70. **Sub topic: Interpreting data in tables and graphs**

    The correct answer is (D).

    Instead of rushing to calculate, let's see if we can eyeball and eliminate some of the incorrect options.

    Note that "percentage change" can be either positive (increase) or negative (decrease).

    It is the (change ÷ initial) × 100

    As x 100 is a common factor, all we care about is the ratio change/initial.

    From the given options, notice that the changes (numerators) from 2 – 3 and 3 – 4 are the same (straight line).

    As the initial amount (denominator) is less at 3 AM than at 2 AM, we can eliminate (A).

    Similarly, between 6 – 7 and 7 – 8, we are able to eliminate 7 – 8, or (E) (larger denominator for the same numerator).

    Let's now look at the remaining options:

    (B) 3 AM – 4 AM: (3/90) x 100

    (C) 5 AM – 6 AM: (1/86) x 100

    (D) 6 AM – 7 AM: (3/85) x 100

    A quick look eliminates (B) as 3/90 < 3/85

    As 1/86 < 3/85, the correct option is (D).

71. **Sub topic: Interpreting data in tables and graphs**

    The correct answer is (B), (D).

    Percentage increase = (Increase/Initial) × 100

    Let's evaluate the options:

    (A) 2012 to 2014:
    $\frac{300-220}{220} \times 100 = 36.36\%$ (not in the range asked)

    (B) 2011 to 2016:
    $\frac{300-200}{200} \times 100 = 60\%$ (in the range asked)

    (C) 2013 to 2018:
    $\frac{380-250}{250} \times 100 = 52\%$ (not in the range asked)

    (D) 2011 to 2019:
    $\frac{400-200}{200} \times 100 = 100\%$ (in the range asked)

    (E) 2012 to 2020:
    $\frac{400-200}{200} \times 100 = 100\%$ (not in the range asked)

    (F) 2015 to 2019:
    $\frac{400-310}{310} \times 100 = 29.03\%$ (not in the range asked)

72. **Sub topic: Interpreting data in tables and graphs**

    The correct answer is (D), (E), (F)

    Total revenue generated in 2019 = $40,000

    Therefore, revenue generated from the sale of smart watches of this particular brand must be greater than 50% of $40,000.

    In other words, the revenue generated from the sale of smart watches of this particular brand must be greater than $20,000

    Price of the watch in 2019 = $400.

    Therefore, to earn a revenue of $20,000, the number of watches sold = $20,000/$400 = 50

    So the number of smart watches of the said brand sold in that year must be **greater than** 50, but **less than or equal to** 100 (as the total revenue is $40,000).

    Only options (D), (E) and (F) are in this range.

73. **Sub topic: Interpreting data in tables and graphs**

    The correct answer is (D).

    Number of students preferring Sea Salt in 2018-19 = 30% of 200 = 60

    As this is double the number of students preferring that flavour in 2019-20,

    Number of students preferring Sea Salt in 2019-20 = 60/2 = 30

    Percentage of students preferring that that flavour in 2019-20 = (30/240) × 100 = 12.5%

    Difference in percentage = 30% − 12.5% = 17.5%

74. **Sub topic: Measures of Center**

    The correct answer is (E).

    The mean number of students per year (m) = (120 + 150 + 170 + 200 + 240)/5 = 176

    Median (M) is the middle number between 120, 150, 170, 200 and 240 = 170

    So we need to answer the question: what percent of 170 is 176?

    This is (176/170) × 100 = 103.5%

75. **Sub topic: Interpreting data in tables and graphs**

    The correct answer is (C).

    Let the number of students in college X be n and the total number of college students in city A be N.

    Number of Physics majors in college X = 35% of $n = 0.35n$

    Number of Physics majors in city A = 28% of $N = 0.28N$

    Therefore, 50% of all Physics majors in city A = 50% of $0.28N = 0.14N$

    As per the given condition, $0.35n = 0.14N$

    Therefore, $n/N = 0.14/0.35 = 2/5$

76. **Sub topic: Interpreting data in tables and graphs**

    The correct answer is (D).

    Central angle of Mathematics majors in city A = 30% of 360° = 108°

    Central angle of Economics majors in college X = 14% of 360° = 50.4°

    Difference = 108° − 50.4° = 57.6°

    This is (57.6°/50.4°) × 100 percent greater than the central angle of Economics majors in college X

    ≈ 114.3%

77. **Sub topic: Measures of Center**

    The correct answer is (A).

    The team won in those matches in which the number of goals scored > the number of goals conceded.

    As per the scatterplot, the scores in those matches were as follows:

Goals scored	Goals conceded
2	0
3	2
1	0
2	1

    Mean number of goals scored = (2 + 3 + 1 + 2)/4 = 2

    Mean number of goals conceded = (0 + 2 + 0 + 1)/4 = 3/4

    Required ratio = 2 : 3/4 = 8:3

78. **Sub topic: Interpreting data in tables and graphs**

    The correct answer is (B).

    From the given scatterplot we have the following information:

Goals scored	Goals conceded
1	1
2	0
3	2
1	2
1	0
0	2
2	1
3	3
2	2
0	1

Total number of goals scored = 15

Total number of goals conceded = 14

Difference = 1

79. **Sub topic: Measures of Center**

The correct answer is (A).

Goals scored	Goals conceded	Goal difference
1	1	0
2	0	2
3	2	1
1	2	−1
1	0	1
0	2	−2
2	1	1
3	3	0
2	2	0
0	1	−1

To find the median of goal differences, we need to sort the data:

−2, −1, −1, 0, 0, 0, 1, 1, 1, 2

Median is the mean of the 5th and 6th numbers in the sorted list above = $(0 + 0)/2 = 0$

80. **Sub topic: Conditional Probability**

The correct answer is (C).

Let the relative frequency of 'Vegetarian' be x and that of 'Vegan' be y.

As relative frequencies add up to 1, we have

$x + y + 0.375 = 1$

Or, $x + y = 0.625$

Again, $x:y = 4:1$ (given)

Or, $x = 4y$

So we have $4y + y = 0.625$

Or, $5y = 0.625$

Or, $y = 0.625/5 = 0.125$

And $x = 0.125 \times 4 = 0.5$

Therefore, the relative frequency of 'Vegetarian' = 0.5, out of a total of 400 people surveyed.

Therefore, number of people who said they are vegetarians = $0.5 \times 400 = 200$

Chapter 7

Exercise #1

Questions: 12 | Time: 21 minutes

This Exercise includes *12 practice questions*. The questions cover all the question types as explained in Chapter 2 and may fall into any of the following categories - Arithmetic, Algebra, Geometry or Data Analysis. You will find answers and detailed explanations towards the end of this chapter.

1.

The arithmetic mean of a, b, c and 24 is M, and the arithmetic mean of a, b, c, and d, is N.
The arithmetic mean of b, c, d, and 24 is (M + N).

Quantity A	**Quantity B**
$d - a$	4N

- Ⓐ Quantity A is greater.
- Ⓑ Quantity B is greater.
- Ⓒ The two quantities are equal.
- Ⓓ The relationship cannot be determined from the information given.

2.

Two salespeople bought TV sets for resale from different wholesalers. Susan made a profit of 24% after selling the TV set at $148.80, while Christina sold her TV at a loss of 4% less than the percent of Susan's profit, or $96.00 total.

Quantity A	**Quantity B**
Susan's buying price	Christina's buying price

- (A) Quantity A is greater.
- (B) Quantity B is greater.
- (C) The two quantities are equal.
- (D) The relationship cannot be determined from the information given.

3.

Let $x < 0$, $y > 0$ and $|x| > y$.

Quantity A	**Quantity B**
$\dfrac{2x^2 + y}{2y + x^3 + 3}$	$\dfrac{x + 2y^2}{2y + x^2 + 3}$

- (A) Quantity A is greater.
- (B) Quantity B is greater.
- (C) The two quantities are equal.
- (D) The relationship cannot be determined from the information given.

Exercise #1

Questions 4 and 5 are based on the following data:

Number of reported cases of AIDS in Bangkok has increased each year since 1991. The two bars for each year represent the number of cases diagnosed respectively in the first and second half of the year. The following table gives the fatality percentages among the cases corresponding to each half year. Most of patients who were diagnosed before 1996 as having AIDS have already died.

Percentage of AIDS cases Resulted in Death

	1991	1992	1993	1994	1995	1996	1997
1st Half	92	89	90	83	80	70	47
2nd Half	93	89	89	83	77	58	33

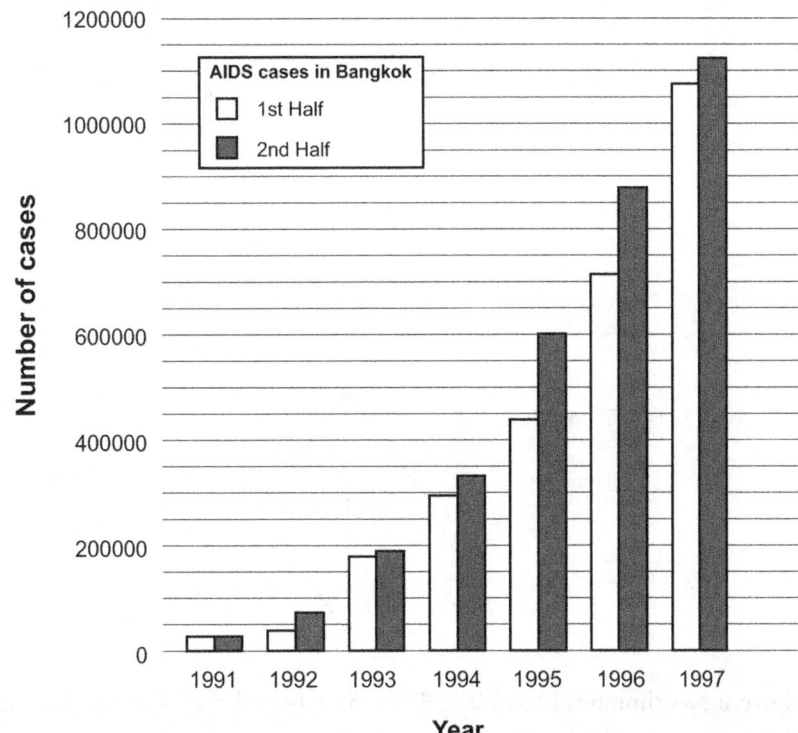

4. The approximate percentage increase of the reported cases in the first half of 1997 as compared to the second half of 1995 is

   (A) 90
   (B) 95
   (C) 70
   (D) 83
   (E) 93

5. In 1994 the increase in the number of reported cases in the second half of the year as compared to the first half is

   (A) 150000
   (B) 75000
   (C) 50000
   (D) 100000
   (E) 125000

6. At the grocery store, an apple costs $1.34, an orange costs $0.47, and a banana costs $0.19. How much did Helen pay for 5 apples, 3 oranges, and 7 bananas?

   (A) $7.70
   (B) $9.44
   (C) $10.56
   (D) $11.74
   (E) $30.00

7.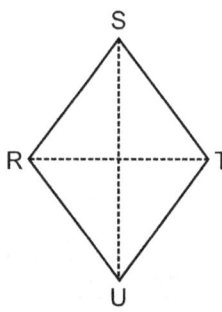

   The diagram above shows rhombus RSTU. If ∠ RST = 5x − 14 and ∠ UST = 2x + 4, what is the value of x?

   (A) 2.5
   (B) 4
   (C) $5\frac{1}{3}$
   (D) 18
   (E) 22

Exercise #1

8. 8, 9, 12, 17, 24 ...

   In the preceding sequence, a certain pattern determines each of the subsequent numbers. What is the next number in the sequence?

   - (A) 41
   - (B) 35
   - (C) 33
   - (D) 30
   - (E) 29

9. If the volume and the total surface area of a cube are equal, how long must the edge of the cube be?

   - (A) 2 units
   - (B) 3 units
   - (C) 4 units
   - (D) 5 units
   - (E) 6 units

10. 150 regular size chocolate bars include 10 lbs. of sugar total. When promotional size bars are made 20% more sugar is needed. How many pounds of sugar will be required to make 250 promotional size chocolates?

    ☐ lbs

11. Andrew tells David, "If you give me $100 then I will have twice the money that you have". David, in turn tells Andrew, "If you give me $10, I shall have six times the amount you have".

Quantity A	**Quantity B**
Original amount with Andrew + Original amount with David	Original amount with David + Amount borrowed from Andrew

    - (A) Quantity A is greater.
    - (B) Quantity B is greater.
    - (C) The two quantities are equal.
    - (D) The relationship cannot be determined from the information given.

12.

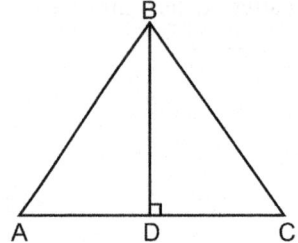

Note: Figure not drawn to scale

In the preceding figure, BD ⊥ AC, AB = 34, BD = 30, and BC = 34. What is the length of AC?

- Ⓐ 8
- Ⓑ 18
- Ⓒ 30
- Ⓓ 32
- Ⓔ 34

Exercise #1

Answers and Explanations

1. **Topic: Algebra**

   Sub topic: Algebraic Expressions

   The correct answer is (C).

   (1) $a + b + c + 24 = 4M$

   (2) $a + b + c + d = 4N$

   Subtract.

   (3) $24 - d = 4M - 4N$

   (4) $b + c + d + 24 = 4M + 4N$

   Subtract (2) from (4).

   (5) $24 - a = 4M$

   Subtract (3) from (5).

   $d - a = 4N$

2. **Topic: Arithmetic**

   Sub topic: Profit & Loss

   The correct answer is (C).

   Susan's selling price = $148.80 to get a profit of 24%

   Buying price percentage = 100% and

   Selling price = % buying price + % profit = 100 + 24 = 124%

   Susan's buying price = $\frac{100}{124} \times \$148.80 = \$120.00$

   Christina's selling price = $96 to get a loss of 24% − 4% = 20%

   Buying price percentage = 100% and

   Selling price = % buying price − % loss = 100 − 20 = 80%

   Christina's buying price = $\frac{100}{80} \times 96 = \$120$

   Therefore, the two quantities are equal; the correct option is C.

3. **Topic: Algebra**

   Sub topic: Inequalities

   The correct answer is (A).

   Since $x < 0$, $x^2 > 0$ Given that $|x| > y$, $x^2 > y^2$ and $2x^2 > 2y^2$

   Since $x < 0$, $y > 0$, $x < y$ hence $2x^2 + y > 2y^2 + x$.

   $x < 0$ implies that $x^3 < 0 > x^2$, thus $2y + x^3 + 3 < 2y + x^2 + 3$

   Therefore, Quantity A =

   $\frac{2x^2 + y}{2y + x^3 + 3} > \frac{x + 2y^2}{2y + x^3 + 3}$ = Quantity B

4. **Topic: Data Analysis**

   Sub topic: Interpreting data in tables and graphs

   The correct answer is (D).

   Number of reported cases in the first half of 1997 = 1100000

   Number of reported cases in the second half of 1995 = 600000

   Increase as a percentage

   $= \frac{1100000 - 600000}{600000} \times 100$

   $= \frac{5 \times 100}{6} = 83.3\% \cong 83\%$

5. **Topic: Data Analysis**

   Sub topic: Interpreting data in tables and graphs

   The correct answer is (C).

   In 1994, the number of cases reported in the first half = 250000 and the number of cases reported in the second half = 300000. Hence, the increase = 50000.

6. **Topic: Arithmetic**

   Sub topic: Integers

   The correct answer is (A).

Helen bought 5 apples, 3 oranges and 7 bananas. Each apple costs $1.34. Each orange costs $0.47. Each banana costs $0.19.

To calculate the total that Helen paid, we need to calculate how much Helen paid for each kind of fruit and then add the totals together.

Based on this table, Helen paid $9.44 for the fruit. The answer is B.

Items	Cost per Item	Number of Items	Total cost for Item
Apples	$1.34	5	5 × $1.34 = $6.70
Oranges	$0.47	3	3 × $0.47 = $1.41
Banana	$0.19	7	7 × $0.19 = $1.33
			$9.44

7. **Topic: Geometry**

    Sub topic: Quadrilaterals

    The correct answer is (E).

    The diagonals of the rhombus bisect the angles. The measure of ∠RST is thus twice the measure of ∠UST. Use this relationship to create an equation and solve for x.

    ∠RST = 2(∠UST)

    $5x - 14 = 2(2x + 4)$

    $5x - 14 = 4x + 8$

    $x - 14 = 8$

    $x = 22$

8. **Topic: Arithmetic**

    Sub topic: Sequences of Numbers

    The correct answer is (C).

    In the series 8, 9, 12, 17, 24

    $9 - 8 = 1$

    $12 - 9 = 3$

    $17 - 12 = 5$

    $24 - 17 = 7$

    Therefore, the difference between the next term and 24 must be 9, or

    $x - 24 = 9$

    $x = 33$

    Therefore, the next term in the series must be 33.

9. **Topic: Geometry**

    Sub topic: Three-Dimensional Figures

    The correct answer is (E).

    Let x equal the length of a side of the cube. The volume $v = x^3$, and the surface area $s = 6x^2$, Therefore, $x = 6$.

10. **Topic: Arithmetic**

    Sub topic: Percent, Ratio, Rate

    The correct answer is 20lbs.

    If 150 promotional size chocolates are made they need $10 \times 1.2 = 12$ lbs. of sugar. (1.2 represents a quantity increased by 20% in decimal form). Using simple ratio proportion,

    $$\frac{12}{15} = \frac{x}{250}$$
    $x = 20$

11. **Topic: Algebra**

    Sub topic: System of Equations

    The correct answer is (A).

    The original amount with Andrew = $x

    The original amount with David = $y

    If Andrew gives $10, then the amount left with Andrew = $(x - 10)

    If David gives $100, then the amount left with David = $(y - 100)

    Andrew tells David, "If you give me $100 then I will have twice the money that you have".

    $x + 100 = 2(y - 100)$

$x + 100 = 2y - 200$

$x = 2y - 200 - 100$

$x = 2y - 300$ (Equation 1)

David, in turn tells Andrew, "If you give me $10, I shall have six times the amount you have".

$y + 10 = 6(x - 10)$

$y + 10 = 6x - 60$

$y = 6x - 60 - 10$

$y = 6x - 70$ (Equation 2)

Substituting the value of x from equation 1 in equation 2:

$y = 6(2y - 300) - 70$

$y = 12y - 1800 - 70$

$y = 12y - 1870$

$1870 = 12y - y$

$11y = 1870$

$y = \frac{1870}{11} = \$170$

Substituting the value of y in equation 1:

$x = 2(170) - 300$

$x = 340 - 300$

$x = \$40$

Original amount with Andrew = $40

Original amount with David = $170

Quantity A: Sum of the original amount with Andrew and the original amount with David = 40 + 170 = $210

Quantity B: Sum of the original amount with David and the amount borrowed from Andrew = 170 + 10 = $180

Quantity A is greater.

12. **Topic: Geometry**

    Sub topic: Triangles

    The correct answer is (D).

    Since AB = BE = 34, ΔABC is an isosceles triangle and altitude BD will bisect AC. Since ΔBDC is right triangle, use the Pythagorean Theorem, which says

    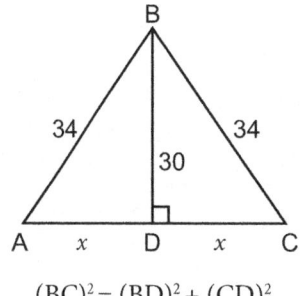

    $(BC)^2 = (BD)^2 + (CD)^2$

    $(34)^2 = (30)^2 + x^2$

    $1{,}156 = 900 + x^2$

    $x^2 = 1{,}156 - 900$

    $x^2 = 256$

    $x = \sqrt{256} = 16$

    Therefore, CD = 16 = AD

    AC = AD + DC

    16 + 16

    =32

This page is intentionally left blank

Chapter 8

Exercise #2

Questions: 15 | Time: 26 minutes

This Exercise includes *15 practice questions*. The questions cover all the question types as explained in Chapter 2 and may fall into any of the following categories - Arithmetic, Algebra, Geometry or Data Analysis. You will find answers and detailed explanations towards the end of this chapter.

1. An integer whose cube root is also an integer is called a perfect cube. i.e., 216, 343, 512 are perfect cubes as their cube roots will be 6, 7 and 8 respectively. Which of the below options shall not necessarily be a perfect cube, assuming integers m and n are perfect cubes?

    - (A) $8m$
    - (B) mn
    - (C) $mn + 216$
    - (D) $-m$
    - (E) $(m - n)^9$

2. The length and the width of a rectangle is 10cm and 8cm respectively, if the side of a square is 6cm, find the ratio of the area of the rectangle to that of the square.

    - (A) $\frac{20}{9}$
    - (B) $\frac{3}{1}$
    - (C) $\frac{10}{3}$
    - (D) $\frac{3}{2}$
    - (E) $\frac{5}{3}$

3.

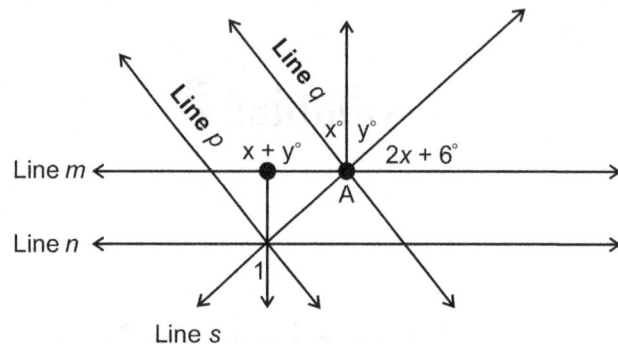

In the figure above Point A is on Line m. Line m and Line n are parallel. Line p and Line q are parallel. If $x°$ is three less than $y°$, what is the measure of $\angle 1$?

- Ⓐ 28°
- Ⓑ 31°
- Ⓒ 59°
- Ⓓ 62°
- Ⓔ Cannot be determined

4. If a store purchases several items for $1.80 per dozen and sells them at 3 for $0.85, what is the store's profit on 6 dozen of these items?

- Ⓐ $4.20
- Ⓑ $5.70
- Ⓒ $9.60
- Ⓓ $10.60
- Ⓔ $20.40

5. Andrew wants to build a new house. According to the blue-print, the length and width of the hall are $(x - 5)^2$ and $(10 + x)$ respectively and the length and the width of the library are $(x - 5)$ and $x^2 - 5$ respectively. The hall and the library are equal in area.

Which of the following statements could be true?

Select all that apply.

- [A] The area of the library is 196 sq. feet.
- [B] The value of x is 4.5 feet.
- [C] The area of hall is 304 sq. feet.
- [D] The sum of the area of the hall and the library is 608 sq. feet.
- [E] The value of x is 9 feet.
- [F] The sum of the area of the hall and the library is 392 sq. feet.

Exercise #2

6.

The sum of the roots of the equation $3x^2 - 5x - k(x - 2) - 2 = 0$ is -3.

Quantity A　　　　　　　　　　　　　　**Quantity B**

K　　　　　　　　　　　　　　The greatest root of $x^2 + 9x - 22 = 0$

- Ⓐ　Quantity A is greater.
- Ⓑ　Quantity B is greater.
- Ⓒ　The two quantities are equal.
- Ⓓ　The relationship cannot be determined from the information given.

7. Angela has nickels and dimes in her pocket. She has twice as many dimes as nickels. What is the best expression of the amount of money she has in cents if x equals the number of nickels she has?

- Ⓐ　$25x$
- Ⓑ　$10x + 5(2x)$
- Ⓒ　$x + 2x$
- Ⓓ　$5(3x)$
- Ⓔ　$20(x + 5)$

8.

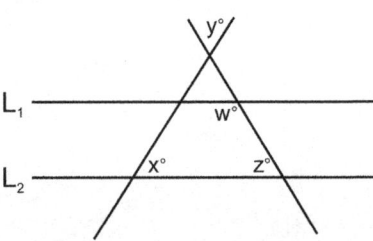

If $L_1 \parallel L_2$, $x = 60°$, and $w = 2z$, then $y + w =$?

- Ⓐ　60°
- Ⓑ　90°
- Ⓒ　120°
- Ⓓ　150°
- Ⓔ　180°

9.

A cylindrical canister has the radius r and the height h. A second cylindrical canister has the same radius r as the first canister, but different height. The surface area of the second canister is twice the surface area of the first canister.

Quantity A	**Quantity B**
The volume of the second canister	The volume of a cone with the same radius r as the first canister, and with a height equal to $6h$

- Ⓐ Quantity A is greater.
- Ⓑ Quantity B is greater.
- Ⓒ The two quantities are equal.
- Ⓓ The relationship cannot be determined from the information given.

10. A reduction of 25% in the price of eggs will enable Peter to buy 4 dozen more for $9.60. What was the original price per dozen?

    $ [   ]

11. What is the area of a square inscribed in a circle whose circumference is 16π?

    - Ⓐ 512
    - Ⓑ 256
    - Ⓒ 128
    - Ⓓ 64
    - Ⓔ 32

12. 6" 2" 10" 2" 5"

    Above are the measures of rainfall for five consecutive days during the winter. For the measure of those five days, which of the following is true?

    I   The median equals the mode.
    II The median equals the arithmetic mean.
    III The range equals the median.

    - Ⓐ I only
    - Ⓑ II only
    - Ⓒ III only
    - Ⓓ I and II only
    - Ⓔ I and III only

Exercise #2   233

13.

Given: $\dfrac{n}{mn} + \dfrac{m}{mn} = \dfrac{p}{p^2+1}$ and $m + n = p^2$

Quantity A   **Quantity B**

$p + p^3$ $mn - 1$

- (A) Quantity A is greater.
- (B) Quantity B is greater.
- (C) The two quantities are equal.
- (D) The relationship cannot be determined from the information given.

Question 14 is based on the following diagram:

Marketing Budget for 1999

14. If the total budget is twice the present, the ratio of expenditure on packaging to trade discounts is most nearly

- (A) 5 : 6
- (B) 1.2 : 1
- (C) 1 : 2
- (D) 6 : 5
- (E) None of these

15.

Two shaded regions are shown below: Which shaded area is larger? Use π = 3.14

Quantity A

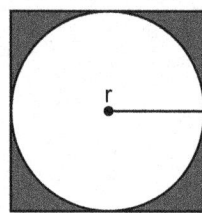

Quantity B

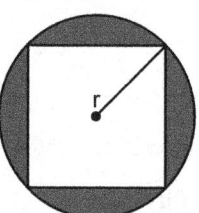

- Ⓐ Quantity A is greater.
- Ⓑ Quantity B is greater.
- Ⓒ The two quantities are equal.
- Ⓓ The relationship cannot be determined from the information given.

Exercise #2   235

Answers and Explanations

1. **Topic: Arithmetic**

    Sub topic: Integers

    The correct answer is (C).

    A perfect cube will have prime factors that are in groups of 3.

    Let us look at the options.

    Option A is 8*m*. 8 is the cube of 2, and *m* is a cube, and so the product will also be a cube.

    Option A is *mn*. m is a cube and n is a cube. Hence, the product *mn* will also be a cube.

    Option C is *mn* + 216. *mn* is a cube and 216 is a cube. However, their sum need not be a cube.

    Option D is – *m*. *m* is a cube and hence - *m* will also be a cube.

    Option E is $(m - n)$. $(m-n)^9 = \left[(m-n)^3\right]^3$. Hence, $(m - n)^9$ will also be a cube.

2. **Topic: Geometry**

    Sub topic: Quadrilaterals

    The correct answer is (A).

    Area of the rectangle = $10 \times 8 = 80 cm^2$

    Area of the square = $6^2 = 36 cm^2$

    The ratio of the area of rectangle: square = 80:36, which reduces to 20:9.

    The correct option is A.

3. **Topic: Geometry**

    Sub topic: Lines & Angles

    The correct answer is (E).

    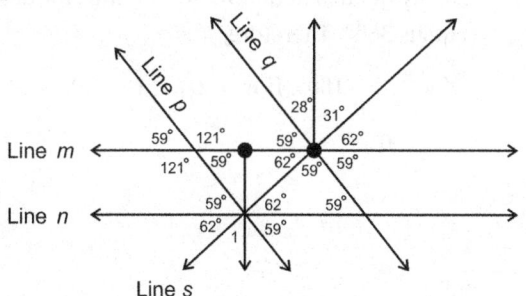

    Find the measure of the angles given in terms of *x* and *y*. The sum of all four angles is 180° and *y* = *x* + 3.

    $(x + y) + x + y + 2x + 6 = 180°$

    $\{x + (x + 3)\} + x + (x + 3) + 2x + 6 = 180°$

    $6x = 168°$

    $x = 28°$

    Now use your knowledge of angle relationships to determine the measure of ∠1. We know the sum of ∠1 and an adjacent angle are 59°, but there is no way to determine the measure of ∠1 with the given information. The answer cannot be determined.

4. **Topic: Arithmetic**

    Sub topic: Percent, Ratio, Rate

    The correct answer is (C).

    The selling price for 1 dozen at 3 for $0.85 is 3 × 4 = 12 = 1 dozen = $0.85 × 4 = $3.40

    Therefore, 6 dozen will yield $3.40 × 6 = $20.40.

    The store's cost for 6 dozen at $1.80 per dozen is $1.80 × 6 = $10.80

    Therefore, the profit on 6 dozen of these items will be $20.40 - $10.80 or $9.60.

5. **Topic: Geometry**

    Sub topic: Geometric Areas

    The correct answers are (C), (D) and (E).

    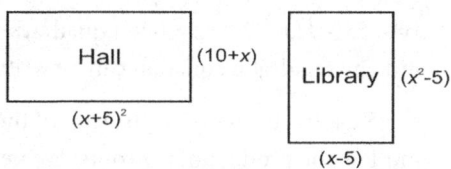

    The hall and the library are shaped like a rectangle.

    The formula for calculating the area of rectangle is: Area = Length × Width

    Area of hall = $(x - 5)^2 \times (10 + x) = (x^2 - 10x + 25)(10 + x)$

$= 10x^2 - 100x + 250 + x^3 - 10x^2 + 25x$

$= x^3 - 75x + 250$

Area of library $= (x - 5) \times (x^2 - 5) = x^3 - 5x^2 - 5x + 25$

Area of hall = Area of library

$x^3 - 75x + 250 = x^3 - 5x^2 - 5x + 25$

$x^3 - x^3 + 5x^2 - 75x - 5x + 250 - 25 = 0$

$5x^2 - 70x + 225 = 0$

$x^2 - 14x + 45 = 0$ ----- (Dividing the equation by 5)

Factor, finding two numbers that add to get −14 and multiply to get 45. The numbers that multiply to get 45 are 1 and 45, 3 and 15, and 5 and 9. To add -14, use −5 and −9. Thus, the factors are $(x - 5)(x - 9) = 0$, so $x - 5 = 0$ and $x - 9 = 0$. Therefore, x could equal 5 or 9.

$x = 5$ is not correct as when we plug it in for the value of length of hall and the library, the length becomes 0, which is not possible.

Only 9 is the correct value.

Hence the area of hall $= (x - 5)^2 \times (10 + x) = (9 - 5)^2 \times (10 + 9) = 4^2 \times 19 = 16 \times 19 = 304 ft^2$

Since area of hall and library are equal, the sum of their areas is equal to $304 + 304 = 608 ft^2$

Options C, D and E are correct.

6. **Topic: Algebra**

   Sub topic: Quadratic Equations

   The correct answer is (A).

   $3x^2 - 5x - k(x - 2) - 2 = 0$ is a quadratic equation, and any quadratic equation can be written as:

   $x^2 + Sx + P = 0$ where S is the sum of the roots and P is the product of the roots. We need to bring it to this form.

   $3x^2 - 5x - k(x - 2) - 2 = 3x^2 - 5x - kx + 2k - 2 = 0$

   If we divide by $3 \rightarrow x^2 - \dfrac{x(5+k)}{3} + \dfrac{2(k-1)}{3} = 0$

We know the sum of the roots is

$3 \rightarrow -\dfrac{5+k}{3} = -3 \rightarrow k = 4$

The quantity on the right is also a quadratic equation that can be factorized into $(x + 11)(x - 2) = 0$

This means x must be either −11 or 2. So the greatest root is 2, which is less than 4.

Hence the quantity on the left is greater, so the correct answer is A.

7. **Topic: Algebra**

   Sub topic: Systems of Equations

   The correct answer is (A).

   The number of nickels that Angela has is x. Therefore, the total value of those nickels (in cents) is 5x. Angela also has twice as many dimes as nickels, or 2x. The total value in cents of those dimes is 2x(10), or 20x. Adding together the value of the nickels and dimes gives $5x + 20x$, or $25x$.

8. **Topic: Geometry**

   Sub topic: Lines & Angles

   The correct answer is (E).

   Since $L_1 \parallel L_2$, the corresponding angles formed on lines L_1 and L_2 are equal.

   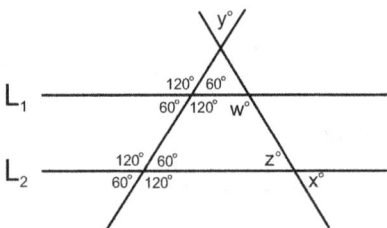

   In any quadrilateral, the sum of interior degrees equals 360°. Therefore,

   $\angle w + \angle z = 180°$. If $w = 2z$, $\angle w = 120°$, and $\angle z = 60°$.

Exercise #2

Therefore,

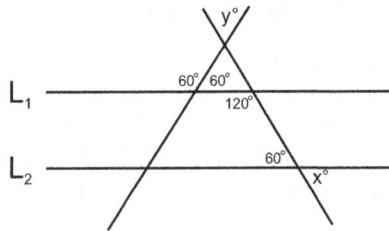

∠y = 60° (since there are 180° in a triangle). So, the sum of y + w = 60° + 120° = 180°.

The correct answer is E.

9. **Topic: Geometry**

   Sub topic: Three-Dimensional Figures

   The correct answer is (A).

   The volume of the first cylindrical canister with radius r and height h is calculated with the formula:

   V = πr²h

   The surface area of the first canister is calculated with: SA = 2πr² + 2πrh

   We are told that the second canister has the same radius r and its area is twice the area of the first canister. Let h_2 be the height of the second canister.

   2πr² + 2πrh₂ = 2 × (2πr² + 2πrh)

   If we divide both sides by 2πr

   r + h₂ = 2r + 2h → h₂ = r + 2h

   We can now substitute h_2 in the formula for calculating the second canister's volume

   Volume of the second canister = πr² (r + 2h)

   The volume of a cone is calculated with the formula: V = πr² $\frac{h}{3}$

   We are told that the cone has the same radius r as the first canister and its height = 6h

   Volume of the cone = πr² $\frac{6h}{3}$ = πr² 2h

   If we compare the volume of the second canister πr²(r + 2h) to the volume of the cone πr² 2h → r + 2h > 2h → the volume of the second canister is greater than the volume of the cone.

Hence the left column is greater than the right column and (A) is the correct answer.

10. **Topic: Arithmetic**

    Sub topic: Percent, Ratio, Rate

    The correct answer is $0.80.

    Let the initial cost of eggs will be $\frac{\$x}{dozen}$

    New price is $\frac{\$0.75x}{dozen}$. In either case Peter spends $9.6 so initially he buys $\frac{\$9.60}{x}$ dozen eggs and now he is able to buy $\frac{\$9.60}{0.75x}$ dozen eggs for the same price, which happens to be 4 dozen more than what he bought initially.

    Expressing the statement mathematically,

    $4 + \frac{\$9.60}{x} = \frac{\$9.60}{0.75x}$

    This gives x = $0.80

11. **Topic: Geometry**

    Sub topic: Area, Perimeter, and Volume

    The correct answer is (C).

    Circumference = πd.

    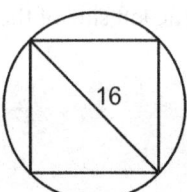

    16π = πd

    d = 16

    Diameter of circle = diagonal of square

    Area of square = $\frac{1}{2}$ (product of diagonals)

    = $\frac{1}{2} d_1 \times d_2$

    = $\frac{1}{2}$(16)(16) = 128

    Therefore, the area of the square is 128.

    Alternate method: assume x for side of square.

Using Pythagorean Theorem for isosceles right triangles gives $x^2 + x^2 = 162$, $2x^2 = 256$, and $x^2 = 128$, which is the area of the square.

12. **Topic: Data Analysis**

    Sub topic: Measures of Center

    The correct answer is (B).

    II only. The arithmetic mean is the average (sum divided by number of items), or $6 + 2 + 10 + 2 + 5 = 25$ divided by $5 = 5$.

    The median is the middle number after the numbers have been ordered: 2, 2, 5, 6, 10.

    The median is 5.

    The mode is the most frequently appearing number: 2.

    The range is the highest minus the lowest, or $10 - 2 = 8$.

    Therefore, only II is true: The median 5 equals the mean 5.

13. **Topic: Algebra**

    Sub topic: Algebraic Expressions

    The correct answer is (A).

    Combine the fractions on the left side of the first equation as follows:

    $\frac{n}{mn} + \frac{m}{mn} = \frac{p}{p^2+1}$

    $\frac{m+n}{mn} = \frac{p}{p^2+1}$

    $\frac{p^2}{mn} = \frac{p}{p^2+1}$

    Cross-multiply.

    $mnp = p^2(p^2+1)$

    Divide each side by p.

    $mn = p(p^2+1)$

    Distribute p over the parentheses.

    $mn = p^3 + p$

    Since $mn = p^3 + p$, then $p^3 + p > mn - 1$. Therefore, (A) is the correct answer.

14. **Topic: Data Analysis**

    Sub topic: Percent, Ratio, Rate

    The correct answer is (A).

    Given the marketing budget above, the ratio of expenditure on trade discounts to packaging is most nearly: $54.6 : 67 = 546 : 670 = 1 : 1.2$ or $5 : 6$.

15. **Topic: Geometry**

    Sub topic: Circles/Quadrilaterals

    The correct answer is (B).

    Let us calculate the area of the shaded region in Quantity A.

    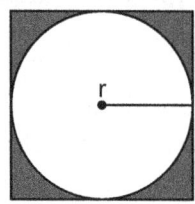

    In Quantity A, a circle of radius r is inscribed in a square.

    From the figure, we can see that the length of the side of the square will be the same as the diameter of the circle.

    That is, side of square = $2r$.

    Area of the shaded region = Area of square - Area of circle

    $= (2r)^2 - \pi r^2$

    $= r^2(4 - \pi)$

    $= 0.86r^2$ ...(i)

    Now let us find the area of the shaded region in the Quantity B.

    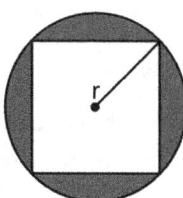

    In Quantity B, a square is inscribed inside a circle of radius r.

    From the figure, we can see that the length of the diagonal of the square will be the same as the diameter of the circle.

Hence, diagonal of square = 2r.

side of square = $\frac{diagonal}{\sqrt{2}}$

$= \frac{2r}{\sqrt{2}}$

$= \sqrt{2}$

Area of the shaded region = Area of circle − Area of square

$= \pi r^2 - \sqrt{2r} \times \sqrt{2r}$

$= \pi r^2 - 2r^2$

$= r^2 (\pi - 2)$

$= 1.14\ r^2 \ldots$(ii)

Comparing the two areas, we can see that Quantity B has the larger area.

This page is intentionally left blank

Chapter 9

Exercise #3

Questions: 12 | Time: 21 minutes

This Exercise includes *12 practice questions*. The questions cover all the question types as explained in Chapter 2 and may fall into any of the following categories - Arithmetic, Algebra, Geometry or Data Analysis. You will find answers and detailed explanations towards the end of this chapter.

1. Given that
   $y = (x^2)^3 - 5^x$. If $x = 4$, then the value of y will be

   ☐

2.
   A team of 3 people take 3 weeks and 2 days to complete a certain job. Every week has 6 working days and each working day is of 8 hours.

Quantity A	**Quantity B**
Number of days required to complete the job if 4 people working for 6 hours each day to complete the job	Number of days required if 5 people work to complete the job. 3 people work 8 hours a day, while 2 others work for 3 hours a day

   Ⓐ Quantity A is greater.
   Ⓑ Quantity B is greater.
   Ⓒ The two quantities are equal.
   Ⓓ The relationship cannot be determined from the information given.

3. If $a > b$, and $ab > 0$, which of the following must be true?

   I $a > 0$

   II $b > 0$

   III $\dfrac{a}{b} > 0$

   (A) I only

   (B) II only

   (C) III only

   (D) I and II only

   (E) I and III only

4.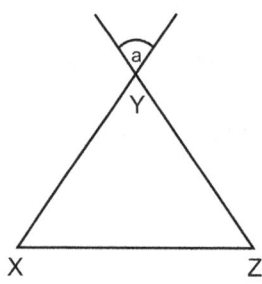

   In $\triangle XYZ$, $XY = 10$, $YZ = 10$, and $\angle a = 84°$. What is the degree measure of $\angle Z$?

   (A) 96°

   (B) 84°

   (C) 48°

   (D) 42°

   (E) 24°

5. Maria plans to make sandwiches for a picnic. She has three types of bread from which to choose (rye, sourdough, and white), four types of meat from which to choose (salami, bologna, ham, and pastrami), and three types of cheese from which to choose (Swiss, cheddar, and jack). If Maria will use only one type of bread, one type of meat, and one type of cheese on each sandwich, how many different kinds of sandwiches can Maria make?

   (A) 3

   (B) 4

   (C) 10

   (D) 17

   (E) 36

Exercise #3

6.

Given: $\dfrac{x^2 + y^3}{x + y} = x + y$ for $x \neq -y$

Quantity A	**Quantity B**
xy	0

- (A) Quantity A is greater.
- (B) Quantity B is greater.
- (C) The two quantities are equal.
- (D) The relationship cannot be determined from the information given.

7.

If a, b, x, and y are all > 1 satisfying $x^{\frac{2}{5}} = a^{-6}$, and $y^{\frac{2}{5}} = b^6$,

Quantity A	**Quantity B**
$(xy)^{\frac{1}{3}}$	$a^4 b^4$

- (A) Quantity A is greater.
- (B) Quantity B is greater.
- (C) The two quantities are equal.
- (D) The relationship cannot be determined from the information given.

8. By what percentage is the average production of wheat less than the average production of rice?

- (A) 62.3
- (B) 71.7
- (C) 41.8
- (D) 38.6
- (E) 52.6

9.

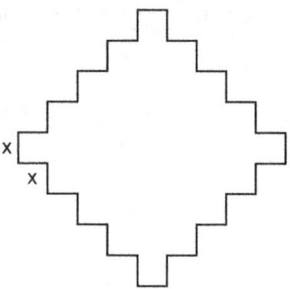

In the figure above, all lines meet at ninety-degree angle, and each segment has a length of x. What is the area of the figure in terms of x?

- (A) $25x$
- (B) $36x$
- (C) $36x^2$
- (D) $41x^2$
- (E) $41x$

10. The average of three numbers is 55. The second is more than twice the first, and the third is 4 less than three times the first. What is the largest number?

- (A) 165
- (B) 88
- (C) 80
- (D) 57
- (E) 28

11.

Inequality 1: $4(x+2) \leq 2(x+5)+14$

Inequality 2: $\sqrt{16-8y+y^2} \leq 9$

Quantity A

x, where x is a solution of Inequality 1

Quantity B

y, where y is a solution of Inequality 2

- (A) Quantity A is greater.
- (B) Quantity B is greater.
- (C) The two quantities are equal.
- (D) The relationship cannot be determined from the information given.

Exercise #3

12. If the diameter of a circle P is 40 percent of the diameter of circle Q, then the area of circle P is what percentage of the area of circle Q?

    (A) 16
    (B) 20
    (C) 40
    (D) 80
    (E) It cannot be determined from the information given.

Answers and Explanations

1. **Topic: Algebra**

   Sub topic: Rules of Exponents

   The correct answer is 3471.

   $y = 4^6 - 5^4 = 4096 - 625 = 3471$

2. **Topic: Arithmetic**

   Sub topic: Time and Work

   The correct answer is (A).

   3 weeks and 2 days works out to 20 days.

   The total work-hours needed to complete the job $= 3 \times 20 \times 6 = 360$

   Quantity A

   When 4 people work for 6 hours each day, they complete 24 work-hours of the job per day.

   To complete 360 work-hours of job, they will take $\frac{360}{24} = 15$ days to complete the job.

   Quantity B

   5 people work to complete the job.

   3 people work 8 hours a day, while 2 others work for 3 hours a day

   The 3-member team completes $3 \times 8 = 24$ work-hours of job in one day.

   The 2-member team completes $2 \times 3 = 6$ work-hours of job in one day.

   Together, the team completes 30 work-hours of job in one day.

   To complete 360 work-hours of job, they will take $\frac{360}{24} = 15$ days to complete the job.

   Hence, Quantity A is greater than Quantity B.

3. **Topic: Algebra**

   Sub topic: Solving Linear Equations and Inequalities

   The correct answer is (C).

   Because a and b must both be positive, or both be negative, choice C is the only answer that must be true.

4. **Topic: Geometry**

   Sub topic: Triangle

   The correct answer is (C).

   Since $XY = YZ = 10$, ΔXYZ is an isosceles triangle and $\angle X = \angle Z$.

   $\angle Y = 84°$ because it forms a vertical angle with the given angle

   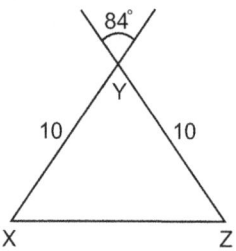

   $\angle X + \angle Y + \angle Z = 180°$

   $\angle X + 84° + \angle Z = 180°$

   $2(\angle Z) + 84° = 180°$

   $2(\angle Z) = 96°$

   $\angle Z = 48°$

   Therefore, the measure of $Z = 48°$

5. **Topic: Data Analysis**

   Sub topic: Counting Methods

   The correct answer is (E).

   Total number of different combinations ("how many different kinds") is found by multiplying the number of ways for each item. Therefore, three different breads times four different meats times three different cheeses $= 3 \times 4 \times 3 = 36$.

6. **Topic: Algebra**

   Sub topic: Equations

   The correct answer is (C).

Exercise #3

Place the expression on the right side over 1 to form a fraction.

$$\frac{x^2 + y^2}{x + y} = \frac{x+y}{1}$$

Having $x \neq -y$, which yields $x + y \neq 0$, set the cross products equal.

$(x^2 + y^2) = (x + y)(x + y)$

Expand the right side using the identity $(a + b)^2 = a^2 + 2ab + b^2$ or the FOIL method.

$x^2 + y^2 = x^2 + y^2 + 2xy$

Subtract $(x^2 + y^2)$ from each side and simplify.

$x^2 + y^2 - (x^2 + y^2) = x^2 + y^2 + 2xy - (x^2 + y^2)$

$x^2 + y^2 - x^2 - y^2 = x^2 + y^2 + 2xy^2 - x^2 - y^2$

$0 = 2xy$

$xy = 0$

Therefore, the correct answer is (C).

7. **Topic: Algebra**

   Sub topic: Exponents

   The correct answer is (A).

   First of all, we need to simply the two equations to get $x(a)$ and $y(b)$.

   In $x^{-\frac{2}{5}} = a^{-6}$, using cross multiplication, we can eliminate the minus signs and get $x^{\frac{2}{5}} = a^6$

   then, $x = a^{6*\left(\frac{5}{2}\right)} = a^{15}$. We also have $y^{\frac{2}{5}} = b^6$,

   $y = b^{6*\left(\frac{5}{2}\right)} = b^{15}$.

   Therefore, $xy = a^{15}b^{15}$, and $(xy)^{\frac{1}{3}} = (a^{15}b^{15})^{\frac{1}{3}}$, which simples to $a^5 b^5$. This is greater than $a^4 b^4$ since all values of a and b are > 1.

8. **Topic: Data Analysis**

   Sub topic: Measures of Center

   The correct answer is (C).

   Average production of wheat

   $= \frac{780 + 795 + 928 + 750 + 978}{5}$

   $= \frac{4231}{5}$

   $= 846.2$

   Average production of rice

   $= \frac{(1125 + 1752 + 1344 + 1404 + 1640)}{5}$

   $= 1453$

   The required percentage $= \frac{1453 - 846.2}{795} \times 100 = 41.8\%$

9. **Topic: Geometry**

   Sub topic: Lines/Quadrilaterals Lines

   The correct answer is (D).

   Breaking the figure into squares of sides x by adding lines gives

   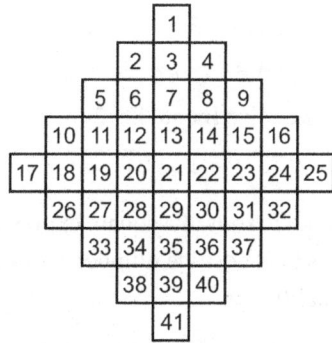

   Remember that each square has area x^2. Then the total area is $41x^2$. Choices A, B, and E are not possible because area must be in square units.

10. **Topic: Arithmetic**

    Sub topic: Averages

    The correct answer is (C).

    Let x = first number, $2x + 1$ = second number, and $3x - 4$ = third number.

    Since the average of the three numbers is 55,

    $\frac{x + (2x+1) + (3x-4)}{3} = 55$

    Multiplying both sides of the equation by 3,

    $x + (2x + 1) + (3x - 4) = 165$

    $6x - 3 = 165$

$6x - 3 + 3 = 165 + 3$

$6x = 168$

$\dfrac{6x}{6} = \dfrac{168}{6}$

$x = \dfrac{168}{6}$

$x = 28 =$ first number

$2x + 1 = 57 =$ second number

$3x - 4 = 80 =$ third number

Therefore, the largest number is 80.

11. **Topic: Algebra**

    Sub topic: Inequalities and Roots

    The correct answer is (D).

    First, we solve Inequality 1:

    $4(x + 2) \leq 2(x + 5) + 14 \rightarrow 4x + 8 \leq 2x + 10 + 14 \rightarrow 2x \leq 16 \rightarrow x \leq 8$

    Then we solve Inequality 2:

    $\sqrt{16 - 8y + y^2} \leq 9 \rightarrow \sqrt{(4-y)^2} \leq 9$

    The square root of a square expression will always be a positive number, so we can write this inequality as:

    $|4 - y| \leq 9 \rightarrow -9 \leq 4 - y \leq 9 \rightarrow -13 \leq -y \leq 5$

    We multiply with (−1) so the inequality sign changes:

    $13 \geq y \geq -5$

Any number equal to, or less than, 8 is a solution of the first inequality, while for the second inequality the solutions are numbers equal to, or greater than, −5 and less than, or equal to, 13.

This means that 13 for instance is a solution for Inequality 2 which is greater than any solution of Inequality 1. However, in another example, 6 is a solution of Inequality 2 which is less than some solutions of Inequality 1 (8 for instance)

The relationship cannot be determined without further information and (D) is the correct answer.

12. **Topic: Geometry**

    Sub topic: Circles

    The correct answer is (A).

    The radius of circle P will also be 40% of the radius of circle Q. Because the area of any circle is πr^2, the radius will be used to compare the area of the two circles. Since

    $40\% = 0.40 = 0.4$

    and $(4)^2 = (0.16) = 16\%$

    Thus, area of circle P will be 16% of the area of circle Q.

Chapter 10

Exercise #4

Questions: 15 | Time: 26 minutes

This Exercise includes *15 practice questions*. The questions cover all the question types as explained in Chapter 2 and may fall into any of the following categories - Arithmetic, Algebra, Geometry or Data Analysis. You will find answers and detailed explanations towards the end of this chapter.

1. Nickels, quarters and dimes are part of a set of twenty-five coins. What is the total value of these set of coins in dollars and cents if, there are three more dimes than quarters and three-times as many dimes as nickels?

    A. $3.65
    B. $3.25
    C. $2.25
    D. $1.65
    E. $1.25

2. At a casino there are three tables. The payoff at the first table is 10: 1; at the second, 30: 1; and at the third, 40: 1. If a woman bets $10 at each table and wins at two of the tables, what is the difference between her maximum and minimum possible gross winnings?

    A. $200
    B. $300
    C. $400
    D. $500
    E. $600

3.

Distance from A to B is 12 *miles*.

Distance from A to C is 10 *miles*.

Quantity A	**Quantity B**
Distance from A to B	Distance from B to C

- (A) Quantity A is greater.
- (B) Quantity B is greater.
- (C) The two quantities are equal.
- (D) The relationship cannot be determined from the information given.

4. If the five vowels are repeated continuously in the pattern *a, e, i, o, u, a, e, i, o, u,* and so on, what vowel will the 327th letter be?

- (A) *a*
- (B) *e*
- (C) *i*
- (D) *o*
- (E) *u*

5. If $5^{x+3} = 3125$, then the value of *x* will be? Write your answer in the answer box.

☐

6. Gasoline varies in cost from $0.96 to $1.12 per gallon. If a car's mileage varies from 16 to 24 miles per gallon, what is the difference between the most and the least that the gasoline for a 480-mile trip will cost?

- (A) $5.12
- (B) $7.04
- (C) $11.52
- (D) $14.40
- (E) $52.80

Exercise #4

7.

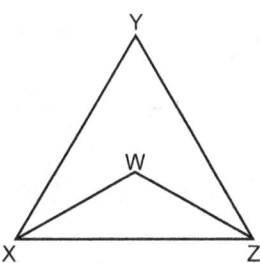

WX and WZ are angle bisectors of the base angles of isosceles ΔXYZ above. If ∠Y = 80°, what is the degree measure of ∠XWZ ?

- Ⓐ 65
- Ⓑ 80
- Ⓒ 100
- Ⓓ 130
- Ⓔ 160

8.

$$n \neq 0$$
$$n \neq -\frac{1}{2}$$
$$n \neq -1$$

Quantity A

$$\frac{1}{1+\dfrac{1}{1+\dfrac{1}{n}}}$$

Quantity B

$$\frac{n+1}{2n+1}$$

- Ⓐ Quantity A is greater.
- Ⓑ Quantity B is greater.
- Ⓒ The two quantities are equal.
- Ⓓ The relationship cannot be determined from the information given.

9.

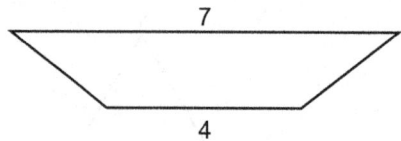

Which of the following could be the area of this trapezoid, if the height is an integer?

Select *all* that apply.

- [A] 11
- [B] 17
- [C] 34
- [D] $\frac{12}{5}$
- [E] $\frac{17}{2}$
- [F] $\frac{11}{2}$
- [G] 33

10. If a book costs $5.70 after 40% discount, what was its original price?

- Ⓐ $2.28
- Ⓑ $6.10
- Ⓒ $7.98
- Ⓓ $9.12
- Ⓔ $9.50

11.

Quantity A

Volume of cube with side 6

Quantity B

Volume of rectangular prism with two dimensions less than 6

- Ⓐ Quantity A is greater.
- Ⓑ Quantity B is greater.
- Ⓒ The two quantities are equal.
- Ⓓ The relationship cannot be determined from the information given.

12.

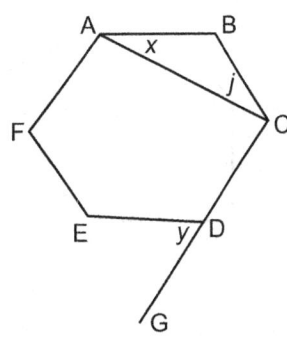

Hexagon ABCDEF is a regular hexagon.

Quantity A	Quantity B
$x + j$	y

- Ⓐ   Quantity A is greater.
- Ⓑ   Quantity B is greater.
- Ⓒ   The two quantities are equal.
- Ⓓ   The relationship cannot be determined from the information given.

13. If x is an integer and $3x + 11$ is even, which of the following must be even?

- Ⓐ x
- Ⓑ $x + 1$
- Ⓒ x^2
- Ⓓ $2x + 1$
- Ⓔ x^3

14.

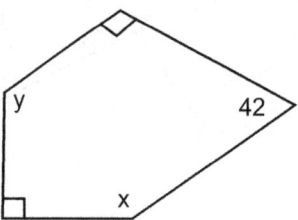

Quantity A	Quantity B
$2x$	$2y$

Ⓐ Quantity A is greater.

Ⓑ Quantity B is greater.

Ⓒ The two quantities are equal.

Ⓓ The relationship cannot be determined from the information given.

Exercise #4

15.

Percentage of candidates enrolled for GRE for various faculty from country X in year 2020

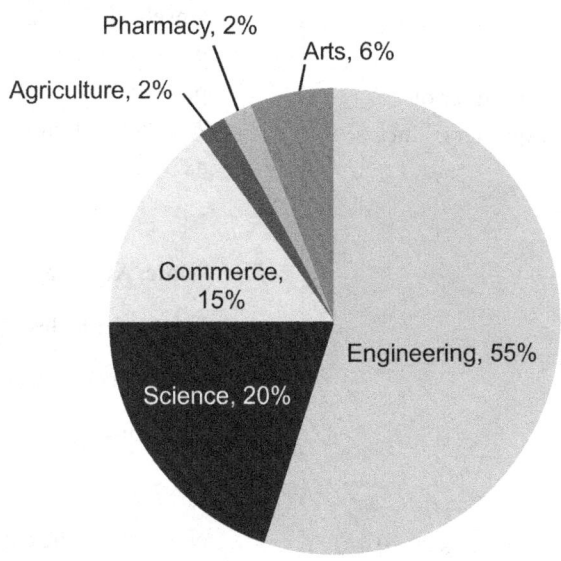

Percentage of candidates who got 300 plus marks in GRE from various faculty from country X in year 2020

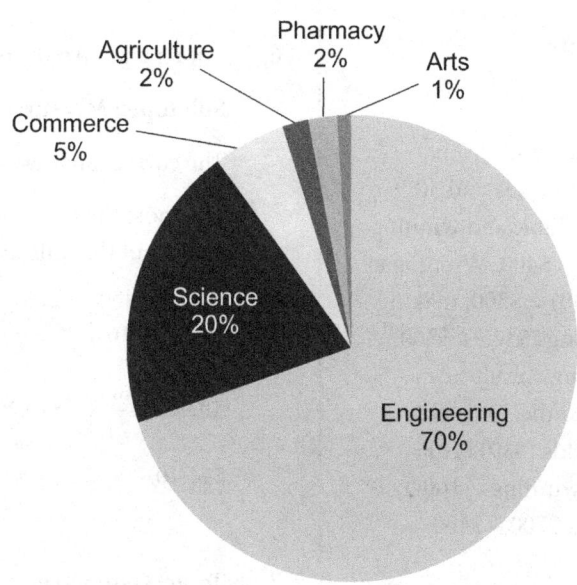

What percent of candidates in the science faculty got over 300 on the GRE?

- Ⓐ 25%
- Ⓑ 30%
- Ⓒ 35%
- Ⓓ 40%
- Ⓔ 45%

Answers and Explanations

1. **Topic: Algebra**

   Sub topic: Systems of Equations

   The correct answer is (A).

   Let n = number of nickels, $3n$ = number of dimes, and $3n - 3$ = number of quarters. Since 25 coins are in the collection,

   $n + 3n + (3n - 3) = 25$

   $7n - 3 = 25$

   $7n = 28$

   $n = 4$ nickels = $0.20

   $3n = 12$ dimes = $1.20

   $3n - 3 = 9$ quarters = $2.25

   Therefore, the total value of collection is $0.20 + $1.20 + $2.25 = $3.65.

2. **Topic: Arithmetic**

   Sub topic: Percent, Ratio, Rate

   The correct answer is (B).

   The maximum winning would result from winning at the tables with 40: 1 odds and 30: 1 odds. Betting $10 at the 40: 1 Table and winning result in a prize of ($10) (40) = $400. Winning at the 30: 1 Table yields ($10) (30) = $300, making the maximum possible winnings $400 + $300 = $700. The minimum winnings result from winnings at the 10: 1 table and the 30: 1 table. Winning at the 10: 1 table yields ($10) (10) = $100, making the minimum winnings $100 + $300 = $400. The difference is $700 – $400 = $300.

3. **Topic: Algebra**

   Sub topic: Relations

   The correct answer is (D).

   Since we know nothing about the placement of A, B, and C, we cannot determine anything about their distances.

4. **Topic: Arithmetic**

   Sub topic: Remainders

   The correct answer is (B).

   Because each letter repeats after every five vowels, divide 327 by 5, and the remainder will determine the vowel in that place of the pattern. Since $327 \div 5 = 65$ with a remainder of 2, indicates that the second vowel (E) will be the 327th letter.

5. **Topic: Algebra**

   Sub topic: Rules of Exponents

   The correct answer is 2.

   First convert 3125 to an exponent with base 5.

   $5^{x+3} = 5^5$

   Now equate the exponents and solve for x

   $x + 3 = 5$

   $x = 2$

6. **Topic: Data Analysis**

   Sub topic: Measures of Spread

   The correct answer is (D).

   The most the trip would cost is when gas costs $1.12 and the mileage is 16mph. Therefore,

   $\$1.12 \times \left(\dfrac{480}{16}\right) = \$33.60$. The least would be

   $\$0.96 \times \left(\dfrac{480}{24}\right) = \$19.20$. The difference is therefore $14.40.

7. **Topic: Geometry**

   Sub topic: Triangles

   The correct answer is (D).

   In isosceles $\triangle XYZ$, $\angle X = \angle Z$.

Exercise #4

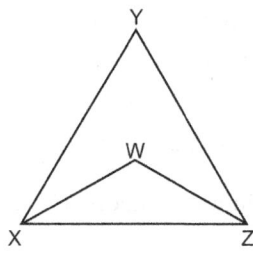

$\angle X + \angle Y + \angle Z = 180°$

$\angle X + 80° + \angle Z = 180°$

$\angle X + \angle Z = 100°$

$\angle X = \angle Z = 50°$

Since WX bisects $\angle$XYZ and WZ bisects $\angle$YZX,

$\angle YXW = \angle WXZ = \angle YZW = \angle WZX = 25°$

Therefore, on $\triangle$XWZ,

$\angle XWZ + \angle WXZ + \angle WZX = 180°$

$\angle XWZ + 25° + 25° = 180°$

$\angle XWZ + 50° = 180°$

$\angle XWZ = 130°$

8. **Topic: Arithmetic**

   Sub topic: Fractions

   The correct answer is (C).

   Simplifying the complex fraction in column A,

   $\dfrac{1}{1+\dfrac{1}{1+\dfrac{1}{n}}} = \dfrac{1}{1+\dfrac{1}{\dfrac{n+1}{n}}} = \dfrac{1}{1+\dfrac{1}{\dfrac{(n+1)}{n}}} = \dfrac{1}{1+\dfrac{n}{n+1}}$

   $= \dfrac{1}{\dfrac{n+1}{2n+1}+\dfrac{n}{n+1}} = \dfrac{1}{\dfrac{n+1+n}{n+1}} = \dfrac{1}{\dfrac{2n+1}{n+1}} = \dfrac{n+1}{2n+1}$

9. **Topic: Geometry**

   Sub topic: Quadrilaterals

   The correct answers are (A), (F) and (G).

   The area is $\dfrac{h(4+7)}{2}$. If h is an integer, then the area must be an integer multiple of $\dfrac{11}{2}$. Answer A would have h = 2, answer F would have h = 1 and answer G would have h = 6.

10. **Topic: Arithmetic**

    Sub topic: Profit and Loss

    The correct answer is (E).

    Let x = original price. Then

    $x - 0.40x = 5.70$

    $0.60x = 5.70$

    $x = 9.50$

    Hence, the book originally cost $9.50.

11. **Topic: Geometry**

    Sub topic: Volumes

    The correct answer is (D).

    Volume of cube with side 6 is $6 \times 6 \times 6 = 216$. Volume of rectangular prism with two dimensions less than 6 is not determinable because the third dimension is needed. Therefore, no comparison can be made.

12. **Topic: Geometry**

    Sub topic: Quadrilaterals

    The correct answer is (C).

    If Hexagon ABCDEF is a regular hexagon, all sides and angles are congruent. First, we need to determine the sum of the interior angles in the hexagon. The sum of the interior angles in a polygon is $(S = (n - 2)180)$

    Number of sides in a Hexagon = 6

    Sum of interior angles = $(6 - 2)180 = 4(180) = 720°$

    The measure of $\angle$B can be calculated by dividing the sum of the interior angles by the total number of angles.

    $\angle B = \dfrac{720°}{6} = 120°$

Now we can calculate the measure of x and j. They are both equal since the sides opposite them are equal.

The degrees in the three angles of a triangle sum to 180°.

$x + j + 120 = 180°$

$x + x + 120 = 180°$

$2x + 120 = 180°$

$2x = 60°$

$x = 30°, j = 30°$

Therefore, Quantity A is 60°.

For Quantity B, the interior angle is 120° just like all interior angles of a regular hexagon. A straight line has an angle measure of 180°. The measure of y is 180 – 120, so y is 60°.

The question can also be evaluated conceptually without calculations by using the knowledge that the interior angles B and D are equal, $x + j$ will be supplementary to B, and y will be supplementary to D. Therefore, $x + j$ must equal y.

Both quantities are 60°; therefore, the answer is C.

13. **Topic: Arithmetic**

    Sub topic: Integers

    The correct answer is (B).

    Since the sum of two odd integers is an even integer, and $3x + 11$ is even, then $3x$ must be odd. Since the product of two odd integers is an odd integer, then x must be an odd integer. Hence $x + 1$ must be an even integer.

14. **Topic: Geometry**

    Sub topic: Quadrilaterals

    The correct answer is (D).

    First, we need to determine the sum of the interior angles in the pentagon. The sum of the interior angles in a polygon is dictated by the following equation. ($S = (n – 2)180°$)

    Number of sides in a Pentagon = 5

    Sum of interior angles = $(5 – 2)180 = 3(180) = 540°$

    We know all interior angles of the polygon should sum to 540°. Now we can find the measure of x and y.

    $x + y + 90 + 90 + 42 = 540°$

    $x + y + 222 = 540°$

    $x + y = 318°$

    We know that the sum of the angles is 318°, but we are unable to calculate the measure of each individual angle. The answer is D, cannot be determined.

15. **Topic: Data Analysis**

    Sub topic: Interpreting data in tables and graphs

    The correct answer is (D).

    Number of candidates enrolled from faculty of science $= 35000 \times \dfrac{20}{100} = 7000$

    Number of candidates got 300 plus from faculty of science $= 14000 \times \dfrac{20}{100} = 2800$

    Percentage of candidates from faculty of science, who got 300 plus out of total number of candidates enrolled from the same faculty $= \dfrac{2800}{7000} \times 100 = 40\%$

Chapter 11

Exercise #5

Questions: 12 | Time: 21 minutes

This Exercise includes *12 practice questions*. The questions cover all the question types as explained in Chapter 2 and may fall into any of the following categories - Arithmetic, Algebra, Geometry or Data Analysis. You will find answers and detailed explanations towards the end of this chapter.

1.

At a store, all shoes are being marked off 30% and all bags are marked off 25%.

Quantity A

Sale price of a pair of shoes that originally cost $80

Quantity B

Sale price of a bag that originally cost $75

- Ⓐ Quantity A is greater.
- Ⓑ Quantity B is greater.
- Ⓒ The two quantities are equal.
- Ⓓ The relationship cannot be determined from the information given.

2.

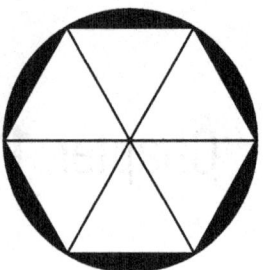

In the figure above, six equilateral triangles with sides of 1 are joined to form a hexagon. A circle is then circumscribed about the hexagon. What is the area of the shaded region?

- (A) $\pi - \dfrac{\sqrt{3}}{2}$
- (B) $\pi - \dfrac{3\sqrt{3}}{2}$
- (C) $\pi - \dfrac{\pi\sqrt{3}}{2}$
- (D) $2\pi - 3\sqrt{3}$
- (E) $2\pi - 3\sqrt{3}$

3. For how many integers' values of x will the value of the expression $3x - 4$ be an integer greater than 4 and less than 250?

- (A) 86
- (B) 85
- (C) 84
- (D) 83
- (E) 82

4. Two uniform dice marked 1 to 6 are tossed together. The probability of the total 7 in a single throw is

- (A) $\dfrac{5}{36}$
- (B) $\dfrac{5}{12}$
- (C) $\dfrac{2}{31}$
- (D) $\dfrac{1}{6}$
- (E) None of these

Exercise #5

5.

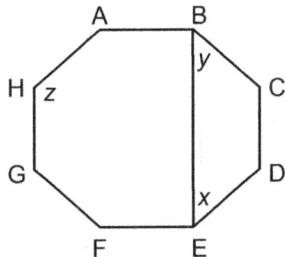

Polygon ABCDEFGH is a regular octagon.

Quantity A	**Quantity B**
$x + y$	$z - y$

- Ⓐ   Quantity A is greater.
- Ⓑ   Quantity B is greater.
- Ⓒ   The two quantities are equal.
- Ⓓ   The relationship cannot be determined from the information given.

6. Dolly's age is 15 years. Pinky is 1/3 years older than Dolly's current age. How many years ago was Pinky twice as old as Dolly was then? Write your answer in the answer box.

7.

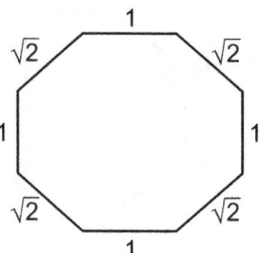

Note: - Figure not drawn to scale.

The sides of an octagon alternate in length. As pictured above, each side with Length 1 is next to a side of length $\sqrt{2}$. What is the area of the octagon?

- Ⓐ 5
- Ⓑ 6
- Ⓒ 7
- Ⓓ 8
- Ⓔ 9

8. What is the area of the square with vertices at the points (0, 2), (0, –2), (2, 0), and (–2, 0)?

- Ⓐ 4
- Ⓑ 6
- Ⓒ 8
- Ⓓ 12
- Ⓔ 6

Exercise #5   263

Questions 9 and 10 are based on the following chart:

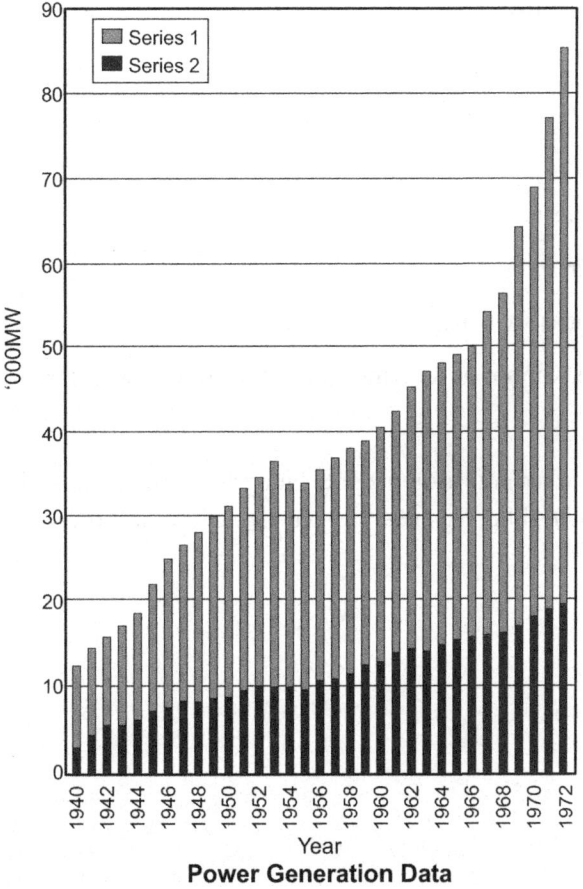

Power Generation Data
Series 1: Hydro   Series 2: Gas

9. In which of the following years was the increase maximum over the previous year in the installed capacity of hydro?

    (A) 1969
    (B) 1960
    (C) 1968
    (D) 1965
    (E) 1944

10. Number of times the installed capacity of gas decreased over the previous year is

    (A) once
    (B) twice
    (C) thrice
    (D) four times
    (E) never

www.vibrantpublishers.com

11.

Quantity A	Quantity B
$(5.32)(0.453) - \dfrac{4.328}{0.5}$	$\dfrac{6.3452}{0.2} - (12.56)(0.45)$

- Ⓐ Quantity A is greater.
- Ⓑ Quantity B is greater.
- Ⓒ The two quantities are equal.
- Ⓓ The relationship cannot be determined from the information given.

12. A cylindrical roller 12 inches long is dipped into blue paint, and then rolled for one complete revolution over a white wall. If the area of the blue region is 48 square inches, what is the radius, in inches, of the roller?

- Ⓐ $\dfrac{2}{\pi}$
- Ⓑ $\dfrac{4}{\pi}$
- Ⓒ 2
- Ⓓ 4
- Ⓔ 2π

Answers and Explanations

1. **Topic: Arithmetic**

   Sub topic: Profit and Loss

   The correct answer is (B).

   We need to determine the price of each item. Shoes are 30% off and bags are 25% off. We need to multiply the original cost by the percent discount written as a decimal. Then subtract that amount from the original price.

   Quantity A: Original Price = $80, discount = 30% = 0.30

   Amount of Discount = $80 × 0.30 = $24

   Price of item = $80 − $24 = $56

   Quantity B Original Price = $75, discount = 25% = 0.25

   Amount of Discount = $75 × 0.25 = $18.75

   Price of item = $75 − $18.75 = $56.25

   The cost of the item in Quantity B is greater; therefore, the answer is B.

2. **Topic: Geometry**

   Sub topic: Quadrilateral

   The correct answer is (B).

   To find the area of the shaded region, simply subtract the area of the hexagon from the area of the circle. The area of the circle = πr^2.

   Since the radius of the circle is 1, its area is $\pi(1)^2 = \pi$. Since you know that the area of the hexagon must be subtracted from the area of the circle or π, you can eliminate choices (D) and (E). The hexagon is composed of six equilateral triangles, so six times the area of one triangle will give you the area of the hexagon. The area of a triangle is one half base times height. The base of each triangle is 1, but you have to solve for the height. Dropping a perpendicular line from the top vertex of a triangle to its base divides it into two triangles. Since the hypotenuse of each is 1 and the other leg of each is $\frac{1}{2}$, it is a 30:60:90 right triangle and the remaining side must be $\frac{\sqrt{3}}{2}$.

   That means the area of one equilateral triangle is

   $$\left(\frac{1}{2} \times 1 \frac{\sqrt{3}}{2}\right) = \frac{\sqrt{3}}{4}$$

   So, the area of the hexagon is $6 \times \frac{\sqrt{3}}{4} = \frac{3\sqrt{3}}{2}$

   Therefore, the area of the shaded region is

   $\pi - \frac{3\sqrt{3}}{2}$, choice (B).

3. **Topic: Arithmetic**

   Sub topic: Integers

   The correct answer is (E).

   For the expression $3x - 4$ to be greater than 4 and less than 250,

   $4 < 3x - 4 < 250$

   Add 4,

   $4 + 4 < 3x - 4 + 4 < 250 + 4$

   $8 < 3x < 254$

   Divide by 3,

   $\frac{8}{3} < \frac{3x}{3} < \frac{254}{3}$

   $\frac{8}{3} < x < \frac{254}{3}$

   Since x is an integer, $x = 3, 4, 5...82, 83, 84$. Hence there are 82 integer values of x.

4. **Topic: Data Analysis**

   Sub topic: Probability

   The correct answer is (D).

   In a single throw with two dice, 7 can be obtained in the following 6 ways:

   (6, 1), (1, 6), (5, 2), (2, 5), (4, 3), (3, 4) and total number of ways = $6^2 = 36$

   Therefore, required probability = $\frac{6}{36} = \frac{1}{6}$

5. **Topic: Geometry**

   Sub topic: Polygons

   The correct answer is (C).

   It is given that the polygon is a regular octagon meaning that all sides and angles of the octagon are congruent. We need to determine the sum of the interior angles in an octagon. ($S = (n - 2)180°$)

   Number of sides in an Octagon = 8

   Sum of interior angles = $(8 - 2)180 = 6(180) = 1080°$

   The measure of one angle in the octagon can be calculated by dividing the sum of the interior angles by the total number of angles.

   Measure of one interior angle = $\frac{1080°}{8} = 135°$

   Therefore, z is 135°.

   Polygon BCDE is an isosceles trapezoid. Therefore, the base angles are congruent.

   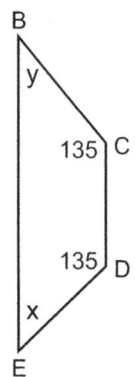

   The sum of the angles in a quadrilateral is 360°.

   $x + y + 135 + 135 = 360°$

   $x + y + 270 = 360°$

   $x + y = 90°$

   $x = 45°$

   $y = 45°$

   Both x and y are congruent, so both are 45°.

   Quantity A: $x + y = 45° + 45° = 90°$

   Quantity B: $z - y = 135° - 45° = 90°$

   Both quantities are 90°.

   Therefore, the answer is (C).

6. **Topic: Algebra**

   Sub topic: Ages

   The correct answer is 10.

   Pinky will now be 20 years old since $\frac{4}{3}$ of 15 is 20.

   10 years ago, Pinky was twice as old as Dolly was since Pinky would have been 10 (20 - 10 = 10) and Dolly would have been 5 (15 - 10 = 5)

7. **Topic: Geometry**

   Sub topic: Polygons

   The correct answer is (C).

   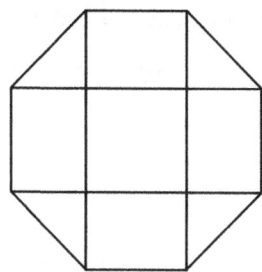

   Divide the octagon into pieces whose areas you can find. Drawing perpendiculars from the top to the bottom and from left to right breaks the figure into 5 squares and 4 right triangles, as shown above. Each of the squares has side length 1, for an area of $1^2 = 1$. Each of the right triangles is equal to half a square (they are isosceles right triangles with legs of length 1) and have an area of $\frac{1}{2}$.

   So, the total area is $5(1) + 4\left(\frac{1}{2}\right)$ = 5 + 2 = 7.

8. **Topic: Geometry**

   Sub topic: Quadrilateral/Triangles

   The correct answer is (C).

   Make a quick sketch of the figure. You can see that each side of the square is also the hypotenuse of a right triangle. Solve for the hypotenuse of one of these triangles, say the one in the first quadrant. Each leg of the triangle falls on one of the axis, so it's easy to see that each has length 2.

Two equal legs make it an isosceles right triangle. And its hypotenuse is equal to a leg times $\sqrt{2} = 2\sqrt{2}$. The area of a square is equal to a side length squared, or $\left(2\sqrt{2}\right)^2 = 8$.

9. **Topic: Data Analysis**

   Sub topic: Interpreting data in tables and graphs

   The correct answer is (A).

   In 1969 installed capacity of hydro increased from 15 thousand MW to 17 thousand MW.

10. **Topic: Data Analysis**

    Sub topic: Interpreting data in tables and graphs

    The correct answer is (B).

    In 1954, decrease of 1 thousand MW and in 1965 decrease of 0.5 thousand MW over the previous year were observed in the installed capacity of gas.

11. **Topic: Arithmetic**

    Sub topic: Numbers

    The correct answer is (B).

    We need to work out the values for Quantity A and Quantity B before we can determine the answer.

Quantity A: $(5.32)(0.453) - \dfrac{4.328}{0.5} = 2.40996 - 8.656 = -6.24604$

Quantity B: $\dfrac{6.3452}{0.2} - (12.56)(0.45) = 31.726 - 5.652 = 26.074$

Quantity B is greater, so B is the answer. This example can be approximated as a quick check to be sure you did not make a calculation error. Quantity A is roughly $(2 - 8)$ or -6. Quantity B is roughly $(30 - 6)$ or 24.

12. **Topic: Geometry**

    Sub topic: Three-Dimensional Figures

    The correct answer is (A).

    Visualize the situation: rolling a cylindrical paint roller on the wall produces a rectangular region of blue paint, with one side of length 12. The length of its other side will be equal to the circumference of the roller. Since the area of the region is 48, the circumference must be $48 \div 12 = 4$. Circumference equals $2\pi r$, where r is the radius. Therefore $2\pi r = 4$, $r = \dfrac{4}{2\pi} = \dfrac{2}{\pi}$.

This page is intentionally left blank

Chapter 12

Exercise #6

Questions: 15 | Time: 26 minutes

This Exercise includes *15 practice questions*. The questions cover all the question types as explained in Chapter 2 and may fall into any of the following categories - Arithmetic, Algebra, Geometry or Data Analysis. You will find answers and detailed explanations towards the end of this chapter.

1. Conglomerate Corp manufactures hubcaps in 3-different factories. How many days would it take to manufacture a million hubcaps if these factories produce hubcaps in the following ratios:

   The first two factories can manufacture a hundred thousand hubcaps in 15 days while the third factory is thirty percent faster.

   (A) 38
   (B) 42
   (C) 44
   (D) 46
   (E) 50

2. If $m^4 + n^4 = 0$, what is the value of $9m - 5n$?

   (A) 9
   (B) 5
   (C) 4
   (D) 0
   (E) −1

3.

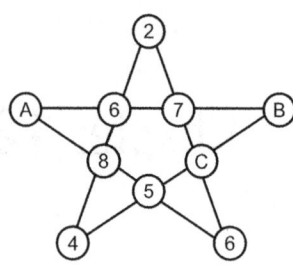

If the sums of four circles along any line segment of the star above are equal, then B =

Ⓐ 3

Ⓑ 4

Ⓒ 6

Ⓓ 7

Ⓔ It cannot be determined from the information given.

4.

Quantity A	**Quantity B**
$\dfrac{1}{3} \div \dfrac{5}{9} + \dfrac{2}{5} \times \dfrac{4}{7}$	$\dfrac{1}{3} \div \dfrac{5}{7} + \dfrac{4}{5} \times \dfrac{4}{7}$

Ⓐ Quantity A is greater.

Ⓑ Quantity B is greater.

Ⓒ The two quantities are equal.

Ⓓ The relationship cannot be determined from the information given.

5.

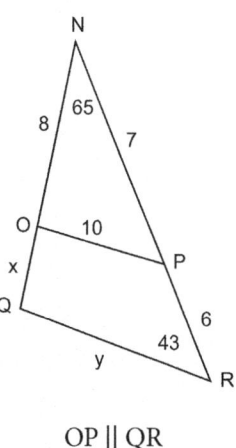

OP ∥ QR

Quantity A	**Quantity B**
Length of QR	Length of NQ

- Ⓐ Quantity A is greater.
- Ⓑ Quantity B is greater.
- Ⓒ The two quantities are equal.
- Ⓓ The relationship cannot be determined from the information given.

6. Tickets numbered from 1 through 50 are placed in a container, and one ticket will be selected at random. What is the probability that the ticket selected will have a number on it divisible by 3?

- Ⓐ $\dfrac{1}{5}$
- Ⓑ $\dfrac{1}{5}$
- Ⓒ $\dfrac{3}{10}$
- Ⓓ $\dfrac{8}{25}$
- Ⓔ $\dfrac{1}{3}$

7. Which of the following statements must be true?

   Select *all* that apply.

   I. If n^2 is even, then n^3 is even.

   II. If $2n$ is even, then n is odd.

   III. If n is even, then $2n - 1$ is odd.

   A. I only
   B. II only
   C. III only
   D. I and II only
   E. I and III only
   F. I II and III

8. In a certain examination 60% of the students passed in Mathematics, 74% passed in English and 18% failed in both English and Mathematics. If 416 students passed in both these subjects, then what will be the total number of students who took the exam?

   A. 740
   B. 770
   C. 800
   D. 820
   E. 840

9. In a class of 83 students, 72 are present. What percentage of the student is absent? Provide answer up to two significant digits in the answer box.

   [ ]

10.

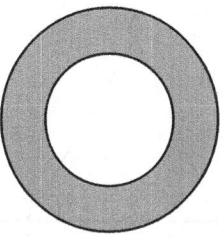

The radius of the inner circle is *r*, and the distance from the inner circle to the outer circle is also *r*.

Quantity A

The area of the unshaded portion

Quantity B

The area of the shaded portion

- Ⓐ   Quantity A is greater.
- Ⓑ   Quantity B is greater.
- Ⓒ   The two quantities are equal.
- Ⓓ   The relationship cannot be determined from the information given.

11.

$$x = 4, y = 20, z = -5$$

Quantity A

$z^{-3} + 2(xy)$

Quantity B

$(xy)^2 \div y - z$

- Ⓐ   Quantity A is greater.
- Ⓑ   Quantity B is greater.
- Ⓒ   The two quantities are equal.
- Ⓓ   The relationship cannot be determined from the information given.

12.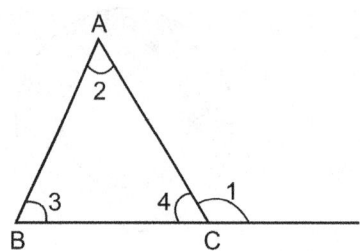

If ABC is a triangle, the measure of angle 1 is 124°, and the measure of angle 2 is 46°, then what is the measure of angle 3?

- Ⓐ 46°
- Ⓑ 56°
- Ⓒ 78°
- Ⓓ 124°
- Ⓔ 132°

13. Emma had some oranges, by adding $\frac{5}{3}$ of these the total became 80. How many oranges Emma had before?

- Ⓐ 40
- Ⓑ 30
- Ⓒ 35
- Ⓓ 25
- Ⓔ 20

14. Which of the following statements are false?

   Select all that apply.

   - A $[7 - (5 + 4)^2 \div 3] + 10 = -10$
   - B $6^2 + [18 \div 2 \times 3 - 7] = 32$
   - C $(4 - 1)^2 + [(9 - 4)(7 - 10) - 6] = -12$
   - D $[9 \div 3^2 - 4]^2 + 10 = 35$
   - E $2^3 \times 5^2 \div 10 - 6^2 = -16$
   - F $(4^2 + 5) + [4 \times 6 \div 3 - 3^2]^5 = -21$

15.

A six-sided number cube is rolled two times.

Quantity A

The probability of rolling a number greater than 1 on the first roll and a prime number on the second roll

Quantity B

The probability of rolling an even number on the first roll and a factor of six on the second roll

- Ⓐ Quantity A is greater.
- Ⓑ Quantity B is greater.
- Ⓒ The two quantities are equal.
- Ⓓ The relationship cannot be determined from the information given.

Answers and Explanations

1. **Topic: Arithmetic**

   Sub topic: Percent, Ratio, Rate

   The correct answer is (D).

   First, calculate the rates of production per day. Two of the factories each make 100,000/15 ≅ 6667 hubcaps per day. The third plant makes 1.3 × 6667 ≅ 8667 hubcaps per day. The total production rate is 8667 + 2(6667) = 22,001 hubcaps per day. At that rare, it would take 45.5 days to produce a million hubcaps.

2. **Topic: Arithmetic**

   Sub topic: Exponents and Roots

   The correct answer is (D).

   For any numbers m and n, $m^4 \geq 0$ and $n^4 \geq 0$.

   Since $m^4 + n^4 = 0$, then both $m = 0$ and $n = 0$. Therefore $9m - 5n = (9)(0) - 5(0) = 0$.

3. **Topic: Algebra**

   Sub topic: Integers

   The correct answer is (C).

   The full line of the numbers on the star shows you that:

   Each group of four circles must sum to 2 + 6 + 8 + 4, or 20.

   Therefore, A + 8 + 5 + 6 = 20 and A = 1. Therefore, 1 + 6 + 7 + B = 20

   Hence B = 6.

4. **Topic: Arithmetic**

   Sub topic: Order of Operations

   The correct answer is (B).

   Evaluate each expression for Quantity A and Quantity B to determine the answer. We are adding, subtracting, multiplying, and dividing fractions.

   - Add/Subtracting Fractions: Get a common denominator for both fractions, combine the numerators, and simplify the fraction.

   - Multiplying Fractions: Multiply straight across the numerator and denominator to obtain your answer.

   - Dividing Fractions: Keep the first fraction. Change the division to multiplication and take the reciprocal of the second fraction. Simplify.

   Quantity A: $\frac{1}{3} \div \frac{5}{9} + \frac{2}{5} \times \frac{4}{7} = \frac{1}{3} \times \frac{9}{5} + \frac{2}{5} \times \frac{4}{7} =$

   $\frac{9}{15} + \frac{8}{35} = \frac{63}{105} + \frac{24}{105} = \frac{87}{105}$

   Lowest common denominator is 105.

   Quantity B: $\frac{1}{3} \div \frac{5}{7} + \frac{4}{5} \times \frac{4}{7} = \frac{1}{3} \times \frac{7}{5} + \frac{4}{5} \times \frac{4}{7} =$

   $\frac{7}{15} + \frac{16}{35} = \frac{49}{105} + \frac{48}{105} = \frac{97}{105}$

   Lowest common denominator is 105.

   Both answers have the same denominator, but the numerator is greater in quantity B, hence the answer is B.

5. **Topic: Geometry**

   Sub topic: Congruent and Similar Figures

   The correct answer is (A).

   Because OP ∥ QR, we know ΔNQR ~ ΔNOP. Therefore, we can conclude the following segments are proportional.

   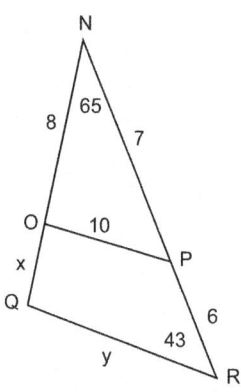

Exercise #6

$$\frac{NQ}{NO} = \frac{QR}{OP} = \frac{NR}{NP}$$

$$\frac{8+x}{8} = \frac{y}{10} = \frac{7+6}{7}$$

$$\frac{8+x}{8} = \frac{y}{10} = \frac{13}{7}$$

To solve the following proportions, we should have two different equations that we can solve using cross multiplication.

6. **Topic: Arithmetic**

   Sub topic: Sequences of Numbers

   The correct answer is (D).

   In the set of numbers from 1 to 50 inclusive, there are 16 numbers divisible by 3: 3, 6, 9... 48. Therefore, the probability that a ticket selected will have a number divisible by 3 is $\frac{16}{50} = \frac{8}{25}$

7. **Topic: Arithmetic**

   Sub topic: Integers

   The correct answer is (E).

   Let's evaluate each statement separately.

   Statement I must be true: Raising an even number to a power will always result in an even number. Eliminate choices (B) and (C) since they do not include statement I.

   Statement II isn't always true: If $2n = 8$, $n = 4$. Since this statement isn't always true, eliminate choice (D).

   Statement III must be true: 2n will always result in an even number (whether n is odd or even) and when you subtract 1 from any even number, the result will always be an odd number.

   Therefore, choice (E) is correct.

8. **Topic: Algebra**

   Sub topic: Set Theory

   The correct answer is (C).

   Assume total number of students be 100.

   Failed in Mathematics = 100 – 60 = 40

   Failed in English = 100 – 74 = 26

   Failed in both subjects = 18

   Failed students in any of the subjects = 40 + 26 – 18 = 48

   Students who pass in both the subjects = 52

   If 52 passed, then total number of students = 100

   If 416 passed, then total number of students = $\left(\frac{100}{52}\right) \times 416 = 800$

9. **Topic: Arithmetic**

   Sub topic: Percent, Ratio, Rate

   The correct answer is 13.

   Absent students = 83 – 72 = 11

   Percentage of the absent students = $\left(\frac{11}{83}\right) \times 100 = 13.25$

   Reducing up to two significant digits it will be 13.

10. **Topic: Geometry**

    Sub topic: Area, Perimeter, and Volume

    The correct answer is (B).

    The unshaded area is πr^2.

    The area of the shaded portion is $\pi(2r)^2 - \pi r^2 = 4\pi r^2 - \pi r^2 = 3\pi r^2$

11. **Topic: Arithmetic**

    Sub topic: Order of Operations

    The correct answer is (A).

    Substitute the values of x, y, and z into both expressions, simplify and compare.

    Quantity A:

    $z^{-3} + 2(xy)$

    $= (-5)^{-3} + 2(4)(20)$

    $= -125 + 160$

    $= 35$

Quantity B:

$(xy)^2 \div y - z$

$= [(4)(5)]^2 \div 20 - (-5)$

$= [20]^2 \div 20 - (-5)$

$= 400 \div 20 - (-5)$

$= 20 - (-5)$

$= 25$

Quantity A is greater than Quantity B.

12. **Topic: Geometry**

    Sub topic: Triangles/Lines & Angles

    The correct answer is (C).

    Angle 1 and $\angle ACB$ are supplementary angles then $\angle ACB$ will be $180° - 124° = 56°$.

    As sum of all three angle of a triangle is 180° then angle 3 will be $180° - (56° + 46°) = 78°$.

13. **Topic: Arithmetic**

    Sub topic: Divisibility

    The correct answer is (B).

    Suppose the number of oranges Emma had before = x

    Then according to the condition,

    $x + 5\frac{x}{3} = 80$

    $3x + 5x = 240$

    $x = 30$

14. **Topic: Arithmetic**

    Sub topic: Order of Operations

    The correct answers are (B), (C) and (E).

    To evaluate using order of operations, we need to use PEMDAS.

    P: Parenthesis

    E: Exponents

M/D: Multiplication and Division done from Left to Right.

A/S: Addition and Subtraction done from left to right.

Evaluate each expression to determine which statement is false.

A. $[7 - (5 + 4)^2 \div 3] + 10 = -10$

   $[7 - (5 + 4)^2 \div 3] + 10$

   $= [7 - (9)^2 \div 3] + 10$

   $= [7 - 81 \div 3] + 10$

   $= [7 - 27] + 10$

   $= -20 + 10$

   $= -10$

B. $6^2 + [18 \div 2 \cdot 3 - 2] = 32$

   $6^2 + [18 \div 2 \cdot 3 - 7]$

   $= 36 + [18 \div 2 \cdot 3 - 7]$

   $= 36 + [9 \cdot 3 - 7]$

   $= 36 + [27 - 7]$

   $= 36 + [20]$

   $= 56$

C. $(4 - 1)^2 + [(9 - 4)(7 - 10) - 6] = -12$

   $(4 - 1)^2 + [(9 - 4)(7 - 10) - 6]$

   $= (3)^2 + [(5)(-3) - 6]$

   $= 9 + [-15 - 6]$

   $= 9 + [-21]$

   $= -12$

D. $[9 \div 3^2 - 4]^2 + 10 = 35$

   $[9 \div 3^2 - 4]^2 + 10$

   $= [9 \div 9 - 4]^2 + 10$

   $= [1 - 4]^2 + 10$

   $= [-3]^2 + 10$

   $= 9 + 10$

   $= 19$

Exercise #6

E. $2^3 \cdot 5^2 \div 10 - 6^2 = -16$

$2^3 \cdot 5^2 \div 10 - 6^2$

$= 8 \cdot 25 \div 10 - 36$

$= 200 \div 10 - 36$

$= 20 - 36$

$= -16$

F. $(4^2 + 5)[4.6 \div 3 - 3^2]^5 = -21$

$(4^2 + 5)[4.6 \div 3 - 3^2]^5$

$= (16 + 5)[4 \cdot 6 \div 3 - 9]^5$

$= (21)[24 \div 3 - 9]^5$

$= (21)[8 - 9]^5$

$= 21[--1]^5$

$= 21[-1]$

$= -21$

15. **Topic: Data Analysis**

Sub topic: Elementary Probability

The correct answer is (A).

The probability of two independent events occurring is equal to the product of the individual event probabilities.

Quantity A:

Rolling a # > 1: 2, 3, 4, 5, 6 or $\frac{5}{6}$

Rolling a prime #: 2, 3, 5 or $\frac{3}{6}$. One is neither prime nor composite.

Quantity B:

Rolling an even number: 2, 4, 6 or $\frac{3}{6}$

Rolling a factor of six: 1, 2, 3, 5 or $\frac{4}{6}$

Without multiplying you can see that Quantity A, $\frac{15}{36}$, is greater than Quantity B, $\frac{12}{36}$.

The quantity of A is greater than the quantity of B.

This page is intentionally left blank

Chapter 13

Exercise #7

Questions: 12 | Time: 21 minutes

This Exercise includes *12 practice questions*. The questions cover all the question types as explained in Chapter 2 and may fall into any of the following categories - Arithmetic, Algebra, Geometry or Data Analysis. You will find answers and detailed explanations towards the end of this chapter.

1.

$$x \leq -1, y \geq 1, 2 < z \leq 4$$

Quantity A	**Quantity B**
$xy - z$	$xz + y$

   Ⓐ   Quantity A is greater.
   Ⓑ   Quantity B is greater.
   Ⓒ   The two quantities are equal.
   Ⓓ   The relationship cannot be determined from the information given.

2.

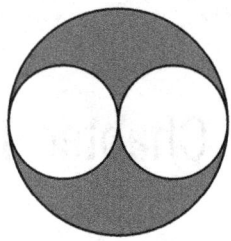

R is the radius of the large circle, and r the radius of the smaller circles.

Quantity A	**Quantity B**
The area of the unshaded portion	The area of the shaded portion

- Ⓐ Quantity A is greater.
- Ⓑ Quantity B is greater.
- Ⓒ The two quantities are equal.
- Ⓓ The relationship cannot be determined from the information given.

3.

Quantity A	**Quantity B**
300	26% of 960

- Ⓐ Quantity A is greater.
- Ⓑ Quantity B is greater.
- Ⓒ The two quantities are equal.
- Ⓓ The relationship cannot be determined from the information given.

4. Length of a rectangle is 3cm less than the double of its width. If perimeter of the rectangle is 96cm then what will be its width and length?

- Ⓐ 16cm & 29cm
- Ⓑ 15cm & 27cm
- Ⓒ 14cm & 25cm
- Ⓓ 13cm & 23cm
- Ⓔ 17cm & 31cm

Exercise #7

5. If $8^x = 128^3$, what will the value of x be?

    (A) $\frac{7}{3}$

    (B) $\frac{5}{3}$

    (C) 5

    (D) 7

    (E) 21

6. Which month will it be after 132 weeks of September?

    (Assume 4 weeks = 1 month)

    (A) June

    (B) August

    (C) September

    (D) October

    (E) November

7. If Kelly received $\frac{1}{3}$ more votes than Mike in a student election, which of the following could have been the total number of votes cast for the two candidates?

    Select all that apply.

    [A] 12

    [B] 14

    [C] 3

    [D] 21

    [E] 8

    [F] 7

    [G] 2

    [H] 4

    [I] 16

    [J] 10

8.

a, *b* and *c* are consecutive even integers.

Quantity A   **Quantity B**

$a + b + c$ $3a + 6$

Ⓐ Quantity A is greater.

Ⓑ Quantity B is greater.

Ⓒ The two quantities are equal.

Ⓓ The relationship cannot be determined from the information given.

9.

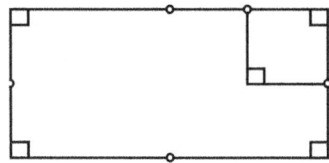

Length of the rectangle is twice as its width, and the measure of one side of the square is one half as the width of the rectangle. The perimeter of the square is 8.

Quantity A   **Quantity B**

Area of Rectangle   32

Ⓐ Quantity A is greater.

Ⓑ Quantity B is greater.

Ⓒ The two quantities are equal.

Ⓓ The relationship cannot be determined from the information given.

Exercise #7

Questions 10 and 11 are based on the following chart:

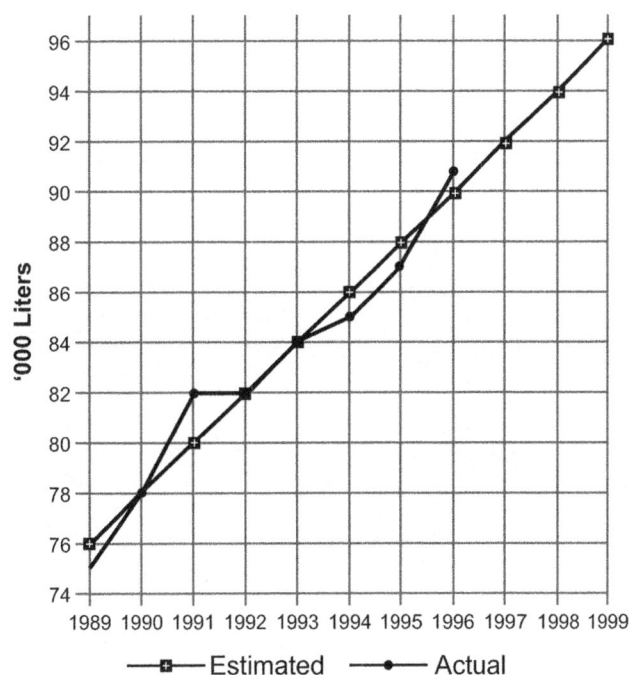

10. The average of the actual values is most nearly (in '000 liters)

    (A) 83

    (B) 85

    (B) 79

    (D) 80

    (E) 81

11. The ratio of the range of actual value to the range of trend value is

    (A) 8 : 7

    (B) 7 : 8

    (C) 7 : 9

    (D) 4 : 5

    (E) 5 : 4

12. Of the total number of days in a week, what fraction of them occurs only 52 times in a leap year?

   Ⓐ $\frac{1}{7}$

   Ⓑ $\frac{2}{7}$

   Ⓒ $\frac{3}{7}$

   Ⓓ $\frac{4}{7}$

   Ⓔ $\frac{5}{7}$

Exercise #7 287

Answers and Explanations

1. **Topic: Arithmetic**

   Sub topic: Numbers

   The correct answer is (D).

   Based on the above conditions, x is less than or equal to -1, so x is always a negative number. y is greater than or equal to 1, so y is always positive. z can be any positive number between 2 and 4.

   Quantity A: $xy - z = (-)(+) - (+) = (-) - (+) = -$

   Quantity A will always be negative.

   Quantity B: $xz + y = (-)(+) + (+) = (-) + (+)$

   This quantity can either be positive or negative depending on the value of x times y and z. We cannot determine which quantity is greater, xy or z. Therefore, we don't know whether the resulting number is negative or positive. The answer is D and cannot be determined based on the information given.

2. **Topic: Geometry**

   Sub topic: Circles

   The correct answer is (C).

   The two smaller circles are the same size, and so each has a diameter equal to R, and so a radius $= \frac{R}{2}$. The combined area of the two smaller circles is $2\pi \left(\frac{R}{2}\right)^2 = \frac{\pi R^2}{2}$.

   The area of the large circle is πR^2, so the shaded portion has area $\pi R^2 - \frac{\pi R^2}{2} = \frac{\pi R^2}{2}$. The answer is C.

3. **Topic: Arithmetic**

   Sub topic: Percentage

   The correct answer is (A).

   Without using the calculator, we can quickly determine 26% of 960 by diving by four to obtain 25% and adding 1% or 9.6.

   Quantity A:

   300

   Quantity B:

   $960 \div 4 = 240$; $240 + 9.6 = 249.6$

   Quantity A is greater than Quantity B.

4. **Topic: Geometry**

   Sub topic: Polygons

   The correct answer is (E).

   Let width $= x$

   Then length $= 2x - 3$

   Perimeter $= 2(x + 2x - 3) = 6x - 6$

   According to the condition

   $6x - 6 = 96$

   $x = 17$cm

   width $= 17$cm and length $= 31$cm

5. **Topic: Arithmetic**

   Sub topic: Exponents and Roots

   The correct answer is (D).

   To solve, first convert $8^x = 2^{3x}$. Next, convert $128^3 = 2^{7 \times 3} = 2^{21}$

   Now relate the two exponents and solve for x.

   $3x = 21$

   $x = 7$

6. **Topic: Arithmetic**

   Sub topic: Divisibility

   The correct answer is (A).

   $\frac{132}{4} = 33$ months

   $\frac{33}{12} = 2$ years and 9 months

   9 months later from September will be June.

7. **Topic: Algebra**

   Sub topic: Applications

   The correct answers are (B), (D), and (F).

   Let M be the number of votes cast for Mike. Then Kelly received $M + \left(\frac{1}{3}\right)M$, or $\left(\frac{4}{3}\right)M$ votes. The total number of votes cast was therefore "votes for Mike" + "votes for Kelly" or $M + \left(\frac{4}{3}\right)M = \frac{7M}{3}$.

   Because M is number of votes, it cannot be a fraction – specifically, not a fraction with a 7 in the denominator. Therefore, the 7 in the expression $\frac{7M}{3}$ cannot be cancelled out. As a result, the total number of votes cast must be a multiple of 7. Among these answer choices, the multiples of 7 are (B) 14, (D) 21 and (F) 7.

8. **Topic: Arithmetic**

   Sub topic: Integers

   The correct answer is (C).

   The values of a, b, and c differ by 2 as they are consecutive even integers. Let $a = a$, $b = a + 2$, $c = a + 4$.

   Now substitute these variables into Quantity A, simplify, and compare.

   Quantity A:

   $a + b + c$

   $a + (a + 2) + (a + 4)$

   $3a + 6$

   Quantity B:

   $3a + 6$

   The quantity of A is equivalent to Quantity B.

9. **Topic: Geometry**

   Sub topic: Quadrilaterals

   The correct answer is (C).

   Use the following notation in solution process:

   m = Length of the rectangle

   n = Width of the rectangle

   a = Side of the square

   P = Perimeter of the square

   Q = Perimeter of the rectangle

   Translate the given facts in the same order listed above.

   (1) $m = 2n$

   (2) $n = 2a$

   (3) $P = 8$

   Also, using the formulas of perimeters of square and rectangle, we have

   (4) $P = 4a = 2(2a)$

   (5) $Q = 2(m + n)$

   Replace (2) and (3) in (4)

   (6) $8 = 2n$

   Divide each side by 4.

   (7) $n = 4$

   Apply (7) in (1) and simplify.

   $m = 2(4) = 8$

   Having measures of a length and a width of the rectangle, calculate its area.

   $A_{rectangle} = mn = (4)(8) = 32$

   The two quantities are equal.

10. **Topic: Data Analysis**

    Sub topic: Measures of Center

    The correct answer is (A).

    Total of eight actual values = (75 + 78 + 82 + 82 + 84 + 85 + 87 + 91) = 664. Average = $\frac{664}{3}$ = 83.

11. **Topic: Data Analysis**

    Sub topic: Measures of Spread

    The correct answer is (A).

Exercise #7

The range of actual values = 91 − 75 = 16. The range of trend values = 90 − 76 = 14. Ratio = 8 : 7

12. **Topic: Arithmetic**

    Sub topic: Divisibility

    The correct answer is (E).

    There are 366 days in a leap year. $\frac{366}{52} = 7$, with a remainder of 2. Therefore, 2 of the 7 days in the week occur 53 times in a leap year, and the remaining 5 occur 52 times, so choice (E) is correct.

This page is intentionally left blank

Chapter **14**

Exercise #8

Questions: 15 | Time: 26 minutes

This Exercise includes *15 practice questions*. The questions cover all the question types as explained in Chapter 2 and may fall into any of the following categories - Arithmetic, Algebra, Geometry or Data Analysis. You will find answers and detailed explanations towards the end of this chapter.

Questions 1 and 2 are based on the following data:

1.   What is the average number of watches sold in the specialty store per day?

   Ⓐ   327

   Ⓑ   331

   Ⓒ   329

   Ⓓ   298

   Ⓔ   281

2. The ratio of percentage increase in sales on Wednesday and percentage increase in sales on Saturday over average sales is

   (A) 1 : 1
   (B) 17 : 13
   (C) 13 : 15
   (D) 21 : 17
   (E) 17 : 15

3. Which of the following ordered pairs (*a*, *b*) is NOT a member of the solution set of $2a - 3b = 6$?

   (A) (6, 2)
   (B) (−3, −4)
   (C) (3, 0)
   (D) $\left(4, \frac{2}{3}\right)$
   (E) (0, 2)

4. A circle has the same area as a square with side of length $\frac{1}{\pi}$. What is the diameter of the circle?

   (A) $\frac{1}{\sqrt{\pi}}$
   (B) $\frac{2}{\sqrt{\pi}}$
   (C) $\frac{1}{\pi\sqrt{\pi}}$
   (D) $\frac{1}{\pi\sqrt{\pi}}$
   (E) $\frac{1}{\pi^3}$

5. There are between 60 and 70 eggs in a basket. If they are counted out 3 at a time there are 2 left over, but if they are counted out 4 at a time there is 1 left over. How many eggs are in the basket?

   (A) 61
   (B) 62
   (C) 65
   (D) 68
   (E) 69

Exercise #8

6.

Quantity A	Quantity B
$\dfrac{x^7 \times y^{\frac{3}{4}}}{y^{-4} \times \left(x^{\frac{2}{3}}\right)^3 \times y^6}$	$\dfrac{(y^8)^{\frac{1}{2}} \times x^{\frac{1}{4}} \times y^{\frac{3}{4}}}{y^6 \times x^{-\frac{3}{4}} \times x^{-6}}$

- Ⓐ Quantity A is greater.
- Ⓑ Quantity B is greater.
- Ⓒ The two quantities are equal.
- Ⓓ The relationship cannot be determined from the information given.

7.

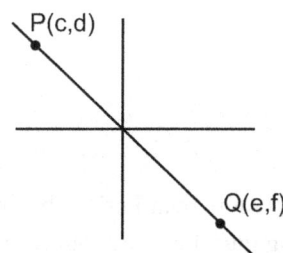

Quantity A	Quantity B
c	d

- Ⓐ Quantity A is greater.
- Ⓑ Quantity B is greater.
- Ⓒ The two quantities are equal.
- Ⓓ The relationship cannot be determined from the information given.

8.

The point (a, b) is on the x-axis

Quantity A
a

Quantity B
b

- Ⓐ Quantity A is greater.
- Ⓑ Quantity B is greater.
- Ⓒ The two quantities are equal.
- Ⓓ The relationship cannot be determined from the information given.

9. In a fraction of two positive numbers if we subtract 1 from both numerator and denominator the fraction reduces to $\frac{4}{3}$ and if we add 1 in numerator and denominator then it reduces to $\frac{9}{7}$. Write the original fraction in the answer box.

☐
☐

10. Ed and Lori go shopping. Ed spends $30 more than Lori in the first store and Lori spends $12 less than Ed in the second store. Which of the following must be true about Lori's total spending in the two stores compared to Ed's?

- Ⓐ Lori spent $\frac{2}{5}$ less than Ed.
- Ⓑ Lori spent $18 less than Ed.
- Ⓒ Lori spent $21 less than Ed.
- Ⓓ Lori spent $42 less than Ed.
- Ⓔ Lori spent $42 more than Ed.

11. Pam makes pies and jam pints with strawberries. This year, Pam had s grams of strawberries, of which she utilized 40% to make pies and the rest for jam pints. Each pie needs p grams of strawberries while each jam pint needs j grams. Choose the following option that gives the total jam pints Pam can make?

    (A) $\dfrac{2s}{5p}$

    (B) $\dfrac{2s}{5j}$

    (C) $\dfrac{3s}{5j}$

    (D) $\dfrac{3p}{5s}$

    (E) $\dfrac{3sj}{5}$

12. A pair of dice is rolled. If the two numbers appearing on the dice are different, what is the probability that the sum of them is at most 4?

    (A) $\dfrac{2}{15}$

    (B) $\dfrac{13}{15}$

    (C) $\dfrac{14}{15}$

    (D) $\dfrac{1}{6}$

    (E) $\dfrac{1}{15}$

13.

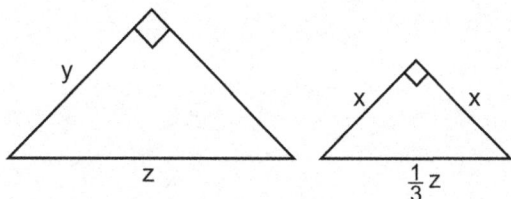

Note: Figure not drawn to scale.

In the figures above, what is the value of y in terms of x?

(A) $\sqrt{2}x$ (approximately 1.41x)

(B) 2x

(C) $2\sqrt{2}x$ (approximately 2.83x)

(D) 3x

(E) $3\sqrt{2}x$ (approximately 4.24x)

14.

An apartment building has 5 floors, one of which has only 2 apartments. Each of the other floors have 4 apartments.

Quantity A	**Quantity B**
3 times the number of floors in the building	The number of apartments in the building

- (A) Quantity A is greater.
- (B) Quantity B is greater.
- (C) The two quantities are equal.
- (D) The relationship cannot be determined from the information given.

15. Sarah's weight is 25 pounds more than that of Tony. If together they weigh 205 pounds, what will be the weight of Sarah and Tony approximately in kilograms?

    Assume 1 pound = 0.4535 kilograms

    Select all that apply.

    - [A] 41
    - [B] 48
    - [C] 50
    - [D] 52
    - [E] 56
    - [F] 45

Answers and Explanations

1. **Topic: Data Analysis**

   Sub topic: Measures of Center

   The correct answer is (A).

   Total number of watches sold over the week

   = 220 + 323 + 385 + 356 + 310 + 370

   = 1964

   Average sales per day = $\dfrac{1964}{\text{No. of days}} = \dfrac{1964}{6} =$ 327

   Please note that one must not take the number of days as 7 as clearly Sunday seems to be a holiday in this case.

2. **Topic: Data Analysis**

   Sub topic: Measures of Spread

   The correct answer is (B).

   Percentage increase on Wednesday over average sales = $\dfrac{385 - 327}{327} \times 100$

   = 17.7%

   Percentage increase on Saturday over average sales = $\dfrac{370 - 327}{327} \times 100$

   = 13.15%

   The ratio = 17.7 : 13.15 ≅ 17 : 13

3. **Topic: Algebra**

   Sub topic: Graphs of Functions, Equations, and Inequalities

   The correct answer is (E).

   In the ordered pair (0, 2), $a = 0$ and $b = 2$. For $2a - 3b$,

   $2(0) - 3(2) = 0 - 6 = -6 \neq 6$

   Therefore, the ordered pair (0, 2) is not a member of the solution sets of $2a - 3b = 6$.

4. **Topic: Geometry**

   Sub topic: Area, Perimeter, and Volume

   The correct answer is (D).

   The formulas to use in this problem are:

   Divide both sides by π^3.

   Area of a square = s^2

   Area of a circle = πr^2

   Diameter = $2r$

   Area of square of side $\left(\dfrac{1}{\pi}\right) = \left(\dfrac{1}{\pi}\right)^2 = \dfrac{1}{\pi^2}$

   We want to find radius of circle whose area equals $\dfrac{1}{\pi^2}$

   Substitute πr^2 for the area of the circle.

   Area of circle = Area of square

   $\pi r^2 = \dfrac{1}{\pi^2}$ Solve for r. Multiply both side by π^2

   $\pi r^2 (\pi r^2) = \pi^2 \left(\dfrac{1}{\pi^2}\right) = \pi^3 r^2 = 1$

   $r^2 = \dfrac{1}{\pi^3}$

   $\sqrt{r^2} = \sqrt{\dfrac{1}{\pi^3}}$ Take square root on both the sides

   $r = \dfrac{\sqrt{1}}{\sqrt{\pi^3}} = \dfrac{1}{\sqrt{\pi^2 \cdot \pi}} = \dfrac{1}{\pi\sqrt{\pi}}$ Simplify the radical

   $d = 2r; \; d = \dfrac{2}{\pi\sqrt{\pi}}$

   The answer is (D).

5. **Topic: Arithmetic**

   Sub topic: Divisibility

   The correct answer is (C).

   The integers between 60 and 70 that have a remainder of 2 when divided by 3 can be found as follows:

   61 ÷ 3 = 20 R1

   62 ÷ 3 = 20 R2

   63 ÷ 3 = 21 R0

64 ÷ 3 = 21 R1

65 ÷ 3 = 21 R2

66 ÷ 3 = 22 R0

67 ÷ 3 = 22 R1

68 ÷ 3 = 22 R2

69 ÷ 3 = 23 R0

Notice that remainders for a divisor of 3 can only be 0, 1, or 2.

So, when 4 is the divisor, the remainders can only be 0, 1, 2, or 3.

60 ÷ 4 = 15 R0

61 ÷ 4 = 15 R1

62 ÷ 4 = 15 R2

63 ÷ 4 = 15 R3

64 ÷ 4 = 16 R0

65 ÷ 4 = 16 R1

65 satisfies both conditions.

The answer is (C).

6. **Topic: Arithmetic**

   Sub topic: Exponents and Roots

   The correct answer is (C).

   Simplify both expressions and compare. When exponents with like bases are multiplied, the powers are added. When exponents with like bases are divided, the powers are subtracted. When exponents are raised to power, the powers are multiplied.

   Quantity A:

   $$\frac{x^7 \times y^{\frac{3}{4}}}{y^{-4} \times \left(x^{\frac{2}{3}}\right)^3 \times y^6}$$

   $$= \frac{x^7 \times y^{\frac{3}{4}}}{y^{-4} \times x^2 \times y^6}$$

   $$= \frac{x^7 \times y^{\frac{3}{4}}}{x^2 \times y^2}$$

   $$= x^5 \times y^{-1\frac{1}{4}}$$

   Quantity B:

   $$\frac{\left(y^8\right)^{\frac{1}{2}} \times x^{\frac{1}{4}} \times y^{\frac{3}{4}}}{y^6 \times x^{-\frac{3}{4}} \times x^{-4}}$$

   $$= \frac{y^4 \times x^{\frac{1}{4}} \times y^{\frac{3}{4}}}{y^6 \times x^{-\frac{3}{4}} \times x^{-4}}$$

   $$= \frac{y^{4\frac{3}{4}} \times x^{\frac{1}{4}}}{y^6 \times x^{-4\frac{3}{4}}}$$

   $$= y^{-1\frac{1}{4}} \times x^5 = x^5 \times y^{-1\frac{1}{4}}$$

   Quantity A is equal to Quantity B.

7. **Topic: Geometry**

   Sub topic: Coordinate Geometry

   The correct answer is (B).

   Since d is above X-axis, it must be positive, and c, being to the left of the Y-axis, must be negative.

   Therefore, $c < d$ because all negatives are less than all positive.

8. **Topic: Arithmetic**

   Sub topic: Number Line

   The correct answer is (D).

   The fact the point $(α, b)$ is on the x–axis implies that $b = 0$. It says nothing about $α$.

   Since $α$ could be either positive or negative, the relationship between $α$ and b cannot be determined.

9. **Topic: Algebra**

   Sub topic: Algebra Exercises

   The correct answer is $\frac{17}{13}$.

   Let the numerator be x and the denominator be y.

According to the first condition $\dfrac{x-1}{y-1}=\dfrac{4}{3}$

Solving for x

$x=\dfrac{4y-1}{3}$

According to the second condition $\dfrac{x+1}{y+1}=\dfrac{9}{7}$

Solving it

$7x + 7 = 9y + 9$

Substituting the value of x in this

$7\left(\dfrac{4y-1}{3}\right)+7=9y+9$

Solve for y

$y = 13$,

Substitute back into $x=\dfrac{4y-1}{3}$ and solve for x

$x=\dfrac{4(13)-1}{3}$

$x = 17$

This gives an original fraction of 17/13.

10. **Topic: Arithmetic**

    Sub topic: Estimation

    The correct answer is (D).

    Let the amount Lori spends in each store be x. Ed spends $30 more than Lori does in the first store, or $x + 30$. In the second store, Lori spends $12 less than Ed does, so Ed spends $x + 12$. Therefore, Lori spends a total of $2x$ while Ed spends $2x + 42$, making choice (D) correct.

11. **Topic: Arithmetic**

    Sub topic: Integers

    The correct answer is (C).

    To determine how many pints of jam Pam can make, simply divide the amount of berries set aside for jam by the number of grams required for each pint. If she uses 40 percent of the strawberries for pies, that means she has 60 percent or $\dfrac{3}{5}s$ to use for jam. Each pint requires j grams: $\dfrac{3}{5}s \div j = \dfrac{3s}{5j}$

12. **Topic: Data Analysis**

    Sub topic: Elementary Probability

    The correct answer is (A).

    Two dice are rolled and the number appearing on the dice are different. Consider the events P and Q such that,

    S = The numbers appearing on the dice which are different.

    Q = The sum of the numbers appearing on the dice which is at most 4.

    S = (1, 2), (1, 3), (1, 4), (1, 5), (1, 6),

    (2, 1), (2, 3), (2, 4), (2, 5), (2, 6),

    (3, 1), (3, 2), (3, 4), (3, 5), (3, 6),

    (4, 1), (4, 2), (4, 3), (4, 5), (4, 6),

    (5, 1), (5, 2), (5, 3), (5, 4), (5, 6),

    (6, 1), (6, 2), (6, 3), (6, 4), (6, 5),

    $n(S) = 30$

    Since the sum of the numbers is at most 4, the sum can be 2, 3 or 4.

    Q = (1, 1), (1, 2), (2, 1), (1, 3), (1, 3), (2, 2)

    Out of these we will consider the cases when the numbers on the dice are different. So, the favorable outcomes are:

    (1, 2), (2, 1), (1, 3), (3, 1)

    Or, $n(E) = 4$

    So, the required probability is $P=\dfrac{n(E)}{n(S)}=\dfrac{4}{30}=\dfrac{2}{15}$

13. **Topic: Geometry**

    Sub topic: Triangles

    The correct answer is (D).

    Both figures are isosceles right triangles, so they are similar. Corresponding lengths of figures are proportional. Since the ratio of the hypotenuses z and $\dfrac{1}{3}z$ is 3:1, the ratio of the legs must also be

3:3. Therefore, leg y of the larger triangles must be 3 times as great as leg x of the smaller triangle, and $y = 3x$.

14. **Topic: Data Analysis**

    Sub topic: Estimation

    The correct answer is (B).

    This question is really not so much a matter of mathematics as just common sense. Indeed, you can probably solve it easily just by counting on your fingers (or multiplying and adding). First, Quantity A must be 15 since $5 \times 3 = 15$. As for Quantity B, since there is 1 floor with 2 apartments and 4 floors with 4 apartments, the total number of apartments in the building is 18. So, Quantity B is greater.

15. **Topic: Arithmetic**

    Sub topic: Divisibility

    The correct answers are (A) and (D).

    If we subtract 25 pounds from total 205, then in remaining 180 pounds, their weights are equal. So, weight of Sarah will be 90 + 25 = 115 pounds.

    In kilograms it will be $115 \times 0.4535 = 52.15$kg, it comes to approximately 52 kg.

    Weight of Tony will be 205 − 115 = 90 pounds = $90 \times 0.4535 = 41$kg.

Chapter 15

Exercise #9

Questions: 12 | Time: 21 minutes

This Exercise includes *12 practice questions*. The questions cover all the question types as explained in Chapter 2 and may fall into any of the following categories - Arithmetic, Algebra, Geometry or Data Analysis. You will find answers and detailed explanations towards the end of this chapter.

1. Lara, Olivia, and Emma divide $620 among themselves. Lara receives $\frac{2}{3}$ of the amount that Olivia gets and Olivia receives $\frac{2}{5}$ of the amount that Emma gets. So, what will be the approximate amount that Lara receives?

   $

2.

   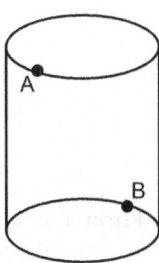

   A cylinder with a height of 5 units and radius of 2 units is showing above. Determine the longest possible distance (straight-line) between points A and B, assuming point A lies on the circumference of the top of the cylinder and point B lies on the circumference of the bottom of the cylinder.

   Ⓐ 3
   Ⓑ 5
   Ⓒ 7
   Ⓓ $\sqrt{29}$
   Ⓔ $\sqrt{41}$

3. The average (arithmetic mean) of six numbers is 16. If five of the numbers are 15, 37, 16, 9, and 23, what is the sixth number?

    (A) −20
    (B) −4
    (C) 0
    (D) 6
    (E) 16

4.

Quantity A	Quantity B
The number of cents in $8n$ dimes	The number of cents in $5n$ quarters

   (A) Quantity A is greater.
   (B) Quantity B is greater.
   (C) The two quantities are equal.
   (D) The relationship cannot be determined from the information given.

5.

$$x < y$$

Quantity A	Quantity B
$(x - y)^2$	$x^2 - y^2$

   (A) Quantity A is greater.
   (B) Quantity B is greater.
   (C) The two quantities are equal.
   (D) The relationship cannot be determined from the information given.

6.

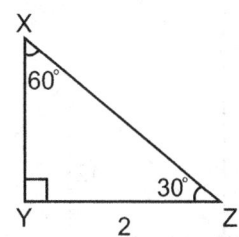

Note: Figure not drawn to scale

Quantity A	Quantity B
XY	$3\sqrt{2}$

- Ⓐ Quantity A is greater.
- Ⓑ Quantity B is greater.
- Ⓒ The two quantities are equal.
- Ⓓ The relationship cannot be determined from the information given.

7. The average (arithmetic mean) of five numbers is 8. If the average of two of these numbers is –6, what is the sum of the other three numbers?

- Ⓐ 28
- Ⓑ 34
- Ⓒ 46
- Ⓓ 52
- Ⓔ 60

8.

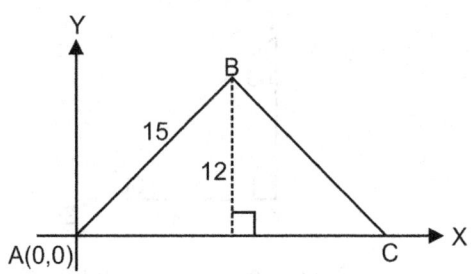

In the figure above, side AB of △ABC contains which of the following points

- Ⓐ (3, 2)
- Ⓑ (3, 5)
- Ⓒ (4, 6)
- Ⓓ (4, 10)
- Ⓔ (6, 8)

9. Win : loss ratio of a basketball team is 3:1. After they won 6-straight games, the ratio changed to 5:1. How many games did the team win before it won the 6-straight games?

- Ⓐ 3
- Ⓑ 6
- Ⓒ 9
- Ⓓ 15
- Ⓔ 24

Exercise #9

Questions 10 and 11 are based on the following chart:

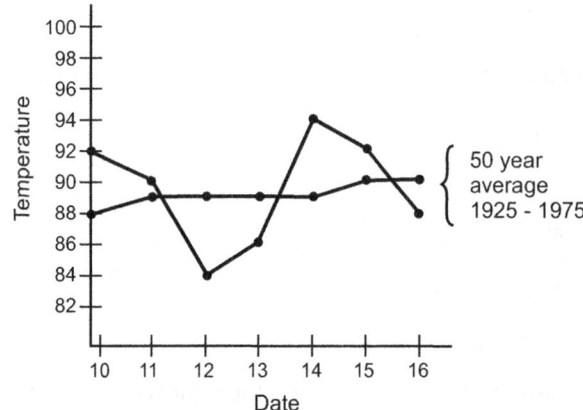

10. What was the percent increase in the maximum temperature from July 12 to July 14, 1979?

    (A) 10
    (B) 10.6
    (C) 11.9
    (D) 84
    (E) 94

11. According to the graph, the average maximum temperature in Los Angeles for the week of July 10 to 16, 1979, was

    (A) much less than the 50-year average for 1925-1975.
    (B) approximately equal to the 50-year average for 1925-1975.
    (C) much greater than the 50-year average for 1925-1975.
    (D) greater than any individual maximum reading for all dates given.
    (E) less than any individual maximum reading for all dates given.

12.

a, b, and c are positive integers

$(b+c)^a = 81$

$a \neq b \neq c$

Quantity A	Quantity B
a	$b + c$

- Ⓐ Quantity A is greater.
- Ⓑ Quantity B is greater.
- Ⓒ The two quantities are equal.
- Ⓓ The relationship cannot be determined from the information given.

Exercise #9

Answers and Explanations

1. **Topic: Algebra**

   Sub topic: Relations

   The correct answer is $85.5.

   Let Emma get x then

   Olivia will get $\frac{2x}{3}$

   and Lara will get $\frac{4x}{15}$

   According to the condition

   $\frac{4x}{15} + \frac{2x}{3} + x = 620$

   $x = 320.7$

   Share of Lara will be $85.5

2. **Topic: Geometry**

   Sub topic: Three Dimensional Figures

   The correct answer is (E).

   Sketch in length AB. Drop a perpendicular from A down to the bottom circumference of the cylinder and call this point C. Then connect C to B and you have right triangle. The height of this triangle is AC, which is the height of the cylinder or 5. The base of this triangle is CB, which is the diameter of the cylinder. Since the radius of the cylinder is 2, its diameter is 4. To solve for AB, use the Pythagorean Theorem:

   $5^2 + 4^2 = AB^2$

   $41 = AB^2$

   $\sqrt{41} = AB$

3. **Topic: Data Analysis**

   Sub topic: Measures of Center

   The correct answer is (B).

   Average × Number of terms = Sum of terms

   $16 \times 6 = 15 + 37 + 16 + 9 + 23 + x$

   $96 = 100 + x$

   $-4 = x$

4. **Topic: Algebra**

   Sub topic: Estimation

   The correct answer is (A).

   Since there are 10 cents in each dime, the number of cents in $8n$ dimes is $10(8n) = 80$. Since there are 25 cents in each quarter, the number of cents in $3n$ quarters is $25(3n) = 75n$.

   Hence, the number of cents in $8n$ dimes is greater than the number of cents in $3n$ quarters. Or you can disregard the n, since it is the same positive number on each side. Thus, you are actually comparing 80¢ in Quantity A and 75¢ in Quantity B.

5. **Topic: Algebra**

   Sub topic: Exponents and Roots

   The correct answer is (D).

   Substituting $x = 0$ and $y = 1$,

   $(x - y)^2 \,[?]\, x^2 - y^2$

   $(0 - 1)^2 \,[?]\, (0)^2 - (1)^2$

   Then $1 > -1$

   Now, Substituting $x = -1$ and $y = 0$

   $(-1 - 0)^2 \,[?]\, (-1)^2 - (0)^2$

   $(-1)^2 \,[?]\, (-1)^2$

   Then $1 = 1$

   Since different values give different comparisons, no comparison can be made.

6. **Topic: Geometry**

   Sub topic: Triangles

   The correct answer is (B).

   The ratio of the sides of 30°–60°–90° triangle is 1, 2, $\sqrt{3}$, and since the side opposite 30° is 2, the side opposite 90° is 4. Compare each quantity by squaring the number outside and multiply by the numbers under radical.

   $2\sqrt{3} \,[?]\, 3\sqrt{2}$

$\sqrt{3.4}\;\boxed{?}\;\sqrt{2.9}$

$\sqrt{12} > \sqrt{18}$

7. **Topic: Data Analysis**

   Sub topic: Measures of Center

   The correct answer is (D).

   Average × Number of terms = Sum of terms

   The sum of all five numbers is $8 \times 5 = 40$

   The sum of two of these numbers is $(-6) \times 2 = -12$

   So, the difference of these two sums, $40 - (-12) = 52$, is the sum of the other numbers.

8. **Topic: Geometry**

   Sub topic: Triangles

   The correct answer is (E).

   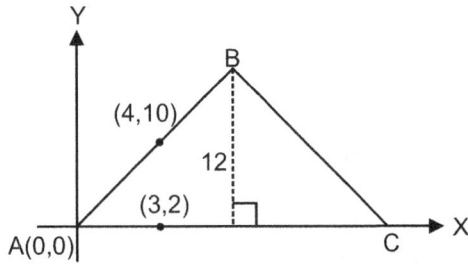

   To solve this problem, you need to figure out the ratio between the *x* and *y* values in line segment AB. If you look at the figure, AB is the hypotenuse of a right triangle with a side of 12. Without even using the Pythagorean Theorem, you can tell that this triangle is one of the favorite right triangles: a 3: 4: 5. So this has to be a 9: 12: 15 triangle, and the coordinates of point B are (9, 12). All the points on line segment AB are in a ratio of 9 and 12 (which is the same as 3 to 4). The only answer with that ratio is E(6, 8).

9. **Topic: Arithmetic**

   Sub topic: Percent, Ratio, Rate

   The correct answer is (B).

   And yet again the slow way to solve a word problem like this is to set up equations.

   Letting *w* and *l* represent the number of wins and losses respectively, the slow method of setting up equations would yield the following:

   $$\frac{w}{l} = \frac{3}{1}$$

   $$\frac{w+6}{l} = \frac{5}{1}$$

   Faster way to solve the problem:

	Before		After	
	Wins	Losses	Wins	Losses
1.	3			
2.	6			
3.	9	3(3 : 1)	15	3(5 : 1)
4.	15			
5.	24			

   Bingo! We found the answer on the first try! If C didn't work, we'd move up or down depending on whether the result was too small or too big.

10. **Topic: Data Analysis**

    Sub topic: Interpreting data in tables and graphs

    The correct answer is (C).

    The increase was $94 - 84 = 10$. The percent increase is found by dividing the increase from the original amount. Thus,

    $$\frac{10}{84} = 11.9\%$$

11. **Topic: Data Analysis**

    Sub topic: Measures of Spread

    The correct answer is (B).

    The maximum temperature for July 10 to 16, 1979, were 92, 90, 84, 86, 94, 92, and 88. These averages to just under 90°. The 50-year average is also just under 90°.

12. **Topic: Arithmetic**

    Sub topic: Integers

    The correct answer is (D).

    There are only two ways for a positive integer to a positive power to equal 81 : 9^2 or 3^4. Thus, $(b + c)^a$ could be, say, $(3 + 6)^2$ or it could be $(1 + 2)^4$. In the first case $b + c$ is greater than a. But in the second instance, $b + c$ is less than a. Therefore, the answer is D.

This page is intentionally left blank

Chapter **16**

Exercise #10

Questions: 15 | **Time: 26 minutes**

This Exercise includes *15 practice questions*. The questions cover all the question types as explained in Chapter 2 and may fall into any of the following categories - Arithmetic, Algebra, Geometry or Data Analysis. You will find answers and detailed explanations towards the end of this chapter.

1.

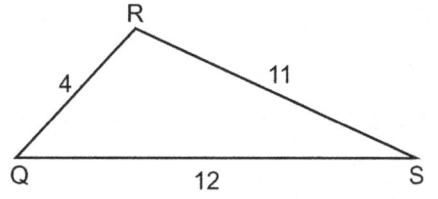

Quantity A

The area of ΔQRS

Quantity B

The perimeter of ΔQRS

- Ⓐ   Quantity A is greater.
- Ⓑ   Quantity B is greater.
- Ⓒ   The two quantities are equal.
- Ⓓ   The relationship cannot be determined from the information given.

www.vibrantpublishers.com

2.

Set A: {2, –1, 7, –4, 11, 3}

Set B: {10, 5, –3, 4, 7, –8}

Quantity A

The median of set A

Quantity B

The average (arithmetic mean) of Set B

- Ⓐ Quantity A is greater.
- Ⓑ Quantity B is greater.
- Ⓒ The two quantities are equal.
- Ⓓ The relationship cannot be determined from the information given.

3.

$$\begin{array}{r} R \\ +S \\ +T \\ \hline 1W \end{array}$$

In the addition problem above, R, S, and T are different digits that are multiples of 3, and W is a digit.

Quantity A

W

Quantity B

8

- Ⓐ Quantity A is greater.
- Ⓑ Quantity B is greater.
- Ⓒ The two quantities are equal.
- Ⓓ The relationship cannot be determined from the information given.

4. $\frac{1}{4}$ boys and $\frac{1}{6}$ girls play soccer at the Union High School, The ratio of boys : girls is 2 : 1. Calculate the fraction of students playing soccer.

- Ⓐ $\frac{1}{24}$
- Ⓑ $\frac{5}{24}$
- Ⓒ $\frac{2}{9}$
- Ⓓ $\frac{1}{3}$
- Ⓔ $\frac{5}{12}$

Exercise #10

5. A fair coin is tossed 100 times. The probability of getting tails an odd number of times is

   (A) $\frac{1}{2}$

   (B) $\frac{1}{8}$

   (C) $\frac{3}{8}$

   (D) $\frac{1}{33}$

   (E) $\frac{3}{4}$

6. In $\triangle MNP$, $\angle M$ is 65° and $\angle P$ is 40°. Q is a point on side MP such that $NQ \perp MP$. Of the following line segments, which one is the shortest?

   (A) MN

   (B) NP

   (C) PQ

   (D) NQ

   (E) MQ

7. Given that $\dfrac{\{(x+y)(x-y)+y^2\}}{8} = 2$, what are the possible values of x?

   Select *all* that apply.

   [A] −8

   [B] −6

   [C] −4

   [D] −2

   [E] 0

   [F] 2

   [G] 4

   [H] 6

   [I] 8

8.

Quantity A	Quantity B
$\dfrac{\sqrt{897(x^2)^3}}{x^{-1}}$	$30(x^6)^{\frac{1}{3}}x^5$

Ⓐ Quantity A is greater.

Ⓑ Quantity B is greater.

Ⓒ The two quantities are equal.

Ⓓ The relationship cannot be determined from the information given.

9.

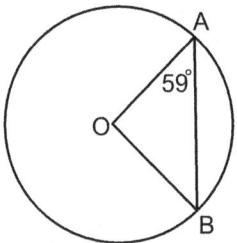

Note: - Figure not drawn to scale.

A and B are points on the circle with center O.

Quantity A	Quantity B
OA	AB

Ⓐ Quantity A is greater.

Ⓑ Quantity B is greater.

Ⓒ The two quantities are equal.

Ⓓ The relationship cannot be determined from the information given.

10.

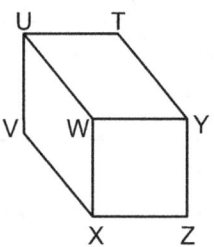

Note: Figure not drawn to scale

Each dimension of the rectangular solid above is an even number. The area of face TUWY is 20, and the area of face WXZY is 8

Quantity A

Total surface area of the rectangular solid

Quantity B

Volume of the rectangular solid

- Ⓐ Quantity A is greater.
- Ⓑ Quantity B is greater.
- Ⓒ The two quantities are equal.
- Ⓓ The relationship cannot be determined from the information given.

11. Tom is t years old, which is 3 times Becky's age. In terms of *t*, after how many years Tom will be just twice as old as Becky?

- Ⓐ $\dfrac{t}{3}$
- Ⓑ $\dfrac{t}{2}$
- Ⓒ $\dfrac{2t}{2}$
- Ⓓ t
- Ⓔ $\dfrac{3t}{2}$

12.

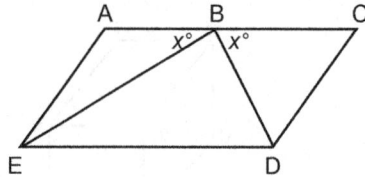

Note: Figure not drawn to scale.

In the figure above, AC ∥ ED. If the length of BD = 3, what is the length of BE?

- Ⓐ 3
- Ⓑ 4
- Ⓒ 5
- Ⓓ $3\sqrt{3}$
- Ⓔ It cannot be determined from the information given.

13. A magician can double the number of coins given to her in 1 minute. I give her a certain number of coins and after an hour she has a box full of coins. When was the box $\frac{1}{4}$ filled?

- Ⓐ 15 min
- Ⓑ 30 min
- Ⓒ 58 min
- Ⓓ 45 min
- Ⓔ 35 min

14. A coin was flipped 20 times and came up heads 10 times. If the first and last flips were both heads, what is the greatest number of consecutive heads that could have occurred?

- Ⓐ 1
- Ⓑ 2
- Ⓒ 8
- Ⓓ 9
- Ⓔ 10

Exercise #10

Question 15 is based on the following chart:

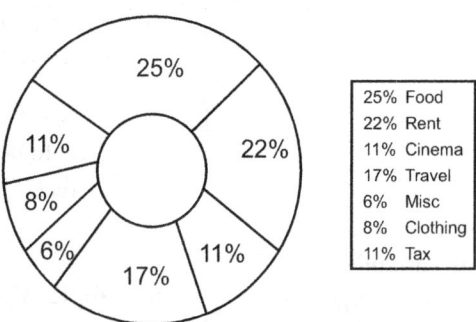

Distribution of expenses

15. Which of the following items amount to the same expenditure as on food?

    Ⓐ Tax, clothing and miscellaneous

    Ⓑ Travel, cinema and miscellaneous

    Ⓒ Cinema and travel

    Ⓓ Rent and miscellaneous

    Ⓔ Rent and cinema

Answers and Explanations

1. **Topic:** Geometry

   Sub topic: Triangles

   The correct answer is (B).

   First, draw a line segment from point R perpendicular to QS. This is the altitude of ΔQRS, and it must be less than 4. The formula for the area of a triangle is $\frac{1}{2} \times \text{base} \times \text{height}$.

   The base is 12, and if the height were 4, the area would be 24. Since the height is actually less than 4, the area must be less than 24. You don't have to find the actual value of area, though. Whatever the area is, the perimeter (the sum of all the sides) is 27. Quantity B is bigger regardless of the exact value of Quantity A.

2. **Topic:** Data Analysis

   Sub topic: Measures of Center

   The correct answer is (C).

   Remember, the median of a group of numbers is the number that is exactly in the middle of the group when the group is arranged from smallest to largest. To find the median of set A, you have to put the numbers in order: –4, –1, 2, 3, 7, and 11. Since there are only six numbers, you have to take the average of the two middle numbers, 2 and 3. The average of 2 and 3 is 2.5. To find the average of set B, add up all the numbers and divide by six, because there are six numbers. The sum of the numbers in set B is 15 divided by 6 is 2.5. So, the quantities are equal.

3. **Topic:** Data Analysis

   Sub topic: Integers

   The correct answer is (D).

   Because you're told that R, S, and T are digits and different multiples of 3, most people will think of 3, 6, and 9, which add up to 18. That makes W equal to 8, and Columns A and B equal.

   There's another possibility. 0 is also a multiple of 3. So, the three digits could be 0, 3, and 9, or 0, 6 and 9, which give totals of 12 and 15, respectively. That means W could be 8, 2 or 5.

   Since the columns could be equal, or Column B could be greater, answer choice (D) must be correct.

4. **Topic:** Algebra

   Sub topic: Percent, Ratio, Rate

   The correct answer is (C).

   The student body is $\frac{2}{3}$ male and $\frac{1}{3}$ female. So $\left(\frac{1}{4} \times \frac{1}{3}\right) + \left(\frac{1}{6} \times \frac{1}{3}\right) = \frac{1}{6} + \frac{1}{18} = \frac{2}{9}$ of the student body plays soccer.

5. **Topic:** Data Analysis

   Sub topic: Elementary Probability

   The correct answer is (A).

   The total number of cases is 2^{100}. The number of favorable ways is $_{100}C_1 + {_{100}C_3} + \ldots + {_{100}C_{99}} = 2^{100-1} = 2^{99}$. Therefore, the probability of the required event is $\frac{2^{99}}{2^{100}} = \frac{1}{2}$

6. **Topic:** Geometry

   Sub topic: Triangles

   The correct answer is (E).

   Draw a quick sketch. Label the important information.

   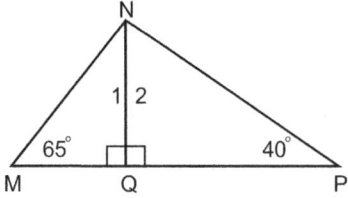

   MN and NP are the hypotenuses of ΔQNM and ΔQNP. Therefore, these are greater than MQ, NQ, and QP (the hypotenuse is the longest side

Exercise #10   319

of a right triangle). So, eliminate MN and NP. NQ > MQ, since ∠QMN(65°) > ∠MNQ(25°) (the longest side is opposite the greatest angle in a triangle).

Eliminate NQ, Similarly, since ∠QNP(50°) > ∠NPQ(40°), QP > NQ. Eliminate QP.

Therefore, the answer is MQ, the only remaining line.

The answer is (E).

7. **Topic: Algebra**

   Sub topic: Quadratic Equations

   The correct answer is (C).

   $\dfrac{\{(x+y)(x-y+y^2)\}}{8} = 2$

   $(x+y)(x-y) + y^2 = 16$

   $x^2 - y^2 + y^2 = 16$

   $x^2 = 16$

   $x = \{-4, 4\}$

   So, the possible values of x are -4 and 4.

8. **Topic: Algebra**

   Sub topic: Exponents

   The correct answer is (B).

   Left side (if we only look at the expression containing x) $= \dfrac{(x^2)^3}{x^{-1}} = \dfrac{x^6}{\frac{1}{x^1}} = x^6 x^1 = x^7$

   Right side (if we only look at the expression containing x) $= (x^6)^{\frac{1}{3}} x^5 = x^2 x^5 = x^7$

   Thus, the expressions containing x are equal in the left and right columns. This implies any differentiation should come from the remaining numerical part of the expressions.

   If we look at the right column, 30 can also be written as $\sqrt{900}$.

   Thus $\sqrt{900}$ is greater than $\sqrt{897}$ (no calculation is needed). Consequently, the right column is greater than the left column. Hence the correct answer is B.

9. **Topic: Geometry**

   Sub topic: Triangles

   The correct answer is (B).

   Since OA and AB are both radii of circle O, they are equal. In a triangle, angles opposite equal sides are also equal, so ∠OAB = ∠OBA = 59°. The angles of a triangle sum to 180°, so ∠AOB = 180 − 2(59°) = 62°. Since the angle opposite AB is greater than the angle opposite OA, AB is greater.

10. **Topic: Geometry**

    Sub topic: Three-Dimensional Figures

    The correct answer is (A).

    Since the area of face TUWY is 20, the dimensions must be 2 × 10.

    Remember, each dimension must be an even number. The dimension of face WXZY must therefore be 2 × 4. Since edge WY is common in both faces, the dimensions of face UVXW are 10 × 4.

    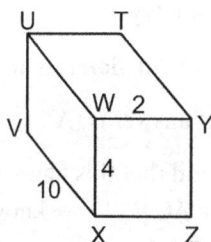

    The surface of the rectangular solid is

    2 × 10 = 20 (doubled) = 40
    + 2 × 4 = 8 (doubled) = 16
    + 10 × 4 = 40 (doubled) = 80 = 136

    Volume equals 2 × 10 × 4 = 80

    Therefore, the surface area is greater.

11. **Topic: Arithmetic**

    Sub topic: Integers

    The correct answer is (A).

    Set up a chart.

	Now	In x years
Tom	t	$t+x$
Becky	$\frac{t}{3}$	$\frac{t}{3}+x$

    Let x = the number of years from now.

    If Tom is t years old he is 3 times as old as Becky, then Becky must be $\frac{t}{3}$ years old.

    In x years, Tom will be $t + x$ years old and Becky will be $\frac{t}{3} + x$ years old.

    Set up an equation based upon your chart.

    In how many years will Tom be twice as old as Becky?

    $t + x = 2\left(\frac{t}{3} + x\right)$ Distribute $t + x = \frac{2t}{3} + 2x$

    Solve for x

    $\frac{t}{3} = x$

    The answer is (A).

12. **Topic: Geometry**

    Sub topic: Quadrilaterals and other Polygons

    The correct answer is (A).

    Keep in mind that this figure is not drawn to scale. Since AC || ED, we know that the following angles are equal:

    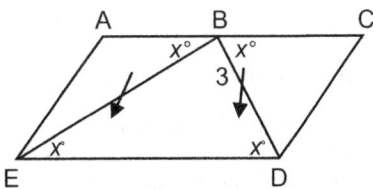

    Since ΔEBD has equal angles, the opposing sides are also equal. Therefore, BE = BD = 3.

13. **Topic: Data Analysis**

    Sub topic: Estimation

    The correct answer is (C).

    In 60 min - box is full.

    In 59 min - box is half filled.

    In 58 min - box is $\frac{1}{4}$ filled.

    Hence C.

14. **Topic: Data Analysis**

    Sub topic: Elementary Probability

    The correct answer is (D).

    If the first and last flips were heads, we could have 9 consecutive heads, followed by 10 consecutive tails and the final head.

15. **Topic: Data Analysis**

    Sub topic: Interpreting data in tables and graphs

    The correct answer is (A).

    Tax, Clothing and miscellaneous = 11 + 8 + 6 = 25% = $\frac{1}{4}$ th of his income which is the expenses on food.

Chapter 17

Exercise #11

Questions: 12 | Time: 21 minutes

This Exercise includes *12 practice questions*. The questions cover all the question types as explained in Chapter 2 and may fall into any of the following categories - Arithmetic, Algebra, Geometry or Data Analysis. You will find answers and detailed explanations towards the end of this chapter.

1.

It is given that
$$\frac{b+6}{4b^2} + \frac{3}{2b^2} = \frac{b+4}{8b^2}$$

Quantity A

$\dfrac{b+6}{4b^2}$

Quantity B

$\dfrac{b+4}{8b^2}$

- Ⓐ Quantity A is greater.
- Ⓑ Quantity B is greater.
- Ⓒ The two quantities are equal.
- Ⓓ The relationship cannot be determined from the information given.

2. Which of the following numbers are equal to 1?

   Select *all* that apply.

A	100 percent of 1
B	400 percent of 0.4
C	80 percent of $1\frac{3}{4}$
D	5 percent of $\frac{1}{5}$
E	1 percent of 1
F	300 percent of $\frac{1}{3}$

3.

   If $6a - 2b = -7$ and $b > 300$

Quantity A	**Quantity B**
The smallest value of a	84

   - (A) Quantity A is greater.
   - (B) Quantity B is greater.
   - (C) The two quantities are equal.
   - (D) The relationship cannot be determined from the information given.

4.

   If x is a real number and $f(x) = \frac{x^2}{2}$ and $g(x) = [x]$,
   where $[x]$ is the greatest integer less than or equal to x

Quantity A	**Quantity B**
$f(g(-2.5)) - g(f(2.5))$	2.5

   - (A) Quantity A is greater.
   - (B) Quantity B is greater.
   - (C) The two quantities are equal.
   - (D) The relationship cannot be determined from the information given.

Exercise #11

5. Solve for $x: 4^{3x+6} = 8^{6x+12}$

   (A) 2
   (B) 4
   (C) −4
   (D) 6
   (E) −2

6. A stone is vertically thrown up in the air. Its velocity is given by $v = 40 - 20t$ where t is the time in seconds. When will the velocity be between 20 metres per second and 30 metres per second?

   (A) $0.6 < t < 1.1$
   (B) $0.7 < t < 1.2$
   (C) $0.4 < t < 1$
   (D) $0.8 < t < 1.3$
   (E) $0.5 < t < 1$

7. In the diagram at the right what is the value of $b - a$?

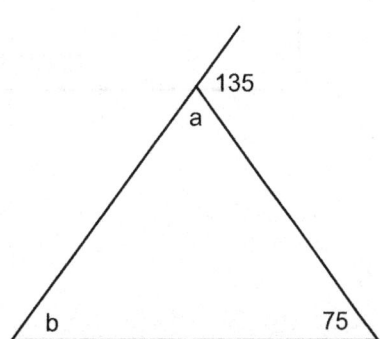

   (A) 10°
   (B) 15°
   (C) 20°
   (D) 25°
   (E) 30°

8.

If $4x + 7y + 5z = 33$

and $2x + 5y + 4z = 24$ then

Quantity A	Quantity B
$y + z$	5

- Ⓐ Quantity A is greater
- Ⓑ Quantity B is greater
- Ⓒ The two quantities are equal.
- Ⓓ The relationship cannot be determined from the information given

9.

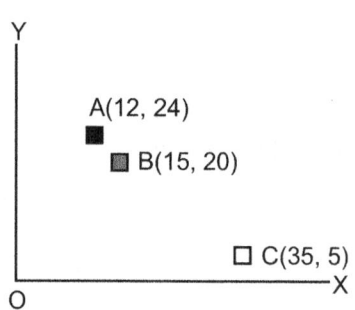

Quantity A	Quantity B
The square of the distance between the points A and B	The distance between the points B and C

- Ⓐ Quantity A is greater.
- Ⓑ Quantity B is greater.
- Ⓒ The two quantities are equal.
- Ⓓ The relationship cannot be determined from the information given.

Exercise #11

10.

p, q and r are three distinct positive integers such that their product pqr = 385.

Quantity A	Quantity B
The value of $p + q + r$	22

- Ⓐ Quantity A is greater.
- Ⓑ Quantity B is greater.
- Ⓒ The two quantities are equal.
- Ⓓ The relationship cannot be determined from the information given.

11.

In the xy coordinate plane $y = x\sqrt{5}$ is equation of a line. $P(x_1, y_1)$ is a point on the line

Quantity A	Quantity B
x_1	y_1

- Ⓐ Quantity A is greater.
- Ⓑ Quantity B is greater.
- Ⓒ The two quantities are equal.
- Ⓓ The relationship cannot be determined from the information given.

12.

A invested a certain amount in bank P for two years under the simple interest and got $1200 as interest and B invested the same amount in bank Q for two years under the same rate under the compound interest compounded yearly and got $1290 as interest.

Quantity A	Quantity B
The invested amount by each	$3000

- Ⓐ Quantity A is greater
- Ⓑ Quantity B is greater
- Ⓑ The two quantities are equal.
- Ⓓ The relationship cannot be determined from the information given.

Answers and Explanations

1. **Topic: Algebra**

   Sub topic: Algebraic Expressions

   The correct answer is (B).

   $$\frac{b+6}{4b^2} + \frac{3}{2b^2} = \frac{b+4}{8b^2}$$

   $$\frac{b+6}{4b^2} + \frac{3}{2b^2} - \frac{b+4}{8b^2} = 0$$

   $$\left(\frac{b+6}{4b^2}\right) \times 2 + \left(\frac{3}{2b^2}\right) \times 4 - \left(\frac{b+4}{8b^2}\right) = 0 \text{ Make}$$

   denominators the same.

   $$\left(\frac{2b+16}{8b^2}\right) + \left(\frac{12}{8b^2}\right) - \left(\frac{b+4}{8b^2}\right) = 0$$

   $$\frac{2b+12+12-b-4}{8b^2} = 0$$

   $$\frac{b+20}{8b^2} = 0$$

   $b + 20 = 0$ Cross multiplying $8b^2$ and 0

   $b = -20$

   Quantity A: $\frac{b+6}{4b^2}$ Substituting the value of b

   $$\frac{-20+6}{4 \times (-20)^2} = \frac{-14}{4 \times 400} = \frac{-14}{1600} = -0.00875$$

   Quantity B: $\frac{b+4}{8b^2}$ Substituting the value of b

   $$\frac{-20+4}{8 \times (-20)^2} = \frac{-16}{8 \times 400} = \frac{-16}{3200} = -0.005$$

   Quantity B is bigger.

2. **Topic: Arithmetic**

   Sub topic: Percent, Ratio, Rate

   The correct answers are (A) and (C).

   A. $100\% \times 1 = \frac{100}{100} \times 1 = 1$

   B. $400\% \times 0.4 = \frac{400}{100} \times 0.4 = 1.6$

   C. $80\% \times 1\frac{1}{4} = \frac{80}{100} \times \frac{5}{4} = 1$

   D. $5\% \times \frac{1}{5} = \frac{5}{100} \times \frac{1}{5} = \frac{1}{100}$

   E. $1\% \times 1 = \frac{1}{100} \times 1 = \frac{1}{100}$

   F. $300\% \times 3 = \frac{300}{100} \times 3 = 9$

3. **Topic: Algebra**

   Sub topic: Solving Linear Equations and Inequalities

   The correct answer is (A).

   $6a - 2b = -7$

   $2b = 6a + 7$

   $b = \frac{6a+7}{2}$

   $b > 300$

   $\frac{6a+7}{2} > 300$

   $6a + 7 > 600$

   $6a > 593$

   $a > \frac{593}{7}$

   $a > 84.71 > 84$

   So Option: A

4. **Topic: Algebra**

   Sub topic: Functions

   The correct answer is (B).

   $g(-2.5) = -3$ { Note : it is not -2}

   $f(g(-2.5)) = f(-3) = \frac{(-3)^2}{2} = \frac{9}{2} = 4.5$

   $f(2.5) = \frac{(2.5)^2}{2} = \frac{6.25}{2} = 3.125$

   $g(f(2.5)) = g(3.125) = 3$

   $f(g(-2.5)) - g(f(2.5)) \, 4.5 - 3 = 1.5$

5. **Topic: Algebra**

   Sub topic: Exponential Operations

   The correct answer is (E).

Exercise #11

Given: $4^{3x+6} = 86^{x+12}$

4^{3x+6} can be written as $2^{2(3x+6)} = 2^{6x+12}$

and 8^{6x+12} can be written as $2^{3(6x+12)} = 2^{18x+36}$

$2^{6x+12} = 2^{18x+36}$

Since bases are the same exponents will also be the same.

Hence $6x + 12 = 18x + 36$

$12x = -24$

$x = -2$

6. **Topic: Algebra**

   Sub topic: Solving Linear Equations and Inequalities

   The correct answer is (E).

   Given $v = 40 - 20t$

   We have to find t when v is between 20 and 30.

   $20 < v < 30$

   $20 < 40 - 20t < 30$

   $-20 < -20t < -10$

   $-2 < -2t < -1$

   $-1 < -t < -0.5$

   $1 > t > 0.5$

   $0.5 < t < 1$

7. **Topic: Geometry**

   Sub topic: Angle Measurement

   The correct answer is (B).

   Since angle A and the external angle make a linear pair, $a + 135° = 180°$, thus $a = 45°$. The triangle angle sum property says that $a + b + 75° = 180°$, so $45° + b + 75° = 180°$. Thus, $b = 180° - 120° = 60°$, and $b - a = 60 - 45° = 15°$.

8. **Topic: Algebra**

   Sub topic: Systems of Equations

   The correct answer is (C).

   One may be tempted to answer as D, since there are only 2 equations in 3 variables. But a careful approach will give the answer as C.

   Given

   $4x + 7y + 5z = 33$ --------- (1)

   $2x + 5y + 4z = 24$ -------- (2)

   Multiplying the equation (2) by number 2, we get

   $4x + 10y + 8z = 48$ --------- (3)

   Subtracting (1) from (3) we get

   $3y + 3z = 15$

   $y + z = 5$

9. **Topic: Geometry**

   Sub topic: Coordinate Geometry

   The correct answer is (C).

   The distance between two points is given by $D = \sqrt{dx^2 + dy^2}$ where:

   dx is the difference between the x coordinates of the points

   dy is the difference between the y coordinates of the points

   In this case:

   AB = $\sqrt{(15-12)^2 + (20-124)^2} = \sqrt{3^2 + 4^2} = \sqrt{25} = 5$

   $(AB)^2 = 5^2 = 25$

   BC = $\sqrt{(35-15)^2 + (5-20)^2} = \sqrt{20^2 + 15^2} = \sqrt{625} = 25$

   Quantities A and B both equal 25, so the correct answer is (C).

10. **Topic: Arithmetic**

    Sub topic: Factorization

    The correct answer is (A).

    385 can be factorized into $385 = 5 \times 7 \times 11$

    This being the prime factorization it is unique.

    So $p = 5, q = 7, r = 11$.

    $p + q + r = 5 + 7 + 11 = 23$

11. **Topic: Algebra**

    Sub topic: Graphs of Functions, Equations, and Inequalities

    The correct answer is (D).

    When $x_1 = 0$, $y_1 = 0$. So $x_1 = y_1$

    When $x_1 = 1$, $y_1 = \sqrt{5}$. So $x_1 < y_1$

    When $x_1 = -1$, $y_1 = -\sqrt{5}$. So $x_1 > y_1$

    So the relationship cannot be determined from the information given.

12. **Topic: Arithmetic**

    Sub topic: Percent, Ratio, Rate

    The correct answer is (A).

    Under simple interest, the interest is calculated only on the principal; whereas, under the compound interest scheme, interest on interest is also calculated.

    So for SI, the interest for the first and the second year would be the same ($600)

    But for CI, the interest for the first year will be $600 and the second year would be $690 ($1290–$600).

    That means under CI, for the second year an extra interest of $90 is received. That is nothing but the interest on interest.

    So under CI, $90 is interest for $600 for one year.

    We know that, interest $= \dfrac{PTR}{100}$, where P = 600, T = 1 year.

    First, we will find R.

    $R = \dfrac{\text{interest} \times 100}{T \times R} = \dfrac{90 \times 100}{1 \times 600} = 15\%$

    NOW original principal (say) Q is given by the equation

    $\dfrac{Q \times T \times R}{100} = \text{interest}$

    $\dfrac{Q \times 1 \times 15}{100} = 600$

    So original Principal $= \dfrac{600 \times 100}{1 \times 15} = \$4000$

Chapter 18

Exercise #12

Questions: 15 | Time: 26 minutes

This Exercise includes *15 practice questions*. The questions cover all the question types as explained in Chapter 2 and may fall into any of the following categories - Arithmetic, Algebra, Geometry or Data Analysis. You will find answers and detailed explanations towards the end of this chapter.

1. The following pie charts show (1) the percentage of students in various courses P, Q, R, S, T and U and (2) the percentage of girls in various courses P, Q, R, S, T and U in a central university. Study the pie charts carefully and answer the question.

   Percentage of students in various courses P,Q,R,S,T and U in Central University

   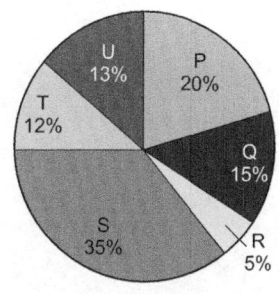

   Percentage of girls in various courses

   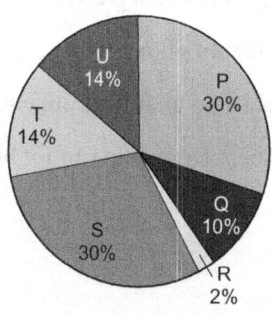

   If the total number of students is 12000 and two third of the students are girls, for which pair of courses the number of boys the same.

   - (A) R and U
   - (B) T and U
   - (C) P and S
   - (D) Q and S
   - (E) S and U

www.vibrantpublishers.com

2. x, y, and z are consecutive positive integers greater than 1, not necessarily in that order, which of the following is (are) true?

   Select all that apply.

   I $x > z$

   II $x + y > z$

   III $yz < xz$

   IV $xy < y + z$

   A I only
   B II only
   C II and III only
   D II and IV only
   E III and IV only
   F IV only

3. Point P has the coordinates (–4, 5) and point Q has the coordinates (4, –5) on the same rectangular coordinate plane.

   Quantity A   **Quantity B**

   Distance of P from origin (0, 0)   Distance of Q from origin (0, 0)

   A Quantity A is greater.
   B Quantity B is greater.
   C The two quantities are equal.
   D The relationship cannot be determined from the information given.

Exercise #12

4. Toy train cars made of blocks of wood either 6 inches long or 7 inches long can be hooked together to make longer trains. 6 inches trains can be hooked only in pairs. Which of the following train lengths can be made by hooking together the 6-inch train cars, 7-inch train cars, or a combination of both?

   Select all that apply.

   |A| 30 inches
   |B| 31 inches
   |C| 40 inches
   |D| 46 inches
   |E| 38 inches
   |F| 53 inches
   |G| 51 inches
   |H| 59 inches

5. John will be y years old x years from now. How old will he be z years from now?

   (A) $y - x + z$

   (B) $y + x + z$

   (C) $y + x - z$

   (D) $y - x - z$

   (E) $x + z - y$

6.

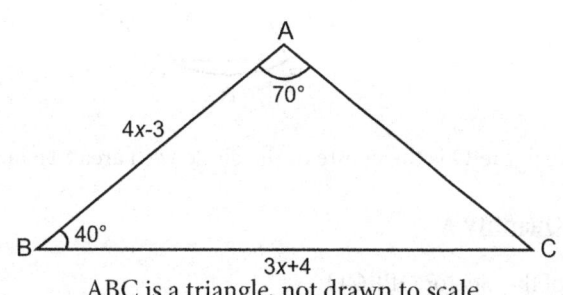

ABC is a triangle, not drawn to scale.

Quantity A	**Quantity B**
x	7

(A) Quantity A is greater.

(B) Quantity B is greater.

(C) The two quantities are equal.

(D) The relationship cannot be determined from the information given.

7. The following table shows the number of books sold by five different stores in three different years in a city.

Shop Number	2018	2019	2020
Shop 1	3000	4200	5200
Shop 2	2400	4000	3200
Shop 3	4000	2000	2800
Shop 4	1200	3200	2400
Shop 5	5000	6000	2000

In which shop is the highest percentage CHANGE of the number of books sold from the year 2018 to 2019?

- Ⓐ Shop 1
- Ⓑ Shop 2
- Ⓒ Shop 3
- Ⓓ Shop 4
- Ⓔ Shop 5

8.

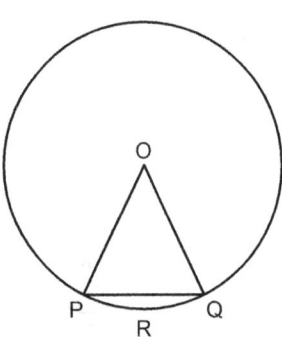

In the above figure O is the centre of the circle with area 81π and angle ∠POQ = 40°

Quantity A   **Quantity B**

Perimeter of the Sector OPRQO   3π + 18

- Ⓐ Quantity A is greater.
- Ⓑ Quantity B is greater.
- Ⓒ The two quantities are equal.
- Ⓓ The relationship cannot be determined from the information given.

9.

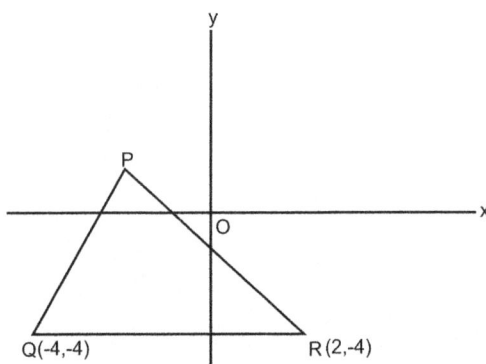

In the coordinate plane given above, the area of triangle PQR is 18 square units.

Quantity A	Quantity B
Y coordinate of P	1

- Ⓐ Quantity A is greater.
- Ⓑ Quantity B is greater.
- Ⓒ The two quantities are equal.
- Ⓓ The relationship cannot be determined from the information given.

10. If in an office $\frac{1}{2}$ of the staff commute by bus, $\frac{1}{3}$ commute by motorbike, $\frac{1}{12}$ commute by car and remaining 100 walk, then what is the total number of staff in that office?

11.

There are 500 employees in an organization. For a charity they donated a total of $9000. If 300 employees donated at least $15 and 180 employees donated at least $20, and x is the maximum average amount the remaining 20 employees could have donated.

Quantity A	Quantity B
x	$40

- Ⓐ Quantity A is greater.
- Ⓑ Quantity B is greater.
- Ⓒ The two quantities are equal.
- Ⓓ The relationship cannot be determined from the information given.

12. Andrew and Ben play in the same cricket team of Indian Premier League. In the last season, Ben scored 3 more centuries than Andrew, but together they scored less than 9 centuries. What is a possible number of centuries Ben scored?

    (A) 1
    (B) 2
    (C) 4
    (D) 7
    (E) 8

13.
    From all the words formed using all the letters of the word CARE, one word is selected at random.

Quantity A	**Quantity B**
The probability that the chosen word will have consonants next to each other	$\frac{1}{3}$

    (A) Quantity A is greater.
    (B) Quantity B is greater.
    (C) The two quantities are equal.
    (D) The relationship cannot be determined from the information given.

14. A problem on probability in the GRE quantitative section is given to A, B C and D for solving independently. If the probabilities of solving the problem by A, B, C and D are 60%, 70%, 80% and 90% respectively, what is the probability that the problem will be solved?

    (A) 0.9188
    (B) 0.9326
    (C) 0.9424
    (D) 0.9976
    (E) 0.9820

15.

Quantity A	Quantity B
$(2)^4 (8)^{-\frac{2}{3}}$	$(4)^{\frac{5}{2}} (16)^{-\frac{3}{4}}$

Ⓐ Quantity A is greater.

Ⓑ Quantity B is greater.

Ⓒ The two quantities are equal.

Ⓓ The relationship cannot be determined from the information given.

Answers and Explanations

1. **Topic: Data Analysis**

   Sub topic: Interpreting data in tables and graphs

   The correct answer is (A).

   Total number of students = 12000

   Total number of girls = $\frac{2}{3} \times 12000 = 8000$

Course	Number of boys
P	20% of 12000 – 30% of 8000 = 2400 – 2400 = 0
Q	15% of 12000 – 10% of 8000 = 1800 – 800 = 1000
R	5% of 12000 – 2% of 8000 = 600 – 160 = 440
S	35% of 12000 – 30% of 8000 = 4200 – 2400 = 1800
T	12% of 12000 – 14% of 8000 = 1440 – 1120 = 320
U	13% of 12000 – 14% of 8000 = 1560 – 1120 = 440
	Number of Students in R = Number of Students in U = 440

2. **Topic: Arithmetic**

   Sub topic: Integers

   The correct answer is (B).

   Adding any two of three consecutive positive integers greater than 1 will always be greater than the other integer. Therefore, II is true. The others cannot be determined because they depend on values and/or the order of x, y, and z.

3. **Topic: Geometry**

   Sub topic: Distance and Midpoint

   The correct answer is (C).

   The distance between two points (x_1, y_1) and (x_2, y_2) on the coordinate plane is given by $\sqrt{(x_2-x_1)^2 + (y_2-y_1)^2}$.

   The distance between the points (–4,5) and (0,0)
   $= \sqrt{(0-(-4))^2 + (0-5)^2} = \sqrt{16+25} = \sqrt{41}$.

   The distance between the points (4,–5) and (0,0)
   $= \sqrt{(0-(4))^2 + (0-(-5))^2} = \sqrt{16+25} = \sqrt{41}$.

   The correct answer is (C).

4. **Topic: Arithmetic**

   Sub topic: Divisibility

   The correct answers are (B), (C), (E) and (H).

   The table gives the number of train cars that need to be hooked to get the train lengths.

Total train length	No. of 6-inch trains	No. of 7-inch trains
30 inches	5	
31 inches	4	1
40 inches	2	4
46 inches	3	4
38 inches	4	2
53 inches	3	5
51 inches	5	3
59 inches	4	5

   It is given that 6-inch train cars come in pairs. Options A, D, F, and G require that odd number of 6-inch train cars be hooked together. However, they can be hooked only in pairs.

   Hence, the correct answers are B, C, E, and H.

5. **Topic: Arithmetic**

   Sub topic: Integers

   The correct answer is (A).

   Since John will be x years old y years from now; he is $y - x$ years old now.

   Therefore, z years from now he will be $y - x + z$ years old.

Exercise #12

6. **Topic: Geometry**

   Sub topic: Triangles

   The correct answer is (C).

   $\angle C = 180° - 40° - 70° = 70° = \angle A$

   Therefore triangle ABC is Isosceles

   Hence AB = BC (Sides opposite to equal angles)

   $\Rightarrow 4x - 3 = 3x + 4$

   $\Rightarrow x = 7$

7. **Topic: Arithmetic**

   Sub topic: Percent, Ratio, Rate

   The correct answer is (D).

   Shop 1: 4200 – 3000 = 1200 ; $\frac{1200}{3000} \times 100 = 40\%$

   Shop 2: 4000 – 2400 = 1600; $\frac{1600}{2400} \times 100 = 66.67\%$

   Shop 3: 2000 – 4000 = –2000; $\frac{-2000}{4000} \times 100 = -50\%$

   Shop 4: 3200 – 1200 = 2000: $\frac{2000}{1200} \times 100\% = 166.67\%$

   Shop 5: 6000 – 5000 = 1000: $\frac{1000}{5000} \times 100\% = 20\%$

   If we take the absolute value of the increase/decrease we can see the maximum change is in shop 4

8. **Topic: Geometry**

   Sub topic: Area, Perimeter, and Volume

   The correct answer is (B).

   Area of the circle $= 81\pi$

   If r is the radius, then $\pi r^2 = 81\pi$

   $\Rightarrow r = 9$

   Length of arc PRQ

   $= \frac{40}{360} \times 2\pi \times r = \frac{40}{360} \times 2\pi \times 9 = 2\pi$

   Perimeter of the Sector OPRQO

   $= 2\pi + 9 + 9 = 2\pi + 18$

9. **Topic: Geometry**

   Sub topic: Area, Perimeter, and Volume

   The correct answer is (A).

   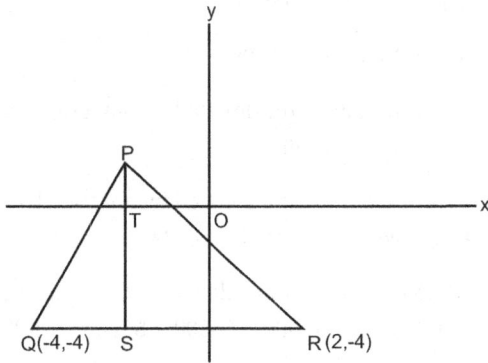

   Since y coordinates of Q and R are same, QR is parallel to x axis.

   Length of QR = 6 units (4 + 2)

   If h is the height of the triangle then

   $\frac{1}{2} \times base \times height = 18$

   $\Rightarrow \frac{1}{2} \times 6 \times h = 18$

   $\Rightarrow h = 6$ units

   $\Rightarrow PS = 6$ units

   BUT $TS = 4$ units

   $\therefore PT = 6 - 4 = 2$ units

   Hence y coordinate of $P = 2$

10. **Topic: Data Analysis**

    Sub topic: Conditional Probability

    The correct answer is (C).

    If x is the number of staff, then

    $\frac{1}{2}x + \frac{1}{3}x + \frac{1}{12}x + 100 = x$

$$\frac{11}{12}x + 100 = x$$

$$x - \frac{11}{12}x = 100$$

$$x = 1200$$

11. **Topic: Data Analysis**

    Sub topic: Measures of Spread

    The correct answer is (A).

    Total donation = $9000

    Minimum amount donated by 300 employees = $300 \times 15 = \$4500$

    Minimum amount donated by another 180 employees = $180 \times 20 = \$3600$

    MAXIMUM amount donated by remaining 20 employees = $9000 - \$4500 - \$3600 = \$900$

    MAXIMUM average amount donated by 20 employees = $\frac{\$900}{20} = \$45$

12. **Topic: Algebra**

    Sub topic: Systems of Equations

    The correct answer is (C).

    Let the number of centuries Ben scored: B and the number of centuries Andrew scored: A!

    We know that Ben scored 3 more centuries than Andrew did, so: $B = A + 3$

    And we know that together they scored less than 9 centuries: $A + B < 9$

    We are being asked for how many centuries Ben might have scored: B

    Now

    $A + B < 9$

    $B = A + 3$, so: $A + (A + 3) < 9$

    $2A + 3 < 9$

    $2A < 9 - 3$

    $2A < 6$

    $A < 3$

    Andrew scored less than 3 centuries, which means that Andrew could have scored 0, 1 or 2 centuries.

    Ben scored 3 more centuries than Sam did, so Ben could have scored 3, 4, or 5 centuries.

    In the answer choices only 4 is there. So option C

13. **Topic: Data Analysis**

    Sub topic: Elementary Probability

    The correct answer is (A).

    Total number of words formed using all the letters of the word CARE = 4! = 24

    We aim to get all the words those will have consonants next to each other

    Place the consonants, R and C in a box, so that they will move always together.

    RC- First unit

    A and E are second and third units

    Now, the number of units = 3

    These 3 units can be arranged in 3! ways.

    But the consonants, between themselves, can be arranged in 2! ways.

    $\therefore$ Required arrangements = $3! \times 2! = 12$

    Required probability = $\frac{12}{24} = \frac{1}{2}$

    $\frac{1}{2} > \frac{1}{3}$, So option A

14. **Topic: Data Analysis**

    Sub topic: Elementary Probability

    The correct answer is (D).

    The probability that the problem will be solved

    = Probability that at least one will solve

    = 1 − probability that none of them solve

    = 1 − [(1 − 0.6) (1 − 0.7) (1 − 0.8)(1 − 0.9)]

    = 1 − (0.4 × 0.3 × 0.2 × 0.1)

    = 1 − 0.0024

    = 0.9976

Exercise #12

15. **Topic: Arithmetic**

    Sub topic: Exponents

    The correct answer is (C).

    To solve this problem, we need to use the following two properties to evaluate each expression.

    - $a^{-n} = \dfrac{1}{a^n}$

    - $a^{m/n} = \sqrt[n]{a^m} = \left(\sqrt[n]{a}\right)^m$

    Quantity A:

    $$(2)^4 (8)^{-\frac{2}{3}} = \dfrac{(2)^4}{(8)^{\frac{2}{3}}} = \dfrac{16}{\left(\sqrt[3]{8}\right)^2} = \dfrac{16}{(2)^2} = \dfrac{16}{4} = 4$$

    Quantity B:

    $$(4)^{\frac{5}{2}} (16)^{-\frac{3}{4}} = \dfrac{(4)^{\frac{5}{2}}}{(16)^{\frac{3}{4}}} = \dfrac{\sqrt{4^5}}{\sqrt[4]{16^3}} = \dfrac{\left(\sqrt{4}\right)^5}{\left(\sqrt[4]{16}\right)^3} = \dfrac{2^5}{2^3} = \dfrac{32}{8} = 4$$

    Both quantities are equal, so the answer is C.

This page is intentionally left blank

Chapter 19

Exercise #13

Questions: 12 | Time: 21 minutes

This Exercise includes *12 practice questions*. The questions cover all the question types as explained in Chapter 2 and may fall into any of the following categories - Arithmetic, Algebra, Geometry or Data Analysis. You will find answers and detailed explanations towards the end of this chapter.

1.

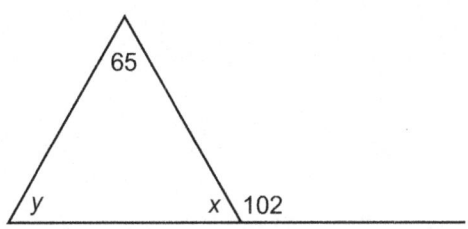

Quantity A

$2x + y$

Quantity B

$x + 2y$

- Ⓐ Quantity A is greater.
- Ⓑ Quantity B is greater.
- Ⓒ The two quantities are equal.
- Ⓓ The relationship cannot be determined from the information given.

2. If $(x + 1)$ times $(2x + 1)$ is an odd integer, then x must be

    Ⓐ an odd integer

    Ⓑ an even integer

    Ⓒ a prime number

    Ⓓ a compose number

    Ⓔ a negative number

3. Given that $y - x^2 + 3x + 7 = 0$

    If x is a positive multiple of 5, then which of the following could be possible values of y?

    Select *all* that apply.

    ☐ A 3
    ☐ B 62
    ☐ C 173
    ☐ D 243
    ☐ E 333
    ☐ F 642
    ☐ G 1113
    ☐ H 1563

4.

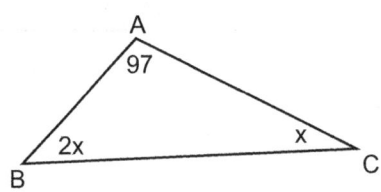

Quantity A	**Quantity B**
The length of AB	The length of AC

Ⓐ Quantity A is greater.

Ⓑ Quantity B is greater.

Ⓒ The two quantities are equal.

Ⓓ The relationship cannot be determined from the information given.

Exercise #13

5.

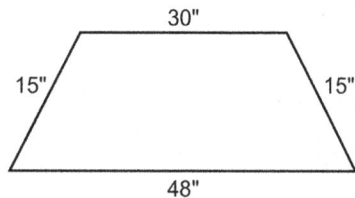

What is the area of the preceding trapezoid in square inches?

- Ⓐ 108
- Ⓑ 234
- Ⓒ 368
- Ⓓ 468
- Ⓔ 585

6.

Pamela covers a distance of 400 kilometers from city A to city B taking altogether 6 hours. Part of her journey is covered at 60 km/h and the remaining part at 80 km/h. how many hours did she travel at 60 mph?

Quantity A	**Quantity B**
The number of hours she travelled at 60 mph	4

- Ⓐ Quantity A is greater.
- Ⓑ Quantity B is greater.
- Ⓒ The two quantities are equal.
- Ⓓ The relationship cannot be determined from the information given.

7.

Alex and Ben joined a company and their initial salaries were same. Alex got a hike of 43% after one year and another 43% after one more year. Though Ben did not get any hike after one year, his salary was doubled after two years.

Quantity A	**Quantity B**
Alex's salary after two years of joining the company	Ben's salary after two years of joining the company

- Ⓐ Quantity A is greater.
- Ⓑ Quantity B is greater.
- Ⓒ The two quantities are equal.
- Ⓓ The relationship cannot be determined from the information given.

8.

Quantity A	Quantity B
The simplified value of $\dfrac{(125)^{\frac{2}{3}} \times (729)^{\frac{1}{2}}}{(27)^{\frac{2}{3}}}$	75

- (A) Quantity A is greater.
- (B) Quantity B is greater.
- (C) The two quantities are equal.
- (D) The relationship cannot be determined from the information given.

Study the following Bar graph and answer the following 2 questions.

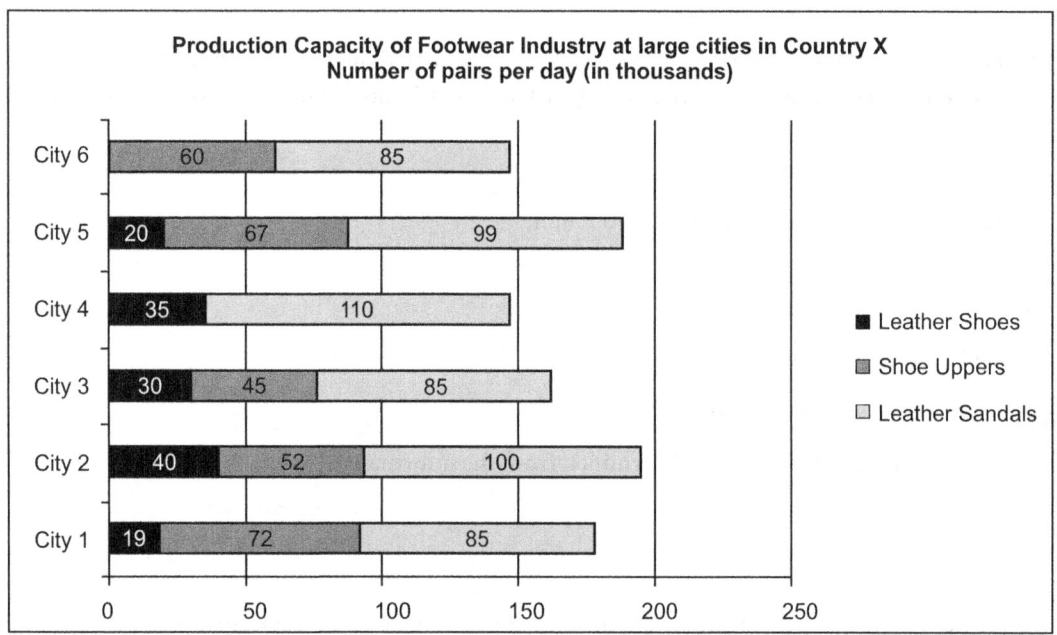

9. The ratio of the capacities per day of the total leather shoes to shoe uppers is given by

- (A) 9:17
- (B) 14:31
- (C) 18:37
- (D) 15:29
- (E) 23:47

Exercise #13

10. In City 5 the production of leather shoes, shoe uppers and leather sandals are 70%, 85% and 90% of the capacity respectively. The combined percentage of **unutilized** capacity in City 5 is approximately equal to

    Ⓐ 11%

    Ⓑ 89%

    Ⓒ 86%

    Ⓓ 14%

    Ⓔ 17%

11.

In the following figure QR = 12 units

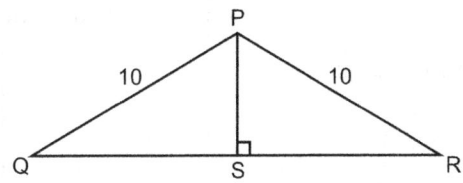

Quantity A	Quantity B
Length of PS	7.5

Ⓐ Quantity A is greater

Ⓑ Quantity B is greater

Ⓒ The two quantities are equal.

Ⓓ The relationship cannot be determined from the information given.

12.

Number X is 80% more than number Y and which is 40% less than number Z.

Quantity A	Quantity B
X	108 % of Z

Ⓐ Quantity A is greater

Ⓑ Quantity B is greater

Ⓒ The two quantities are equal.

Ⓓ The relationship cannot be determined from the information given.

Answers and Explanations

1. **Topic: Geometry**

   Sub topic: Triangles

   The correct answer is (A).

   To calculate the measure of x and y we need to know the following properties:

   - All interior angles of a triangle have a sum of 180°.
   - Two adjacent angles that form a straight line have a combined angle measure of 180°.

   We can now write the following equations:

   $x + 102° = 180°$

   $x + y + 65 = 180°$

   We can solve for x using the first equation, and then solve for y.

   $x + 102 = 180°$

   $x = 78°$

   $78 + y + 65 = 180°$

   $143 + y = 180°$

   $y = 37°$

   Now we can calculate Quantity A and Quantity B by substituting in the values of x and y.

   Quantity A: $2x + y = 2(78) + 37 = 193°$

   Quantity B: $x + 2y = 78 + 2(37) = 152°$

   Quantity A is greater; therefore, the answer is A.

2. **Topic: Arithmetic**

   Sub topic: Numbers

   The correct answer is (B).

   Solve this problem by plugging in simple numbers. Start with 1, an odd integer.

   $(1 + 1)$ times $(2.1 + 1)$

   $= (2)$ times $(2 + 1)$

   $= 2.3$

   $= 6$ (not odd)

   Now, try 2, an even integer.

   $(2 + 1)$ times $(2.2 + 1)$

   $= (3)$ times $(4 + 1)$

   $= 3.5$

   $= 15$ (an odd integer)

3. **Topic: Algebra**

   Sub topic: Algebraic Expressions

   The correct answers are (A), (C), (E) and (G).

   Solving the equation $y = x^2 - 3x - 7$

x	$y = x^2 - 3x - 7$
5	3
10	63
15	173
20	333
25	543
30	803
35	1113
40	1473
45	1883
50	2343
55	2853
60	3413
65	4023

4. **Topic: Geometry**

   Sub topic: Triangles

   The correct answer is (B).

   In a triangle, the angles can be organized by the smallest angles to the largest angles. The side opposite the smallest angle is the shortest side of the triangle just as the side opposite the largest angle is the longest side.

   $\angle B > \angle C$

Therefore, the sides opposite should follow the same inequality which is $AC > AB$. Quantity B is greater, so the answer is B.

5. **Topic: Geometry**

   Sub topic: Quadrilaterals

   The correct answer is (D).

   Since the area of a trapezoid = $\frac{1}{2} \times h \times (b_1 + b_2)$, we need to find the altitude, h. Draw altitudes in figures as follows:

   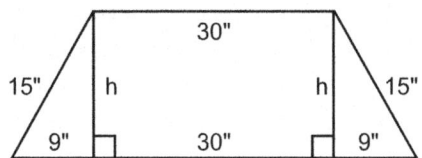

   Since the triangles formed are right triangles, use the Pythagorean Theorem, which says

   $c^2 = a^2 + b^2$

   $15^2 = 9^2 + h^2$

   $225 = 81 + h^2$

   $h^2 = 225 - 81$

   $h^2 = 144$

   $h = \sqrt{144} = 12$ inches

   Hence the area of the trapezoid will be

   $\frac{1}{2} \times h \times (b_1 + b_2) = \frac{1}{2} \times 12 \times (30 + 48)$

   $= (6)(78)$

   $= 468$ square inches.

6. **Topic: Arithmetic**

   Sub topic: Percent, Ratio, Rate

   The correct answer is (C).

   Let the first part of journey be covered in t hours.

   Second part covered in $6 - t$ hours.

   $60(t) + 80(6 - t) = 400$

   $3t + 4(6 - t) = 20$

   $-t = -4$

   $t = 4$ hours.

7. **Topic: Arithmetic**

   Sub topic: Percent, Ratio, Rate

   The correct answer is (A).

   Let $100 be the salary of Alex and Ben when they joined the company.

   Alex's salary after 1 year = $143

   Alex's salary after 2 years = $143 × 143% = $204.49

   Ben's Salary after 2 years = $200 (double)

8. **Topic: Arithmetic**

   Sub topic: Exponents

   The correct answer is (C).

   We know $a^m \times a^n = a^{m+n}$ and $(a^m)^n = a^{mn}$

   Consider $(125)^{\frac{2}{3}} = (5^3)^{\frac{2}{3}} = 5^2$

   $(729)^{\frac{1}{2}} = (3^6)^{\frac{1}{2}} = 3^3$

   $(247)^{\frac{2}{3}} = (3^3)^{\frac{2}{3}} = 3^2$

   Now $\dfrac{(125)^{\frac{2}{3}} \times (729)^{\frac{1}{2}}}{(27)^{\frac{2}{3}}} = \dfrac{5^2 \times 3^3}{3^2} = 5^2 \times 3^1 = 75$

9. **Topic: Data Analysis**

   Sub topic: Interpreting data in tables and graphs

   The correct answer is (C).

   Required ratio $= \dfrac{19 + 40 + 30 + 35 + 20 + 0}{72 + 52 + 45 + 0 + 67 + 60} = \dfrac{144}{296} = \dfrac{18}{37}$

10. **Topic: Arithmetic**

    Sub topic: Percent, Ratio, Rate

    The correct answer is (D).

    Total Capacity (in thousands) in City 5 = 20 + 67 + 99 = 186

Utilized capacity (in thousands) = 20 × 0.70 + 67 × 0.85 + 99 × 0.90 = 14.00 + 56.95 + 89.10 = 160.05

Percentage of utilized capacity = $\frac{160.05}{186}$ × 100% = 86.05% = 86% (Approx)

Percentage of unutilized capacity = 100% − 86% = 14% (Approx)

11. **Topic: Geometry**

    Sub topic: Triangles

    The correct answer is (A).

    PQR is an isosceles triangle

    Hence the perpendicular PS will divide QR in to two halves.

    Hence QS = = 6 units.

    In right triangle PQS, by Pythagorean Theorem,

    $PS^2 = PQ^2 − QS^2$

    $PS^2 = 10^2 − 6^2 = 64$

    PS = 8 units

12. **Topic: Arithmetic**

    Sub topic: Percent, Ratio, Rate

    The correct answer is (C).

    Let Z be 100

    Y = 40% less than Z = 60

    X = 80% more than Y = $\frac{180}{100}$ × 60 = 108.

    Hence X is 8 % more than Z

    i.e. X = 108 % of Z

Chapter 20

Exercise #14
Questions: 15 | Time: 26 minutes

This Exercise includes *15 practice questions*. The questions cover all the question types as explained in Chapter 2 and may fall into any of the following categories - Arithmetic, Algebra, Geometry or Data Analysis. You will find answers and detailed explanations towards the end of this chapter.

1.

The figure above is formed of two equal circles and a square. If each circle has an area of 18π, what is the perimeter of the square?

(A) 9
(B) 12
(C) 18
(D) 24
(E) 36

www.vibrantpublishers.com

2.

Two pipes T and P supply water at a rate of 1,200 cubic centimeters per minute and 2.16 liters per minute, respectively.

Quantity A	**Quantity B**
Volume of water supplied when T runs for 3 minutes continuously	Volume of water supplied when P runs for 2 minutes continuously

Ⓐ   Quantity A is greater.

Ⓑ   Quantity B is greater.

Ⓒ   The two quantities are equal.

Ⓓ   The relationship cannot be determined from the information given.

3.

Quantity A	**Quantity B**
Number of degrees in the interior angles of a pentagon	500°

Ⓐ   Quantity A is greater.

Ⓑ   Quantity B is greater.

Ⓒ   The two quantities are equal.

Ⓓ   The relationship cannot be determined from the information given.

4. What will be the smallest possible number which when divided by 5 has remainder 3 and when divided by 7 has remainder 2? Ignore the quotients in both the cases and write the answer in answer box.

☐

Exercise #14

5.

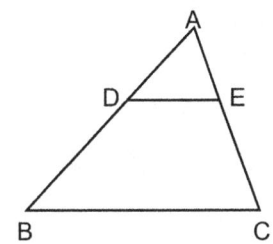

Note: Figure not drawn to scale.

In the figure above, DE is parallel to BC and AD = $\frac{DB}{2}$. If the perimeter of △ABC is 24, what is the perimeter of △ADE?

- Ⓐ 6
- Ⓑ 8
- Ⓒ 12
- Ⓓ 16
- Ⓔ 48

6. For which values of x is the statement $x^3 > x^2$ true?

- Ⓐ all x
- Ⓑ $x > 0$
- Ⓒ $x > 1$ or $x < -1$
- Ⓓ $-1 < x < 1$
- Ⓔ $x > 1$

7.

Quantity A	Quantity B
$18 \div 3 \times 6 - 2 - 3^2$	$18 + 6 \div 3 \times 2 + 2^3$

- Ⓐ Quantity A is greater.
- Ⓑ Quantity B is greater.
- Ⓒ The two quantities are equal.
- Ⓓ The relationship cannot be determined from the information given.

8. A 16-inch by 36-inch piece of material is to be cut into equal circles, with the least amount of material left over. What is the amount of material that remains if the largest possible circles are cut from the material?

    Ⓐ 576 (π – 1)

    Ⓑ 4 (144 – π)

    Ⓒ 144π

    Ⓓ 144 – π

    Ⓔ 144 (4 – π)

9.
$$\frac{m^4}{3} = 27$$

Quantity A m

Quantity B 4

Ⓐ Quantity A is greater.

Ⓑ Quantity B is greater.

Ⓒ The two quantities are equal.

Ⓓ The relationship cannot be determined from the information given.

10.

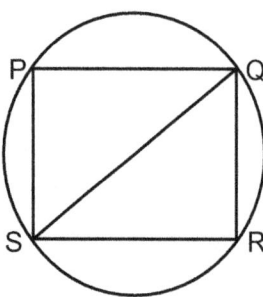

In the figure the area of the circle is 6.25π square units and PQRS is a rectangle with length PQ = 4 units. What is the area of the rectangle PQRS?

Ⓐ 12 Square units

Ⓑ 12 π Square units

Ⓒ 16 Square units

Ⓓ 16 π Square units

Ⓔ 8 Square units

Exercise #14

11.

If $[(a)] = (1 + a)^2 + 2$ for all numbers a

Quantity A   **Quantity B**

$[(b)]$ $[(-b)]$

- Ⓐ Quantity A is greater.
- Ⓑ Quantity B is greater.
- Ⓒ The two quantities are equal.
- Ⓓ The relationship cannot be determined from the information given.

12.

In the figure the area of the circle with center O is 81π square units

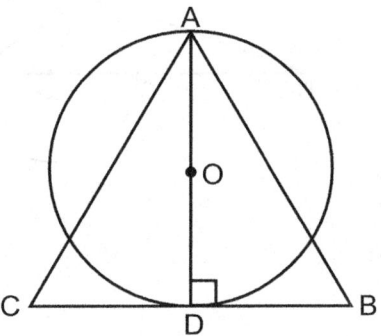

Quantity A   **Quantity B**

Area of Equilateral triangle ABC $96\sqrt{3}$

- Ⓐ Quantity A is greater.
- Ⓑ Quantity B is greater.
- Ⓒ The two quantities are equal.
- Ⓓ The relationship cannot be determined from the information given.

13.

1200 kg of apples is purchased for $3000. It is sold in such a way that after selling the whole quantity, the quantum of loss is equal to the amount obtained by selling 300 kg of apples.

Quantity A	**Quantity B**
$1.80	Sales price per kg of apples

Ⓐ Quantity A is greater.

Ⓑ Quantity B is greater.

Ⓒ The two quantities are equal.

Ⓓ The relationship cannot be determined from the information given.

14.

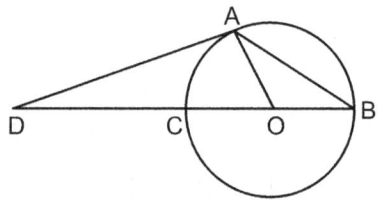

Quantity A	**Quantity B**
∠AOB	∠ADB

Ⓐ Quantity A is greater.

Ⓑ Quantity B is greater.

Ⓒ The two quantities are equal.

Ⓓ The relationship cannot be determined from the information given.

15.

   x, y and z are consecutive even integers and $z > y > x$.

Quantity A	**Quantity B**
$\dfrac{xy + yz}{y}$	$\dfrac{xz + yx}{z - 1}$

   Ⓐ Quantity A is greater.
   Ⓑ Quantity B is greater.
   Ⓒ The two quantities are equal.
   Ⓓ The relationship cannot be determined from the information given.

Answers and Explanations

1. **Topic: Geometry**

    Sub topic: Circles/Quadrilaterals

    The correct answer is (D).

    When dealing with combined figures, look for pieces they have in common. If you sketch in a line connecting the centers of the circles, you'll see that it is also a diagonal of the square.

    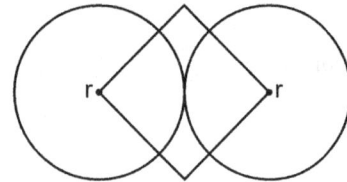

    This line is composed of a radius of each circle; since the circles are equal their radii are equal and the diagonal equals 2r. The area of a circle is 18π. So πr2 = 18π, r2 = 18 and r = $\sqrt{18}$ = $\sqrt{9} \times \sqrt{2}$ = $3\sqrt{2}$. Therefore, the diagonal is $6\sqrt{2}$.

    The diagonal is of a square is equal to a side times $\sqrt{2}$. (Since it is essential ratio of 1: $\sqrt{2}$) since the diagonal is $6\sqrt{2}$ the side of the square must be 6. Perimeter of a square is equal to 4s = 4(6) = 24

2. **Topic: Geometry**

    Sub topic: Area, Perimeter, and Volume

    The correct answer is (B).

    The rate for pipe T is $\frac{1200 cm^3}{minute}$ but $1000 cm^3$ = 1 liter

    Hence, $\frac{1200 cm^3}{minute} = \frac{1200 cm^3}{1000 cm^3 / l}$ per minute = 1.2 l/minute

    Now that all rates are in liters per minute, we compute the quantities:

    Quantity A: T runs for 3 minutes, so we calculate: $\frac{1.2 l}{min} \times 3 min = 3.6 l$

    Quantity B: P runs for 2 minutes, so we calculate:

    $\frac{2.16 l}{min} \times 2 min = 4.32 l$

    By comparison, quantity B is greater; the correct option is B.

3. **Topic: Geometry**

    Sub topic: Angle Measurement

    The correct answer is (A).

    To find the number of degrees in the interior angles of a pentagon, use the formula 180 × (n − 2), where n is the number of sides. Therefore, 180 × (5 − 2) = 180 × 3 = 540°

    540° > 500°

    Another method would be to draw the pentagon and break it into triangles connecting verticals (lines cannot cross), as shown here.

    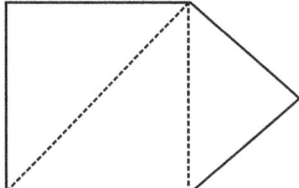

    Multiplying the number of triangles (3) by 180° (degrees in a triangle) gives the same result, 540°.

4. **Topic: Arithmetic**

    Sub topic: Divisibility

    The correct answer is 23.

    x ÷ 5 remainder 3

    x ÷ 7 remainder 2

    The smallest number is 23. 23 divided by 5 gives a quotient of 4 and a remainder of 3. 23 divided by 7 gives a quotient of 3 and a remainder of 2.

5. **Topic: Geometry**

    Sub topic: Triangle

    The correct answer is (B).

    Since DE is parallel to BC, ∠ADE = ∠ABC and ∠AED = ∠ACB. Since both ΔADE and ΔABC

Exercise #14

contain A, all three of their angles are equal and they are similar. The sides of similar triangles are proportional. Since AD = $\frac{DB}{2}$, 2AD = DB

Since AB = AD + DB, AB = 3AD, and AD = $\frac{1}{3}$ AB.

Since the perimeter of ΔABC = 24, the perimeter of ΔADE = $\frac{1}{3}$(24) = 8

6. **Topic: Arithmetic**

   Sub topic: Integers

   The correct answer is (E).

   When $x = 0$, then $x^3 = x^2 = 0$, so choices (A) and (D) are incorrect. When x is a positive fraction, then $x^3 < x^2$; for example, $x = \frac{1}{2}, \left(\frac{1}{2}\right)^3 = \frac{1}{8} < \left(\frac{1}{2}\right)^2 = \frac{1}{4}$

   So, choice (B) is incorrect. When x is negative and x^2 is positive (a negative raised to an odd power is always negative and a negative raised to an even power is always positive), then $x^3 < x^2$ and choice (C) is therefore incorrect. Only when $x > 1$ will the inequality be true.

7. **Topic: Arithmetic**

   Sub topic: Order of Operations

   The correct answer is (B).

   To evaluate using order of operations, we need to use PEMDAS.

   P: Parenthesis

   E: Exponents

   M/D: Multiplication and Division done from Left to Right.

   A/S: Addition and Subtraction done from left to right.

   We will evaluate each quantity.

   Quantity A:

   $18 \div 3 \times 6 - 2 - 3^2$

   $= 18 \div 3 \times 6 - 2 - 9$

   $= 6 \times 6 - 2 - 9$

   $= 36 - 2 - 9$

   $= 25$

   Quantity B:

   $18 + 6 \div 3 \times 2 + 2^3$

   $= 18 + 6 \div 3 \times 2 + 8$

   $= 18 + 2 \times 2 + 8$

   $= 18 + 4 + 8$

   $= 30$

   Quantity B is greater, so the answer is B.

8. **Topic: Geometry**

   Sub topic: Area, Perimeter, and Volume

   The correct answer is (E).

   The amount of material that will remain after the circles are cut out is the area of the entire piece of material, minus the total area of the circles that were cut out. The total area of the circles that were cut out will be equal to the area of one of the circles times the total number of circle.

   To minimize the amount of wasted material, the diameter of the circle cut out should divide evenly into both the length and width of the cloth. Therefore, what you're really looking for is the greatest common factor of the length and width. To find the greatest common factor of 16 and 36, break down each number to its prime factorization and then multiply together all the prime factors that the two have in common. In this case, 16 and 36 share 2 prime factors of 2, so their greatest common factor is 4. Since 4 goes into 16 and 36 nine times, a total of (4)(9) = 36 circles with diameter of each circle is 4, its radius is 2 and the area of each circle is πr^2. Since the diameter of each circle is 4, its radius is 2 and the area of each circle is $\pi \times (2)^2 = 4\pi$. So, the material that will be left over is $(36)(16) - 36(4\pi) = 36(16 - 4\pi) = (36)(4)(4 - \pi) = 144(4 - \pi)$.

9. **Topic: Arithmetic**

   Sub topic: Exponents and Roots

   The correct answer is (B).

   If you multiply both sides by 3, you find that $m^4 = 81$. Therefore, m can equal 3 or –3. In either case, m is less than 4.

10. **Topic: Geometry**

    Sub topic: Area, Perimeter, Volume

    The correct answer is (A).

    PQRS is rectangle. It means angle P and angle R are right angles. That again means diagonal QS is a diameter of the circle.

    Given area of circle = 6.25π square units.

    If r is the radius then $\pi r^2 = 6.25\pi$

    $r^2 = 6.25$

    $r = 2.5$

    Diameter QS = $2 \times 2.5 = 5$ units

    But PQ = 4 units (Given)

    By Pythagorean Theorem

    $PS^2 = QS^2 - PQ^2$

    $PS^2 = 5^2 - 4^2 = 25 - 16 = 9$

    $PS = 3$

    Now area of rectangle PQRS = $3 \times 4 = 12$ square units.

11. **Topic: Arithmetic**

    Sub topic: Integers

    The correct answer is (D).

    $[(a)] = (1 + a)^2 + 2$ for all numbers a

    $[(b)] = (1 + b)^2 + 2$

    Suppose b = 5

    $[(b)] = [(5)] = (1 + 5)^2 + 2 = 38$; $[(-b)] = [(-5)] = (1 - 5)^2 + 2 = 18$; $[(b)] > [(-b)]$

    Suppose b = –7

    $[(b)] = [(-7)] = (1 - 7)^2 + 2 = 38$; $[(-b)] = [(7)] = (1 + 7)^2 + 2 = 51$; $[(b)] < [(-b)]$

    Suppose b = 0

    $[(b)] = [(0)] = (1 - 0)^2 + 2 = 3$; $[(-b)] = [(0)] = (1 + 0)^2 + 2 = 3$; $[(b)] = [(-b)]$

    Hence option D

12. **Topic: Geometry**

    Sub topic: Area, Perimeter, Volume

    The correct answer is (A).

    Area of the circle = 81π

    If r is the radius, $\pi r^2 = 81\pi$

    $r = 9$

    Diameter AD = 18

    Triangle ABC is equilateral.

    Angle ADB = 900

    Hence AD becomes altitude of ABC.

    If a is the side of the equilateral triangle then altitude AD = $\frac{\sqrt{3}a}{2}$ [formula]

    So $\frac{\sqrt{3}a}{2} = 18$

    $a = \frac{36}{\sqrt{3}}$;

    $a^2 = \frac{1296}{3} = 432$

    By formula area of the equilateral triangle

    $\frac{\sqrt{3}a^2}{4} = \sqrt{3} \times \frac{432}{4} = 108\sqrt{3}$

13. **Topic: Arithmetic**

    Sub topic: Estimation

    The correct answer is (A).

    Let the sales price of apple per kg be $x

    According to the question

    Total Purchase price – Total Sales Price = Loss

    Now Total purchase price = $3000

Exercise #14

Total sales price = $1200x

Loss = Amount obtained by selling 300 kg of apples = $300x

Hence 3000 − 1200x = 300x

3000 = 1500x

x = $2

14. **Topic: Arithmetic**

    Sub topic: Triangles

    The correct answer is (A).

    Since ∠AOB is a central angle, it equals the measure of AB, and since ∠ADC is outside the circle but connects

    to AB, it is less than half of AB. Therefore, ∠AOB > ∠ADC

    Alternate method: The external ∠AOB must be larger than either of the remote interior angles.

15. **Topic: Arithmetic**

    Sub topic: Integers

    The correct answer is (A).

    The values of x, y, and z differ by 2 as they are consecutive even integers and x is the smallest.

    Let $x = x, y = x + 2, z = x + 4$.

    Now substitute these variables into the expressions, simplify, and compare.

    Quantity A:

    $$\frac{xy + yz}{y}$$

    $$= \frac{x(x+2) + (x+2)(x+4)}{x+2}$$

    $$= \frac{x^2 + 2x + x^2 + 4x + 2x + 8}{x+2}$$

    $$= \frac{2x^2 + 8x + 8}{x+2}$$

    $$= \frac{2(x^2 + 4x + 4)}{x+2}$$

    $$= \frac{2(x+2)^2}{x+2}$$

    $$= 2(x+2)$$

    $$= 2x + 4$$

    Quantity B:

    $$\frac{xz + yx}{z-1}$$

    $$= \frac{x(x+4) + (x+2)x}{(x+4)-1}$$

    $$= \frac{x^2 + 4x + x^2 + 2x}{x+3}$$

    $$= \frac{2x^2 + 6x}{x+3}$$

    $$= \frac{2x(x+3)}{x+3}$$

    $$= 2x$$

    Compare:

    $2x + 4 \;?\; 2x$

    $4 \;?\; 0$

    $4 > 0$

    The Quantity A is greater than Quantity B.

This page is intentionally left blank

Chapter 21

Exercise #15
Questions: 11　|　Time: 20 minutes

This Exercise includes *11 practice questions*. The questions cover all the question types as explained in Chapter 2 and may fall into any of the following categories - Arithmetic, Algebra, Geometry or Data Analysis. You will find answers and detailed explanations towards the end of this chapter.

1. If $a^2b = 12^2$, where b is odd, then a is divisible by all of the following EXCEPT

    Ⓐ　3
    Ⓑ　4
    Ⓒ　6
    Ⓓ　9
    Ⓔ　12

2. 5-liters of water is emptied from tank-A into tank-B. Another 10-liters is emptied from tank-A to tank-C. If tank-A had 10-liters extra water compared to tank-C, how many extra liters does tank-C have now compared to tank-A?

    Ⓐ　0
    Ⓑ　5
    Ⓒ　10
    Ⓓ　15
    Ⓔ　20

3.

A two-pound box of brand A costs $7.88.

A three-pound box of brand B costs $11.79.

Quantity A

Cost per pound of Brand A

Quantity B

Cost per pound of Brand B

- Ⓐ Quantity A is greater.
- Ⓑ Quantity B is greater.
- Ⓒ The two quantities are equal.
- Ⓓ The relationship cannot be determined from the information given.

4.

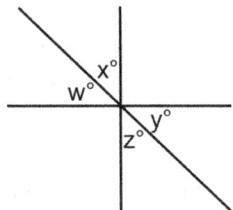

Quantity A

90 − (w + x)

Quantity B

90 − (y + z)

- Ⓐ Quantity A is greater.
- Ⓑ Quantity B is greater.
- Ⓒ The two quantities are equal.
- Ⓓ The relationship cannot be determined from the information given.

5. 0.1% percent of m is equal to 10% of n, then m is what percent of $10n$?

- Ⓐ $\frac{1}{1000}$%
- Ⓑ 10%
- Ⓒ 100%
- Ⓓ 1,000%
- Ⓔ 10,000%

6. In a certain examination 60% of the students passed in Mathematics, 74% passed in English and 18% failed in both English and Mathematics. If 416 students passed in both these subjects, then what will be the total number of students who took the exam and also number of students who passed in Mathematics and English?

   Select *all* that apply.

A	770
B	800
C	830
D	400
E	480
F	574
G	592
H	600

7. A reduction of 2% in taxation enables him to increase his expenditure by one per cent on each of the items, cinema and travel. Then a ratio of 1:2:3 is maintained on the expenditures incurred on which of the following items.

   - A   Travel, miscellaneous and cinema
   - B   Miscellaneous, cinema and travel
   - C   Miscellaneous, tax and clothing
   - D   Miscellaneous, travel and cinema
   - E   None of the above

8.

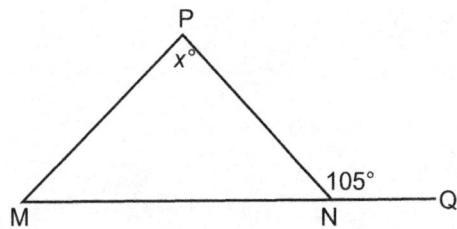

   In the figure above, MQ is a straight line. If PM = PN, what is the value of x?

   - A   30
   - B   45
   - C   60
   - D   75
   - E   90

9.

$$15 - x < 2$$
$$2y < 24$$

Quantity A	Quantity B
x	y

- (A) Quantity A is greater.
- (B) Quantity B is greater.
- (C) The two quantities are equal.
- (D) The relationship cannot be determined from the information given.

10.

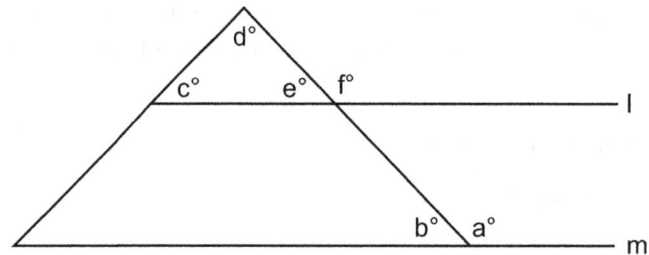

In the figure above, if *l* || *m*, which of the following must be equal to *a°*?

- (A) b + c
- (B) b + e
- (C) c + d
- (D) d + e
- (E) d + f

Exercise #15

11.

A triathlon athlete practices for competition. He swims *s* miles in *t* hours and runs *r* miles in another *t* hours and finally cycles *c* miles in another *t* hours. 5 miles per hour (mph) equals approximately 8 kilometers per hour (kmph)

Quantity A

Average speed of the athlete in kilometers per hour

Quantity B

$\dfrac{5(s+r+c)}{24t}$

- Ⓐ Quantity A is greater.
- Ⓑ Quantity B is greater.
- Ⓒ The two quantities are equal.
- Ⓓ The relationship cannot be determined from the information given.

Answers and Explanations

1. **Topic: Arithmetic**

   Sub topic: Exponents and Roots

   The correct answer is (D).

   Note first this is an EXCEPT question. Now, since $a^2b = 12^2$, and b is an odd integer, let's see what we can come up with. The first value for b that occurs to us is 1, so we get the following:

   $a^2b = 12^2$

   $(a^2)(1) = 12^2$

   $a^2 = 12^2$

   $a = 12$

   If a equals 12 it is divisible by 1, 2, 3, 4, 6, and 12. So the only choice that remains is D.

2. **Topic: Geometry**

   Sub topic: Three-Dimensional Figures

   The correct answer is (D).

   Tank A originally contained 10 more liters of water than tank C, so represent the initial number of liters in each tank in terms of tank A:

   Tank A = a

   Tank C = $a - 0$

   5 liters of water are poured from A to B, and additional 10 liters are poured from A to C. A total of 15 liters are removed from tank A, so it now contains $a - 15$ liters of water. 10 liters are added to tank C, so it now contains $a - 10 + 10 = a$ liters. So, tank C contains 15 more liters of water than tank A.

3. **Topic: Arithmetic**

   Sub topic: Divisibility

   The correct answer is (A).

   $7.88 divided by 2 equals $3.94.

   $11.79 divided by 3 equals $3.93.

4. **Topic: Geometry**

   Sub topic: Coordinate Geometry

   The correct answer is (C).

   We should notice first that we are definitely not in a position to say the magnitude of the unlabeled angles is 90°. But we need not make the assumption! We know that $w = y$ and $x = z$ because vertical angles are equal. Therefore, we are subtracting equal quantities from both sides of the comparison, a maneuver which, as we have already seen, will neither upset the balance of the original equality nor interfere with the direction of the in equality. This leaves us with 90 on both sides of the comparison, so we conclude that the original comparison must have been an equality.

5. **Topic: Arithmetic**

   Sub topic: Percent, Ratio, Rate

   The correct answer is (D).

   It's time to plug in values for m and n and make use of our translation approach to solving percent problems. We're working with a small percent, so plug in big number for m.

   Let's say $m = 2,000$. So, 0.1% of 2000 =

   $\frac{0.1}{100} \times \frac{2000}{1} = 2$. Therefore, 10% equals 2; rewrite this as $\frac{10}{100} \times n = 2$

   Solving for n, you get $n = 20$. Now, translate the rest of the problem: "m is what percent of $10n$" can be written as $2000 = \frac{x}{100} \times 200$

   Now just solve for x, which equals 1000. The answer is 1000%.

6. **Topic: Algebra**

   Sub topic: Set Theory

   The correct answers are (B), (E) and (G).

   Assume total number of students to be 100.

   Failed in Mathematics = 100 − 60 = 40

   Failed in English = 100 − 74 = 26

Failed in both subjects = 18

Failed students in any of the subjects = 40 + 26 − 18 = 48

Students who will pass in both the subjects = 52

If 52 passed, then total number of students = 100

If 416 passed, then total number of students will be $\left(\dfrac{100}{52}\right) \times 416 = 800$

Number of students who passed in English = $0.74 \times 800 = 592$

Number of students who passed in Mathematics = $0.60 \times 800 = 480$

7. **Topic: Data Analysis**

   Sub topic: Interpreting data in tables and graphs

   The correct answer is (B).

   After reduction of 2% in tax: 11% − 2% = 9%. Increase of 1% each on cinema and travel amount to 12% on cinema and 18% on travel.

8. **Topic: Geometry**

   Sub topic: Angle Measurement

   The correct answer is (A).

   ∠PNM is supplementary to ∠PNQ, so ∠PNM + 105° = 180°, and ∠PNM = 75°. Since PM = PN, ∆MPN is isosceles and ∠PMN = ∠PNM = 75°. The interior angles of a triangle sum to 180°, so 75 + 75 + x = 180, and x = 30.

9. **Topic: Algebra**

   Sub topic: Solving Linear Equations and Inequalities

   The correct answer is (A).

   Solving 15 − x < 2

   15 − x − 15 < 2 − 15

   −x < −13

$$\dfrac{-x}{-1} > \dfrac{-13}{-1}$$

$x > 13$

(Note: Inequality is reversed when dividing by a negative number.)

Solving 2y < 24

$$\dfrac{2y}{2} < \dfrac{24}{2}$$

$y < 12$

Therefore, $x > y$.

10. **Topic: Geometry**

    Sub topic: Angle Measurement

    The correct answer is (C).

    $a = f$, since all the obtuse angles formed when two parallel lines are cut by the transversal are equal.

    f is an exterior angle of the small triangle containing angles c, d, and e.

    The sum of all angles of a triangle is 180. So, we have $c + d + e = 180$ or $c + d = 180 − e$.

    Since f is external to the triangle, we can say $e + f = 180$ or $f = 180 − e$ or $a = 180 − e$ (since $a = f$).

    From the above three statements, we can say, $a = c + d$, the answer is (C).

11. **Topic: Arithmetic**

    Sub topic: Percent, Ratio, Rate

    The correct answer is (A).

    Average speed = $\dfrac{\text{Total distance}}{\text{Total time}} = \dfrac{s+r+c}{t+t+t}$ miles

    per hour = $\dfrac{(s+r+c)}{3t}$ miles per hour

    $= \dfrac{8}{5} \times \dfrac{(s+r+c)}{3t}$ kilometers per hour =

    $= \dfrac{8(s+r+c)}{15t}$ kilometerss per hour >

    $\dfrac{5(s+r+c)}{24t}$ kilometers per hour

NOTES

Made in the USA
Monee, IL
12 May 2025